WOMEN ADMIRING A WATCH.

IN JAPAN.

My Last Cruise
or
Where We Went
&
What We Saw
THE OLD JOHN
VOLCANO ISLAND
JAPANESE JUNK
CAMOENS GROT
PAGODA WHAMPOA
PHILADELPHIA
PUBLISHED BY J.B. LIPPINCOTT & Co.

THE

NORTH PACIFIC SURVEYING AND EXPLORING EXPEDITION;

OR,

MY LAST CRUISE.

WHERE WE WENT AND WHAT WE SAW:

BEING AN ACCOUNT OF

VISITS TO THE MALAY AND LOO-CHOO ISLANDS, THE COASTS OF CHINA, FORMOSA, JAPAN, KAMTSCHATKA, SIBERIA, AND THE MOUTH OF THE AMOOR RIVER.

BY

A. W. HABERSHAM,

LIEUT. U. S. NAVY,

AND LATE OF THE NORTH PACIFIC SURVEYING AND EXPLORING EXPEDITION.

PHILADELPHIA:

J. B. LIPPINCOTT & CO.

LONDON: TRÜBNER & CO.

1857.

Entered according to Act of Congress, in the year 1857, by
J. B. LIPPINCOTT & CO.
in the Clerk's Office of the District Court of the United States for the Eastern District of Pennsylvania.

TO

The Memory

OF

MY BROTHER OFFICERS

WHO PERISHED IN THE UNFORTUNATE

BRIG-OF-WAR PORPOISE.

PREFACE.

ONE of the most prolific sources of loss to the merchant, and, through him, to the world at large, exists in the incorrectness of many of the charts by which his ships are sailed. There are also many coasts of which we have no charts at all, and there are various currents with whose strength and direction we do not pretend to be acquainted.

Besides, there are some few branches of our common family of whom we know little or nothing, and there is also a vast extent of the earth's surface yet awaiting the first pressure of the explorer's foot.

To test the accuracy of charts extant, to prepare others of unknown coasts, to follow the trackless path of the wayward current, to lift the veil that hung between civilization and the customs and habits of isolated tribes and nations, and to collect data from unfrequented parts of our globe for the advancement of science, the Government of the United

States sent out the North Pacific Surveying and Exploring Expedition; and the following pages are simply intended to show where it was that we went, and what it was that we saw, while engaged in the attainment of these objects.

And now, in presenting them to the public, I advance but one claim to its approbation: *i.e.* their contents, though limited, and confined mostly to personal observation while serving successively on board of several vessels of the squadron, are *strictly matter-of-fact*, and, though slightly coloured by the excitement of feeling consequent upon my having participated in most of the scenes of peril and adventure which they will be found to contain, yet is the colouring honest, and not at all calculated to impart incorrect impressions.

THE AUTHOR.

CONTENTS.

CHAPTER XI.

CHAPTER XII.

CHAPTER XIII.

CHAPTER XIV.

CHAPTER XV.

CHAPTER XVI.

CHAPTER XVII.

CHAPTER XVIII.

CHAPTER XIX.

CHAPTER XX.

CHAPTER XXI.

CHAPTER XXII.

CHAPTER XXIII.

CHAPTER XXIV.

CONCLUSION.

MY LAST CRUISE.

CHAPTER I.

INTRODUCES THE READER TO THE EXPEDITION, AND CARRIES HIM TO THE CAPE OF GOOD HOPE; AFTER WHICH HE IS TAKEN BACK TO THE CAPE DE VERDE ISLANDS, AND FROM THENCE AGAIN TO THE CAPE OF GOOD HOPE.

THE United States Surveying and Exploring Expedition to the North Pacific, China Seas, &c. &c. sailed from the port of Norfolk on the 21st of June, 1853, and commenced its wandering and perilous cruise.

It was commanded by Commander Cadwallader Ringgold, of the navy, and consisted of the five following vessels, viz.:—

The sloop-of-war Vincennes, (flag-ship,) of eight hundred tons, ten guns, and some two hundred men.

The screw-steamer John Hancock, of five hundred and thirty tons, three guns, and seventy men.

The brig-of-war Porpoise, of about four hundred tons, five guns, and some seventy men.

The schooner J. Fenimore Cooper, of eighty-eight tons, one gun, and twenty men.

And lastly, the store-ship John P. Kennedy, of five

hundred and twenty tons, three guns, and forty men. On board of the last sailed the writer of the present volume.

The first four of these vessels proceeded to Simon's Bay, Cape of Good Hope, *viâ* the island of Madeira, while the latter touched at the Cape de Verde Islands on her way to the same destination. On the 20th of September we had all joined company at that extreme of Southern Africa, and were expecting soon to continue our voyage, when to our extreme chagrin it was announced that every vessel of the squadron, with the exception of the little "Cooper," was in need of extensive repairs: we had been sent to sea in a miserably unseaworthy condition. Of course these repairs were at once entered upon with energy and spirit; but such was their extent, and such the difficulty of obtaining skilful workmen and proper material at that port, that it was not until the 9th of November that we once more found ourselves clear of the headlands and fairly pointed for the *locale* of our future work.

The passage of the Kennedy as far as Porto Praya, Cape de Verde Islands, was remarkably pleasant, though presenting but two occurrences worthy of note. These were meteorological phenomena, the following description of which I take from my journal under date of July 1:—

"The last two nights have each been remarkable for an interesting display of meteorological phenomena. The first of these, as seen night before last by Mr. Kennon, the master, consisted of a meteorite or fire-ball, which, commencing its flight in the vicinity of the constellation of the Scorpion, measured a segment of at least sixty degrees, and finally exploded into a dozen or more burning fragments, each of which was distinctly observed obeying the laws of gravity. The light emitted during its flight, previous to the explosion, was a greenish blue of rare brilliancy, that pained the eye by its unexpected appearance and intensity of power, and illuminated our decks as effectually as if a blue-light had been burnt on each mast-head and yard-arm. At the time of its explosion it could not have been distant more than a mile, and yet he heard no attendant report. It was like the bursting of an immense rocket, and as the flaming fragments fell in curves towards the sea he listened in vain for the expected sound.

"The second of these was seen by Captain Collins and myself last night, while the first watch was dragging to its close.

"Though undoubtedly the most rare and singular of the two, it offered scarcely any ground for description. It was without motion, and wanted the beautifully-variegated colour of the former. It presented a most perfect representation of the human eye, though visible for not more than a second at the utmost. We distinctly saw it contract and dilate twice during that limited period, immediately after which the lids, as it were, closed, and shut it out from view."

What now was this phenomenon? A comet without a train or more than a momentary existence? A shooting star or meteorite without motion? or an *ignis fatuus* in mid-heaven? One more conversant with the stars than I must answer the question. * * *

Upon our arrival at Porto Praya, on the 14th of July, we proceeded to get in a supply of wood and water; while thus engaged, a limited opportunity only was offered us for making observations. I find the following remarks in my journal in regard to that port:—

"Soon after letting go the anchor, we proceeded to raft our water-casks and tow them on shore, where we employed negroes, *the slaves of negroes*, to fill them and float them out to the boats. And here let me say a word in regard to 'watering ship' at this and other similar ports.

"The process, though not at all impracticable, is attended by many disagreeable, often fatal, drawbacks. On account of the heavy and constant surf which lines their coasts, boats can only land at particular points; and, when these points do not happen to be near a stream of fresh water, you have to land on the open beach. In this case it becomes necessary for boats with water-casks in tow to let go their anchors some distance outside of the surf, and then drop in towards this latter as far as is consistent with safety. The line by which the casks have been towed is then cast adrift, when the latter are quickly washed upon the beach, while the crew jump overboard, wade on shore, and roll them through the hot sand or over the slippery shingle to the watering-place. There they are filled, and, the bungs being tightly driven, they are rolled back to the beach, rafted together a second time, and finally towed back to the ship, where several men in a boat pass slings around them, hook on the yard-tackle, and they are hoisted on board.

"We find but one small coasting-vessel at anchor, though the consul tells us that he has seen as many as a hundred from his parlour-window, most of which were whalers. We are told that the only article with which ships are ever freighted from Porto Praya is a dye-wood, or rather dye-moss, if I may so call it. It is of the lichen family, grows upon the rocks and trees in the shape of a heavy, dense moss, and yields a rich purple colour. This colour, however, though beautiful beyond conception in its richness, is, unfortunately, not durable. For export it is bruised between stones and then combined with lime and urine. Its proper name is Rocella tinctoria, and the quantity annually exported does not exceed fifty or sixty tons a year.

"Yesterday Captain Collins called away his gig, gave out that he was going on shore, and offered a passage to any of the mess who might feel like going along. So Purser Ritchie and myself took advantage of it, and were pulled to the landing. We then indulged in a hot walk of twenty minutes along the beach and up the stony road of the bluff, and at the end of that time found ourselves in the roomy and well-ventilated apartments of the American Consulate.

"There we looked around in vain for Mr. Morse, the acting consul, and finally settled down into his large armchairs and commenced to recover a reasonable amount of coolness; after which we partook of his stone-filtered water, and, despairing of his speedy return, sallied out to accomplish the main object of our visit,—to see our washerwoman, and reimpress it upon her mind that our clothes must be on board before the hour of sailing.

"The purser and myself were now walking through Porto Praya for the first time, while the captain, being an old cruiser on the African station, guided us through the narrow and filthy streets. We observed that the houses were mostly built of rough stone, were two-storied, and possessed of a singularly-unfinished appearance. They had to me the look of houses that had been hurriedly built while the art of masonry was yet in its infancy.

"I have said that the 'streets were narrow and filthy;' they were also disgraced by the shameless gambols of naked children of all colours, and the loitering presence of indolent, half-dressed adults of both sexes. One of the latter, a girl of at least fifteen, and clothed in the *lightest possible* style, lounged by us with a bold and inquisitive stare, and without the least evidence of shame or attempt at concealment.

"A walk of ten minutes through such streets and scenes as these took us to our journey's end, when we entered a half-finished house of rough stone-masonry, and were presented by the captain to three females, a mother and her two daughters,—old friends of his, and *pro tem.* our washerwomen. He introduced them jestingly as 'one of the first families of the place,' and gave as his reasons that the mother and her elder daughter slept on a bedstead that had been ordered all the way from Lisbon, and that the younger one had married the 'military commander' of the place. This latter was a young African, an advocate of the long-cherished desire of some of our ultra abolitionists for the amalgamation of the African and Caucasian races, and was, I heard, as noble a specimen of the 'buck' order as one would wish to see.

"I looked upon the olive complexion, the sparkling

eyes, and the delicate form of the negro's wife, and felt an involuntary prayer rise to my lips:—'Lord, that such a revolting relationship may never exist in the great world that lies over the Western waters.' She was the first white woman I had ever seen who had placed her hand in that of a thick-lipped, long-heeled negro.

"We soon concluded our business and again continued our walk. We saw nothing more than has been written of by dozens of previous writers, and I will therefore step at once upon the beach on our return to the boat. We experienced a sense of indescribable relief as we left the dirty streets and thin half-clad occupants behind us, and drew long breaths of the freshening sea-breeze before it had been contaminated by their ever-exhaling miasma.

"That night I kept the mid-watch; and, while it was rolling slowly by, a ship's light made its appearance around the point to seaward, and shortly after the dark hull, lofty spars, and white sails of a frigate loomed through the surrounding gloom, holding her steady way across our stern.

"'Ship ahoy!' hailed a hoarse voice.

"'Hillo!' I answered.

"'What ship's that?'

"I gave our name, and the hoarse voice returned theirs.

"She proved to be the United States frigate Constitution; old Charles Stewart's bridge to his Nelson-like reputation,—'Old Ironsides,' as she was affectionately called by those who had sailed in her over that glorious path. As she crossed our stern and rounded to on our quarter, she burnt a blue-light to satisfy herself as to the locality, and shone out, a noble specimen of the concentration of war's power on the sea, while the lambent flame lit up her double row of guns and brought out in bold relief her dark and heavy rigging.

"The next day we talked with old friends; with messmates of bygone years. We talked of our wandering and perilous cruise, of the strange people we were going to see, of the lapse of time, and of our final return. We talked as if death were a thing of the past, as if there was no possibility of his striding through our midst and carrying away in his fleshless grasp hearts that then beat strong with youth and the glowing hope of that final return. We talked of all this, and of much more, and the next day again unfurled our sails to the friendly trade-wind, and urged our old ship from those barren shores.

"The breeze falling light as we got away from the land, it took us two days to sink the peak of Fogo Island, which, with its elevation of nine thousand seven hundred and fifty-nine feet, offers a beautiful landmark to the navigator. At the end of this time, however, it sank slowly below the northern board, and we bade adieu to land until the Cape of Good Hope should break the even surface of a more southern horizon. Things now went on very smoothly until we had crossed the line and ran to the southeast trades, when we fell in with a heavy swell from that direction, which indicated a probable gale. Warned by this friendly forerunner, we were on our guard, and when it came it found us ready. Still, we had a hard time of it; we were as near foundering as was pleasant, and came out of it with the loss of our deck-

"IT WAS TIME TO THINK OF LIGHTENING HER."

load,—a heavy loss to the expedition, as it consisted of all our spare spars.

"This gale itself was nothing remarkable: it was the really awful height and steepness of the seas that alarmed us. I look back to it now and wonder how we lived through it, and, as I wonder, I shudder. At one time we took on board such a sea that the old ship hesitated to lift it up; had another followed it, we must have gone down. It was time to think of lightening her; so we, at the risk of various broken legs, cut adrift the forty tons of deck-load, and managed to get it overboard at the cost of a *single* leg: the owner of that *one*, however, made noise enough to bring up the doctor without his hat, who soon abused him into silence, after which he splintered it with tender care, and got him comfortably stowed away in a cot. Poor H——, rough of speech and tender of heart! We lingered sadly under a granite shaft which rears itself over your narrow home in the unknown land of the Eastern heathen.

"At the end of three days the weather moderated, after which we had a calm, and, finally, a fine breeze on the quarter: we made all sail and boomed away towards our longed-for port.

"No one can tell how much we enjoyed the first day's moderating weather. We had suffered so terribly during the gale from the effects of bilge-water that some of the mess had been thrown on the sick-list by it; and, now that fair weather was returned, we knew its fumes would settle down with the sea. It had a fair sweep at us as long as the gale lasted; for, having to batten down all of the hatches, we were without both light and air; and when the battens were at length removed, the hatches opened, and the cool, fresh ocean air, and the bright light of a sunny day permitted to enter our long-closed apartments, we found that our white-paint-work was entirely ruined. It was as black as ink,—a kind of *bluish* black,—and most unpleasantly damp and greasy to the touch.

"Our first object was to get our bedding and clothes up on deck for an airing, and our second to get our mess and state-rooms as dry and free from bilge-water as possible. We therefore commenced breaking out our clothes; and our horror may be imagined when we found that the blackening fumes had ruined most of our uniforms, and had rendered unfit for use (previous to passing through the hands of the washerwoman) the greater part of our under-clothing. A cry arose as general as that which swelled through Egypt for the loss of the first-born: *no one had escaped.* Some of us lost hundreds of dollars from the effects of the destroying effluvia; all had lost something.

"In a few days another gale crossed our path, then another calm, then another fair wind: finally, we rubbed our eyes one fine morning and looked upon the blue outlines of Africa's extreme southern point, and the next day we were well in with the land. Here we were again headed off by a three days' spell of bad weather, at the expiration of which we stood in for the harbour of Simon's Town, and were so fortunate as to pick up Mr. John Koutze, the pilot, who took us into a snug anchorage just as another gale was beginning to sing through our rigging. We were the first arrival: they knew nothing of the rest of the squadron."

CHAPTER II.

WE RECEIVE A VISIT WHICH IS NOT INTENDED TO INQUIRE AFTER OUR HEALTH, AND MAKE THE ACQUAINTANCE OF "LIEUTENANT PAGET, R.N.;" AFTER WHICH THE PURSER AND MYSELF "SMELL A RAT" AND FIRE AT A CATBIRD, TO THE INFINITE TERROR OF SOME HOTTENTOT WOMEN.

WE had scarcely let go our anchor when we were boarded by one of the boats of the English frigate, the officer of which stepped over the side as if he had lately suffered from an attack of rheumatism, or pride of birth, it was hard to say which. He introduced himself as Lieutenant Paget, Royal Navy, and was immediately conducted down to the captain by the affable officer of the deck, with the intention of making him known. We found the captain and doctor engaged in some general conversation, and I was just preparing to introduce my friend with a proper amount of *empressement*, when he anticipated me:—"Lieutenant Paget, sir, of the Royal Navy. Happy to see you, sir. The admiral's compliments,—ahem! ah!—"

"Glad to see you on board, Lieutenant Paget. Permit me to present to you Dr. Hamilton," replied the captain, with one of his easy smiles.

Now, "Lieutenant Paget" must have thought that the captain took him for the port health-officer, or he must have been greatly wanting in politeness,—one of the two; for, instead of shaking hands with the man of pills, or noticing the introduction by the ramrod-like bow usual on such occasions, he gave an affected start, and, in the drawling tone cultivated by many would-be high-bred Englishmen, observed,—"Ar-ar-rea-l-ly, but—ar-r, in fact, ar-r—I didn't come—ar-r—to inquire after the health." After which he indulged in a few *quite commonplace* remarks, drank a glass of wine, and was bowed over the side. The doctor subsequently remarked, in a confidential manner, that he never in his life felt more like doing any thing than, at that moment, like knocking his confounded "ar-r-s" down his cockney throat: nevertheless, he controlled himself, and left the cabin in a high state of disgust with England, the English, and with Lieutenant Paget, R.N., in particular.

Two days after our arrival, the Vincennes hove in sight, came in to her anchorage very prettily, and made signal for our captain to repair on board. Day after day they now dropped in; first the little Cooper, then the Porpoise, and, finally, the old John Hancock. On the 20th of September we were again together.

Then it was that we discovered the dilapidated condition of our own vessel; while the Vincennes, Porpoise, and Hancock were each reported as being in want of repairs. We commenced; and I think, before the last bill was sent in, the repairs of the "squadron" must have ranged as high as $20,000, and we just from the outfitting care of the navy-yards of New York and Norfolk.

While all this work was going on, and we necessarily detained in our sheltered anchorage, Purser Ritchie and myself one day took it into our heads to take a tramp over the hills in search of some unfortunate antelope, "hundreds" of which, we had been told, were easily to be found. Stimpson, the energetic naturalist of the Vincennes, had also spoken of several flocks of quail; and we therefore looked forward to returning with any quantity of game. The purser had a shaky-looking seventeen-dollar American gun, that he had bought to destroy can vas-back ducks with on the Chesapeake Bay some years back, and I was provided in pretty much the same style; the only difference being that mine had been bought several years later, and for only *fifteen* dollars. We were jested unmercifully by the mess whenever we appeared with those dangerous weapons, and so always found it convenient to get off upon our hunts as quietly as possible. This being our first attempt, we were off our guard, and came in for an extra allowance:—

"There go the two Nimrods! Now we'll feast on game!" exclaimed a disagreeably-loud voice,—so loud that the whole mess were at once upon us.

"Just see how the purser shoulders old bust-proof!" exclaimed a sarcastic voice.

"Habersham, you'd better walk astern of old bust-proof: he'll go off backwards with the first heavy load," remarked a voice of friendly caution.

"That wont make it any better for the purser," remarked another. "Habersham's gun only cost *fifteen* dollars, and is warranted to shoot through both ends."

Through these and similar salutations we ran the gauntlet of our admiring messmates, turned a deaf ear to all that we were not *forced* to hear, and, finally, found ourselves stowed away in the stern-sheets of the dingy and out of reach of their attentions. The dingy was pulled by two very small boys encased in very tight trousers, who got us on shore after a while by the greatest exertion, and then returned despondingly on board to repair damages.

We at once made for the hill-side and commenced beating the bush for antelope with the most "new-broom"-like energy; and, to have seen us as we thus started, one would have thought that we were following a most reliable pointer, and that we were expecting a bird to rise under our noses at every step, so ready were our guns and so watchful were our eyes. As I now look back upon that tramp and recall its various drawbacks, it seems without exception the most disagreeable thing of the kind that I ever undertook. Such a total absence not only of game but even of animal life! and such walking as it was *along* the sides of those rugged hills! I shall never forget the feeling of satisfaction with which I went to bed that night.

Imagine the sloping side of a mountain-range three miles in length, covered by a thick undergrowth reaching up to one's shoulders; millions of loose round stones underfoot; stationary rocks in the shape of o'erhanging cliffs and huge boulders around and overhead; deep ravines every one or two hundred yards, running from the ridge to the sea,—a regular alternation of ridge and ravine; and imagine us walking over those loose stones which we could not see, and through those thick and tangled bushes which we could just see over, and one has a very fair idea of the "hard road" which we had to travel. And travel it we *did*, with a pelting rain and strong wind in our faces, and growing disgust in our hearts.

After thus walking along the side of this rocky mountain for a mile or more, and just as disgust had grown about as strong as expectation, we stopped under the lee of one of the huge boulders, to draw a moment's breath and wonder where all the antelope could be, and where the ground was upon which Stimpson had started a flock of quail and killed ten of them.

Now, while we were thus wondering without deriving the slightest satisfaction from it, we noticed a gentleman of Hottentot visage approaching us with a spy-glass in his right hand, through which he had probably long since satisfied himself as to the likelihood of our being persons who *carried tobacco;* for he had no sooner joined us and made a polite bow, than he commenced to express himself at some length in favour of the consumption of said article, and ended by indicating a perfect readiness on his part to accept a small piece of it, "if we happened to have any." The fact of this personage living in an English colony will account for his speaking the language.

I had a small tobacco-box in my pocket containing a quantity of John Anderson & Co.'s "fine-cut;" and that I offered freely, knowing how much one often longs for a single "chew," and hoping, moreover, to loosen the honest strings of his tongue in regard to the whereabouts of the game.

I was right in both my impression as to his longing for a chew and as to the loosening of his tongue in regard to the game, though I cannot say much for the amount of honesty about this latter. He glanced doubtingly at the fine-threaded preparation at first, but had no sooner carried it to his nose than his whole face relaxed into a confiding smile of the utmost complacency, under cover of which he put at least half of my supply into his capacious mouth, and was at once seized with a severe fit of coughing, the result of his being unacquainted with the particular knack of using that valuable but likely-to-choke-you luxury. Then, after recovering himself in a measure, and with a face that would doubtless have been red had it not been almost black naturally, he commenced to tell us that "between the spot on which we stood and the house of Mr. John Koutze, the pilot, there was no lack of game, but that a great difficulty sometimes existed *in finding it;* that he felt confident, however, that, in spite of this difficulty, we could, by continuing our walk a mile or two farther, start up several spring-boke and any number of quail: he himself had just passed over the ground and seen several." He ended by telling us most emphatically, and with an air of great apparent candour, that "he liked Americans," and that we might thank our nationality for the information just received. Englishmen, he said, were "no good," but *Americans*—ah!—he sighed a deep sigh, which, combined with a look,—such a look!—was doubtless intended to produce another chew; but the purser and myself had both been around Cape Horn already, and were now rounding that of Good Hope; so the box remained unopened.

At first we thought that by "spring-boke" he must mean the ordinary African hare; but, upon our intimating as much, he hooted at the idea, assuring us that "he no speky lie," and that they stood as high as the knee, and had horns. At this we concluded they must be antelope;

and, upon his saying that he had heard them called by that name, expectation put disgust to a precipitate flight, imparted fresh vigour to our limbs, and carried us bravely over the huge potato-patch.

During this time we *saw one rat;* and, just as we had crossed a deep ravine and were looking up at the rugged path we were called upon to ascend, we *smelt another:* we began to think we had been humbugged; and so disgust rallied, overcame expectation beyond further hope, and caused us to make the best of our way down the ravine to the beach, along which ran a fine hard road from Simonstown to the pilot's country residence.

Once clear of the rough walking, we gave up all idea of hunting farther, and, remembering an invitation which Mr. Koutze had extended to us to visit him, took it leisurely along towards his cottage.

Now, however, that we were no longer hunting, it seemed that we were to begin to burn powder; for we had not walked a hundred yards along our fine road, before it took us across a little rivulet that followed the windings of one of those interminable ravines, crossed the road, and then disappeared through the thick bushes, down, down, into the most snaky-looking locality that we had yet seen.

"Hillo! there's a catbird!" exclaimed Ritchie, in an excited whisper.

"Where?" I asked, in the same tone.

"Where? In the bushes! Don't you see him?"

"No, I don't!"

"Nor I either, now! *confound* it! He's got away. Suppose you fire into the bushes at random and let me take him on the wing as he comes out. We must carry *something* back at any rate."

So I fired into the bushes; and oh! such a scream as saluted our affrighted ears in return! one would have thought that half the women in Africa had been shot all over except in their tongues and throats, and that the other half were helping them to scream.

"There! now you've done it!" exclaimed my instigator, as he took to his heels and ran with a speed indicating any thing but his having tired himself over the potato-patch. "*Come on*, man!"

I did not wait for a second invitation, but followed his example with the spasmodically-braced muscles of alarmed excitement. We really thought I might have killed some one; and the cruelty of running away without rendering him, her, or them, any aid that might have been in our power, did not strike us until after we had put several hundred yards between us: then we called a halt, concluded to return, and did so nearly as fast as we had left.

We found that I had fired pellmell in among a dozen or more Hottentot washerwomen, without drawing a drop of blood or otherwise harming them, except by a slight stinging; and, when we had acknowledged the mistake, they rubbed themselves, seemed perfectly satisfied, and went quietly on with their washing, while we bade them a smiling adieu and continued on our way to the pilot's. He received us quite warmly, treated us to as much pure fresh milk, butter, and bread as we could dispose of, showed us all through his whaling establishment, and ended by asking us to dinner. This latter we declined, however, as it was getting late and our walk was long; but we consented to a second attack upon the before-mentioned viands, plus a glass of fine old rum, during the discussion of which he found time to assure us that there were not, had not been for years, and were never again expected to appear, a dozen quail on that side of the mountain, and that as for "spring-boke," *they never* crossed the ridge,—a piece of information rather calculated to strengthen a suspicion as to the veracity of our Hottentot friend which had assailed our minds at the time of our "smelling a rat."

We now started upon our return, but had not walked five minutes before we were overtaken by about the hardest shower of rain that I ever stood under; and I do really believe that if the gentleman of colour who expressed himself so freely in favour of Americans had passed at that moment, he would have been startled, by an explosion of fire-arms and a sharp pain about six inches below his waist, into a far different conclusion as to American character; at the same time that the purser would have found himself minus a load of powder, a cap, two patent wads, and an ounce or more of mustard-seed shot. Fortune favoured him, however, and he went to bed(?) that night weighing some half-ounce less than if we had met. We reached the ship just before dark, and stepped at once into a perfect hotbed of annoying observations.

"Hillo! here comes old bust-proof and his master," said one.

"And Habersham and his fifteen-dollar gun!" exclaimed another.

"And *not* a feather!" put in a third. "Fine hunters *you* are, to-be-sure." And thus were we passed around, until I really began to feel rather small and cheap than otherwise.

"Now, stop your talking for a moment," said the purser, "while I tell you of our hunt." He then gave them a very flowing account of it, imitated the screaming part to perfection, and ended pretty much as follows:—

"We saw during that tramp much more than you did who remained on board. We saw hard walking, oceans of the most beautiful and brilliant, but *odorless*, wild flowers, huge rocks hundreds of feet above the present sea-level, the general form and appearance of which indicated beyond a doubt that they had been at some remote period subjected to the wearing action of a constant surf. Hence, one may reasonably conclude that the sea has retired, or that the rocks have been lifted to their present elevation by some powerful convulsion of nature. We saw all of this and much more, not forgetting the catbird and the terrified females; and what is there more distressingly beautiful than terrified females (pretty ones, I mean) upon the verge of several fainting-fits?"

He stopped for want of breath, gave old bust-proof to his boy to clean, and retired into his den amidst the cheers of the audience.

There were two things that surprised us greatly on our arrival at this port, and those were the almost total absence of natural trees of every description, and the great abundance of sweet oranges. Though able from our mast-head to overlook quite an extensive section of the southern point of Africa, and see natural shrubs and undergrowth in abundance, I much doubt if the eye could have rested upon *a dozen trees* which had not been transplanted.

Some of the shore mechanics, however, who were working on board, told us that there was no lack of timber farther down the coast, and that it existed in considerable variety. The kind most esteemed by them for working into vessels is something between the teak of India and the live oak of Georgia and Florida; but there is a wide difference in one respect, *i. e.* in the smell, which places it entirely out of the power of even the most superficial observer to confound it with either. When moist, this smell is absolutely sickening; and, if you attempt to burn it while in that condition, the fumes drive all, even the *most* seasoned noses, from the immediate vicinity of the fire. I can give no idea of that odour, unless it be by comparing it to a combination of sulphur and assafœtida, and even that does not do it justice.

On account of this peculiar property, the early settlers indorsed it with a name which will not bear translation into the English of the present day, but which, a hundred years since, when people were not so particular, would have been called "ye stinke-woode;" and this I regard as the most appropriate of names, inasmuch as it gives you a better idea of the wood than could otherwise be obtained, except through the medium of the sense of smell, —a source of information to which no one has ever been known to apply twice.

The Mandarin orange of China, as well as the well-known species of the West Indies, flourish here in great perfection,—a rather singular fact when the latitude is taken into consideration. As far as my own experience carries me, the northern shore of the Mediterranean and this extremity of Africa are the only high latitudes where this fruit is cultivated in the open air.

Simon's Town and Cape Town—the former situated on the east side of the Cape of Good Hope, and the latter on its west side—are the two settlements of the English on this extremity of the continent, and are often confounded. They are, notwithstanding, separated by the entire width of the promontory, which is there some twenty miles wide, and are totally different; Cape Town being the door through which pass both exports and imports, while Simon's Town is simply *a naval station*, and, like all other naval stations, a small town has spread itself around the walls of the dock-yard: *nothing* more.

Unlike most English ports, we found this latter without a good beef-market. The article can be obtained in any quantity, but its poor quality renders that fact almost a misfortune. In the words of the doctor, "a little of it went a great way." We seldom had it on the mess-table, therefore, but devoted ourselves to the mutton, which was equally plentiful, cheap, and certainly the best mutton I ever ate,—that of even the Valley of Virginia not excepted.

The population of Simon's Town is only several hundred, who live in some eighty or a hundred neatly-whitewashed houses that presented a striking contrast to those we had lately left at Porto Praya. Among them I counted four churches, five government buildings, sixteen grog-shops, three taverns, &c. &c. I don't know, therefore, that I can well give the place a name for any great morality; for, while four churches require a certain amount of true or worldly religion to keep them up, the sixteen grog-shops, the three hotels, and the &c. &cs., call for even a greater amount of sin and dissipation. Each one of the churches to which I have alluded was the place of worship of different denominations. In the first place, there was the Church of England, composed of most of the "first people of the place,"—evidently *the fashionable church*, the place where the richest dresses and the brilliant uniforms were to be seen. Then came the Mormons, with their seducing doctrines; next the Methodists; and both last and least came the Roman Catholics. With the exception of the Mormons', these churches are attended by persons of all classes; but the prolific followers of Joseph Smith, with very few exceptions, have succeeded in turning from the way of darkness(?) only members of a certain race. The "Cape Malay," a people of whom I had never heard before our arrival, grasped eagerly at the demoralizing doctrine of a plurality of wives, and crowded around the sacred men who could uncurb the bit of sensuality and render null and void the restraining laws of bigamy.

And I was informed by Mr. Holmes, the American consul at Cape Town, that, although the converts to that creed were generally persons of no individual influence, still, from the simple fact of the contagion spreading far and wide, it was rapidly becoming of importance from the sheer force of numbers. The same gentleman also informed me that upon the first arrival of the two "elders" at Cape Town they had paid him a visit, wishing him, as the American consul, (they themselves being Americans, who had been sent from the Great Salt Lake to "preach the word,") to back them up with his countenance through the colony, and that he had been forced to politely deny their request. He *did not* tell me, however, that he had said to them, "Well, gentlemen, your request is rather a singular one; but if you will return to-morrow you shall have an answer." And he further neglected to tell me what that answer was. "I have thought seriously over your *very* singular request, Messrs. Mormons," he said, "and I think it a humbug, (your religion, I mean;) and, as the representative of the great American people, *I can't support a humbug. Good*-morning, gentlemen!"

And this last interpretation of the affair I got from a married friend of his, who seemed to think that Mrs. H. had had something to say about the Mormons and their institutions during the night which followed their first interview with him. So much for the commencement of Mormonism in Africa.

CHAPTER III.

WE MAKE UP A PARTY TO VISIT CAPE TOWN, AND TAKE OUR SEATS IN A CHARIOT —WE READ POETRY IN FOUR LANGUAGES, AND THINK THAT IT MUST BE A FINE THING TO BE A MORMON—WE MAKE THE ACQUAINTANCE OF AN EAGER GENTLEMAN, AND CONCEIVE A HIGH IDEA OF THE HOSPITALITY OF CAPE TOWN.

AFTER having been a week or more at anchor, several of us concluded to pay a visit to Cape Town. A party was therefore made up, consisting of Dr. Stuart, of the Porpoise, Lieutenant Bliss, of the "Old John," and Mr. Lea and myself, from the Kennedy. Our mode of conveyance consisted of a two-wheeled vehicle, a Dutch driver by the name of Peter, four fearfully-rawboned animals that had four legs each and were evidently more like horses than any thing else, and a certain amount of traces, bridles, reins, and whips. This uncertain "turn-out" was dignified by the name of the "Mail-coach,"—a high-sounding title which had alone carried confidence to our unsuspecting hearts and caused us to *pay for our seats in advance.* And now, when I add that this "mail-coach" was without springs, just like an old ox-cart, and that nine unfortunates were crowded into it, some skeptic may be so bold as to say that a two-wheeled vehicle without springs, and drawn by horses, would be apt to spill said nine unfortunates out of its stern while being hauled up a hill; and so, for the information of that awful class of society, I will add yet something more about our *vehicle.*

True, it only had two wheels: but then an ox-cart has no more; and it is a well-known fact that this latter cannot tilt backwards—turn a half back-somerset—without entailing serious inconvenience on the oxen that draw it.

"Yes, but oxen are yoked, and horses are *hitched*," remarks the skeptic.

"Not always, by any means," is my reply. The oxen with us are yoked to their carts, and at the Cape the carts are yoked to the *horses:* that's the only difference. It sounds singular, truly; yet, let us see how they accomplish it.

In our case, the four animals were hitched up exactly as four horses are generally attached to a wagon, with the single addition of a curved and flat bar of iron, which was secured to the pole just back of the fore-legs of the after-ones, and which fit under them just as snugly as the half of a hoop would around a barrel.

And thus much for the ingenious peculiarities of the "mail-coach" that ran daily between Simon's Town and Cape Town, and in which we were induced to "make ourselves comfortable" when we saw that there was no help for it.

It was not long before I was struck with the ingeniousness of the foregoing device for preserving the parallelism of two planes; but I could not help hinting to Peter of a fear which had arisen with it in my mind as to the consequences which might result in case of a stumble.

"Lord bless you, sir!" was his reply: "vy, that's the very time ven it comes in. Don't you see, it a'n't likely as how they'll both fall at oncet? and so t'other holds t'other up." I was struck with the force of his argument, and, lighting a cigar, began to make notes of things in general as they crossed our heavy path. And now I will show the reader how it was that we got into our singular vehicle, and how the "animals" were persuaded to make a start.

It was at the Fountain Inn, the head-quarters of the mail-coach line, that we had agreed to rendezvous; and, having assembled there at sunrise on the appointed morning, we exchanged four shillings sterling for as many cups of warm water, about seven grains of coffee, half an ounce of rancid butter, and four slices of stale bread, which we called breakfast; and then, providing ourselves with a bunch of Manilla cheroots each, climbed up to our seats, and told Peter that he was at liberty to "crack his whip."

Upon receiving this piece of information, the individual to whom it was addressed produced a strange sound, somewhat between a whistle, a grunt, and an exclamation of surprise, which, much to our astonishment, acted like a charm upon the four raw-boned animals. Without waiting to impart a gradual motion to the "coach," they started it with a jump; and, since Jupiter, the goddess of Fortune, or some youthful member of the rising generation, had put a large stone immediately in front of our left wheel, we started with a most awful jolt, which, on account of the absence of springs, was enabled to give the warm water, grains of coffee, stale bread, and half-ounce of rancid butter, a very fair idea of what they had to expect should our road prove rough.

By the time we had driven a mile, both the doctor and myself were on very sociable terms with our Saxon driver; and, before I proceed any further in this veritable narration, I will, for the benefit of all unfortunate "mail-coach" passengers, relate the devices we resorted to to overcome his lofty reserve of manner,—*i. e.* the stupid air of importance which small people filling small stations often assume towards better people who are for the time-being at their mercy. Who is there who at some time has not been offended, has not had his comfort uselessly interfered with, by the conductor of a railroad, the mate of a mail-steamer, or the driver of a "mail-coach"?

In the first place, then, knowing that I was driving over a strange road with a hungry note-book in my pocket, I saw the necessity of being on communicative terms with some person who could answer questions; and, as Peter was the only one in the coach who *could* answer said questions, he "was the man" to be thawed. Now, as soon as I had brought the doctor to my way of thinking, we commenced the attack, I being armed with the ability to drive even four "animals" in hand, and with a bunch of cheroots; while the great medicine-man shook aloft a much more terrible weapon of offence in the shape of a pocket-pistol,—not one of the murdering inventions of Messrs. Sharpe, Colt, or Allen, but a reasonable, single-barrelled fellow, who only had one true aim, which was to keep always full of good old brandy.

With these as our weapons, we soon overcame the enemy's reserve, I having offered to drive for him while he poured out the doctor's brandy, and subsequently handed him a cigar with an overcoming suavity of manner. Our ammunition was not half expended before his face was wreathed in smiles and his tongue loosened into absolute loquaciousness.

"What!" he exclaimed, in answer to a question which the doctor now hazarded,—"what! Don't you know what that fence is made of?"

The doctor puffed his cheroot, and assured his "Christian friend" that he was indeed in a state of blissful ignorance as to the material of which it was composed.

"Why, them's *whale*-ribs, and they lasts longer than any *wood* you can find."

"Do they, indeed?" smiled the man of pills; but he *said* nothing. It is astonishing how far a pleasant smile will go. This one seemed to tickle Peter amazingly: he again indulged in the strange sound which we had heard at starting, and then his tongue ran from subject to subject with amazing agility. At last he came down to his domestic affairs, and every one in the coach was soon aware of the following facts connected with them.

Peter was a married man. Peter had no children. Peter never *expected* to have any children. Peter's wife didn't love him. Peter never went home more than once a year. Peter was a new and zealous advocate of the Mormon doctrine. Peter thought that woman was made for man, and not man for woman. And last, but not least apparently, Peter was desperately in love with a feminine whose name was *not* Mrs. Peter.

About the time that he had enlightened us thus far, the "mail-coach" came to a halt in front of a most singular sign. It was at least ten feet square, and hung from a long pole that projected over the door of an unpretending wayside inn. It was intended to tell the traveller all that he had to expect, without putting him to the trouble of asking questions. On its double face there was painted a house, in the open window of which stood a half-emptied bottle and an inverted glass: the door also was open, supposed to be the exponent of the boundless hospitality which awaited the wayfarer upon entering. There was also on its face the figure of a Charles II. cavalier, with a shepherd's crook in his warlike hand, and a most feline-looking dog crouching at his feet. There was, moreover, a horseshoe nailed on its bottom-edge, to scare away all Dutchmen's ghosts; two verses of poetry in the centre, to tell the nature of the "treatment" that was to be expected; and, finally, written under the feet of the cavalier, the following sentence:—"The Gentle Shepherd of Salisbury Plain." The poetry, which was written in English, French, Latin, and Dutch, is well worthy of preservation. It was "got up" at the shepherd's especial request by an English army-officer who was fond of fun. Here is how it reads:—

"'LIFE'S BUT A JOURNEY; LET US LIVE ON THE ROAD,' SAYS THE GENTLE SHEPHERD.

"Multum in parvo, pro bono publico;
Entertainment for man and beast all of a row.
Lekker Kost as much as you please;
Excellent beds, without any fleas.

"Nos patriam fugimus; now we are here,
Vivamus, let us live, by selling beer.
On donne à boire et à manger ici:
Come in and try it, whoever you be."

Upon drawing up in front of the establishment from which this rare signboard was hung, we were received by the Gentle Shepherd of Salisbury Plain in person, and had it not been for a forewarning of Peter's in regard to the quality of his "lekker," we would most certainly have been inveigled, by his polite invitation and bland smiles, into entering his bar-room and paying him a shilling sterling each. As it was, however, we contented ourselves with congratulating him upon the non-existence of fleas in his beds, (as per signboard,) wished him a polite good-morning, and drove out of hearing before he could command words to express himself pleased or annoyed by our remarks. We inferred the latter to be the case, however, from the fact of his looking very red in the face and shaking his fist at our retreating conveyance, as well as from a comment indulged in by Peter upon his appearance:—"Vell now, old man's mad, I *tell* you."

"Never mind the old shepherd, Peter; you take another drink of this good brandy, and then crack your whip: we're getting late," said the doctor.

So Peter smilingly complied, and then once more "got off" the "undetermined sound."

It is twenty-one miles from Simon's Town to Cape Town, and the first seven miles that we had driven over was the best of roads at one time and the worst of roads at another. It was what is understood by a "beach-road," so that the hauling was over hard sand at low-water and through hub-deep sand at high-water: the latter happened unfortunately to fall to our lot. The last fourteen miles, however, we travelled over the most beautiful road *I ever saw*, and I do not think that I ever rode over a beautiful road before with such true pleasure. This was owing to the fact of our "chariot" (Peter even called it "the chariot" sometimes) being minus springs; for I could not avoid imagining the horrible succession of jolts to which we should have been forced to submit had we been running over any but a perfectly-macadamized road.

In addition to the perfect smoothness of this road, we found, after passing the Half-way House, an avenue of fine old oaks spreading their branches between us and the sun, which, meeting overhead and twisting among each other in every imaginable form, formed a cool, shady drive, that was crossed every now and then by a noisy little stream of limpid mountain-water, that washed our tires and added to the general coolness of the road. This avenue reached almost to Cape Town: it must have been eight miles long. And just imagine an avenue of heavy, solid old oaks of that length: it was a perfect treat to drive through it. And then the numbers of the fair sex (?) that we were continually passing,—some of them quite pretty, and, again, some of them horribly ugly. They were of all colours, too. They were white, copper-coloured, black, and undetermined, and seemed to resort to this avenue as their favourite morning walk.

I soon began to be attracted by Peter's manner as we fell in with these fair pedestrians: I noticed that if they were young and pretty, our newly-fledged Mormon *invariably knew them*, whereas, if they were the contrary, such was never the case. To some of the former he would give a nod; to others, a "good-morning, miss!" while with others again I even saw him go so far as to indulge in a wink; but, when either age or ugliness drew towards us, he always found that his horses were not going fast enough, that it was necessary to gather up his reins, shake his dilapidated whip, and produce the startling noise, the "undetermined sound." And if they came towards him too closely, as if *determined* to catch his eye, he would even turn his head to answer an imaginary question, thus presenting his back to their anxious gaze. Noticing all of this, I could not help hinting that I feared Mrs. Peter had good cause to avoid doting on him; but he replied, with great earnestness of manner, that the greater part of them were Mormons, and consequently his spiritual sisters. So I thought, "What a fine thing it must be to be a Mormon!" and thereafter held my peace.

Previous to our arrival at the Gentle Shepherd's, we had passed a small sea-side village, called Cork Bay, which Peter told us was inhabited entirely by whale-fishermen and their families. We subsequently saw another of those whaling-establishments at Cape Town. These two, with that which we had previously visited at the pilot's, comprised all that we could hear of in the locality.

Those engaged in the business do not own vessels which they send in search of the whale, but accomplish most of their work in open boats. They lounge about the beach until some unfortunate whale is discovered in the bay, when they man their boats, attack him with harpoon and lance, and, if victorious, tow him to the beach, where he is hauled up by oxen, stripped of his blubber, and otherwise roughly handled. We were told that they were getting very scarce of late years, however, and that the business no longer held out the promise of even a reasonable gain. We now ceased to wonder where so many whale-ribs had come from, the road having been lined with fences made of them, during the first part of our drive.

Talking of hauling the whale up with oxen reminds me that I there saw as many as sixteen of the latter yoked to a single cart; and we were subsequently informed by the consul that they could travel without difficulty as far as forty or fifty miles a day before a heavy load. They are yoked like those of South America, the yoke being lashed on in front of the horns.

Shortly after leaving the whale-rib fences behind us, we began to find a more elevated country; and soon after this we pulled up in front of the "Half-way House," where we exchanged our "piles of bones" for four others, that looked even more unpromising than the first, but which astonished us by getting over the beautiful road with a very fair speed. We now began to see rich, tasteful, and romantic-looking country-seats peering through the planted woods on either side of our avenue, also two or three small villages, and as many brick-kilns. These latter produce a very inferior brick, however, if I may judge from those which came under my inspection. The country-seats belong to the more wealthy residents of Cape Town, are of the English style, and are generally surrounded by extensive groves of pine-trees, planted in rows like Indian corn. As we drove along between those beautifully laid-out grounds, we were more than ever struck with the absence of natural foliage.

At last we began to enter Cape Town, after a drive of three hours and twelve minutes, and, having taken rooms at the "Masonic," commenced preparing for an official visit to Mr. Holmes, the consul. He received us with great politeness, and, as is usual on such occasions, the visit terminated with an invitation to dinner, at "six sharp;" and we were just being bowed out of the consulate, when a most gentlemanly-looking Englishman of some fifty years entered, and was introduced to us as Mr. Eager. The name of this gentleman seemed most appropriate; for he took advantage of the first pause in the renewed conversation to ask us to dine with him at "six sharp," which caused us to smile as we told him of "six sharp" No. 1, and begged him to accept it as our excuse. He seemed quite disappointed at this, and begged us to let him have the pleasure of our company at the same hour on the following day; but there, also, three of us were forced to disappoint him, as our leave expired at that time. The doctor, however, accepted "with pleasure," and, after pointing out the most pleasant direction for strolling, our polite acquaintance took his leave. We never subsequently met his equal: we hope to meet him again.

Having nothing to do but hunt for what was to be seen, we followed the direction he had pointed out, and soon arrived at a stone gateway that opened into a most shady and picturesque walk. It proved to be some five hundred yards in length by about fifty feet in width, and was limited on either side by closely-planted oaks of gigantic proportions, the same apparently that had sheltered us on our way down. Had not the days of Aladdin's lamp and ring been among those of the past, one might readily have imagined this second avenue of noble trees to have been a section of that beautiful road that had been transplanted for our express benefit.

At the far-end of this walk we found another gateway, which, like the first, was guarded day and night by ramrod-like sentries, whose particular business it is to salute officers and to keep out brindled cows, fierce dogs, and, what is nearly as bad, presuming rowdies, so that ladies and children may enjoy a quiet walk without the fear of encountering the attentions of either of the foregoing parties.

On the left of this delightful promenade is located the Government house and grounds, while the space on the right is occupied by a botanical garden. Both of these are enclosed by tasteful fencing; and when you get half-way up the avenue you come to two gates,—the one directly facing the other,—before which two more dressed-up ramrods walk up and down and bore all who pass in uniform, by "presenting arms" with a clang that often startles weak-minded officials into a state of nervous politeness and takes away greatly from the pleasure of any one's walk. This soon became such a bore that we were glad to get out of our feathers and emerge once more from the "Masonic" in the reasonable costume of free and enlightened citizens. Previous to this, however, we used said feathers to open the gates of the garden, through the well-kept walks of which we lounged, to the intense admiration of a dozen or more nurses and probably double the number of children, until the arrival of the hour for lunch.

During this lounge we did not notice any foreign plants or flowers; but those indigenous to the country were both so numerous and beautiful that their presence was not at all necessary. We were told by the keeper that that garden was not supported by either the home, colonial, or city treasury, but by the voluntary subscription of various families, who thus secure to themselves and friends a quiet, retired spot in which to stroll at pleasure. Then each of these subscribers has furnished him any number of tickets, which are presented to "distinguished strangers" to gain them admission; but, in spite of this, there are shingle-notices stuck up and through the garden to the effect that "strangers are admitted without tickets," so one would say they are of no use. When the music is under way, however, the shingle-notices cease to be of effect, and the ticket is required. Some of our officers found themselves in a most mortifying situation on this account: they were in uniform, the garrison-band was in full blast, and the garden was crowded with "the families." Of course they made for the gate with as dignified a step as possible, to join in the scene, when invidious Fate, in the shape of the gate-keeper, stopped them, and asked for their tickets.

Of course they could only look angry or sheepish, and they chose the former; but old Fate was not to be alarmed. They were therefore about to act like sensible men and retire, when several of the officers of the garrison, seeing their dilemma, left the ladies who were hanging on their arms, and advanced to their assistance; but their efforts were of no avail, and they were forced to return to the fair ones, while our fellows walked off in a state of disgusted sheepishness. The English officers seemed as much mortified, however, as they were, and a few days later a long apology reached the squadron from his excellency the governor, in which he attributed all the blame to the stupidity of the gate-keeper.

Well, as soon as we had got out of our uniform, we

again sallied out, this time in search of a bookstore, where we hoped to find a standard work that we were in search of. We were surprised to find but one establishment of the kind, and at being there informed that they only imported similar works "*to order.*" I could not help comparing this yawning reply, the store, and the "importer" himself, with the Yankee bookseller of the present day. I could not help thinking how in a port like that, where no duties were levied, the latter would soon open their eyes to the "Young America" way of carrying on that business.

We now returned to the hotel, where we found several Dutch officers, whose vessel had reached Simon's Bay since our arrival, engaged in discussing a late lunch in the only sitting-room. Of course we had to intrude our company upon them or retire to our rooms; so we chose the former. It is a singular fact that naval men, of whatever nation, become acquainted as the most natural thing in the world: in the present case, five minutes had not elapsed before several bottles of ale were consumed and double the number of cheroots ignited. Then we commenced to talk of our past and future movements quite smoothly; and when they left in the "mail-coach" a half-hour later, one would have imagined that we were old acquaintances. We learned one thing from those gentlemen which struck us as being but just and reasonable:—their men-of-war are kept seven or eight years in commission when once sent to a distant colony like Batavia, (they were then on their homeward-bound voyage from that station,) and after that, such officers as desire it may retire from service on reduced pay;—a proceeding which, if applied to our own navy, would render it both effective and *comfortable.*

Table Mountain has been drawn so often both by pen and pencil, and Cape Town, which slumbers at its base, is so well known, that I shall pass lightly over both and hasten on to other regions.

We met Mr. Holmes at the appointed hour, enjoyed a very fair dinner, and had the pleasure of conversing during said enjoyment with Captain Jamison, R.N., an accomplished Englishman, and a man of great general and local information. Having resided over twenty years in the colony, and being known as a gentleman of unexceptionable character, I feel that I may safely give circulation to parts of his very instructive conversation.

Among other things, he told us that the tribe of Kaffirs proper did not number over forty thousand fighting-men, but that in their conflicts with the English they could double or treble that number by calling in other South Africans, drawn chiefly from the Bushmen and another tribe the name of which has escaped me. The Hottentots, he said, were almost extinct. In regard to wild animals and reptiles, he said that the cheetah, the leopard, and the antelope, still existed in the vicinity in considerable numbers, but that a lion was now very rarely encountered. Puff-adders were abundant, and the cobra di capello was often killed on the mountain-sides measuring from ten to fourteen feet.

This latter was a piece of information that sounded much more agreeably to my ear at that time than it would have done some days previous, when the purser and myself were "smelling a rat" at the head of a deep ravine, with at least half a mile of undergrowth between us and the open road.

Captain Jamison next spoke of the great superiority of the Kaffir over the Bushman, and placed the latter in turn over the Hottentot. "The Kaffir," he said, "has considerable mind, is brave, and differs from the negro in many essential points: in colour he approaches the Moor. The Bushman is 'regular negro,' passably brave, but of no mental capacity; while the Hottentot is remarkable for nothing but high cheek-bones and a most marvellous development that would put to shame the most exaggerated of old-fashioned bustles."

Somehow or other the conversation here turned upon Peter, our Mormon driver; and the captain laughingly gave us a short history of him. Peter, he said, was widely known as a clever and obliging fellow, but, like Joseph Bagstock, he was "sly, sir,—devilish sly." Having been unmercifully "kicked" by a young lady of Dutch parentage, he had rushed to the feet of a Hottentot belle and dragged her to the nuptial broomstick in a state of mind bordering upon desperation. Alas for Peter! He had not been married a week before he made the startling discovery that he was not her "first love;" and this, combined with the fact of his brandy-bottle always giving out when he still thought that it should be half full, produced a gradual change in his feelings which finally resulted in his embracing the Mormon faith. Poor Peter! I'll venture to say that you still sit behind those piles of bones, still urge them ahead with that ejaculation of surprise.

It was a late hour when we shook hands with our host,

and the next day at 2 P.M. we were again in the "chariot," on our return to Simon's Town. During this drive we were struck with the great number of brilliantly-plumaged birds that crossed our path, as well as by the fact that none of them seemed to be of the singing order. I asked Peter the reason of this, and he replied that they had given up singing since the English had taken the country from his people,—an answer which caused a young female in a linsey-woolsey garment of very limited length to say, "What a vag Mr. Peter is!" "What's it to you?" asked the latter, turning sharply around and scowling upon her with crushing disdain. The lady was not pretty. We are again on board ship. So much for Cape Town and—Peter.

CHAPTER IV.

WE LEAVE SIMON'S TOWN AND SAIL FOR BATAVIA, WHERE WE RECEIVE A VISIT THAT *DOES* RELATE TO OUR HEALTH, AND SEE A REMARKABLE GUN; AFTER WHICH WE LISTEN TO SEVERAL ASTONISHING ACCOUNTS FROM AN ENGLISH RESIDENT, AND AGAIN PUT TO SEA.

IT is the 9th of November, and we are again getting up our anchor. The Hancock and Cooper sailed some days since for Batavia, and we are now to follow them in the Kennedy, while the Vincennes and Porpoise proceed to Hong-Kong *viâ* Australia. From Batavia we are to proceed in company with the first two vessels to the neighbouring Straits of Gaspar, survey them, and then join the Vincennes and Porpoise at Hong-Kong. And now, before we leave Simon's Town, let me say a word in regard to the "Cape Malay."

Surprised to find this race in such numbers so far away from their island-homes, I questioned Captain Jamison on the subject, and learned that when the Cape was in possession of the Dutch they had been imported from the islands of Sumatra, Borneo, &c. as slaves, and that, being remarkably prolific, they had increased tenfold. That when the English succeeded the Dutch, and they were emancipated and thrown on their own resources, they had turned their attention to making honest livelihoods, and were now very creditable members of society. I could not but compare their conduct and success as freemen with the conduct and failure of the African slave of my own land when similarly released.

There was another subject—one of nature's numerous phenomena—that excited both our surprise and admiration while anchored off Simon's Town.

The whole surface of the harbour would at times be covered by a greasy, frothy, variously-coloured substance, that gave the water a most uncleanly appearance during the day, but which at night caused it to resemble a lake of molten gold. How deep it extended we could not tell, possibly the whole depth of the harbour.

We had observed the same phenomenon while approaching the coast, and had at first been at a loss what to attribute it to. The whole sea was sprinkled with the variously-hued patches, and as we sailed through them we left a wake of fire that was apparent even under the glare of the mid-day sun. It was like sailing over a painted sea in the daytime; and at night, when the seas lifted up their lambent crests in all directions, the effect was truly grand. We subsequently attributed their existence to the presence of vast masses of a migrating infusoria, the minute and phosphorescent forms of the largest of which we could readily detect in a drop of the water by placing it under an ordinary magnifier.

And now when we again "launched out upon the sea"—we, and the Vincennes, and the poor doomed Porpoise—we looked around in vain for those living fields—those green and golden and purple plains—which had extended for miles around us and been composed of *an infinite number of living animals*,—animals which exist only in the microscopic world, and which are of such infinitesimal dimensions that *we are told* five millions may pass through the eye of a cambric-needle at the same time without elbowing each other. So much for the Cape of Good Hope; —with its ugly women, songless birds, and odorless flowers.

I have already remarked that it was November 9, and that we were again at sea. The first day out, while we were all three running along before a glorious breeze, the Vincennes suddenly lost a man overboard, and a most lively scene ensued while picking him up. Helms were shoved hurriedly down, studding-sails slapped and flapped in the most approved style, boats were lowered, ships came up into the wind, and, finally, the unfortunate clumsy was rescued from "a watery grave." Night closed around us, and we parted company: the Vincennes and Porpoise to skirt the coral reefs of southern latitudes, and we to make the best of our way to Batavia.

One of those singular accidents which sailors in particular are disposed to regard in a miraculous light now occurred on board, and gave us something to talk about. We were eating our first sea-breakfast: all of the mess, save the officer of the deck, were at the table, and the ship was beating slowly to the eastward against a light breeze. Suddenly our assistant hydrographer, Mr. Samuel Potts, of Washington, remarked that he had "dreamed a dream" about his box of clothes, which, having failed to reach him before sailing from home, his friends had promised to ship to China. "I dreamt," he said, "that we were lying becalmed near a merchant-ship, that we lowered a boat and boarded her, and that the boat returned with my box." Nothing more was said or thought on the subject for several hours, when, strange to say, we found ourselves becalmed within a mile or two of a deeply-laden bark which showed American colours.

"That fellow looks as if he might be from New York, with a load of coal and a few stray newspapers," remarked Russell, the third lieutenant. "I'm going to ask for a boat to board him."

So he asked, got a boat, boarded the strange sail, *and returned with Mr. Potts's box.* She proved to be the bark Roebuck, of Baltimore, eighty-four days out, loaded with coal for Perry's squadron.

Our passage to Batavia presents little of interest to the general reader. I take a few extracts from my journal, simply to avoid slighting that portion of the cruise.

"Nov. 15.—Lat. 35° 37′ S., long. 28° 25′ E. A fresh breeze from south to southeast. Weather overcast and cloudy, the water of a greenish tinge. The following birds have hovered around the ship during the day:—albatross, Cape-pigeons, gulls, blue jays, (a sea-bird resembling its shore-namesake,) sheer-waters, sea-crows, petrels, and whale-birds; not so many by far as yesterday. Where have they gone to? They generally hang by a ship to pick up the scraps that are thrown over by the cooks, and I have been often struck by the uncertainty of their presence. I have at length attributed it to the proximity of other ships; for I have noticed that whenever a vessel comes in sight they invariably become scarce. They soar to such heights that many miles of space that are below our horizon become open to them, besides which they have a clearer sight than man, and instinct in addition. The consequence is that they always see a ship first; and I feel confident that the approach of many vessels might be predicted by following the old Roman idea of consulting the flight of birds."

"Nov. 16.—Saw a school of white porpoises during the afternoon watch, who played about us with great ease, darting ahead or astern as it pleased them, though we were running at the rate of ten knots. One of the men—Corcoran, an old whaler—got a harpoon over the bow, and put it entirely through one of them; but our speed was so great that it tore out with the first jerk, and the wounded animal started frantically off at right angles and was followed by the entire school. He marked his path by a bloody streak."

"Nov. 18.—The weather has been dark and threatening for the last twenty-four hours, and the barometer sinking with a determined uniformity unpleasant to behold. We knew that 'something was in the wind,' but thought we should be able to drag along quite comfortably under double reefs or something of that sort. We contented ourselves, therefore, with hauling up the mainsail, stowing the jib, and setting the topmast-staysail; but it soon came a little harder than we had bargained for, and it was 'up helm and run before it' with unpleasant suddenness. We now shortened sail to a close-reefed maintopsail and foresail, and 'let her slide.' This latter sail was new, and therefore gave us no concern, but the topsail was half worn and not to be trusted. Suddenly the cyclone (it was blowing fearfully by this time) boxed around forward of the beam, and the old maintopsail blew into a hundred pieces. The lee sheet-block was snapped off with the report of a young cannon, and went singing to leeward with furious velocity. 'Hard up the helm, to keep her before the gale:' and, as the wheel turned heavily around, I saw a beautiful sight. It had been blowing a moderate gale for the last twelve hours; a heavy swell had been rolling directly *against* it, and the gale of course had got up its own sea, which ran against and on top of the swell. Now this sudden shifting of the wind brought its new direction almost at right angles with both sea and swell, besides getting up a *cross*-sea; and, as one of the former came tumbling on our quarter, (the ship herself hopping about like an India-rubber ball,) a violent squall got under its curved crest, and, lifting it bodily up, seemed all at once to change from a squall to a furious whirlwind. The result can be better imagined than described. This vast volume of water, held in suspension, as it were, by a powerful current of air that seemed to revolve upon its own axis, and lifting itself between us and the dazzling rays of a meridian sun, reflected the various hues of the rainbow for a moment, and then, torn and scattered into giant drops and driving mist, made the sea foam under its descent and saturated us with its whirling spray. It was a beautiful sight, and, though in or near the centre of one of the dreaded cyclones, we took time to admire it."

"Nov. 21.—I borrowed 'old bust-proof' from the purser this morning and went on deck to shoot an old Cape-albatross, gray with age, and measuring at least twelve feet from pinion to pinion. He swept within thirty or forty yards of me several times, but could never be persuaded to 'turn his back' so that the shot might penetrate up along his feathers. He was evidently a very polite old gentleman, or he had a great weakness for his tail,—it was hard to say which. I was forced, therefore, to fire as he presented his side in turning, and this I did several times with no effect; he did not even shake his valued tail. The No. 4 shot evidently glanced from the smooth and polished coating. At last he forgot his breeding, turned his tail upon me, and was notified of his breach of etiquette through the agency of both barrels. This seemed to cause him considerable annoyance for a short time, but at the end of a minute he ceased to shake his caudal appendage and became as majestic in his movements as ever. I now went below and got some BBB shot, determined to 'try the virtue of stones;' and, like the boy in the apple-tree, he came down at the first summons. I looked at his heavy body and snowy plumage as he floated by, and felt a pang of remorse for having so wantonly destroyed so noble a bird."

"Nov. 27.—Here comes a 'fish-story.' One of our old quartermasters, Peterson by name, told me a few moments since, with the most serious face in the world, that a whale had come as close as ten paces to the ship during his watch, and that he was as long as the ship—within a few feet. I asked him how much he meant by 'a few feet,' and was amused at his answering, 'Ten or twelve, sir!' He thus made his whale over a hundred feet long, and evidently believed what he was saying.

"'His wake was like that of a ship,' he said; 'and when he lifted to blow, his head was at least ten feet above the sea.' I give his yarn a place here because the old fellow would not *imagine* any thing unless for a 'consideration;' and, if there is such a thing as a whale over a hundred feet long, I believe he has seen him, in which case it is worth mentioning."

"Dec. 4.—I observed indications of a strong current on the tops of the heavy westerly swells as they rolled by us. One of them which I measured roughly from the mizzen-rigging—my eye being elevated twenty feet above the sea-level—proved to be ten feet high, or twenty feet from its top to the bottom of the valley, and to be about one hundred yards from the one that followed it. Its velocity was about thirty feet a second. These swells, so different from the short ones of the Atlantic and other confined bodies of water, came under our stern with a power acquired from the immense stretch of space over which they roll, and lift the ship upon their rising breast, urging her ahead with an increased velocity, and leaving us bow up and stern down, to be similarly treated by the next in turn. Ugly companions they would be among the broken rocks of a lee shore." And now for the Malay Islands.

It was on the 24th of December, 1853, that we sighted that of Java, and the next morning we were at anchor off the town of Anger, situated on its western extreme. We stopped there to get a pilot, if possible, to take us on to Batavia; and, though there was none to be found at that time, we bought a late coast-chart from the authorities, by which we worked up to Batavia the next day. We found the Hancock and Cooper already there, and the following day the former left for our surveying-ground,—distant now only a few hours' sail,—ordering us to follow as soon as possible. We had been at sea forty-six days, and were amply prepared to enjoy the few short hours thus considerately granted us.

Let me make an extract from my journal in regard to Anger.

We had anchored near it during the night—"At daylight a beautiful sight spread itself out before us: a low, undulating country, backed by the blue mountains of the interior, and fronted by dense groves of the cocoanut, of the mangosteen, and of the banana, had taken the place of our interminable sea-horizon, and refreshed the vision while it also promised an abundant supply of the most delicious fruits.

"While I yet admired this grateful change through a glass, a dozen or more Malay boats pulled alongside of us, whose occupants soon gave us to understand that they were a most noisy set of people. Their boats were laden to their gunwales with fruit, vegetables, and animals of a dozen different species,—live stock in abundance for the table, and various unknown animals to tempt the curiosity of the naturalist.

"We found every thing very cheap:—chickens one dollar the dozen; eggs ditto the hundred; and the fruit absolutely being thrown away. Everybody smiled complacently, looked ahead two hours, and made an imaginary breakfast upon broiled chickens, soft-boiled eggs, and——mangosteens."

Reader, have you ever eaten a mangosteen? It is by far the most delicious fruit in the world; it puts the cheremoya of Peru to the blush, and doesn't show strawberries-and-cream the shade of a chance: it is worth living even in the East to eat the mangosteen. "While I was opening one of them and putting the four sections into my mouth one after the other in rapid succession, I was saluted by a young Javanese of Mongolian cast of features, rather below the middle size, and showing a horribly-black set of teeth—black as ink—when he wished to appear amiable. He told me that he was the second captain of the port, and that he had called to pay his respects and see *if we wanted any thing.* I subsequently found that he was a dealer in poultry, &c.; and as soon as he found we *didn't want any thing*—having been previously supplied—he took himself off in high dudgeon. Before he went, however, I had, with my usual curiosity, questioned him as to the colour of his teeth, and been told that all of his people's teeth were the same, resulting from the excessive chewing of the betel-nut.

"I liked the looks of their boats and canvas. They were very cleanly built, and were propelled by both oars and sails. The former were very short and broad, almost paddles, and the latter—which generally consisted of a single or double lug—were made of grass-matting sewed together, that was lighter and more flexible even than canvas.

"Like most half-civilized or savage people, the occupants of these boats expressed themselves in quick, loud, and energetic language, accompanied by violent and frequent gesticulation. To stand at a distance and see several of them carrying on an ordinary conversation, a stranger would imagine them upon the verge of a free fight."

While approaching Batavia, the wind was very light,

and the sun so hot as to make the deck *unbearable* for a person with thin soled-shoes. I again turn to my journal:—

"At 1.45 P.M. we beat through the narrow passage that separates the small island of Amsterdam from that of Java, and escaped going on shore by the skin of our teeth: the fine working-qualities of our ship were all that saved us. There are more small islands around us now than I ever saw before,—mere knots of earth with little or no elevation, a very dense growth of wood, and averaging probably five hundred feet in circumference."

I subsequently learned that these islands are let out by the Dutch authorities to the highest bidder, who then cuts the wood and supplies the market of Batavia.

"They seem to be densely populated; and the houses—which are low, and built of bamboo and grass—are situated in snug-looking, shady nooks, and seemed so cool and airy from our heated decks, that one almost forgot the half-blistered feet upon which he was backing and filling around in search of a shady spot upon which to put them. As I write, I hear the laughing voice of our assistant hydrographer:—'I say, doctor, you should have been with us when we landed at Anger this morning: there were more than a hundred Malays on the beach to receive us, and I know I could have carried all the clothes they had on, on my left arm, at a single load. They seemed to think that nature, like beauty, "when unadorned was adorned the most."'"

Poor fellows! One of them now slumbers in the fathomless depths of the coral sea; and the other,—his honest heart beat its final throb upon the unknown shore of heathen Japan, and, as his wasted frame was lowered into its Christian grave amidst the urned ashes of infidel millions, the words of hope—"I am the Resurrection and the Life"—floated solemnly through the silent air, and told the lounging priests of the Buddhist temple that reared its quaint form over the stranger's grave, that the reign of their gods of stone was drawing to a close.

"We have just anchored between our two consorts, and have already been boarded by the boat of a Dutch man-of-war, the officer of which speaks English perfectly. He has been so polite as to give us some useful information in regard to this proverbially-unhealthy port. He says that their squadron, consisting of five steamers and a frigate, has at present several hundred men and officers in the hospital,—cases of Java fever,—and that as a sanitary measure all vessels anchoring here are advised to observe the following rules.

"Firstly: to have natives to pull in their boats, so as to expose the men as little as possible:—

"Secondly: to do no work between 10 A.M. and 4 P.M. that takes the men out from under the awnings.

"Thirdly and lastly: to spread the latter as soon as the sun begins to dissipate the overcast sky, to keep them spread until the sky again becomes overcast in the evening, and then to trice them up so that the heat may radiate from the deck before night. In that way, he said, they managed to keep so cool as often to be able to get to sleep before midnight: neglect these precations and the lower decks would be like ovens. We thanked our adviser, and he took his leave."

I shall say little in regard to Batavia: the road has

been travelled too often. I turn to my journal and select the few following extracts:—

"The ship's sides and decks are so hot that one almost melts in his bunk, and to sleep on deck in the dew is said to be certain sickness."

Bliss, the third lieutenant of the Hancock, and myself had determined to go on shore.

"We had at our disposal one of that vessel's boats, over which was spread a fine awning, and which was pulled by Malay boatmen hired by Captain Rodgers *from the Government* for the small consideration of one rupee each a day. A rupee is equal to from thirty-six to forty cents, and each man must pay fifteen of those cents to the authorities for being so kind as to hire him out. Thus he has only some twenty-two or three left as payment for pulling about all day under a broiling sun. This, however, is good pay; for ten doits—three cents—will give him food for a day, and then he has the rest to gamble with. They are the greatest gamblers I ever saw, except, perhaps, the Chinese.

"After pulling a mile or more from the ship, we reached the mouth of a canal, up which we passed to the landing. We were told that it was a most dangerous thing to cross the bar at its mouth when it was blowing fresh, as there was always a bad sea breaking, and hundreds of sharks and crocodiles ready to pick up the inmates of a swamped boat.

"These animals, it seems, abound in great numbers about the bar,—the sharks outside and the crocodiles inside,—and feed upon the refuse of the city as it is swept down to them by a two-knot current, sometimes making a dessert of some capsized unfortunate. The shark never crosses the bar, and the crocodile never goes up higher than the first houses; so the natives bathe in perfect security in the part of the canal running through the city. The water of this stream is of a dirty grayish-white colour, holds in suspension the sweepings of the city, and smells horribly. One would scarcely imagine it conducive to cleanliness to bathe in it; and yet it is the *water furnished to shipping for drinking-purposes.* It is also used —after passing through stone filterers—by the entire population of Batavia,—a fact which causes many 'first-comers' to say very little about thirst for several days after their arrival.

"I judged, from various indications, that the Dutch have these people in complete subjection. Even the natives, their own fellows, who are so fortunate as to be in the Government employ, are respected, feared, and obeyed as though they were superior beings. This was exemplified even in the conduct of our temporary boatmen, who, when we would get fouled among other boats,—the canal was always crowded,—cleared a track for us with curses, threats, and frequent blows, and were scarcely scowled upon in return. I thought this strange, as my previous idea of the Malay character was that of a wild, untamable, treacherous, and warlike race."

We have landed at the lower town, and hired a conveyance to take us up to the city.

"Our carriage was a comfortable, strongly-built, double buggy, that ran on four very small and solid wheels and was drawn by two very small and solid horses,—horses about the size of a large Shetland pony. Our driver was a Malay, who was very warmly clad for that country. He had on a large oval-crowned straw hat, a gown-like garment of fancy calico, and was protected from the sun by the extensively-projecting roof of the vehicle. He carried a long whip, which, he told us, the law required him to crack at every bridge, corner, or approaching carriage, and, further, that at night every carriage had to drive before a blazing torch, held aloft by a man who rode behind. All of this was to guard against the risk of unpleasant contacts. Unfortunately, he did not thus enlighten us until we had rewarded him with an extra rupee for putting himself into a perspiration in his endeavours to 'make good time,' as we thought, while in reality it was the law which caused him to crack his whip at such a fearful rate. At first we could not imagine what could make every one in such a hurry: every coachman that we passed was cracking his long whip over the heads of his apparently crack-proof ponies."

After driving a half-mile or so, we pass through an enclosure in which are the Government storehouses.

"While passing through these grounds, Bliss pointed out to me a heavy gun, apparently a thirty-two-pounder, which he said a Dutch officer had told him was much reverenced by the native women.

"It seems that, like the ancient Athenians, these people have an idea that *effect* may exist without *cause;* or, rather, when the occurrence of a certain every-day event is looked for in vain, it may be brought about by prayers, offerings to some deity, or the observance of some superstitious form. The Malay ladies therefore, having invested this gun with some miraculous power, are under the impression that they have only to recline upon it for a few moments, invoke the assistance of its powerful influence, stick their offerings in the ground at its rear, and then return home with an *almost* certainty of their prayers being answered. 'The Dutchman said that that gun had been there ever since the English had given up the colony,' continued Bliss, 'and that there is no telling how much longer it will remain. See there, the flowers and fruit and pieces of gilded paper lying around the breech!'"

I had taken a chew of "betel-nut," and, having never heard of the fruit before, inquired concerning it, and wrote in my journal as follows:—

"The betel-nut is used by the natives of both sexes, very much as we use cavendish,—the only difference being that they swallow much of the saliva. It is a stimulant, and is said to impart strength when weak from hunger, without any unpleasant reaction. It grows upon a tall, shaft-like tree, which often attains a height of from one hundred to one hundred and fifty feet. It is perfectly free from branches, knots, or even great irregularities of the bark. It is a single shaft from the ground until within a few feet of the top, when a few branches shoot out and produce the nut. One of them might be taken by a stranger for a very tall and straight cocoanut-tree. The preparation which they chew, and which is generally supposed to be simply a piece of the nut, is composed of equal parts of lime, the leaf, and the nut. It has an acrid, burning taste at first, and is far from unpleasant. The burning sensation proceeds from the leaf.

"The use of this nut gives to its consumers a most disgusting appearance about the mouth. They carry the 'quid' between the lower front-teeth and the lip; and, as it is often as large as the half of one's thumb, and dyes the lips and inner membrane a bright red, they look as if they had just received a crushing blow in the mouth. It is passing strange that while the juice thus stains the mouth *red* it should convert the teeth into ebony. I asked one of our boatmen why he chewed it, and he said it was to make their teeth black. *Dogs* had white teeth, he said, and they wished to be different from dogs. He gave as another reason that they were ordered to do so by their Koran; but this I do not believe, as they get their Koran from the Arabs."

We had made the acquaintance of a Mr. L. M. Squires, an American resident of eleven years, and who subsequently joined the Hancock in the capacity of assistant naturalist. We were smoking our cheroots in the porch of the Amsterdam Hotel.

"While we were thus smoking in the cool evening breeze, we were joined by several gentlemen, acquaintances of Mr. Squires's, and who were presented to us. The usual comments on the state of the weather were got off with happy success, and then every one began to wait for his neighbour to say something else. Finally, one of the new arrivals, an Englishman, asked me, abruptly, if I had ever seen a native under the influence of the 'muck.'

"'The what?' I asked.

"'*The muck!* the *running muck.*'

"I replied in the negative, adding that I had never before heard the expression.

"He expressed great surprise at this, and proceeded to tell us that the running muck was often productive of many deaths.

"I thought this a rather singular piece of information to come by itself, but contented myself with observing, 'You don't say so!'

"The Englishman cleared his throat, swelled very large, called for a glass of ''arf-and-'arf,' and continued as follows:—

"'Some few of the natives here consume quantities of opium in various forms; and the result is that, in due course of time, their features become sharp, the skin is drawn over them like parchment, and, losing their minds, they become more ferocious and bloodthirsty than the tigers themselves. Armed with the long and flexible kreiss, (a sharp dirk-knife, whose edges are wavy and of beautiful temper,) they rush frantically from their houses, and run as swiftly as their limbs will carry them,—sometimes naked, sometimes clothed, always mad. Rushing through the crowded streets in this way, their only aim seems to be to destroy life,—stabbing, biting, cursing, kicking every one whom chance throws across their path.

"'As soon as he is seen in this state, terror proclaims the news far and wide. "Amoak! amoak!" is screamed by the whole population, just as "fire! fire!" is in our own cities. Every man grasps the first weapon that comes to hand, and follows the flying path of the common enemy. *Very long* spears are, however, preferred to the shorter kreiss; and with these they pen him up in a corner, and lance him to death with as much or more gusto than they would a tiger. As many as forty persons were once killed by one of these maniacs before he could be "cornered;" and yet there is no law against the use of opium.' "

The word "muck" is a corruption of the Javanese "amoak," to kill; and this latter is seldom heard, except when some poor wretch is ranging the frightened town with strained muscles and starting eyes, and with death closing around his path at every stride.

In regard to tigers, another of the party remarked that as many as eighteen hundred had been killed on the island in a single year; but I subsequently learned that eleven hundred was the greatest number for one year. The Government pays so much a head for each one that is destroyed, and keeps a regular account of the number. These animals are very destructive to cattle, and numbers of the natives also lose their lives yearly by them.

In the interior of Java there is yet a native prince, who holds his power from the Dutch, receives a regular salary, and keeps up the shadow of their ancient customs. He has the title of Soolctan, and we somehow found ourselves talking about him. My journal says:—

"Out of his salary he must support an army of at least two thousand men, as quite that number is required to make up one of his grand tiger-hunts. Then he has his household expenses, his harem, his dancing-girls, &c. Singular beings are these dancing-girls. Taken at a tender age from the mother's care, they are turned over to a class of men whose only duty it is to arrive at the one end of having their bones and muscles in such a state, by the time they are matured, as to admit of the form being thrown into almost any position. They are described as happy, cheerful creatures, in spite of the cruelty of their early training."

One more extract in regard to Java, and I have done. We were talking of pirates—Malay pirates—who hung around Gaspar Straits,—the very place we were going to survey. The subject was interesting, especially to nervous people who were about to venture among them:—

"'They are getting scarce, now, since war-steamers have visited us,' remarked one of the party. 'It is only once or twice a year that we hear of their attacking a ship: still, they are known to exist in numbers. You will have to look out for them in your little schooner: they would make short work of *her*.' I thought of the high sides of the Kennedy, and felt comfortable. I little thought that in less than a month I should be ordered, with a boat and six men, to join the Cooper: had I known it, my feelings might have been a shade less placid."

We are again under all sail, beating up for our working-ground.

CHAPTER V.

WE REACH GASPAR STRAITS, AND COMMENCE OUR SURVEY BY FIRING A GUN —I AM ORDERED ON TEMPORARY DUTY, WHICH LASTS FOUR MONTHS AND ENABLES ME TO VISIT SINGAPORE—VAST PREPARATIONS OF AN ALARMIST TO RECEIVE PIRATES, AND THE WAY IN WHICH WE LEARNED THE MEANING OF THE MALAY WORD "MAN-AR-R."

It was on the morning of the 10th of January, 1854, that we fired our first gun for "base by sound." We were in Gaspar Straits, lat. 3° 19′ S., long. 106° 40′ E. The "rear division"—as we called our portion of the squadron—had begun the long-talked-of survey. I will indulge in a few remarks in regard to this work, and then pass on to more interesting matter.

These straits—which are the door through which nine-tenths of the world's trade with China passes—had never been properly surveyed, were said to be full of hidden dangers, and were known to be washed by strong and uncertain currents.

We bent to our task with the spirit and energy of "new brooms,"—worked through rain, wind, sharks, tigers, snakes, &c.—and on the 15th of May it was done. We came out of this work without the loss of a man, and the result of our labours was satisfactory in the extreme. We found *some* parts of *some* charts correct; but, generally speaking, they were woefully out. We found dozens of rocks and shoals where all the charts gave safe water, and we found blue water where all the charts located rocks and shoals. We found, also, evidences of fraud and rascality on the part of ship-masters toward the underwriters. In regard to the latter let my journal speak:—

"Captain Rodgers has just found the wreck of the 'Memnon,' lying off the northwest point of Pulo Leat, (Leat Island.) When the water is smooth and polished, you can look down from a boat and see every thing very plainly; and, as there was a fine, heavy anchor lying under her bow, Bridge hitched on to it with the launch and hoisted it up. It is now on board of the Hancock, and will probably sell in Hong-Kong for two or three hundred dollars: quite a healthy sum to be divided among sixty men the first time they go on shore.

"The captain of this vessel reported, when she was lost, that he 'had struck on a rock that was some miles from any land and put down on no chart:' hence, the underwriters paid the loss. Had they known that an ignorant or careless man had run his ship upon a rock within pistol-shot of a large island during broad daylight, they would have saved their money. Of course, we will hunt no more for the 'Memnon Rock,'—the hidden danger on which the ship was said to have struck."

During the survey we made several discoveries similar to this. We erased from the chart all such imaginary dangers, dotted it with others which really existed and which had previously been unknown, and really accomplished a vast amount of work during the four months that we were engaged upon it. Too much credit cannot be awarded to Commander John Rodgers for the manner in which our work was laid out, or to those who assisted him in its execution.

During these four months we met with various adventures; some amusing, some exciting, others that were full of peril to life and limb. Let me again open my journal:—

"Jan. 14, 1854.—Yesterday morning, the schooner ran under our stern, and hailed us to the effect that Commander Rodgers had ordered an officer and boat to be detached from the Kennedy, to assist in *their* part of the work. There was some hesitation at first as to who the officer should be; but, as I had, unfortunately, once expressed myself in favour of small vessels, I was finally sent. I had a boat and six men placed under me, and was ordered to report myself to Captain Stevens, the worthy officer in charge of the schooner. The latter being too small to stow either my boat or the crew, the former is towed astern at night, while the latter find beds about the spar-deck as best they can. This is all very pleasant as long as fair weather lasts; but when men have been working hard for fourteen hours they don't fancy sleeping in the rain during the remaining ten. Stevens, myself, and Baber, the master, are the only occupants of the cabin; and there are twenty men on the berth-deck, and six about the upper—in spots. So much for our little schooner and her hardy crew. May she steer clear of pirates and heavy seas!"

We have been hard at work for some weeks, are running short of wood and water, and find it necessary to go somewhere to obtain supplies:—

"At 7 A.M. all three vessels got under way and ran down for an anchorage under Selio Island, where we came to, abreast of a stream of fresh water and a perfect forest of seasoned firewood that Stevens had discovered a few days previous. This island is some four miles in length by one in width, and differs from all others we have yet visited in having lakes in its centre and running streams dividing its beach. In consequence of the fresh water, various wild animals abound in its jungle, among which I may mention deer and wild hogs as the most plentiful. There are any number of snakes also; and a greater variety of insects than is pleasant. Of these latter there is a mammoth spider, formidable if only through his size and extreme ugliness. He spreads his heavy web across nine open spaces (the jungle is hardly penetrable) out of ten, coils himself away in its centre, and is ready to dart upon his prey or have his fabric destroyed by the passer-by, as the case may be. Running once after a wounded hog, I was so unfortunate as to get one of them half-way *into my mouth*, and before I could get clear of him I had to shell out of my coat and knock him off; with his long legs he had crawled over upon my back."

A great hunt came off on this island before we carried the vessels there. Baber and myself, wishing to try "camping out," took the boat and remained on it all night, after one of our day's work. The men also were in high glee at the idea of shooting the deer before they were awake: it was a regular spree. We carried with us a camp-kettle, a piece of salt pork, bread, coffee, &c., and, upon arriving at the beach, got our tent pitched and a large fire kindled just as night came on. The tent we made out of the boat's sail; and for a bed we had two thicknesses of cotton canvas between us and the ground.

We made a very comfortable supper, smoked our pipes, lay down with our feet to the fire, and imagined that we were going to sleep. One hour later we were all in the boat, the fire grew dim, and the mosquitos and sand-bugs danced the dance and sung the song of a bloody victory: we had been literally driven off. The next morning we awoke at break of day and proceeded to land.

It had been low-tide when we returned to the boat; it was now quite high: the water had been knee-deep then; it was now over one's head. One of the men, in his sleepy drowsiness, stepped out of the boat to lift the anchor and wade her to the beach. The result may be imagined:—a heavy plunge, much subsequent puffing and splashing, and a great deal of hearty laughing.

It was hardly daylight when we entered the jungle, and we hunted bravely until near noon. During this time we fired at several heavy short-legged deer, put a drove of wild hogs of all ages and sexes to a grunting flight, killed several ugly snakes, and finally returned to the ship in great disgust.

Selio is not inhabited, but is visited periodically by Malay fishermen for the purpose of catching and drying the fresh-water fish which exist in its lakes by shoals. The growth of trees upon it is remarkable, many of them being upward of one hundred and fifty feet high. We killed a number of large wild pigeons in their branches, and subsequently found this bird so plentiful on other islands that two men with muskets killed several hundred as an evening's work.

Two days sufficed to fill us with wood and water, and on the third day we were again at work. And now we experienced a terrible fright on account of old "bust-proof," his master, and Lieutenant Russell. They had left the ship, as usual, at an early hour: it had soon come on to blow hard, the sea had risen with singular rapidity, and twenty-four hours had passed without their return: we began to fear they might have swamped. With his usual readiness of action, Commander Rodgers got up the Hancock's anchor and ran down to leeward in search of them. The next day he returned with their boat in tow.

They had had a hard time; old "bust-proof" was irreparably rusted by the rain, and the others were awfully hungry and distressingly seedy. They had been able to keep the boat afloat only by constant exertion, and were about to succumb when the Hancock hove in sight. Old "bust-proof" didn't go out again for some time.

After we had been working some two months, the schooner was ordered to proceed to Singapore, (distant some three hundred miles,) to communicate with the consul, and return as soon as possible. I was so fortunate as to remain by her during the trip, and on the 7th of March we found ourselves at anchor off that city.

While Stevens and myself were stepping into a sampan to go on shore, a light row-boat pulled alongside, in the centre of which stood a very black Hindoo with a very white turban around his head. He introduced himself as follows:—"Me Mohammed!—consul-man. Plenty, oh! *plenty* letter at consul-house for American man-war." But I will say nothing more of letters; for there was but one for me, and that a half-year old.

We went to the consul's, and thence to the London Hotel, where we tasted a bottle of sour Bordeaux, drank another of pale ale, and engaged a room at two dollars a day.

I will be brief in regard to our treatment while in that city. I will only say that, from the governor down to the ship-chandlers, there seemed to be a determination that we should never dine at the hotel. Such hospitality I never saw before. In company with the consul, we went to call upon the governor's family shortly after our arrival.

"We got into our undress uniform, then into a carriage, which we hired for a dollar a day, and after a five minutes' drive commenced winding around the hill which towers over the city, and upon the crest of which stands the palace. This spiral road was a mile or more in length, and wormed through the tastefully laid-out grounds in the centre of which stood the edifice. We drove through groves of the fragrant nutmeg and of the luscious mangosteen, crushing the precious fruit under our wheels and breathing the perfumed air that cooled our brows. It fully realized my idea of an Eastern scene: it was one of those drives that flush the cheek of the invalid and diffuse a dreamy languor through the frame of health; it was grand. As we thus wound around the hill, we gazed upon a constantly-changing scene. We saw the whole of Singapore twice over; for the palace rose out of the centre of the town almost, overlooking every thing. Thus we looked down upon the city by piecemeal at first, and finally, upon reaching the summit, took in 'the whole' at a revolving glance,—the city, the bay, the opposite land, the back-country with its dense jungle, and the immediate grounds around our feet. This also was grand.

"We were ushered into the reception-room by a fancifully-liveried native, and were soon after met by the ladies. We found Mrs. and Miss Butterworth most accomplished personages, and passed a pleasant fifteen minutes. They showed us a stone which had lately been brought from a mountain in the island of Banca, (one of those around which we were surveying,) and which exerted a powerful influence over the needle: every one called it a loadstone. Stevens, having found that it would not attract a *cambric*-needle, pronounced it a singular iron-ore; and such subsequently proved to be its nature."

We had been riding around in our one-dollar vehicle to see the sights. Here is one of them, a Chinese temple:—

"As we entered through the massive stone-work, we were followed by a dozen or more loafing Chinamen, who stopped their gambling (gambling in the very porch of their temple!) to watch our movements. We were very respectful at first, for fear of alarming their jealousy, throwing away our cigars and taking off our hats. These loafers, however, motioned us to light other cigars and to resume our covering, and were so attentive as to bring us fire. They also spit on the smooth and polished floor, to show us, I suppose, that we were at liberty to do likewise. In addition to all this, they advanced to the chancel and commenced a series of violent bends and gesticulations for our information. They were showing us how they paid their devotions. They stood before a massive altar, decked out after the manner of the Romish Church, having upon its right a colossal statue of a very benign old gentleman, and upon its left a similar one with the most hideously-diabolical expression that I ever saw. The one on the right shone as the concentration of every thing good, and extended his left hand in an endless blessing. He of the left—the rampant power of evil—settled his gaze of eternal hate and defiance upon the averted eye of the first, and grasped a bleeding heart in his uplifted hand. It was to this latter that all the devotions were addressed: no one looked at the other. We gave them a half-crown for putting themselves into a perspiration by their furious pantomime, and continued our drive."

We were driving out to the hospital of Dr. Little, where many of our men were on their backs. It seems that over two months of exposure, toil, and privation, had done its work. Seven out of the twenty men composing the crew had been taken with the fever previous to our arrival, and been sent on shore as soon as possible to give them the benefit of comfortable quarters. Stevens, too, was placed *hors de combat* by a bruised hand, and Baber and myself were taking it turn-and-turn-about to indulge in chills or something of that sort: we were fit for any thing but a return to our labours.

As a general thing, one of us made it convenient to visit our helpless shipmates daily. They were a superior class of men to the general run of sailors; *they could all read*, and they derived great satisfaction from the papers which we took them. This hospital of the doctor's was situated outside of the city, in the midst of his vast nutmeg-plantation; and as we now, in the continuation of our drive, passed through a wide gateway and entered upon the latter sweet-smelling hundred-acre lot, we met the owner on his way into town. He turned and accompanied us back to the hospital, where we found two men delirious but the others doing better. I may as well remark here that, after keeping the schooner at anchor some weeks in hopes of their recovery, we were finally forced to leave three of them in charge of the consul, with instructions to forward them to us should they recover. They *did* recover during the next month, and, having had enough of surveying, took care to forward themselves off by the first ship. They *deserted*, and I could not blame them; for the work on which we were to be steadily engaged for years was enough to break down jackasses, and they were not paid half the wages they could command in merchant-ships for doing half the amount of work. It is to be hoped that Congress will reward the men who were too honest to desert, and who returned to their homes after that miserable cruise with bowed heads and broken frames, the wrecks of what they were at its commencement.

As we returned through his orchard of nutmeg-trees, the doctor indulged us with a few remarks in regard to their culture, &c.; and, as nine people out of ten use nutmeg in *some* form, I will repeat here what was then said about them.

It took the planter twenty years to get his trees well covered with fruit, he said, as he had to raise them from the nutmeg itself. The process was this:—

A man bought a hundred acres of ground, and planted nutmegs over it at a distance of from twelve to twenty feet apart. At the end of eight years the trees have grown and many of them bear fruit, and he can thus tell the male tree from the female. All of the former (one to every dozen females excepted) are now dug up and cast away and another nutmeg planted in their place. Then, at the end of eight more years, another culling process takes place, and more nutmegs are planted. In this way the twenty years are soon consumed.

The doctor added that if either of us would rig a purchase for distinguishing between the male and female nutmeg, we might make millions of money by going around to the different plantations, picking out the latter, and thus enabling men to get a plantation under full headway in eight instead of sixteen or twenty-four years.

"These trees," he continued, "bear all the year through. You must have men to go daily from one to the other, picking the fruit as it ripens. It is generally the first thing done in the morning. In this way each tree will give you several nutmegs daily, probably as many as twelve hundred during the year." So much for nutmegs.

Taking dinner one day with Dr. Little, we were associated with a Captain and Mrs. Francis, the former of whom I could not but admire as a bold seaman and successful trader, while the latter challenged the admiration of every one by her extreme beauty and elegance of manner. They were the last of their band,—this opium-smuggler and his beautiful wife.

"Why don't you give up the trade, Francis?" asked the doctor. "Don't you see that your brig is the only one left out of twenty-two sail? and don't you know that all are beggars who have gone before you?"

"No; I don't know any thing of the sort," replied Francis. "There is ——, and ——, who are comfortable yet; and I have got some thousands of pounds *myself* to fall back upon when I break down. As long as the brig lasts I'm bound to hang by her."

I looked at his wife, and I thought I saw a brightening of the eye and a swelling of the breast as he thus spoke of the future. I looked at him, and saw the last of a resolute and desperate band who for years had defied the Chinese authorities and held the slow poison to the lips of the opium-smoker. I looked, and knew not whether most to admire or condemn this the last of those resolute adventurers, half merchant-captains, half pirates, who had for years devoted themselves to the perilous service of the Calcutta and Bombay merchants. Here is what that service was:—

The demand for opium in China caused great quantities of it to be shipped from Calcutta and Bombay. The Chinese authorities, seeing the injury it was effecting on the whole nation, stationed war-junks along their coasts to prevent its being landed. Reckless men, with armed followers and fast vessels, stepped forward, and engaged to land the poison under the very bows of the war-junks and to bring back silver in return. Their vessels were armed as well as their followers; they received high wages, and threw away their money in riot and dissipation. If necessary, they went through blood: *the opium must be landed at every risk;* the lives of a few dozen Imperial sailors were nothing. While at sea, they kept clear heads, and devoted their entire attention to the one great thing of making a quick passage. Masts and sails were nothing *to them:* time was all they looked to. They gloried in heavy weather when it urged them ahead, and became fretful and desperate when it threw them back. It wanted reckless men to lead such a reckless life. "Prudence is the better part of valour" wouldn't have applied to them.

Our little schooner was a source of wonder and surprise to both the foreign and native population of Singapore. The former pulled around her in their light sampans, admired her beauty, and complimented us upon our reckless hardihood in trusting our lives to such an atom for a cruise around the world; the latter compared her to a large phrau, and accused us of having stolen the lines of that peculiar vessel before building her. Both parties laughed at the idea of her weathering a typhoon: they knew not how much it took to smother a New-York pilot-boat when she lies-to under a close-reefed foresail.

Let me again turn to my journal:—

"A singular worm is to be seen on the surface of this

harbour when the water is smooth and polished, during the absence of all wind. It is from three to four inches in length, has its body made up of a hundred joints apparently, has hundreds of centipede-like legs along its entire sides, is covered with a short fine hair or fuzz, and swims quickly and with a zigzag track. The natives fear their bite greatly, and invariably destroy them when they can. They have bright red eyes, and are altogether most disgusting-looking wretches. One of the boatmen dipped me up several, which I transferred to a bottle full of spirits of wine, much to their annoyance. They died hard, and emitted a bluish fluid, which the natives said was poison. These latter gloated over their spasmodic and protracted efforts to escape from the spirits, pretty much as old sailors admire the expiring agonies of a dying shark."

On the 23d of March, Stevens concluded that he had waited long enough for the sick to recover, and got up the anchor on our return. We had a fair passage to Selio Island, where we were to have fallen in with the Hancock and Kennedy, but, seeing nothing of them, had to start off on a hunt. We found them, at the end of twenty-four hours, snugly stowed away under the lee of a number of pigeon-islands, and, after telling them the news, asked theirs in return.

We found that they had passed through several adventures during our absence, some unpleasant and one quite amusing: but let them speak for themselves.

"Dr. Alexander, of the Hancock, was attacked by sharks while wading on a reef in search of shells, and came near being carried off. Fortunately the water was only knee-deep, and he, retaining his presence of mind, was enabled to keep a pretty firm footing, while by well-directed thrusts with a long bowie-knife, which he drew from his back, he succeeded in keeping them off until the boat came to his assistance. Then he got into her with amazing agility and inquired into his damages. He found himself minus his right boot-leg, a large piece of the right leg of his drawers, and a small piece of the skin from his right calf. The shark had evidently a fancy for his right leg below the knee."

Shortly after this adventure the Hancock ran short of coal and returned to Batavia for more, leaving the Kennedy at Selio Island to make tidal observations. These observations were to be made on a rock known as "White Rock," some miles from the ship and entirely cut off from the island. Lieutenant J. H. Russell was ordered upon the duty, and had with him a small boat, three men, a tent, and cooking-utensils. The boat was also armed and provisioned, as was the general order, in case of some unlooked-for accident, and they got along very smoothly for some days. Let my journal tell the rest:—

"One morning he rubbed his eyes and looked in vain for the boat. Then he called in vain for two of the men. Finally he searched in vain for enough provisions to make a breakfast for himself and his remaining companion, and then began to feel that he had been weathered. Smith and Loughead had loaded the boat with *every thing* edible and drinkable, and departed for 'parts unknown:' our work was too hard for them. This discovery was no sooner made than they began to think they might by some means starve during the next week, and so resorted to several ingenious devices for attracting attention to their situation. A mere accident relieved them during the next day." The ship was immediately got under way for Batavia, from whence a reward was announced among the different islands, which resulted in their final capture and they and the boat &c. being forwarded to us at Hong-Kong. They had landed on an island, in a very hungry and used-up state, and had tried to pass themselves off as shipwrecked sailors; but the police were too well informed as to their true character to admit of their yarn being accepted.

The amusing incident was as follows:—

"The Hancock, having anchored near an island about which she had been surveying during the day, was left in charge of thirty fathoms of chain and the officer of the watch, while every one else had gradually retired to their beds. There had been much talk about this time in relation to 'Malay pirates,' how they boarded ships in their phraus at night, murdered all hands, &c. &c.; and the possibility of such an attack caused us to keep constantly on guard, simply as a measure of prudence. There was really no cause for men of even ordinary firmness to feel nervous, however; but, unfortunately, there was an 'alarmist' on board, who was always imagining his throat cut, a snake under his pillow, or something of the sort; and who never went to bed without screwing in his air-port, (thermometer at 100°,) locking the door of his state-room, and arming himself in the most formidable manner. He had gone to bed this night as usual, with a Sharpe's rifle, double-barrelled gun, two revolvers, a bowie-knife, &c. &c., and was just getting into a doze when the quartermaster's hoarse voice reached him from the deck,—

"'Boat ahoy-y-ye!'

"He grasped his guns, first one and then the other, and finally sat bolt upright, a revolver in each hand.

"'Hey, fellows! what is it?' he asked of several as they passed his room, purposely exclaiming that pirates were approaching.

"'A swarm of phraus are pulling toward us,' answered a hurried voice, as its owner passed rapidly to the upper deck; 'bring your arms along.

"In a few minutes all hands were on deck, gazing curiously toward the suspected objects, while the quartermaster was getting hoarser and hoarser with continued hailing. They looked like boats moving stealthily toward the ship.

"'Hail them in Malay, Mr. Squires,' said Commander Rodgers.

"Squires threw himself back and drew a long breath: —'Phrau man-a-a-ar!'

"No answer. 'They must have some bad object, or they would answer,' hazarded the unsteady voice of a semi-alarmist.

"'Phrau man-a-a-ar!' Still no answer.

"'Say phrau man-ar *ahoy*, Squires,' suggested a laughing voice at his elbow.

"'Get out with your fun!' exclaimed the hailer, in a voice of half-forced jocularity; 'don't you know that man-ar *means* ahoy?'

"A general laugh here caused him to cough nervously and renew the hail:—'Phrau man-a-ar!'

"'Lower a boat, Mr. Bridge,' at length ordered the captain, 'and send her to see what they are; we may hail here all night.' So the boat was lowered and pulled off toward the piratical phraus. They proved to be small floating islets of brushwood and densely packed grass drifting with the current; and the discovery was no sooner made than our alarmist was on deck.

"'Why, where are your guns?' asked one.

"'Jist mind your own bisness, will ye?' Fortunately for the navy, our alarmist subsequently became disgusted with the expedition, and left the service of his country for the retirement of a country-life."

These and many similar incidents were now laid before us in return for the letters we had brought; and, as a kind of dessert to the reunion, they showed us a sick-list which seemed to proclaim the survey at an end: nearly half our force was *hors de combat*, and the other half was composed of men whose overtaxed muscles moved slowly to the daily work Still, we hung to it bravely, and were soon rewarded with the most entire success: the survey of Gaspar Straits was ended. The Hancock and Kennedy left for Hong-Kong, *viâ* Singapore, with their crippled crews, toward its close, and left the Cooper and my boat to fill in a few soundings and sail for the former place direct in a few days. We were destined to pass through some suffering and a vast deal of alarm and anxiety before the expiration of that time; but we knew it not then, and went on our careless way.

CHAPTER VI.

WE ARE DESERTED BY THE HANCOCK AND KENNEDY, AND FIND OURSELVES CALLED UPON TO ENJOY A MOONLIGHT WALK, WHICH PROVES TO BE SO PLEASANT THAT WE CONTINUE THE EXERCISE FOR TWO DAYS—WE VISIT A MALAY VILLAGE, AND ARE CAUTIONED AGAINST THE FEROCITY OF CHINESE DOGS.

WE were now alone,—we and our little schooner, and our still smaller boats,—alone upon the confines of our past working-ground, to linger there a while and then follow our consorts. We immediately entered upon the execution of the task which had been left us; we again commenced the interminable soundings, the frequent angling, the prolonged night-work over the skeleton chart and the smooth deck-board. Time rolled on.

On the evening of a dark and stormy Saturday night we anchored near the island of Banca, spread our thin cotton awning between us and the driving rain, and looked with thankfulness to the day of rest which stood between us and any further work. That night we slept well and refreshingly; Stevens, myself, and Baber, in the contracted cabin, and our twenty-five men upon the far more cramped and uncomfortable berth-deck. The next morning the storm was over, a bright sun ushered in the sacred day and lit up the gloomy depths of the tropical jungle near which we were anchored.

There were tall trees growing out of the dense undergrowth, and patches of short, smooth grass between it and the shining beach. Altogether, it had a most inviting look. So, after we had eaten our plain breakfast and got through with the usual Sunday muster, the captain and Baber took our two boats and landed for a stroll: it was so pleasant to have nothing to do and to stoop for shells upon a shining beach.

The boats pulled in different directions, but returned about the same time; they had a common object drawing them back,—a Sunday dinner. The last of our roosters, an old weather-beaten fellow who had crowed alone for weeks around the limited deck, had breathed his last.

They came back and gave me such glowing accounts of the green grass, and of the rustling of the wind through the tall trees, that I longed myself to roll upon the smooth turf, to pick up shells upon the hard sand beach, and to listen to the rustling of the wind through the overhanging foliage. So another party was arranged, and, after the rooster had been attended to, we got into the cutter and pulled on shore. The party consisted of Stevens, myself, and a number of the crew; and we were all armed with carbine and pistol, though not with any idea of hunting. We armed ourselves simply as a means of defence, for Baber and his whole boat's crew had been chased from a pool of rain-water by "some large animal," while two of the captain's men had seen the tail and hind-legs of a tiger. The captain himself had also seen the tracks of deer, hogs, monkeys, and panthers, or tigers, he could not say which; and, as Tanjong-Brekat (the name of the promontory under which we were anchored) was known far and wide as the haunt of various wild animals, we thought it better to be prepared.

Upon landing, we hauled up the boat above high-water mark, after which Stevens gave orders for all hands to be back by sunset, and cautioned them to keep together as much as possible, as there were known to be both panthers and tigers in the jungle of those large islands. He ended by pointing out the tracks he had seen in the morning, and repeating his caution in regard to their keeping company. The sight of those huge hollows, which had evidently been imprinted since the last tide, caused some of them to glance back at the schooner as they followed a small path that took them through the jungle to the opposite beach: the sight of the tracks had had the desired effect; they kept as close together as the nature of the path would admit.

We now started for a point of the island that was about two miles off, keeping upon the hard sand of the beach, and, with the exception of a few projecting points of rock that caused us to wade through the water, had a cool and shady walk. At the end of a mile we crossed a running stream of cool, fresh water, and, after rounding the point, came upon another. This latter oozed through the sand on our right, and caused us to ascend the elevation to see where it came from. We found a beautiful little pond, into the upper end of which the waters of the low back-land emptied and subsequently worked their way through the sandbank into the sea.

The beach of this pond was of a dark-blue sand, and its inner banks were of a soft and velvet-like turf: the heavy trees spread their densely-leaved branches over it, and shut out the sun even from its centre. It was not more than a hundred yards in circumference, and its waters were singularly clear and limpid. It was one of the most beautiful little natural basins that I ever saw. It looked so cool and inviting that we took off our heavy boots and waded into it up to our knees. Singular to say, the water was very warm, and we soon found it to be swarming with leeches;—a most admirable specimen of leech, too, if we might judge from the activity with which they attacked us. We got to the beach in a very few strides, and pulled them off from our bleeding feet: they had cut through the skin at the first bite. My journal goes on to say:—

"It still wanted a half-hour of sunset when we got back to the boat, and, finding but one man returned, we rolled back on the grass to let the time pass. The men came in slowly, in fours, in threes, never less than *in pairs.* Two were yet missing, and it was already dusk. We waited until dark, and then began to tremble for their safety. The last three men who had come in now spoke up, saying that they had left them on the other beach some three hours back, and that they were still walking away from the boat when they themselves had struck through the jungle, to return by a shorter cut, as they imagined: that was all they knew about them. They themselves, having got lost in the bushes, had climbed a high rock to sight the beach if possible, and while there had fired a gun in hopes that some one would answer them. Their gun had no sooner exploded than an awful roar had burst out near them, causing a hurried flight, as they thought, toward the beach they had left, but which fortunately took them to that on which the boat was.

"We now fired several volleys without any answer, save a dismal howl, and returned on board to get more ammunition and prepare for a night's search. We thought they might have retreated to the branches of some tree along the edge of the other beach, and that if we walked up it several miles, firing volleys and shouting, they might hear us and come out. We feared to penetrate the jungle at night: it would have been madness.

"Another half-hour passed and found us again on shore. We were seven able-bodied men, all armed to the teeth, and confident of being able to face even a tiger: we entered the narrow path and crossed the jungle to the opposite beach. We found their tracks and followed them up the beach for an hour or more, keeping as near the water as possible, so as to have a broad, open space between us and any animal that might spring upon us from the jungle, and firing volleys and shouting every ten minutes.

"At the end of this hour's walk we suddenly lost the tracks, and, going back to regain them, found that they led into the jungle. The pale moon came out about this time and showed us a third track, smaller and rounder than the others,—the track of some animal, an animal that had claws. A thrill of horror passed through our hearts as we bent over this last track: *it followed the others into the jungle*, and the pale moon strove in vain to light us farther; we stopped and trembled.

"About this time one of the men remarked that he

smelt a goat, and another sprang violently from the jungle. We heard a rushing sound, too, like that made by a large animal bursting through the bushes, and the man who had sprung back said, in a faltering voice, that he had seen a tiger. I remembered once hearing Squires say that a tiger smelt like a goat, and felt hope die within me. The captain cast an anxious glance into the dark forest ahead of us, and slowly stepped back to the water's edge. 'Come!' he said; 'there is no use going farther: we will do what we can for them to-morrow.' So we returned on board, and after five hours' sleep were again on the tramp.

"The party was still composed of seven men, and as we struck boldly into the jungle the morning sun gave us but a subdued light,—no ray. We entered in single file, the captain leading and I bringing up the rear,—a most unpleasant station, after I had recalled to mind the fact that a crouching tiger *always waits for the last man.* I began to feel very brave, and to remark, in a careless manner, that 'officers should always take the lead.' The captain only laughed: he imagined very well what I was thinking about.

"We walked all that day, fired volley after volley, and made ourselves hoarse with shouting: still no answer, save an occasional howl similar to the one we had heard the preceding evening. We killed several ugly, flat-headed snakes, a huge, poisonous-looking lizard, and a small deer: the latter we cooked for dinner. We found the jungle getting thicker and becoming broken by swampy flats as we progressed, and had discovered a leaden-coloured snake that seemed to live coiled round the branches of the lower bushes just about as high as we usually carried our heads: this was *particularly* pleasant,—worse even than being the '*last man.*' I think of that walk even now and shudder. It was after dark when we reached the schooner; and we returned without hope. Before turning in it was determined to start again on the morrow, leaving but one well man and the sick to look out for the vessel. We thought to find some sign that could determine their fate; at any rate, we could not give them up without another trial.

"The morrow came, and our swelled feet and aching muscles moved us slowly into the boat. We had walked some twenty miles on the previous day, through the dense jungle and miry swamps, and over broken rocks and abrupt elevations, and were hardly fit for another tramp. We had *wrung* blood from our stockings when we had bathed our feet at dinner-time, and yet sunrise found us again entering the jungle.

"The boat which landed us we sent some miles up the beach, with orders to anchor at a certain point and keep up a regular discharge of musketry until sundown. Three men were detailed for this service, and they were ordered to fire every half-hour.

"The rest of us—ten in number—were fully armed, and carried, in addition to our own provisions, a two-pound tin of meat-biscuit, in case we should find the men in an exhausted state. We now gave up the single-file idea, and tried to spread over a wide area by walking abreast of each other, keeping from ten to twenty paces between each man and the next on either hand; but the utter impossibility of progressing in that style soon demonstrated itself and forced us back to following in each others' tracks. Stevens, myself, and three men, were now all that were left of the previous day's party; two of them, having been unable to move, were left on board, and the fresh hands who had joined us, with Baber at their head, kept up such a brisk pace that it was with difficulty we could keep company. In the course of a few hours, however, they quieted down considerably and gave us the lead again.

"Suddenly, we were brought to a halt in a most gloomy and unpromising locality; a rough, black, perpendicular wall of granite rose directly in front of us, whose height was probably fifty feet, whose broken front was hung with an ivy-like growth, whose right and left extremes disappeared in a jungle more gloomy and closely packed than ever, and whose partially-visible base was washed by a sluggish and half-stagnant pool. No ray of sunlight reached us there; the most that the vertical sun could do was to diffuse a subdued light like that of a stormy evening. Every thing else was bushes and water and rock.

"We had walked long without water, and, as we stopped on the edge of this pool, which was filled with old leaves and limbs of fallen trees, I stooped down to try its taste and temperature. I soon arose without drinking; for a small, three-inch snake, doubtless alarmed at the disturbance, swam away directly from under my mouth. I was only too thankful that he had not swum into it. I now turned around to look for a leaf large enough to make a cup of, and, seeing one of the men passing some I thought would suit, asked him to pick me one. I then turned to find a clear place to dip from,—a place in which three-inch snakes would be apparent if there. In the mean time, the rest of the party had been arrested by the wall farther to the left, and were singing out to know if it could be passed on our side. Suddenly, I was staggering sideways toward my rifle with a confused idea that I should have it in my hands, and my face turned toward my companion.

"A scream—such a scream as never before reached me, such a one as I hope never to hear again—was ringing in my frightened ear its painful notes of agonized terror. It drove the tumultuous blood to my startled heart and sent a shivering feeling of despair through my unnerved limbs. It reached our distant friends and was echoed back by their alarmed rally-cry—'A tiger! a tiger!'—and the sound of rushing feet that bore their owners to the doubtful rescue. It was one of those cries of dire extremity, of helpless agony, that drag man to his fellow-man in spite of difficulty and danger and death. I turned upon the scene with levelled gun.

"It was an awful one: the agony of terror is always awful.

"With bent frame and livid and distorted features, a strong man was gripping between his knees a bleeding hand. Terror had almost deprived him of speech and seemed to have shaken his ordinarily stolid brain. He could only rock himself back and forth and mutter, in a hoarse whisper, 'A snake bit me! a snake bit me! a snake bit me!'

"It was a fearful sight. I looked around me for its author, and in my then excited state of mind quailed

ADVENTURE WITH A SNAKE.

before the angry flash of its leaden eyes. The snake was coiled around the half-stripped twig from which I had requested the man to pull a leaf, and, as the branch sprung back and forth after the violent jerking away of the hand, he moved his flattened head and outstretched neck in keeping with the motion: his whole appearance was indicative of anger and readiness for further combat. I looked upon its flat head, its leaden body, its hostile eye, and its projecting fangs, and then turned to the bleeding hand. I felt that it was one of the deadly sort, and that a few hours more would probably add another to the missing men.

"By this time I had recovered my presence of mind, and knew that the best thing I could do would be to restore his courage a little, and try to get him to suck the wound. This I proceeded to accomplish by the use of sundry abusive epithets, sprinkled here and there by a sneer at his cowardice, which soon gave him something to think about. I then made him drink a pint of raw gin, and ended by forcing his hand to his mouth and telling him to suck it. He shrank from it at first, but finally commenced, after which he sucked so hard as to bring half the blood of his body into his face.

"I then strove to make light of the whole affair, telling him that people were bitten by snakes every day, and that they never made children of themselves; at which he got quite angry, though the force of habit kept him from replying as warmly as he would have been justified in doing.

"'Just see, now, how I will shoot that fellow's head off!' I suddenly exclaimed; and, to give his mind occupation, I commenced blazing away with my revolver, while the snake swung back and forth and watched me with a constant glare. My nerves had been so unstrung that I missed him every time.

"While I was still firing, the captain and the rest of the party came tearing through the jungle, some without their hats and covered with spider-webs, some with rent clothes and cocked guns.

"'Look out!' I cried; 'mind that snake; he's bit Williams, and looks ready for any one else.'

"'Blow him away with your rifle,' said Baber; 'he's swinging about too much for the pistol.' The rest of the party gathered around the wounded man.

"I advanced, and, putting the muzzle within a foot of his head, pulled the trigger. The smoke hung about the thick brushwood for a while and finally passed off. There was no snake to be seen.

"'Hunt for him, boys,' said the captain; 'I want a piece of him to put on Williams's hand.'

"We began peering cautiously into the bushes, moving them aside with our guns and gradually passing in among them. We no longer feared an enemy whom we believed blown in half at least, but thought his mate might be on some other bush. Suddenly one of the men discovered him. 'Stand still, Mr. Habersham!' he exclaimed; 'he's got his eyes on *you.*'

"I immediately acted upon the caution; I don't think I ever stood so still before. The speaker lifted his cutlass and brought him to the ground with a broken back. I had simply jarred him to another branch with my rifle, and the cutlass that had at last brought him down had passed within two feet of my head. He now bit furiously right and left, tried the cutlass, which proved rather hard, and finally sank his fangs into his own broken back; and all the while it seemed that his angry, glittering gaze was fastened on me. I could not but wonder if he recognised in me the enemy who had blown him from his first position.

"The captain took a piece of his flesh, bruised it between two knives, and bound it and a piece of tobacco over the wound. Then he told the man, 'There! it's all right *now*. That'll draw the poison out, *I know;*' and this gravely-asserted result, combined with the pint of gin, so restored the poor fellow's nerves that he took up his carbine and expressed himself ready to continue the march.

"I never saw a more gloomily-desponding set of faces than those which now looked toward the captain. We were almost certain that our two men had been devoured by wild beasts, and now here was a third bitten by a snake which every one inwardly acknowledged to be poisonous: who could tell when this man would drop in convulsions, or who was to be the next victim? Death seemed to lurk on every hand,—in the lair-like caves of the hill-side, in the water we stooped to drink, in the rotten logs under our feet, even in the foliage that constantly brushed our faces: it was horrible.

"'Come! come!' said Stevens; 'we must be getting along; this is our last chance: we shall be broken down to-morrow.' So we passed on around the right of this massive wall, crossed a small ridge, and commenced the passage of an extensive swamp.

"Hours more passed, and we came out suddenly upon

the beach. We threw down our guns under a large oak-tree and stretched ourselves upon the yielding, moss-like grass. We were pretty well used up, some of the party entirely so: Williams, too, complained more and more of his hand, which was now quite swollen. We ate our cold dinner, laid back drowsily for a half-hour, and then prepared to cross the jungle to the opposite beach, where we hoped to find the boat in sight. One of the men, who had taken off his boots when we first stopped, now went to the beach to wash his bleeding feet before putting them on again. Suddenly we heard his voice:—

"'Here's some Malay boats down the beach, sir!'

"This was a very acceptable piece of information. We had been longing to fall in with some of the natives to offer them a heavy reward for the discovery of the men, if alive, and a moderate one for their bones if dead: we thought they would be more likely to succeed in their native wilds than we.

"Every man sprang to his feet with renewed strength and started up the beach,—some, however, very slowly. Among these latter were poor Baber and our interpreter, the former of whom had been suffering from the jungle-fever for the last month, and the latter of whom, having just left a counting-room, was poorly prepared to stand fatigue. In my anxiety to inquire about the men, I walked rapidly ahead, while the captain brought up the others at a more moderate gait.

"A half-hour's walk under the broiling sun (thermometer at 101° on board the schooner) brought me to the nearest phrau, when, as I could not speak the language, I commenced making friendly gestures. The men who were poling her along then shoved in to the beach, when one of them strapped on his parang and came forward to meet me. He approached without distrust, evidently regarding his parang as equal to my Sharpe's rifle, and, after making their usual salam, put his hand on his parang and gazed inquiringly at me.

"I replied to his look by holding up two fingers, then pointing to myself, and finally to the jungle. I wanted him to infer that two of my countrymen were lost in the latter, and he seemed to comprehend at once. He held up one finger, touched his face, and then the brown stock of the rifle; after which he held up a second finger, touched my shirt-wristband, and pointed up the beach. From this I understood that he had seen two men, one white and the other brown, and that they were farther up the beach. Now, as one of the missing men was white, and the other a mulatto, the men he had seen must be those we were in search of; I threw up my cap and gave a whoop that reached the stragglers along the beach and was echoed back by their joyful reply.

"When they came up, Stevens took his seat under a large tree near the jungle, and awaited the approach of 'the headman' of the party, who had for some time been running toward us from the more distant phrau. The interpreter stationed himself at his side, and our party in general cast themselves upon the grass for another rest.

"When the headman arrived, he bent on one knee before the captain, made the same salam, and shook his outstretched hand with marked respect. Then he turned to the interpreter and spoke with great volubility for as much as a minute. This latter soon filled himself with the news, and then commenced the process of disgorging.

"Two of the headman's people, he said, had met the men some miles farther up the beach: they were lost, and knew not which way to turn. Their feet were much swollen and bleeding, their clothes in tatters, and they themselves much exhausted for want of food. They had taken them to their village, given them food, washed their feet, given them a house to live in, and were now on their way to find the vessel to which they belonged. All that they had been able to understand from them were the words 'American phrau' and 'Brikat;' and from those they had concluded that an American vessel was somewhere near Tanjong Brikat. They did not know but that she might be wrecked and in want of assistance: they had come to see.

"Stevens now inquired if there was water off their village deep enough to admit of the schooner visiting it, and, upon being answered in the affirmative, made the headman an offer if he would pilot us around. This was accepted, with the proviso that two of his relatives should be allowed to accompany him, when we at once set out upon our return. One of the natives being sent through the jungle to order the boat to return to the point, the rest of us continued on down the beach, preferring its regular though heavy walking, and the hot sun, to the boggy swamps and confined heat of the jungle. There was a fine breeze blowing outside, but none of it could enter those solid masses of interwoven brushwood.

"On this return-walk we suffered greatly from heat and thirst; so much so, in fact, that Baber and several of the men gave out, and, throwing themselves down on a shady spot, declared that they could go no farther. Several of us therefore pushed on to the nearest water; and, after satisfying our own thirst, returned with two bottles of it to their relief, after which they exerted themselves, and with occasional assistance reached the boat.

"The total revulsion of feeling which had followed the announcement of the two men's safety was amusing in the extreme.

"'Blast their eyes!' said the man who had torn his clothes in rushing to the snake-scene, (all along it had been nothing but 'poor fellows!' 'poor fellows!') 'I wish I had the nigger by the throat; I'd show him what it is to make white people hunt him through the woods for three days.'

"'I wish he had the rest of that snake shoved down his throat!' continued he who had been bitten, and whose wound had been pronounced poisonous, but not fatal, by the natives.

"'I hope the captain pays fifty dollars each for the kind treatment they've had from the natives, and *charges it to their accounts*,' put in the man who had started back so violently from the edge of the jungle on the first night of our hunt.

"'Silence!' exclaimed the captain; 'you ought to be thankful that half of us a'n't dead.'"

I will now pass over several pages of my journal until I come to our arrival on board with the headman and his two relatives:—

"It was quite late when we reached the schooner, and we experienced considerable difficulty in persuading the headman to descend into the cabin. After much pressing, however, he commenced by bearing his weight warily upon the first round of the ladder, then stooping down to get a good look at the place he was descending to, and finally reaching the bottom; for five minutes after which he trod as if he were walking on eggs, trembling violently and glancing around in evident alarm. Presently his alarm subsided into admiration, and he began to examine the satinwood bulkheads, the bookcases, the bunks, &c.; and finally, when the interpreter and his two relations were brought down, he became quite self-possessed and talkative. He could not tire of examining *every thing*. The most ordinary article seemed to excite his curiosity; but that which carried his delight beyond all bounds was the action of a revolver which Baber fired six times in as many seconds and then handed him to examine.

"'Ask him how he likes the cabin,' said Stevens.

"He replied that it was grander than any thing he had ever yet seen. He did not know if he was in a house or on board of a phrau: he should like to bring his father on board very much."

I pass over other pages, and my next extract relates to our visit to their village, off which we anchored that night:—

"It struck 8 P.M. as we left the schooner,—the captain, the interpreter, four men, the natives, and myself. Upon arriving at the beach we found the mouth of an extensive lagoon instead of the bamboo houses which we had been led to expect, and, passing through this and crossing the lagoon itself, we came to the mouth of a narrow and

THE MOUTH OF RANGOU CREEK.

gloomy-looking creek. Here again we were disappointed: there were still no houses; and, as the boat shot into the dark and gloomy opening, the captain whispered me to shoot the native nearest me upon the first sign of treachery. We began to think that we might be paying a moonlight visit to a nest of Malay pirates.

"We found the creek so full of logs and banks, so dark and so narrow, that we could no longer use our oars: we therefore had to 'point' them and pole the boat against the current. I have remarked that it was moonlight; but then the bushes were so thick, both over and around us, that this luminary might as well have been behind a constant cloud: we could scarcely see the oars with which we were poling. Sometimes the hanging bushes would brush us in the face, or catch the upper ends of the oars as they were lifted up; and upon these occasions I could not but wonder if more than one snake might not coil himself around hanging bushes, and if they might not snap at us as we brushed by, or drop down upon us as the oars struck the branches overhead. It was a most exciting moonlight visit.

"After poling a mile or more through this darkness, we came out upon a little basin, on the right side of which was a bamboo wharf. We landed at this wharf, and, leaving two men by the boat with orders to warn off every one unless they heard English spoken, took the other two and the interpreter, and followed the headman up a broad and winding road, which he said led to the long-looked-for village. We were now well in for it: if there was a trap we had only to make a running fight. This was what we thought as we got farther and farther from the boat; but we soon found that our suspicions were totally unfounded: they were a village of the most harmless and friendly people that I ever saw, in spite of their being Malays.

"After five minutes' walk we sighted the first house a few yards on our left, and just as this occurred a large dog made a rush at the interpreter and was driven off by our guides.

"'Take care, captain!" exclaimed the alarmed linguist. 'You'd better get sticks, gentlemen: these Chinamen's dogs are very fierce.' And, suiting the action to the word, he provided himself with a small log—a half-grown tree—and closed up to us, probably to afford us protection. (?)

"We found the village to contain a population of some eighty or a hundred souls, half of whom were Malays and the other half Chinese. They came out in crowds to meet us,—men, women, (very pretty women, some of them,) and children. We shook hands with spasmodic friendship, without regard to age or sex:—we were still in an unpleasant state of doubt as to their true character. We found two styles of houses looming up through the moonlight, one being built on the ground, as is ordinarily the case, and the other elevated on posts to the height of several feet. It was into one of the former of these that we were now ushered with respectful eagerness, and we soon forgot every feeling of distrust.

"Our headman now left us in charge of his Chinese friend and went out in search of his father, with whom he shortly returned and informed us that the wanderers would soon make their appearance. The old Malay saluted us reverently, and then retreated to the side of his son, of whom he seemed very proud.

"And now, while some bad tea is being drunk without either sugar or cream, as we await the men's appearance, let me condense some of the interpreter's remarks in regard to the mixed people among whom we found ourselves so suddenly thrown."

I will preface this condensed matter by a single observation:—As the Irish and German emigrants turn to this land of America by hundreds and thousands, so turn the Chinese to the fertile shores of the Malay Islands. There is one difference, however: they leave their wives behind them and carry their customs with them. The Malays provide them the former, but retain their own prejudices. The two are often, as in the present case, found living together, sometimes for protection, sometimes for trade: the latter was the case in this their town of Rangou.

The headman of these Chinese spoke as follows, through the interpreter:—"Our village is small. It has only about one hundred and thirty souls. We are equally divided, and each people has its own leader. I am the chief among the Chinese: the headman is the chief among the Malays. We are equal, and are elected every year by the people. The old men give us advice when necessary. Your men were brought here in great distress, and we treated them like brothers until they troubled our women, when we told them they should remain in their house or we would tie them. We tried to do our best. Have we done right?"

The captain replied warmly in the affirmative, adding

he was only sorry they had not fulfilled their threat of tying them when they behaved badly; and, as the men entered at the moment and heard themselves thus condemned, they advanced with a most sheepish expression of countenance and waited to be questioned.

"Well, what have you got to say for yourselves?" asked Stevens, severely.

"Got lost, sir. We tried to cross through the woods to t'other beach, and was in them all night," &c. &c. &c. The reader must imagine the rest.

Now came some more hot and tasteless tea; then a general shaking of hands; then the furious barking of dogs; then a dark and dismal poling-match down the winding creek; and finally—the schooner. The next day we were again under way, heading for Gaspar Island, where we filled our water-tanks with rain-water from the cavities of rocks, and finally crowded sail for our port of rendezvous,—Hong-Kong, China,—distant some eighteen hundred miles.

The time passed heavily enough now that we had nothing to do; but two weeks cannot last forever, and we finally found ourselves in smooth water. We entered at night, and our pilot, being a great jackass, allowed us to drift afoul of an English vessel's hawse, which gave us work until the change of tide: then we got clear of her and anchored, kicked the offending Celestial into his boat, and turned in for the night.

CHAPTER VII.

WE ARRIVE AT HONG-KONG, AND FIND MORE REPAIRS WANTED—COMMANDER RINGGOLD RETURNS TO THE UNITED STATES IN BAD HEALTH, AND LIEUTENANT-COMMANDING JOHN RODGERS TAKES THE COMMAND OF THE EXPEDITION —SOMETHING ABOUT HUMAN LIFE AND DUCKS IN CHINA, AND HOW WE WERE LIBERALLY ENTERTAINED BY THE FOREIGN MERCHANTS OF CANTON.

OUR nocturnal arrival once more effected a reunion of the squadron. We found familiar hulls all around us when we went on deck the next morning, and that "first day in port" was devoted to climbing their sea-rusted sides and talking over the events of the last few months. On board of the Vincennes we were shown a huge snake, a boa-constrictor, that had been brought from Batavia by the Kennedy, and which was now confined in a strong bamboo cage on the quarter-deck. As we advanced toward him they were about giving him his breakfast, which consisted of quite a tough-looking old rooster, who struggled violently as they forced him in between two of the slats. Upon being let go he immediately occupied the opposite corner of the cage, and lifted his neck-feathers as roosters do when acknowledging their defeat. There he stood,—feathers, spurs, and all; and I watched curiously for the result. The snake began by fixing a settled glare upon his victim, working his coiled length slowly back and forth, and apparently preparing for a spring.

Suddenly, in the twinkling of an eye, he threw two of those working folds over the frightened bird and drew him into his coil; as near as I could see he had sprung from his head and tail. The rooster gave one frightened cry, and then the folds began to close around him,—closer, —closer. Finally he was mashed into an oblong mass, covered with a glutinous saliva, and swallowed, "tail and all." I wondered if they ever grew large enough to prepare men in that way, and if there was any prospect of our visiting the jungles which they inhabited.

This was all very fine for the snake as long as he had a trembling chicken to deal with; but upon a subsequent occasion, when a fine young roasting-pig was introduced to him, the tables seemed turned. I did not see the latter myself, but was told that the pig ensconced himself in the chicken's corner, and exhibited such a warlike front that the boa was completely nonplussed. They seemed mutually afraid of each other, and remained upon a watchful guard until the former was released from his uncomfortable quarters: a whole night, I think, they were together.

Finding it inconvenient, as well as expensive, to retain the snake alive, he was finally taken on shore to the gardens of the naval-storekeeper, where a noose was passed over his head, then over the limb of a tree, and finally "hauled taut" by Stimpson, the energetic naturalist of the Expedition. In this way he was soon put an end to, after which he was deprived of his skin for future stuffing.

My service in the schooner had now expired, and, when I returned to my long-closed room on board of the Kennedy, every thing looked strange and unnatural: I had been away nearly five months, and bilge-water and the moth had not been idle. The former of these had at length become so unbearable that permission had been asked and received to break out the cargo of stores and try to remedy the evil. The attempt was made, and resulted in the discovery that the ship was rotten,—totally unseaworthy. She was subsequently condemned and turned over to the East India squadron as an armed vessel, to be moored off the city of Canton for the protection of American citizens during the frequent outbreaks of rebel violence.

The Porpoise also had been discovered to be in a very rotten condition, and was undergoing extensive repairs when we arrived. Her captain had been deprived of his command,—very unjustly, it was thought,—and had left for the United States; Lieutenant Henry Rolando, of the Vincennes, succeeded him.

In the mean time Commodore Perry arrived from his famous voyage to Japan, and felt himself called upon to take some action in the affairs of the "North Pacific Expedition." Our squadron was totally separate and distinct from his; but then he was the senior officer present, and, from all that he heard in regard to the health of Commander Ringgold, he felt himself called upon to interfere. A board of surgeons having reported it as "very delicate and in need of quiet and retirement,"—or words to that effect,—he ordered him home, and the command naturally devolved upon Commander John Rodgers, the officer next in rank. And now commenced a total reorganization of our expedition. Captain Collins, Lieutenant Carter, and Dr. Hamilton, of the Kennedy, Captain Rolando, of the Porpoise, and several officers from the other vessels, left us and joined one or more of the vessels of Perry's squadron. The Kennedy was sent up to Canton, and her officers divided among the other vessels to fill vacancies. An indescribable state of uncertainty and confusion existed for weeks: no one knew which vessel to prefer, or where to stop when he had his orders. Every day some officer was getting tired of his ship and applying to be ordered to another; or sickness or a detachment from the squadron would force Commander Rodgers to order some one temporarily to fill the vacancy. We knew not where to keep our clothes, where to pay our mess-bill, hardly where to eat: it was nothing but change—change—change; and, what made it worse, it was nearly all *necessary* change. Finally, things seemed to be settled, and I awoke one morning to find Stevens in command of the Hancock, and myself as her first lieutenant. And now, as the remainder of this book will be chiefly made up from what I saw and did while attached to that vessel, I will give a list of her officers, &c., and then a brief idea of the old tub herself:—

Lieutenant Commanding,	H. K. Stevens,	Captain.
Acting Master,	A. W. Habersham,	Lieutenant.
"	W. Van Wyck,	"
"	H. St. Geo. Hunter,	"
"	E. O. Cares,	Sailing-Master.
Purser,	Geo. H. Ritchie.	
Assistant Surgeon,	Gerard Alexander.	
Draughtsman,	A. E. Hartman.	
First Assistant Engineer,	E. Lawton.	
Second " "	D. B. McComb.	
Third " "	L. Williams.	
Assistant Naturalist,	L. M. Squires.	

The above were the officers of the ship, and, in addition, she had some sixty souls,—petty officers, firemen, seamen, ordinary seamen, landsmen, and boys. And now for the vessel herself. Her description should go on paper; her dimensions should never be lost.

"The Old John," as we soon came to call her, was once an honest old water-tank and anchor-hoy, and for years acquitted herself with deserved *éclat* in that humble vocation. She belonged to the Boston Navy-yard, and was really a very useful vessel. She had a steam-engine in her and a propeller under her stern, and used to scull about the harbour of Boston, to the infinite terror of all catfish. In short, like many other things *in their proper sphere*, she was a marvel of good behaviour and success. After a while, people began to talk of sending her to sea, and she did actually get as far as the West Indies, when her officers, like sensible men, turned around and came back. They had had enough of her.

Then it was said that she wanted length, more sail, &c. &c.; and, while she was thus the subject of doubt and uncertainty, she was selected as one of the contemplated expedition. This was no sooner determined upon than she was subjected to what the Government called "great improvements," after which she was rated as a "screw-steamer of the third class," and proclaimed a seaworthy vessel. These great improvements consisted in her having been lengthened to a fearful extent, while her breadth of beam and power of engine remained the same, and of her having a third mast put in where no mast was wanted. Those were all, and she was then ordered to join the hazardous undertaking of a surveying and exploring voyage around the world.

Even now, as the mind runs back to scenes which were then in the future, seated as I am behind my pen in a strong brick house, and with miles of dry land between me and the waste of waters, I tremble at the dangers which seemed to seek us from every quarter, but which in reality were mostly called into existence by her own want of the usual qualities which constitute a seaworthy vessel.

She was one hundred and seventy feet long, something less than twenty-two feet beam, and drew thirteen feet when full of coal. Heard ever any one of such outlandish proportions? She was bark-rigged, and so crank that forty-five tons of pig-ballast had to be stowed in her to keep her from "turning turtle;" and, even with that great weight to steady her, she would list a half streak either way when a boat was hoisted, and careen as if under a heavy press of sail when lying at anchor across the wind and tide. She would dive into seas when in a gale as if without the most remote idea of ever coming up again, wallowing in the trough, and dipping in whole cataracts at every roll. She had an unpleasant way of carrying her helm *hard up* when lying to in a gale, and in light weather she often amused herself by luffing into the wind with the helm hard up, every thing aft shaking and every thing forward full. In short, she was a disgrace to the country, the laughing-stock of foreign officers, and a constant source of anxiety to those who sailed her. As long as our coal lasted we could manage her very well; but as soon as that gave out we could only

SCENERY AROUND WHAMPOA.

wait for a fair wind. More than once she put me in mind of one of those Chinese junks which make but two trips the year, sailing before the monsoon to their port, and then waiting for the opposite monsoon to bring them back. Without steam she was like a log.

Here I am, then, on board of the "Old John" at last; and, by turning back to the "list of officers," the reader will see that old "bust-proof" and his master are keeping me company. We three kept together during the whole of that eventful cruise, although the former did attempt my life on more than one occasion, and the latter never could be persuaded that the fault was anywhere but in my own carelessness. And now, while we are "preparing for sea," let me touch lightly upon the four Eastern ports of Victoria, Macao, Whampoa, and Canton.

These places all lie within a circle of one hundred miles, Macao, the most central, being in lat. 22° 14′ N. and long. 113° 32′ E., according to Raper. The first is a colony of the English, more generally known under the name of Hong-Kong, and situated on an island of that name; the second, an old colony of the Dutch, and situated on a promontory about half-way between Victoria and Canton; and the fourth, a large city which every one knows to be on the Canton River. Add to this the fact of its having an execution-yard, a small hotel, and a few foreign merchants with their club-room, and the reader knows nearly as much about it as I do: the rest he will see shortly. The third, Whampoa, I mention last because least, and will here make an end of it by simply remarking that it is a Chinese bamboo town, situated a few miles nearer the sea than Canton, and possessing the only dry-dock in that part of China. Heavy ships cannot go above Whampoa on account of a barrier across the river: hence its importance.

The view about Whampoa is beautiful from an upper point of the river. The opposite sketch, from the pencil of Mr. Edward Kern, gives a most truthful idea of it.

Hong-Kong is more of a European settlement than any thing else, and the same is pretty much the case with Macao. The former of these is remarkable as the residence of money-makers of all nations, and a few ramrod-like English soldiers, who—to use the words of an old messmate—walk up and down the Queen's Road, encased—dingy-boy like—in dangerously-tight trousers, and amuse themselves by switching the dust from them with very delicate canes. Macao is remarkable for its pure air, cool temperature, fine summer retreats, and as the residence of Portugal's great epic poet,—the second Milton,—Camoens the beautiful. We visited his cave, the birthplace of his most glorious lines, and went away with sad thoughts of his brief though brilliant advent.

So much for the first three. And now for Canton, the city of a million or more, and the grand centre of butchery, the great slaughter-house through which passes much of the surplus population of China, entering as men and cast out as headless trunks,—the victims of civil war. I again turn to my journal, the Hancock having been ordered up the river for a few days:—

"We left our ship, which was anchored above the 'Factories,' and pulled toward the 'gardens' through such numbers of boats that it was almost impossible to

CAMOENS'S CAVE—(MACAO.)

make any headway. We were half an hour in accomplishing a distance which, had it not been for those closely-packed sampans, could have been passed over in five minutes. While thus elbowing our way through them we passed a junk, upon the bow of which several Chinamen were standing with long bamboo poles in their hands: they seemed to be bearing something clear of their cables,—something which the tide had swept afoul of them. This something proved to be the dead bodies of three Chinamen, bodies without heads,—bodies of men who had been decapitated by either the mandarins or rebels, tied together by the feet, and then cast into the river to save the trouble of burial. They were shoved clear of the cable, and then went drifting on, borne upon the changing flow of the muddy stream, to be returned again by the rising flood, like any useless barrel or water-logged piece of driftwood. Such is life in China. I once heard from good authority that it was no uncommon thing for a person to take the place of the condemned unfortunate, provided said condemned would pay a stipulated amount to the friends of the self-offered victim.

"Leaving this revolting scene behind us, we pulled into a basin on the river's bank, the mouth of which was guarded by a floating log, and the quiet bosom of which was covered by scores of the light egg-like boats known as sampans or Tanka-boats. These admirable little passage-boats are sculled by a single girl generally, though they are often the homes of a whole family. One would be surprised to see the great number of Chinese who *live in boats*. This basin was probably a hundred feet in diameter, and after crossing it we reached a flight of heavy stone steps which led up into the 'gardens.' These probably covered as much as two acres of ground, consisted of a single enclosure, in spite of the plurality of the name, and were quite refreshingly sprinkled by shade-trees and patches of grass. The walks were wide and shady, and paved with large squares of granite, and it was backed by a row of massive buildings after the ordinary warehouse style. These were the 'Factories,' or 'Hongs,'—the great doorways of the world's trade with China, and the 'business-places' of the foreign merchants. *We never entered them.*

"There was also a fine club-house in the left corner of the gardens, but we were equally unfortunate in entering that. It *did not pay* to be polite to officers unless the city was about to be sacked, in which case fighting-men were in great demand for the protection of the property of 'citizens of the United States,' and consequently entitled to proportionate consideration. In spite of all this, the 'Canton merchants' have a great reputation for their 'princely hospitality.' Let us turn to more worthy subjects.

"The most attractive (?) object in Canton is the execution-ground or slaughter-yard. There you may go weekly, almost daily, and see heads fall by the score, sometimes by the hundred. You come to a rude enclosure at the gate of which a crowd of Imperial lancers stand in knots, inside of which kneel the miserable victims, and in the corners of which are piled the heads of former sufferers in various stages of decomposition. Shreds of tangled hair, too,—human hair,—is kicked about under foot, and the snarling dogs linger around

TANKA BOAT AND GIRL.

and tear the flesh from pallid faces or lap their meals from the crimson streams of human blood. The sanguinary and callous executioner strides over and among the bleeding trunks, kicks a head out of his way here, steps into a pool of blood there, and sweeps his dripping sword over the head of the next in turn. Men and women,—sometimes children,—age and ugliness, youth and beauty, suffer without distinction. A head is a head, and so many heads *have been ordered to fall.* The manner in which they obtain the requisite number is hardly to be credited; and yet it is true;—so true that I tell it without fear of contradiction.

"These executions are generally the result of a desire to retaliate upon the rebels for some similar act. When, therefore, it becomes known to the mandarins that the rebels have cut off so many Imperial heads, they at once march out an equal number of prisoners and restore the equilibrium. If they have not enough prisoners, they send a company of troops and seize and bind the first poor dozen or twenty countrymen whom fate throws in their way, bring them into the city, and the next day they are kneeling in the slaughter-yard with bowed heads and fettered limbs. It makes little difference *which side* they are on: they may protest themselves to be the best servants of the emperor, and the only answer is,—

"'Why were you outside of the wall while the rebels have possession of the surrounding country?'

"The stained sword drips again, and a Government notice is pasted up to the effect that 'such and such a great victory has been obtained over the rebels, and that so many prisoners have had their heads cut off.' This notice soon reaches the rebels, and results in similar scenes at their hands. It is hard to say which is the worst, the mandarin or rebel party."

Much sympathy was excited in Europe and America some three years since (in 1853, I think) in favour of these rebels of whom I have been writing. It was asserted that Tai-ping-wang, their leader, was a Christian, a convert of the missionaries, and that his followers were all converted Chinamen, and that their object was to spread the light of the gospel over that heathen land. Now see the true state of the case.

Tai-ping-wang, when a boy, attended the schools of the mission at Shanghae, learned to speak, read, and write English tolerably well, and got a very fair idea of the life and religion of our Saviour. As is often the case, this knowledge did him more harm than good: he cursed and swore, felt himself above other Chinamen of his class, and finally left the school-room for a life of starvation, work, or rascality. The first of these not agreeing with him, he was forced to the second. He engaged as a horse-boy in the employ of some European at Shanghae, but, finding work too troublesome, set his brains to work in the line of rascality. The next thing that we hear of him he is the commander-in-chief of the rebels, calling himself the elder brother of our Saviour, and, as such, claiming the respect and veneration due to a God. He says that Christ and Mahomet were both divine spirits, and that their religions did well enough until *he* came: now, however, he is commissioned to modify their teachings, and none but his is the true doctrine. What his modifications consist of I do not know; I only know the

EXECUTION YARD,
CANTON.

above, which I learned from Bishop Boone, the head of the Episcopal mission in China. But to return to Canton.

We are on our return-trip to Hong-Kong, and I make another extract of something I saw while passing down the river:—

"We were now running along the edge of an extensive rice-field, and the pilot called my attention to a queer-looking boat that was fastened to the bank. 'That is a duck-boat,' he said: 'did you ever see one before?'

"I replied in the negative, and he then pointed out hundreds of ducks working their clumsy way through the half-grown rice.

"'They live in that boat,' he continued, 'with the man and his family who own them,—the people in the middle and the ducks in those side-pens. They are let out to feed whenever the boat drifts by a good place, and when the man whistles they get back as fast as they can. The last one that gets back is whipped.'

"'Whipped?' I exclaimed.

"'Yes; he slaps him hard, and then the next time he doesn't come last.'"

I give the above as it was given to me, and as it is given to almost every one visiting China, and must add, in confirmation of it, something of the kind which I witnessed myself.

We had left this first duck-boat well astern and were approaching a second. The man of this second had apparently "whistled," for his ducks were returning in an awful hurry.

"They were apparently making the most desperate

efforts to regain the boat. Some of them were half flying, half swimming through the mud, weeds, and water of the field; others striking out like good fellows across a little creek that separated them from their home. All seemed anxious to arrive first; and, as they gained the boat's side, they tumbled in, heels over head, without the least apparent regard to life or limb. I watched, with the pilot, to see one of them slapped; but, to his evident chagrin, there seemed to be no 'last duck' that time."

So much for Southern China and ducks. That same night we anchored in Hong-Kong, and began to count the hours that were yet to pass before our departure for more northern latitudes.

CHAPTER VIII.

HOW WE TALKED OF "VISITING PEKIN BY WATER," AND HOW THE "OLD JOHN" AND COOPER WERE PRESSED INTO THE CORPS DIPLOMATIQUE—HOW AN OLD TUB AMUSED HERSELF BY ROLLING HER MASTS OUT, AND HOW A NEW-YORK PILOT-BOAT WEATHERED A GALE—HOW WE VISITED THE GREAT CITY OF FOU-CHOW-FOO, AND HOW WE SAW CORMORANTS CATCHING FISH.

THERE was a great talk in Hong-Kong about this time as to the possibility of a commissioner going to Pekin in person and obtaining an interview with the brother of the sun and moon,—the celestial Heinfung,—the Emperor of all the Chinas. The object of this desired interview was to put into the Imperial ear certain proposals, &c. which could never reach it in writing, or which, reaching, would never be acted upon, from the fact that the mandarins or rebels would stop the despatches, or that the former would influence the Celestial mind against the proposals of the encroaching "Fanqui," or barbarians, as all foreigners are contemptuously called in China.

Many were the schemes projected and abandoned to attain this important interview, until it was finally determined to try and reach Pekin by water. Pekin was situated near the Pi-ho River, and the Pi-ho River emptied into the Gulf of Pichili, and the Gulf of Pichili in turn emptied into the Yellow Sea: why might not vessels-of-war go to the mouth of the Pi-ho, and from there despatch boats, or even smaller vessels, upon a visit to the great capital? and why might not the commissioner go in those boats?

No one could object to this arrangement, because no one had ever been to the mouth of the Pi-ho; and so Mr. Robert McLean, of the United States, and Sir John Bowering, of England, gave it out as their intention to attempt to "reach Pekin by water."

The next thing to be done now was to *find the vessels;* and Commodore Perry, Commander Rodgers, and Admiral Sterling were each called upon to assist the cause. The former placed the steam-frigate Powhatan at the disposal of Mr. McLean, the second gave the "old John" and the little Cooper, while the latter furnished Sir John Bowering with the screw-steamer Rattler and a hired lorcha,—a vessel about the size of the Cooper, but drawing much less water. It was hoped that the two latter might be able to ascend the river with boats in tow, and thus give an air of greater *force* than could have been attained with boats only. These arrangements having been made, we were ordered to prepare for sea with all despatch. We were to go to Shanghae, *viâ* the river Min, and await the arrival of Mr. McLean in the Powhatan, and to take advantage of all opportunities for making surveys. We were detailed on "special service," but that did not prevent our going on with our regular work. The Vincennes herself and the Porpoise were to survey around the Bonin, Loo-Choo, and Japanese islands, and we were all to rendezvous at Hong-Kong in the spring. It was now September, 1854, and we were ready for sea,—the "old John" and the Cooper to sail first. Suddenly, Lieutenants J. H. Russell, of the Porpoise, and William Van Wyck, of the Hancock, imagined that their mutual interests would be consulted by changing ships, and accomplished their wish during the hurry of our departure; and this pregnant exchange was no sooner accomplished than we took the Cooper in tow, and stood out to sea on our stormy road to Shanghae.

We left the Vincennes and Porpoise at anchor. *We have never seen the latter since;* and, as her image floats by me, enveloped in the dismal and shadowy shroud of its unknown fate, it drags with it the names and features of lost friends and messmates, endeared to my heart by scenes of common peril and long years of brotherly association. I close my eyes, and recall those well-remembered features; and, as they crowd before me, they are changed: oh, *how* changed! The startled imagination paints them paled and distorted by the hideous emotions of the last struggle,—a struggle in which man, having exhausted the vast resources of his godlike brain in vain efforts to surmount a danger which is literally insurmountable, folds his arms of useless muscle upon his troubled heart and calmly bides his time to die. I close my eyes, and see those fearful shadows crowd around me, and the burning tear of powerless pity leaks through the unsteady lids and blots the swimming paper. It is a brotherly tear, shed over the unknown fate of generous hearts, who sank in the fathomless depths of the coral sea, or lingered upon the barren rocks of some desert island until life faded slowly from their weakened grasp.

Our passage to Shanghae proved even more stormy

9

than we had expected: it was the equinox, and we had a right to look for heavy weather, but we never imagined that we should suffer as we did. We were soon forced to cast the Cooper adrift, and the second night out we ourselves dipped into a heavy sea and twisted off the head of the bowsprit, rolling out the topgallant-masts at the same time. We had a head-gale to beat up against, and of course made little or no headway; and, in addition to this, Stevens would insist upon our dancing attendance upon the Cooper, lest something might befall her. This unnecessary guardianship I never could understand, as the latter vessel was making a much better weather of it than we were, and a quick passage would have been consulted by letting each of us "make the best of our way."

After losing our masts we rolled fearfully, and for ten days our rooms were afloat. We were shipping seas constantly, and having *the most unpleasant time I ever experienced;* while the Cooper under her close-reefed foresail was riding upon the very crests of the towering seas, and keeping as dry as a bone. More than one eye glanced toward her as the safer as well as the dryer of the two.

Finally, we arrived off the mouth of the river Min, upon the banks of which, and thirty-four miles above the sea, is situated the great and slightly-known city of Fou-chow-foo, or rather Fou-chow City, the word "foo" meaning city. The latitude of the mouth of this river is 26° 08′ N., its longitude 149° 42′ E., and it is situated about half-way between the port we had left and the one to which we were bound. Fou-chow is rapidly becoming the great door of export of the vast empire of which it is one of the largest cities, and as such is entitled to unusual consideration: in addition, it has never before been written of, to my knowledge, hence another claim to being made the subject of the next few pages. I turn to my journal for extracts :—

"It is fortunate that we touch at Fou-chow, for the equinoctial gales have bruised and battered us considerably; they still blow very heavy, and our coal is already running short, we having had to keep up constant steam or drift helplessly to leeward. We will now be able to repair damages and fill our bunkers with wood, possibly with coal.

"While standing in for the supposed mouth of the river with the Cooper in tow, we ran aground on a sand-bank, and while hauling off into deep water were boarded by a number of piratical fishermen, one of whom consented to pilot us in. He anchored us about a mile below the pagoda of Loah-sing-tah shortly after dark.

"This pagoda, which is situated on a pleasantly-wooded elevation near a turn in the river, is twenty-five miles above the sea, and within nine of the city itself. It is one of the lingering monuments of unknown ages, and is at length beginning to crumble beneath the constant action of time and the elements. Here it is that merchant-vessels anchor, receiving their teas by huge cargo-boats which come to them on the ebb-tide and return with the flood. We found the American bark Hungarian at anchor, the captain of which boarded us and hailed our arrival with great joy. We also found a large, heavily-laden English ship, the captain of which offered us a thousand dollars if we would tow him around a certain point upon which he feared being cast by the current: we refused the offer with a show of unwilling dignity, but subsequently did him the service for nothing. He was loud in his thanks, and promised we should hear from his owners when he arrived at Liverpool; but he must either have died on the passage or wilfully neglected us, for we are still waiting: the name of the ship was the 'Lord Warrington.'"

In consequence of advice received from the captain of the Hungarian in regard to the tides, we determined to visit Fou-chow with the next flood. This required us to get up before daylight, and I make a few extracts from the account of our trip:—

"We found two of the light and buoyant sampans of a neighbouring village awaiting us at the gangway, in one of which rowed the pilot, who accompanied us as guide through the crooked streets to the American consulate. These two boats seemed to have been made expressly for our party of six,—who now buttoned out the cool morning air and got into them,—so closely did we fit together along the single thwart-ship seat. Three of us there were in each boat; and we had a bamboo frame overhead, upon which was spread a protecting mat, and two large men and four very small boys to urge us along,—one large man and two small boys in each boat.

"It wanted yet an hour of daylight as the driving flood-tide swept us by the towering pagoda, and the next thing that attracted us was the reveillé of an English opium-receiving ship,—one of the floating but permanently-anchored strongholds whose only duty it is to shelter and dispose of the poison as it is delivered from the 'armed vessels of reckless men' previously spoken of.

"At half-past five it was broad daylight, and we could look around us: the entire sky was of one uniform rosy tint. Even the zenith was of this colour, and the contrast between the brilliant heavens and the deep blue of the distant mountains was magnificent: I never before saw the outlines of the mountains so clearly defined,—never their blue so deep, never the sky so brilliant. They lifted themselves in their stately grandeur far into the morning sky, towering over the hills at their base with protecting care, while these in turn hung over an undulating country that waved itself almost imperceptibly into the low rice-fields along the river-banks.

"Nor was it in one direction alone that this view met the eye; the panorama was perfect. We had ascended the windings of the river sufficiently high to place even high mountains between us and the sea, and now the smooth surface of the river, unbroken by either isle or rock, and slightly rippled by the morning air, presented the appearance of a small lake rather than of a running stream. We had a jutting point below us, another about a mile ahead, and the river itself seemed to widen between them; hence its similarity to a lake.

"As we passed over this quiet basin of water and turned the upper point into another lake, the bosom of the water was no longer unbroken.

"Uncouth-looking boats, with noisy boatmen and flapping sails, were sprinkled plentifully over its saffron-coloured breast, while schools of fish leaped bodily into the air and made the water foam again in their descent.

"The sides of the mountains and hills along this river were literally covered with the sweet-potato vine; and, from their peculiar manner of cultivating it, there could be no loss of soil from the zigzag course of the impoverishing gully.

"Take a flight of steps six hundred feet high, each step being twenty yards broad and six feet higher than the lower one, and ranging from fifty to a hundred yards in length.

"Now, manure well the surfaces of these giant steps, and you get a series of fertile patches. Then, imagine the whole slope of a mountain dug into, smoothed off, 'got up' in that style, and you have an idea of how so many people manage to live in China. Did they only cultivate what we call arable land, half of them would starve. It was a rare sight to turn in whatever direction and see thousands of hill-side acres thus converted into level tracts and rising and retreating before the eye like the successive seats of a vast amphitheatre."

After skipping several pages of my journal, I find the following:—

"Shortly after passing the ruined temple just described, we came to a turn in the river whence we first sighted the famous granite bridge of Fou-chow. And such a bridge as it was!—one oblong mass of apparently-solid granite, with square holes cut at regular intervals to permit the flow of the four-knot tide, and with booths and shops of every description built upon it from one end to the other,—built upon the up-river half of the bridge's surface, while the lower half is given to the thousands who daily cross it. Such bridges are not built in China now; they were built by the men who raised those strange columns known as 'pagodas.' The river at this bridge is two thousand feet wide, and there is an island near its south bank over which the bridge passes. It is only on this island, and within certain limits on the left bank, that the houses of the foreign merchants are allowed to be built."

We were passing under this bridge, and saw a novel sight.

"As we passed under the massive blocks of gray granite upon the foaming breast of the rising tide and shot out into the expanding river beyond, we saw a long low raft of bamboo moored under the lee of the heavy pier to our right, on which were a Chinese fisherman, a basket, a paddle, and five duck-like birds, which we at once imagined to be some of the celebrated 'fishing-cormorants' of the East. We also imagined that this might be our only opportunity for witnessing their singular mode of fishing, and consequently stopped in the hope that the Chinaman would gratify our curiosity. We were not disappointed.

"Scarcely had we 'rounded to,' when he reached out his hand toward the birds, the nearest of whom at once waddled up to him and stepped into his open palm. He now smoothed his feathers with the right hand, bent his mouth to his arched neck for a moment, and then put him upon the edge of the raft. There the bird dipped his bill in the water once or twice, snapped his head from side to side, shook his tail several flirts, and ended by diving suddenly into the turbid water that washed his feet.

"In the mean time, the four remaining cormorants were huddled together on the far end of the raft, drying their feathers, switching their tails, and looking altogether quite cool and comfortable. After being down from ten to fifteen seconds, the absent explorer hopped suddenly out of the water with quite a good-sized fish in his mouth, swam to his master, gave up the half-swallowed prize, and hopped upon his knee, where he shook himself while the fish was being put in the basket. His master then stroked him down as before,—much to his apparent delight,—whispered again in his ear, and placed him once more upon the edge of the raft.

"Again he dived, and again he came up with a fish. He then underwent a similar process of caressing, and was once more placed on the water's edge. Now, however, fortune seemed to have left him. He had no fish when he arose after a protracted absence, and seemed at a loss what to do. He turned himself around in the water several times, keeping his dark eyes fixed on his master's as if asking permission to try it again. Suddenly the latter made a motion with his hand, and down he went. When he came up he brought quite a large fish,—eight inches long, say,—which struggled violently, as though surprised at the unusual situation in which he found himself. He too was put in the basket, the proud cormorant once more caressed, and then placed gently in the centre of the raft instead of upon its edge as formerly.

"This seemed to tell him that his services were no longer required, and that he had acquitted himself with considerable credit; for he moved off to the other end of the raft with the stately step of a conqueror, while the next in turn advanced to supply his place. They seemed to regulate their movements by a nod or motion of the hand from their master. Cormorant No. 2 was not as sprightly a looking bird as his predecessor; nevertheless, he brought up a fish after the first dive, gave a flirt with his expanded tail, and swam to his master to give up the prize. He was taken out as before, relieved of his mouthful, and subsequently placed gently on the edge of the raft. There he sat a few moments perfectly motionless, but, seeming suddenly to see a fish, dropped off like a piece of lead, and nothing more was seen of him for at least fifteen seconds. Then he came to the surface with a spring that took him almost out of the water, but having no fish. His actions now expressed his disappointment almost as plainly as words could have done. He did not swim toward his master as formerly, but kept sculling about in a small circle with his bright, unsteady glance fixed on him, at the imminent risk of twisting off his neck.

"The master pointed down with his finger, and down went the unsuccessful fisherman. Still no fish. Once more, and still no success. Finally, he was taken back upon the raft, slapped soundly on the head, and thrown angrily down. He immediately made tracks for the other end, stumbling heels over head and looking very much ashamed of himself. The next in turn now waddled forward; but, having seen enough, we continued on our way. I could not but wonder at their beautiful training, and, as I saw the unlucky explorer receive his slaps, my mind returned to the Canton River and to what the pilot had told me in regard to the 'last duck.' It began to look like the truth."

Two minutes after leaving the bridge we landed on the south bank, and, after a ten minutes' walk through narrow, dark, and filthy streets, found ourselves ascending an elevation in the rear of the town, upon which was the Consulate. We were received with great politeness, drank a cup of good coffee, and were invited to take a walk before breakfast. My journal says:—

"And now we undertook a walk while breakfast was preparing,—we and the four dogs, slim Mr. Clark, the consul, and extremely stout Mr. Sloan, his jovial partner. We passed through the back-entrance and found ourselves upon the edge of an immense graveyard,—an old graveyard of the oldest nation under the sun: the whole face of the outspreading country was mounds, mounds, nothing but mounds. Away over, on a shady elevation, Mr. Clark pointed out the burial-place that had been allotted to foreigners, and here and there you could see a house, or a solitary tree, or a huge rock; but every thing else was graves,—nothing but graves for miles and miles. Footpaths without number ran over and through these oblong hillocks, and a long heavy grass grew in rare luxuriance over their uneven surface. We walked through those hard-beaten paths and saw hundreds of bare-legged women and children cutting and bundling the grass that shaded their ancestors, and carrying it to the opposite city of eight hundred thousand souls. They looked at our uniform curiously as we passed, and smiled and laughed with great good-nature. During this walk Mr. Sloan gave me much information in regard to the people among whom he was living. He said that it was only six years since any foreigner had been allowed to live there, and that even now they ran the risk of insult and loss of life when going through 'the city.' In consequence of this they generally went in sedan-chairs; but even these had been known to be opened and the occupant spit on in mere wantonness.

"'What did he do?' I asked.

"'Do?' he replied; 'he looked straight ahead, like a sensible man as he was: had he struck his insulter he would have been torn to pieces.'"

I did Mr. Sloan the injustice at the time to think this might be exaggerated, but subsequently had good cause to believe that things were even worse. And now, since our return to the United States, I have seen in the Philadelphia Evening Journal of September, 1856, a long account of the death of a Mr. Cunningham, under the most wanton and unprovoked circumstances. This gentleman had treated us with marked courtesy during our visit to Fou-chow, and was a quiet, inoffensive personage. He was murdered by an infuriated mob of the residents of the small island which I have spoken of as being near the south bank of that river.

I learned further, from Messrs. Clark and Sloan, that the exports from Fou-chow were annually doubling themselves; and that, from the fact of its being the nearest seaport to the great tea-district of China, it must eventually become the great point of export.

After breakfast we took sedan-chairs and were carried over the bridge and into the densely-packed city beyond it. I never before saw such crowds of people as blocked up its narrow streets; and, after we had been carried some three miles, we got out at the head of one of the most quiet-looking to stretch our limbs. We were soon surrounded by a crowd of several hundred; but, though they followed us, laughed at us, and even frowned in some cases, we got back again without being "spit upon." We saw some singular sights in the shops of that no longer "quiet street." My journal says:—

"We entered the open door of this old-curiosity shop as much to avoid the crowd as any thing else, and looked around us to pass the time. The first thing I saw was an oval frame of glass, under which were two *very* ordinary-looking wine-glasses that were evidently regarded by the shopman as rare and valuable. To satisfy my curiosity, I asked him the price of them, and was told five dollars: they could be bought in the United States for fifty cents the dozen, if not less."

We saw also some beautiful specimens of lacquer-ware in another shop:—

"This man, who was a skilful workman, and whose wares were all sent to Pekin (at least a thousand miles) as fast as they left his hands, showed us a tray containing twelve oval lacquered boxes about as large as one's fist, for which he asked fifteen dollars a set: we admired them greatly, buttoned up our pockets, and retreated to our chairs. There were four in a set."

We returned to the Consulate in time for dinner, and the next day were again climbing the wall-like sides of the unfortunate "old John."

We remained at our anchorage near the pagoda several days, during which time we made a partial survey

THE PAGODA OF LOAH-SING-TAH.

of the river, and had the misfortune to lose a highly-esteemed messmate in the person of Acting Lieutenant Henry St. Geo. Hunter. This officer had suffered with the disease of the country for some months, and was now carried off by it in the flower of his manhood. His untimely death cast a gloom over our social board, and deprived the Expedition of a valuable officer. We buried him in the shady graveyard of the foreigners, and paid for the erection of a granite monument over his lamented remains. Poor Hal!

The weather having now moderated and our bunkers being full of wood, we again put to sea with the Cooper in tow, and continued our voyage to Shanghae. It proved but a passing lull, however, and at the end of the first twenty-four hours we again found ourselves beating to windward against a northeast gale. The reader already knows how the "old John" was wont to acquit herself under *such* circumstances. Like a huge disabled crab, she drifted helplessly to leeward, and we thought ourselves more than fortunate when we were able to take shelter in a place called Bullocks' Harbour, which we surveyed and made ourselves comfortable in for the space of twenty-four hours. There we bought four fine bullocks for seven dollars, a large quantity of sweet potatoes for a few pieces of fat pork, and sailed again the next day before a light breeze.

Our glory was short: we had scarcely got sail set when the wind hauled in our teeth again, and we were forced to send down all yards and masts, and steam in under the land to avoid losing ground. This was ticklish work: sometimes we ran in such shoal water that we could see the bottom, and yet if we had kept out from the land we would not have been able to steam against the sea: our only hope was to keep in smooth water, carry as much steam as possible, and try to get to Shanghae before our coal gave out. All the wood which we had taken in at Fou-chow was soon expended, and, before commencing on the remnant of coal, we burnt up all the spare timber about the decks,—chicken-coops, old chairs, pieces of masts, &c. &c., and, finally, the few tons of coal. We reached our port on the 7th of October, with a few bags of coal,—the sweepings of the bunkers. Had we been two hours later, we would have drifted helplessly about until the arrival of a fair wind.

CHAPTER IX.

WE ARRIVE AT SHANGHAE, WHENCE WE SAIL WITH THE COMMISSIONERS FOR THE PI-HO — WE PASS OVER THE YELLOW SEA IN FINE STYLE, ANCHOR IN SIGHT OF THE MOUTH OF THE PI-HO, AND SEND IN THE SMALLER VESSELS — WE FAIL TO "REACH PEKIN BY WATER," AND RETURN IN DISGUST TO SHANGHAE, WHERE THE OLD JOHN'S ENGINE "RUNS DOWN."

UPON our arrival at Shanghae, we found the "Pekin party" awaiting our arrival with the most intense anxiety. Mr. McLean, in particular, having heard a most doleful account of the inefficiency of our "screw-steamer-of-war of the third class," began to give us up, and had made up his mind to sail the next day should we not arrive. The consequence was that we had to work day and night coaling ship, and, when that was accomplished, the Powhatan took both the schooner and ourselves in tow, and walked off with us at the rate of eleven miles an hour. The Rattler followed with the hired lorcha, and thus we boomed it over the smooth and polished surface of the Yellow Sea and the Gulf of Pichili, until one moonlight night we found ourselves anchoring in six fathoms of water and no land in sight.

The next morning we got under way and steamed into four fathoms, when we could just see some low land in the distance, which our observations told us was about the mouth of the Pi-ho River. We had not had a breath of wind since leaving Shanghae, and had come several hundred miles. The sea had been like a broad expanse of polished glass.

The "old John" now began to feel herself of vast importance: we only drew twelve-feet of water, and could consequently go much nearer the river than the other steamers; so we took the lorcha and Cooper in tow and stood in for the land. We ran into thirteen-feet water, and then cast off the vessels, which continued on before a light breeze, the lorcha getting safely into the river, and the schooner, which drew a foot more water, grounding on a bank near its mouth. We were a week getting her in after that,—some of the hardest work I ever engaged in. Then, after both she and the lorcha were safely anchored inside of the mud forts, the secretaries of the commissioners took up their residence on board and communications commenced.

The Chinese seemed very averse to have any thing to say to us at all, and humbugged us to such an extent that some of us advocated the idea of forcing our way up to Pekin and demanding an interview in person. As we were not the confidential advisers of the ministers, however, our opinion had little weight,—none at all, I fear.

Thus passed several weeks; and, while the diplomatists were making themselves hoarse with talking, we made a beautiful survey of the locality,—the schooner attending to every thing inside of the river, and our ship the bar and adjoining coasts. The schooner had Carnes—our sailing-master—and his boat to assist her; and upon one occasion, when they were trying to ascend the river as high as possible, they came to a barrier of junks with only a passage-way of some twenty feet wide between the two tiers, and, upon their attempting to go through it, they were assailed by crowds of Chinese armed with spears and match-locks, and found themselves under the necessity of retreating quietly or shedding blood. They chose the former, as the latter might have put a stop to all communication. Besides, the officers had no orders, and did not feel themselves empowered to "declare war."

We found the Chinese of that region a powerful and athletic set of men, very different from those of more southern latitudes: the women we did not see. Lieutenant Raper, R.N., locates the mouth of this river in lat. 38° 58′ N. and long. 117° 47′ E., and we found ten feet of water on its bar at high-tide and twelve or fourteen fathoms inside. From all that we could see, there was no reason why an ordinary river-steamer might not ascend it to within a few miles of Pekin, this city being situated some distance from the bank.

Our commissioners had one or two grand "powwows" on the beach inside of the river, which we all attended in full uniform, after which they steamed away in disgust, leaving the "old John" and the Cooper to continue the survey toward the Great Wall of China, now only some hundred miles to the northward and eastward of us. As far as I have been able to learn, our "attempt to reach Pekin by water" was followed by no results; but this failure must not be placed at the door of Mr. McLean and Sir John Bowering: it was entirely owing to the determination of the Chinese to keep all foreigners out of the centre of their empire.

We now spent several days working up to the Great

Wall, during which time myself and a boat's crew narrowly escaped drowning. My journal says,—

"At 10 A.M., every thing in the shape of provisions, water, ammunition, &c. being in the boat, and the crew amply provided with pea-jackets and blankets, we shoved off and dropped slowly astern, while the Phenomenon herself (the 'old John') began laboriously to gather her sluggish headway. Soon we heard the engine-bell ring four times, (ahead strong,) and then voices began to die away and faces to be confused by the increasing distance. We were left alone upon the proverbially-treacherous bosom of the Gulf of Pichili, with a clumsy and leaky boat, a six-pounder howitzer mounted forward, a week's provision, (in case of being lost,) and water stowed about in spots, and a dozen ashen oars, one mast and sail, with which to protect ourselves against said proverbial treachery.

"Our orders were to anchor where we were left and make tidal observations during the day, after which we would be picked up by the Phenomenon toward night, —a most unpleasant prospect for a cold, raw day. Down went the anchor, however, as soon as said Phenomenon cleared us, over went the lead, and the monotonous employment commenced. It consisted of sounding every ten minutes, the time and depth of water being noted in lead-pencil at each cast; and the hours passed heavily enough, as may be imagined.

"It was one of the most quiet days I ever passed,—quiet, not only so far as work and noise were concerned, but also in the perfect rest of the elements. Not a passing cloud interposed itself between us and the welcome rays of the sun; not a fitful breath of disturbed air chilled our blood, or darkly ruffled the smooth and placid surface of the sleeping gulf. All was quiet: nature lived her inanimate life around us in the form of water and sky only; for the low land of Pichili, though visible from the deck of the steamer, had sunk below the clearly-defined horizon as we descended into the boat, and the ship herself had slowly steamed from us on her trackless path, until, from a mere speck upon the opposite horizon, she had finally disappeared entirely. Neither the air nor the water showed a sign of life. We were alone upon the motionless surface of an unknown sea, with the silent repose of nature for our only companion. At noon I got an altitude of the sun, and then, leaving the coxswain to note the soundings, stretched out for a nap in the sunny corner of the stern-sheets. An hour passed, and its last minutes found me shivering with cold and gazing anxiously at a lowering change which had come over the face of awakening nature.

"The sea was no longer smooth and polished, but broken by rising waves and of an inky hue; while the sun was hidden by dense masses of driving clouds whose lurid edges indicated the commencement of a northern gale. The wind was already blowing quite fresh, and the boat rolling uneasily in the rising sea, dipping in the spray-crests occasionally, and jerking at her anchor as if asking for more chain. I began to think we might be in an awkward predicament, but kept my fears to myself, and ordered more chain veered. Then we unshipped the howitzer and got it in the bottom, after which she rode easier. Anxious eyes now began to be cast in the supposed direction of the ship, but even her smoke was not to be seen. There was a smoky appearance, truly, but it was that of the rising gale; and, as we wrapped our blankets around our shivering frames, we knew that there was anxiety, and work, and danger,—possibly death,—in the voice of the leaping waves and in those lurid masses of hurrying clouds.

"The water was now coming over the bow quite fast; so we commenced baling, served out an extra allowance of grog, and continued watching for the ship.

"And so another and another hour rolled by, and the gloom of approaching night began to deepen that of the rising gale. Ours was now a most unpleasant situation. The water was swashing over either beam at every roll, curling over the bow at every dive, and giving us sharp work with both buckets to keep it from gaining on us. After a while it did gain on us, and men's faces began to turn pale. I felt that things were getting desperate, and, adjusting a glass, swept the eastern board in the vain hope of catching a glimpse of the expected smoke: there was nothing to be seen but a bank of moving mist.

"Our circle of vision had by this time been narrowed down to a diameter of some two miles, and we were just fearing that the ship might miss us in the fog, when suddenly, like a meteor shooting into the clear sky from behind a passing cloud, she burst through the bank of thickening mist into a glorious full view. She was distant not more than a mile, was smoking like a young volcano, was under a crowd of sail at the same time, and, in short, evidently doing her best to reach us. A long-drawn breath seemed to relieve every one. A few minutes later we were alongside, with the boat half full of water, ourselves soaked to the skin and half numbed with cold, but still *safe.*

"'Glad to see you!' said the captain, as we crawled heavily over the side. 'Bad weather came up very suddenly: didn't it? Never mind; it'll rub off when it gets dry: besides, this is special service, for which Congress is to give us extra pay. Heave the ship to with her head off shore, Mr. Russell.' So much for this unpleasantly-near approach to a long swim."

We now experienced a continued spell of bad weather, which forced us to relinquish the idea of reaching the Great Wall, and drove us with tingling ears from the Gulf of Pichili into the Yellow Sea. I have already remarked that the surface of this sea was like a vast expanse of polished glass when we crossed it in tow of the Powhatan, and that we had not felt a breath of wind during the passage; but now, alas! how changed was the state of affairs! The sea was dark and broken, and gale succeeded gale in place of the endless calm. There were some doubtful islands in this sea which we wished to satisfy ourselves in regard to before returning to Shanghae, and several more days were devoted to searching for them. We were unsuccessful; and, finding time running short, squared away on our return-trip.

This was during the latter part of November, 1854,—the 28th, I think; and that night we had a fearful time. Let me describe it.

Imagine yourself upon the restless ocean with the destroying hurricane breathing its furious breath around your labouring craft; with the rugged rocks and boiling surf of the dreaded "lee shore" looming upon the misty horizon, and warning you of the necessity of "holding your own" against the gale, while friendly miles of space yet lie between you and their fatal dangers. Imagine yourself watching the strained canvas and the complaining spar, the hauling gale, the heavy dive into the green seas, and the distant land, which, as the gale hauls, is fast changing into the dreaded "lee shore." Imagine yourself at the commencement of a dark and stormy night, with the position of your ship but poorly defined upon an unreliable chart, suddenly called upon to run her through a narrow passage, before the gale, while yet its direction enabled you to do so, or remain "hove to" with the strong probability of being wrecked on the rocks before morning. Imagine yourself in circumstances similar to these, and you can readily appreciate our feelings as the shades of such a dark and stormy night closed around us and left us to choose between those two evils.

We had scarcely squared away when the weather, which had been overcast and threatening for some days, came on very thick and heavy, and combined with unknown currents, want of observations, and doubtful charts, to render our position perilous in the extreme. We had been several days without a glance at any celestial body when we kept away, and the consequence was that we did not very well know *where we were running to* at such a grand rate: we might soon find ourselves on a pile of rocks for what we knew; so we wisely hove to under a close-reefed maintopsail, and with just enough steam on to keep the old tub from falling off into the trough of the rapidly-increasing sea. Even with the assistance of steam, however, we did not make half the weather of it that the little Cooper did, who, with her close-reefed foresail only, climbed over the threatening seas with the lightness of a feather and "held her own" beautifully; while we, like a huge crab, drifted bodily to leeward, *as usual.* The consequence of this was that in a very few hours we lost sight of her light, and when we next saw it it was off the town of Shanghae. I turn to my journal for an account of our subsequent doings:—

"We drifted along quite miserably in this way for some time, our decks being no sooner well clear of one sea than another would slap her on the bow, curl over the rail, and sweep aft through the lee gangway. We had taken the precaution to batten down all of the forward hatches before the arrival of night, and at about four bells in the first watch (10 P.M.) began to wish that we had done likewise by the after ones. At that hour a heavy weather-roll brought in a sea over the main chains that deluged the quarter-deck, filled the ward-room and our state-rooms six inches deep, and swashed up into our bunks with so much effect as to soak our beds and awaken us most thoroughly.

"Having the mid-watch ahead, I had turned in an hour before, and was annoyed, though not at all surprised, at my nocturnal bath: it was not the first thing of the kind by any means, and, being easily pleased, I was fast becoming reconciled to it as one of the necessary accompaniments of that interesting cruise. Buckets, dippers, and swabs, were now in great demand, and a quarter-watch—called *quarter*, I suppose, because it *means half* the watch that are on deck—was sent below to pass up the water, while the others helped the carpenter to batten down the offending hatches.

"While the men were thus baling, while the old ship rolled horribly, and while I was turning over my mattress in the partially-successful search for a dry spot upon which to coil myself away for the next two hours,—while all of this was going on, I heard a knock at my state-room door, and then the voice of the quartermaster of the watch:—

"'Mr. Habersham!'

"'Well?'

"'The cap'n wants you, sir.'

"'The mischief he does! How many bells is it?'

"'Gone four, sir!'

"'Very well! Any thing wrong?'

"'No, sir! Only it's a-blowin' a livin' gale, and she's mighty uncomfortable. The cap'n wants you in the cabin with Mr. Russell and the master: they're all over the chart now.'

"'All right!' I exclaimed; but I buttoned up my monkey-jacket over a vast deal of disgust and dissatisfaction as I stepped down into the half knee-deep water, and made my way aft through a confused mass of broken chairs, floating spittoons, and baling men. I never felt so out with the sea, so great a longing to quit it for a shore-profession, as I did during that groping walk; and, as I put my hand upon the cabin-door, my mind was pretty well made up never again to engage in a surveying and exploring expedition around the world.

"'Sorry to disturb you, Mr. H——,' said the captain, as I opened the door and took off my cap; 'but the truth is, we are getting into another of our tight places, and want to advise together as the best course to avoid it.'

"'You haven't disturbed me at all, sir,' I replied; 'the water got the start of you: our rooms are all afloat again in the ward-room.'

"'So I hear. Well, I'm afraid we'll have to steam up and get her off before this gale. We are making such a bad weather of it that we have parted company with the Cooper. The gale blows stronger every minute, and hauls too: if it continues thus for two hours, it will make the coast of China a lee shore. We must run through between the capes before it heads us off, or stand our chance of holding our own sufficiently well to keep off the land. R—— and C—— and myself have been talking it over, and think we'd better run for the China Sea, in spite of the strong chance that exists of our running down one or the other of the capes. We don't know where we are: we have only dead reckoning to work upon, but we think it the best chance. Have you any thing to advise?'

"I looked at Carnes. He had made two black spots on the chart, and joined them by a straight line.

"'We have every reason to suppose that we are on this line,' he said, in answer to my look of inquiry; 'but upon what exact part of it we cannot say. The chances are about two out of three that we are between the spots; hence we may be outside, and, if we are outside and conclude to run, we are lost. We propose steering a south course, which will take us between the capes and into the open sea, if our supposition is right. If I have allowed too much or too little for drift and current, or if the chart is much out, we will strike on the east or west cape, as the case may be. If we remain here and the gale goes on hauling, we will be on a lee shore before morning, and you know what the old beast would do then. My voice is for running on a south course. *Voilà!*—the elephant!'

"He shrugged his shoulders, half Frenchman as he is, and indulged in a muttered imprecation, as the ship made a heavy lurch that almost threw us from our feet.

"'I think, too, that our best chance is in running, sir,' I replied, as Stevens again asked my opinion; 'it's an ugly night, and we are as likely to feel the capes as see them: still, it won't do to remain here.'

"'Well, then, *run it is;* we have the satisfaction of knowing that we are all agreed, at any rate. Tell Mr. Lawton to get up plenty of steam; and have all hands called to wear ship. Goose-wing the foresail, secure every thing about the decks, batten down the cabin sky-light, and let me know when you're ready for putting the helm up. There's an awful sea running, but we must try to find a smooth time, and then get by the trough as soon as possible.'

"So we left him and went on deck, where an active and exciting scene at once commenced. The clear, shrill whistle of our only boatswain's mate first arose over the howling of the gale, and called every man to his station for 'wearing ship.' Then commenced the preparations,—lights floating around the gloomy decks, and only serving to render every thing more gloomy than before; men hurrying here and there; the flapping of sails, the creaking of blocks, the slapping about of the running rigging, and the unnatural voice of the speaking-trumpet striving in vain to make itself heard over the battle of the elements. Nor was this all: the thick sheets of descending rain, the heavy seas which now often broke over half the length of the ship, and the visible darkness, whose gloom, as I have said, seemed only increased by the flitting lights that danced around the decks, combined to render the whole affair any thing but pleasant, and promised us an anxious night.

"The men, too, became frightened, and Russell, who, as second lieutenant, had his station on the forecastle, finding them afraid to ascend even to the foreyard, sprang into the rigging in the hope of shaming them into boldness. The device succeeded, and in twenty minutes from the commencement every thing was ready. The captain now took his position near the wheel, while I climbed into the weather mizzen-rigging and commenced to watch anxiously the towering seas as they rolled by, partly under our keel, partly over our decks. Those were some of the most anxious moments of my whole life, as we thus awaited the arrival of a period of comparative quiet to enable the helm to be put up with safety. It was so dark that we could not see the seas until they were nearly upon us, and we could only hope to *feel*, by the change in the ship's motion, when the proper time was arriving. Finally, I judged it at hand, and, as the old ship recovered herself after a more than usually heavy lurch and dive, gave the orders, 'Hard up the helm! Go ahead strong with the engine! Brace in the after yards! Haul aboard the fore tack!" And then every thing was done that *we* could do. It now became the turn of the head sails, of the helm, and of the propeller, to do the rest. If she went off before the wind previous to the arrival of another heavy sea, we were all right; if she hung in the trough, we would, in all probability, founder in five minutes. In either case, nothing more could be done to help her: the die had been cast.

"I grasped the rigging more tightly, and strained my eyes toward the labouring bow; but every thing was so dark and impenetrable that I could only *hope* that she was falling off. Suddenly I felt the wind drawing abeam, then abaft it. I began to breathe freely. * * * * What a glorious thing a propeller is! When the helm had been put up, the old tub was lying like a log in the troubled ocean, and yet the rushing waters of the whirling screw, acting upon the lee face of the rudder, turned her as upon a pivot, thus bringing both wind and sea abaft the beam sooner than we had any reason to hope for. Yes; the dreaded trough was passed quickly, and yet not a second too soon; for it was no sooner accomplished than the heaviest sea of any that had yet struck us came rolling up under our weather quarter, broke completely over our decks, and caused the old ship to vibrate as if every timber in her had been started.

"It was a beautiful as well as a fearful sight, to see that sea rear its tottering crest over the very quarter, cast itself bodily upon our trembling decks, and then rush forward, half of it in-board, half of it out-board, along our weather bulwarks, sweeping with it arm-chests, gratings, spare spars, yelping dogs, squeaking pigs, empty chicken-coops, struggling men,—in short, every thing that was movable. Some of these it swept completely overboard; others it lodged in the ropes along the bulwarks, or piled

THE SEA THAT STRUCK US ON THE QUARTER.

in a confused mass under and about the launch. All along our weather bulwark it broke also, from the very quarter to the distant stem, pouring in over the rail like a young Niagara, loosening spars from the chains, and twisting off the wing of the crow-like eagle that had for years adorned (?) our bow. It was a fearful shock, and we feared for the ship after it. What would have been our fate had it struck us fair on the beam? At the same time, it was productive of a good result; for, as her stern settled down as its body passed from under us, we were urged forward with a velocity which, combined with the action of the propeller, threw us before both wind and sea and told us that the danger of the trough was passed. We actually astonished the barnacles and rudder-fish by flying before the gale at the rate of eleven knots the hour; and, even after disconnecting the propeller, we found her speed but slightly reduced, so heavy was the gale and sea that drove us ahead.

"And thus we ran the gauntlet of those rugged capes, through that dark night, that blinding rain, that shrieking hurricane, and before those angry seas that growled and broke and rose again under our flying stern. The night seemed longer, and darker, and more dismal, than any night I had ever passed before; but daylight came at last, and with it the conviction of safety. At noon it was clear weather once more, and we got observations that fixed our position on the chart. Then we drew a straight line due north from it; and it was frightful to see how closely we had shaved the left cape,—so closely, that bad steering alone might have cast us upon its hopeless rocks, and then———"

It would be unjust to end this adventure without according due credit to him whose close navigation and sound judgment carried us safely through it,—Mr. E. O. Carnes, the sailing-master of the ship, then a passed-midshipman, and now the occupant of a Wall Street office. The hardships of that cruise, combined with a latent distaste for the sea, disgusted him with the navy and caused him to resign his warrant. Fortunately for the Expedition, he could not hear of the acceptance of his resignation by the Government until our arrival at San Francisco, when he was thrown upon his own resources and allowed to find his way home as best he could.

We now shaped our course for Shanghae, and while entering the Woo-sung River the propeller suddenly "ran down," and forced us to anchor to avoid drifting on shore. We could not imagine what caused this singular stoppage, and resorted to every device to get it to start again. We finally had to blow off steam and trust to our sails to get us up to the city, which was only a few miles off. It took us several days to accomplish this; and we could not but wonder what would have been our fate had it failed us during or immediately after the gale. We were subsequently engaged more than two months repairing it,—a great loss of valuable time, and the source of considerable expense to the Government.

CHAPTER X.

WE HEAR A DISTRESSING RUMOUR AND ARE GREATLY DISPIRITED—WE ARE REQUESTED BY THE MERCHANTS OF SHANGHAE TO ATTACK A PIRATICAL SQUADRON, AND EVINCE A PRAISEWORTHY READINESS FOR ACTION—THE OLD JOHN ASTONISHES THE CHINESE OF THE WAN-CHEW RIVER, AFTER WHICH SHE VISITS FORMOSA AND LIBERATES TWO CHINESE CONVICTS.

WHILE we were working our toilsome way up the Woo-sung River, a painful rumour spread itself around our decks and weighed us down with a shapeless and horrid fear. It was said that the Porpoise was lost; but how the news came, or who had spoken positively of it, no one could tell. A startled feeling of doubt, and surprise, and distressing uncertainty, pervaded every heart.

While in this gloomy state of mind, we were one day greatly relieved by the arrival of the Cooper, whom, it will be remembered, we had left in the Yellow Sea, exposed to the fury of a heavy gale and the dangers of a probable lee shore. We had been so disheartened by the report of the loss of the Porpoise, that our fears for the safety of our little consort had been morbidly increased, and we were now proportionately inspirited by her appearance. She anchored near us to see if she could be of any assistance, (we were aground,) but, finding us obliged to wait the rising of the tide, got under way again and stood on up the river. A few days later we reached the city ourselves, when we received a visit from the consul, who confirmed our worst fears in regard to the Porpoise.

There seemed to be no doubt as to the truth of the rumour. Still, we found it difficult to give up our confidence in her as a sea-boat, or in her officers as skilful and able men. We remained in a painful state of suspense for months.

We now found it necessary to put the Hancock into dock before we could ascertain what affected the propeller, and by the time she got out again the month of December was passed and we found ourselves commencing the year of 1855. We were no sooner ready for sea than a report reached Shanghae that an English opium-clipper was blockaded by pirates in the Wan-chew River; and, as it was only slightly out of our route to the island of Formosa, the captain readily complied with the wish of the merchants that we should touch there on our way and rescue her from their clutches. We consequently hurried our departure, and, after fighting many imaginary battles to get our hands in for "deeds of blood and valour," we arrived at the spot and found that the pirates had retired and that the schooner had gone to sea some days since. We now *re*worked our way through the numerous sand-banks that guard the mouth of that rarely-visited river, and shaped a course for Keilung, a harbour in the northern end of the unknown island of Formosa. But, before I leave Wan-chew, let me say a word in regard to the "sensation" which the "Old John" created among the crowds of astonished Chinese who lined the banks of that river to see a vessel sailing head to wind and current without any apparent motive-power.

Persons who are in the daily habit of seeing a balloon

ascend, of wondering over the strange secrets of electricity, or of witnessing the silent progress of a propeller-steamer, will have to reflect a moment before they can appreciate the feeling of alarmed curiosity which fills the semi-civilized or savage breast when for the first time it beholds such apparent miracles. In the present case, we had our sails furled, were steaming with anthracite coal, which made no smoke, and were running through a strong current and against a light breeze. There was nothing in the world to give ignorant minds the slightest clue as to how we got ahead: they were as much confounded as we would have been to have seen an ox-cart going up-hill by itself. As we thus ascended the winding river, the villages which teemed along its banks poured forth their excited inhabitants to witness the strange spectacle,—men, women, and children, hurrying to the water's edge, watching our mysterious progress, and then returning slowly to their homes as if they had seen enough to think about for the next week. After we had anchored, they approached us warily in their boats, refusing to come alongside, and keeping their eyes on our every movement. They were evidently in doubt as to our terrestrial origin, or rather as to that of the Old John. Finally, we landed at a village abreast of our anchorage, and they began to get more reconciled, closing around us in great numbers and pointing to the ship in continued wonder. They were evidently seeking information, which we could only impart by signs.

While entering this river, we picked up a fishing-boat and compelled one of its owners to pilot us in; and it was he who had anchored us off this village, declaring that we could not get any higher up on account of sunken rocks, the captain having been anxious to anchor near the principal town. We could see from this village quite a large walled town which was between us and the larger city, and Hartman and Williams that evening climbed its wall and promenaded its streets, to the infinite terror of the female and juvenile portions of the population. They described it as being very thinly inhabited,—evidently an old city that was being gradually deserted. The latitude of this river is about 28° N., and its longitude 120° 38′ E. It will never probably be any thing more than a haunt for pirates.

We had a fine run to Keilung, where we fell in with the Cooper,—she having sailed direct for that port,—and where we found quite a snug anchorage for one or two sail. We also found ducks, vegetables, and oranges quite plentiful, the latter being as fine as any I ever ate. We had also been told of the existence of coal a few miles in the interior; but, upon applying to the authorities, (such as they were,) they gave us, as usual, the most evasive answers. The captain was, however, determined to get some specimens; so he and one or two of the mess, with his Chinese steward as interpreter, started back into the country to discover the deposit. They were soon encountered by two men, who offered to guide them to the spot, provided they might be allowed to go to Hong-Kong in the ship; and, as it seemed a simple case of buying and selling, the captain consented. They told him that there was a law forbidding any one to show the way to the coal-mine, upon pain of death; but, upon our arrival at Hong-Kong, we learned that Keilung was a penal settlement of the Chinese, and that those two fellows were convicts who thus escaped their punishment.

I will say nothing more about Formosa for the present. We left its shores about as wise as we were upon our arrival, and it was not until our second visit that we picked up what little information now exists upon the files of the Expedition in regard to it. Upon leaving Keilung for Hong-Kong we kept along the east coast of the island, in the vain search for a reported harbour. There was nothing to be seen but an iron-bound coast with range after range of lofty mountains lifting themselves above the heavy surf that broke along the entire beach. One day we thought we had discovered it: we saw ahead the smoke of distant villages rising back of a bight in the coast which looked very much like a harbour; but, upon approaching it, we found ourselves mistaken. We, however, lowered a boat and attempted to land, but the surf was breaking so furiously that it would have been madness to have entered it. Besides, the beach was crowded by naked and excited savages, whom it was generally reported were cannibals, and into whose company we should consequently have preferred being thrown with reliable arms in our hands. The two convicts, whom the captain had taken in the boat to interpret in case of his being able to land, became so frightened at the savage appearance of those reported man-eaters, that they went on their knees to him, protesting, through the steward, that the islanders had eaten many of their countrymen, and that if he went any nearer they would do the same by him and the boat's crew. Finding it impossible to pass the surf, the boat returned on board, and we squared away for Hong-

Kong, where we arrived on the 13th of February, 1855, and found the Vincennes alone at her moorings. We looked with straining eyes and sinking hearts for the well-known hull and spars of the devoted brig. They were nowhere to be seen. We sighed and closed our glasses with a shudder. *The Porpoise was lost.*

We found that the Vincennes herself had passed through an unusually severe cruise during our separation; and as the unfortunate Porpoise had kept company with her up to a certain time, since when she has not been heard of, I make the following extract from a letter lately received from Lieutenant John M. Brooke, of the Vincennes, in regard to the manner in which they separated, &c.; and I am sorry to say to the friends of those who were lost in her, that this extract contains all we know of her melancholy end:—

"The facts relating to the Vincennes and the Porpoise, and the fate of the latter, are simply these:—

"The two vessels in company were struggling with the northeast monsoons in the China Sea. Occasionally the veering wind and changing barometer indicated the passage of a cyclone: the increasing fury of the wind and these indications governed the courses of the vessels. At length they found themselves between Formosa and the main, and, during the night of the 20th of September, they held on near mid-channel; but in the morning the Vincennes, then to leeward, bore up for the Bashee passage. It was presumed that the Porpoise would follow. While the Vincennes was thus running before the wind, towing hawsers astern to break the sea should she cross the banks, the Porpoise was enveloped in a driving mist and lost to sight. This separation was regarded as of little moment, for the brig was well manned, and her officers, individually and collectively, were men of the first ability and courage:—you knew them all.

"It is generally understood by seamen that sound vessels are safer alone than in company; for the whole attention of the commander may be devoted to the care of his vessel without those modifications of plan required when acting in concert. In those seas the obscurity of the night rendered it difficult to distinguish light, and the sound of cannon would be lost in the roaring of the winds and waves. Therefore, neither surprise nor special anxiety was experienced on that occasion.

"The Vincennes, having passed the Bashee passage, entered the Pacific, and, until her arrival at the Bonin Islands, experienced fine weather. The arrival of the Porpoise—a dull sailer—was daily expected. Meanwhile there came on, at *night*, one of those characteristic storms of the Bonins,—a hurricane or cyclone. It came unheralded, except by the slightly-increased sound of the surf on the outer rocks; and it was not until the fitful gusts that, by their peculiar tone, are recognised by those who have heard it, swept from the hills over the ship, that we were aware of its proximity. Nearly shut in by mountains, the Vincennes, with lower yards and topmasts struck and four anchors down, trembled from the vibration of the masts and rigging. There was no shrill whistling of the wind, but a deep and hollow roar; the crests of the waves were caught up, and whitened the air with drift. The falling barometer and the veering wind presented all the indications of a cyclone sweeping toward the north. It was remarked by the ablest seamen of the Vincennes that she, good sea-boat as she was, would scarcely have survived the hurricane at sea.

"In the confined China Sea—near the Pescadores, the wind blowing toward the coast of China—it would be singular indeed if no vestige of a ship wrecked or lost there should be found. It is not probable that the Porpoise was lost until she reached the vicinity of the Bonins.

"She bore the character of a good sea-boat, but was short and deep in the waist, therefore liable to broach to, or to be brought by the lee,—to fill and founder."

And this is all! This gloomy account, similar to that which was laid before us on our arrival at Hong-Kong, contains in its hopeless lines all that is known of the fate of the time-worn old brig and her crew of near a hundred souls. The subsequent search which was undertaken by the Hancock, and in which we persisted at the imminent risk of our ship and lives, resulted in nothing save disappointment, danger, and loss of time. That dense and driving mist which enveloped her in its shroud-like embrace may have veiled from the curious eyes of her receding consort an unequal conflict, waged between man's godlike brain on the one side and the power of the elements and some untoward accident on the other; or she may have followed the stormy path of her more fortunate consort, and perished within a day's sail of the Bonin Islands. Certain it is that no ordinary combination of circumstances would have sufficed to bring about her uncertain fate. That brig, and the man who controlled her slightest movement with the experienced will of his well-balanced brain, had now rested after the labours of their perilous cruise, had not some insurmountable danger crossed their path, against which all human precautions were of no avail. Peace—eternal peace—be to the glorious manes of those who share her unknown grave, and to those mourning friends whose dearest hopes, whose fond longings for an earthly reunion, are blighted by the withering evidence of time's onward roll! There is no more room for hope.

We were now once more in Hong-Kong,—the Vincennes, ourselves, and the Cooper. Further changes soon began to be talked of as to the officering of the different vessels,—the result of the wasting hand of disease, which was by this time thinning our ranks. We had buried Lieutenant Hunter in the vast burial-ground of Fou-chow-fou, and now Acting-master R. R. Carter, of the Vincennes, was lying dangerously ill at the house of a friend on shore. He was partially restored to health after a protracted illness, and finally succeeded in reaching his Virginia home; but he never again did any duty in the Expedition, nor will he, I fear, ever regain his former strength. After the loss of the Porpoise, the detachment of this accomplished officer was the greatest misfortune that the Expedition experienced.

This vacancy on board the flag-ship caused Lieutenant Russell to be ordered to fill it; and Lieutenant McCullom, having grown tired of keeping guard off Canton, in the Kennedy, was induced to join the Hancock in his place. He was my senior officer, and as such unwillingly relieved me of the combined duties of first lieutenant, boatswain, and gunner of a shaky old steamer at which people looked and wondered that she was still afloat.

We had all been so roughly handled during our late cruise that considerable time was now required for repairs; and while these were going on a third set of astronomical observations were obtained by Lieutenant Brooke, the astronomer of the expedition. They were culminations of the moon, and the mean of the three sets was satisfactory in the extreme. Finally, the spring set in, and found us again ready for sea; and, in order to run over as much space as possible, each vessel was assigned a separate track.

The Vincennes was to proceed, *viâ* the Bonin Islands, to Loo-choo, the Cooper to take in some islands to the northward and eastward of Formosa on her way to the same port, and the Hancock to search for the Porpoise in the Formosa Channel, to survey the southwest and east coast of that island, and then join the other two vessels at their port of destination. From thence we were to proceed by different routes to the port of Hakodadi, island of Jesso,—the Cooper going through the Japan Sea, and the Vincennes and Hancock through a long chain of islands, touching at Simoda, island of Nipon, and finally joining the Cooper at Hakodadi. From thence the Vincennes was to pass along the east coast of Kamtschatka and Asia, through Behring's Straits, and into the Arctic; the Cooper was to examine the Kurile, the Fox, and the Aleutian Islands; and the Hancock to survey the entire circumference of the Okotsk Sea, the great centre of the American whalers. It was understood that the middle of October was to find us again united in the harbour of San Francisco, California.

It was another stormy season as we again put to sea from Hong-Kong, and we had a most uncomfortable time working up against strong northerly gales. As already observed, we were bound to the Pescadore Islands, and thence around the south cape of Formosa. We were hunting for the missing brig, or for a stranded plank or floating cask that should tell us of her fate. We had little or no data to assist us in this search. A black spot pricked upon the chart of the China Sea by Commander Rodgers was our only guide. "It was there we left her," said he: "go and seek our brother-officers, and may Heaven prosper your search!" We arrived at the harbour of Makung on the 26th of March, and remained there two days. Makung is the largest settlement of the Pescadores, and is inhabited by Chinese. We communicated with them through our Chinese servants, could hear nothing of the Porpoise, and left for the coast of Formosa. Upon sighting the latter, we were overtaken by a heavy gale, against which we tried to steam, but, finding ourselves near foundering, put up the helm and ran down along the land toward a village this side of the south cape. As we closed in with the land the wind seemed to head us off, and we were glad to reach our destination without being blown to sea.

And now, before I turn to my journal for a few pages in regard to our experience while coasting around this island, let me enlighten the reader as much as possible in regard to it from other sources. The Encyclopædia Britannica says,—

"The Dutch at an early period established a settlement on this island.

"In 1625, the viceroy of the Philippine Islands sent an expedition against Formosa, with a view of expelling the Dutch. It was unsuccessful. . . . About the middle of the seventeenth century, it afforded a retreat to twenty or thirty thousand Chinese from the fury of the Tartar conquest. . . . In 1653, a conspiracy of the Chinese against the Dutch was discovered and suppressed; and, soon after this, Coxinga, the governor of the maritime Chinese province of Tehichiang, applied for permission to retire to the island, which was refused by the Dutch governor; on which he fitted out an expedition, consisting of six hundred vessels, and made himself master of the town of Formosa and the adjacent country. The Dutch were then allowed to embark and leave the island. . . . Coxinga afterward engaged in a war with the Chinese and Dutch, in which he was defeated and slain. But they were unable to take possession of the island, which was bravely defended by the posterity of Coxinga; and it was not till the year 1683 that the island was voluntarily surrendered by the reigning prince to the Emperor of China. . . . In 1805, through the weakness of the Chinese government, the Ladrone pirates had acquired possession of a great part of the southwest coast."

The Encyclopædia Americana says,—

"The island is about two hundred and forty miles in length from north to south, and sixty from east to west in its broadest part, but greatly contracted at each extremity. That part of the island which the Chinese possess presents extensive and fertile plains, watered by a great number of rivulets that fall from the eastern mountains. Its air is pure and wholesome, and the earth produces in abundance corn, rice, and most other kinds of grain. Most of the India fruits are found here,—such as oranges, bananas, pineapples, guavas, cocoanuts,—and part of those of Europe, particularly peaches, apricots, figs, grapes, chestnuts, pomegranates, watermelons, &c. Tobacco, sugar, pepper, camphor, and cinnamon, are also common. The capital of Formosa is Taiouan,—a name which the Chinese give to the whole island."

In addition to the foregoing extracts from standard authority, we have a most marvellous account of this island from the pen of Mauritius Augustus, Count de Benyowsky, a Polish refugee from Siberian exile, who visited its east coast in 1790 in a small armed vessel containing about one hundred men. The account by this nobleman is interesting in the extreme, but unfortunately he is guilty of one gross and palpable falsehood, which necessarily throws a shade of distrust on his entire narrative. He speaks "of anchoring in several fine harbours on the east coast;" whereas we of the Hancock searched in vain for any such place of refuge along that entire shore. On the north and west coasts they are quite plentiful.

After anchoring in one of these "fine harbours," the count goes on to give us an idea of the people who received him: they were Indians, savages, and very fierce,—so much so that they soon attempted the murder of a party that had visited their village. He now killed a great many of them, got up his anchor, and went to an adjoining harbour, where he was most graciously received for having slain so many of their enemies of the place they had just left. Here he fell in with a prince, who persuaded him into an alliance against another prince, and thus they fought for some time. Finally, he drags himself from the island, much to the distress of the prince his ally, who loads him down with gold and silver. It is impossible to read the count's narrative and say what he *did see.* He was evidently a blood-relative of the Munchausen family.

And now, having shown what others say in regard to Formosa, let us return to the "old John," whom we left at anchor under shelter of its west coast, at the close of a stormy day. Here is what my journal says in regard to our arrival, and to what we saw and did upon the following days:—

"We could see nothing that night save an extensive stretch of white sand-beach backed by a sloping green, in the rear of which we imagined we saw a village slumbering under the deepening shadows of a high range of mountains. But this village existed, many said, only in the vivid imaginations of a few, and it was not until darkness had become sufficiently dark to reflect its many lights that the fact was generally admitted. The next morning, however, we had a most refreshing view spread out before us,—green slopes and waving fields of grain, broken here and there by extensive tracts of table-land, over which we could see the cattle roving in their lazy search for the more tender mouthfuls of the abundant grass.

"It is a beautiful sight for any one to look upon—these landscapes composed of sloping lawns, waving fields, grazing cattle, a village here and there, and the mountain-sides glistening with the sunlit spray of rushing waterfalls. But when to all this is added the fact of one being just from the sea, and gazing upon lands seldom beheld by the eye of civilization, it becomes a scene well calculated to drive the blood through the veins with increased velocity. One feels like rushing wildly through those waving fields, and throwing his salt-impregnated frame into the mountain-stream, or rolling childlike upon the green grass, and feeling himself away from the sea at last.

"This was all very beautiful, very desirable, but unfortunately just then quite unattainable. For the gale still raged through, over, and around it all, most effectually preventing our 'rushing into the mountain-stream or rolling upon the green grass.' So we amused ourselves by overhauling our guns, which had been pronounced perfectly ready for service the night before, adding more ammunition to our already large supply, resharpening our bowie-knives, which had always been like razors, and in the various other useless though ingenious occupations of restless minds. 'Old bust-proof' looked more serviceable that day than I ever saw him before.

"During the night the gale fortunately abated, and the next morning bust-proof and his master, several others of the mess, and myself, ventured into our best-pulling boat and struck out boldly for the beach. It was a hard and wet pull; but something over three-quarters of an hour sufficed to cross the stormy half-mile that separated us, and, as the keel grated with welcome harshness on the sand, we felt ourselves once more on shore. What if the boat *was* half full of water, and we like half-drowned rats? we were still *on shore.*

"We landed upon this strange and crowded beach without fear, simply from the fact that, while yet some distance off, we had readily recognised the natives as Chinese, and, although they were all armed with either the matchlock or bow and arrow, we knew too much of their race to anticipate violence. This crowd, which received us in a most noisy manner, was composed of men, women, and children,—the males of almost every age being armed. We had taken the precaution to bring one of our Chinese mess-boys with us; but, their language being neither the Mandarin, Canton, or Shanghae dialect, he at first found great difficulty in making himself understood. After a while, however, by the aid of the few words common to each and a fearful amount of violent pantomime on our part, we succeeded in exchanging ideas with tolerable freedom.

"From all that we could learn from them in this way, it seems that they exist in a state of perpetual warfare with their savage neighbours of the east coast. The island being very narrow there, the latter find no difficulty in crossing the mountain-ridge which, like a huge backbone, divides the two territories, capturing cattle, making prisoners, burning isolated habitations, and then retreating into their mountain-fastnesses, where they are never followed by their unwarlike victims. Thus we always found the latter armed with sword, matchlock, or bow and arrow, and confining themselves strictly to their

HARTMAN AND THE RED MEN OF FORMOSA.

fields and pasture-grounds. Whenever we evinced a disposition to ascend the bushy sides of the neighbouring hills, they became greatly alarmed, caught hold of our clothes, threw themselves in our paths, and made signs to us that our throats would be certainly cut and we roasted for supper by bad men who were very strong and fierce and who wore large rings in their ears. We did not know what to make of all this at first; but Hartman, who had wandered off by himself in search of snipe, rejoined us shortly before dark, and opened our eyes.

"Having unconsciously wandered over the low land and ascended a neighbouring elevation, he had seated himself upon a fragment of rock, and was admiring the view which opened before him, when his ear suddenly caught a sound as of some animal making its way cautiously through the bushes. He turned quickly, and saw a party of three, whom he had no difficulty in recognising as 'bad men who wore large rings in their ears.'

"Here was a fix for our innocent sportsman: he must either retire with an imaginary tail between his legs, or face boldly the unlooked-for danger. Fortunately, he was a man of nerve, and was moreover armed with a shot-gun, bowie-knife, and revolver. Choosing, therefore, the latter alternative, he arose with a great air of non-she-lan-cy, (as I once heard the word pronounced by an American who had been to Paris,) and advanced to the nearest, a tall, fine-looking fellow, who rested upon his bow and fixed his gaze curiously upon him. Hartman says that he whistled with considerable success portions of a popular air as he thus went, as it were, into the lion's mouth, but never before felt such a longing to be safely on the distant decks of the much-abused 'old John.' He soon joined this princely-looking savage, and as the others drew near he made a careful but hurried survey of their personal appearance, exchanged a Mexican dollar for the bow and arrow of one of them, evidently against the will of the surprised owner, and then leisurely retraced his way until an intervening clump of trees enabled him with safety to call upon his legs to do their duty. It is needless to remark that the vocal music and the air of 'non-she-lan-cy' expired in each other's arms at this point. He ran for a mile or more before evincing the slightest curiosity to know if he was followed."

He described them as being of large stature, fine forms, copper-coloured, high cheek-bones, heavy jaws, coarse black hair reaching to the shoulders, and boasting no clothing save the maro, and a light cotton cloth over the shoulders,—very much like our North American Indians, he thought. No wonder that such a miserable race as the Chinese should hold them in dread: in fact, the only wonder is that they have the courage to remain on the same island. I suppose that our innocent sportsman is the first member of civilization who has had a close view of these reputed cannibals since Benyowsky, the Polish count, cruised along their shelterless shores in 1790, since which time they have been more out of the world even than the Japanese. These singularly-captured bow and arrows are now in the collection of the Expedition.

The setting sun looked upon us as we returned on board, and before he had again shone on those sloping greens we were well on our way around the south point of the island, in search of a landing among the savages in their own country. This, I regret to say, we never found, the whole east coast being one continued line of foaming breakers, that carried death upon their rolling crests to every thing like a boat. Where were the fine harbours of the Count de Benyowsky? The roaring of the surf was our only answer. More than once, however, impelled by our excessive curiosity to learn more of these unknown people, did we attempt to land; and more exciting attempts at shore-going I never participated in. Upon one of these occasions we entered upon the dangerous trial with two of our best boats; but, upon nearly losing the inner one, with all who were in her, we wisely returned on board. We got more than one near view of the savages, however, heard their voices, and answered their signs; but all this only increased our desire to know more of them, for now we saw that they were veritable red men; and what were red men doing on the island of Formosa?

As we pulled back to the ship after our narrow escape, we could not but think it providential that they of the inner boat had failed in landing through the surf; for, even had they succeeded in gaining the beach with whole bones, their arms would still have been rendered unserviceable by salt water, and, had the crowd proved unfriendly, we in the outer boat would certainly have kicked prudence overboard and pulled in to share their fate; and the probability is that we should all have "had our throats cut, and our bodies roasted for supper, by 'bad men who wore large rings in their ears.'"

From what I could see over the distance which separated our boat from the crowded beach, I found the previous description of our "innocent sportsman" substantiated by my own eyes and those of others. We saw an excited crowd of fine-looking men and women, copper-coloured, and possessed of the slightest possible amount of clothing,—the former boasting only a cloth tied around the head, while the latter had but a thin loose garment that seemed to gather around the throat and extended no farther than the knee. Some of the men were armed with bow and arrow, others with very serviceable-looking matchlocks; the women held various articles in their hands, probably for barter, and, as we pulled away after our narrow escape, they evinced their sorrow and desire to trade by loud cries and the most violent gestures. Our Chinese boy had almost fainted from fright as the inner boat backed into the surf in the attempt to land: he could only tremble and cry out, "Dey eat man! dey eat man!" His friends on the other side had evidently impressed him with that unpleasant national characteristic, and hence his fright when apparently about to be rolled helplessly to their feet by a boiling surf.

The same day upon which we made this our last attempt to land among them, we steamed along up their coast, keeping as close as was prudent,—in fact closer,—and examining with our glasses as far back as we could see. In this way we saw small but apparently comfortable stone houses, neatly-kept grounds,—what looked like fruitful gardens and green fields,—all being cultivated by "Chinese prisoners who had not yet been eaten," we were told on the other side; or rather we were told that their friends, when captured, were made to work until needed for culinary purposes.

We were surprised at this air of comfort among half-naked savages, and could not but wonder how they could have built such nice-looking houses, until we finally concluded that their prisoners had been made to turn their hands to masonry as well as gardening. Thus ended our second and last visit to Formosa, and all that we learned in regard to it may be condensed into a few words, viz.:—

We found it two hundred and five miles long by about sixty average width. It runs N. by E. and S. by W., has a range of mountains running along its entire east coast, and is peopled by two different races of men,—Chinese and red men. The former possess the north and west side of the island, the latter the east and south, and they exist in a state of constant hostility. The country in the possession of the former is undulating or low, that of the latter rugged and mountainous. There are harbours on the north and west side, and none on the east. All else is conjecture. So much for Formosa and its mysterious red men. We continued our survey, and arrived at the port of Nappa, island of Great Loo-choo, on the 9th of April. Neither the Vincennes or the Cooper had yet arrived.

CHAPTER XI.

SOMETHING ABOUT THE ANAKIRIMA GROUP OF ISLANDS, AND CLIMBING HILLS—ALSO A WORD IN REGARD TO LOO-CHOOANS, AND TWO MISSIONARIES WHO RESIDED AMONG THEM, AND HOW IT WAS THAT WE LEFT LOO-CHOO AND ARRIVED IN JAPAN.

WE found considerable difficulty in working our way through the sand-banks which guard the harbour of Nappa, as the pilots which Commodore Perry had made the Government promise to keep on the look-out did not approach us until we were near the anchorage. Then two of them boarded us, and begged by signs that we would not report their neglect to the authorities. We could not imagine for some time what caused them to be so much in earnest: we were subsequently enlightened on the subject by a missionary. Let me make an extract from my journal in regard to our arrival at this place:—

"At 4 P.M. we anchored in this harbour,—nine fathoms water and muddy bottom. McCullom, the first lieutenant, was at once sent on shore to see the governor, present our compliments, and ask for a quantity of wood with which we purpose steaming while surveying a neighbouring group of islands. Our coal is already running short; and, remembering how well we steamed with the wood obtained at Fou-chow-fou, we hope to use no more coal for some time.

"McCullom had scarcely reached the beach when a

messenger arrived from the governor, bringing *the card* of his excellency and inquiring most affectionately after the health of the captain. This messenger's name was Nagador, and he was a Loo-choo gentleman of the first water. His bearing was even courtly: he spoke in a low voice, almost a whisper, and possessed a singular air of good-breeding and cunning combined. Our decks were soon crowded by his suite, at least thirty or forty in number, and not a word above a whisper from any one of them: had the same number of Chinese been on board one could not have heard himself speak.

"Nagador spoke English well enough to make himself understood; and there were several others who knew a few words. They had learned it from the missionaries. We find two of these latter here. One is a member of the Church of England,—an Englishman; and the other a priest of that of Rome,—a French Jesuit. Singular to say, the latter is the last-comer in this case. They say they are treated kindly by the natives, but make few converts: time, they hope, will give them success. Those Loo-chooans who speak a little English pronounce it with more ease than any foreigners I ever saw. Unlike the Chinese, they pronounce the letter *r* without difficulty. I remember once being put to the blush by a Chinese servant at Macao: he was handing around a dish of rice, and attracted my attention by a nudge of the elbow, and asking, 'You wanchy lice?' I did not eat any rice that day."

I shall dwell lightly on Loo-choo. Commodore Perry's mammoth narrative leaves little to write about. I will only remark that they are a simple and inoffensive people, rather shy, extremely cringing in manner, and superlatively cunning. As far as my observation went, they have no arms of any description. In cunning, however, they excel even the Japanese. We tried to get some fresh provisions, a few potatoes and chickens, from them, but failed most signally. They complained of poverty, drought, thick population, and finally let us sail with *two goats* which they presented to us. Some of the women are very pretty; but, as they invariably ran, or turned their faces to the wall when too high to be climbed, we saw little but their backs.

As soon as we had filled our bunkers and decks with wood, we steamed over to the Anakirima group of islands,—distant some twenty miles to the eastward of Nappa,—and spent two weeks in surveying them. During this time we were troubled more than ever with our leaking boilers, having often to keep the ship anchored several days after blowing the water out of them to let them get cool enough for workmen to enter: then, probably, immediately after getting steam up again, a new leak would show itself and the same work have to be repeated. This was very harassing to the men and detrimental to the survey; but, like a great many other things, we had to get used to it, for it continued till the last day of the cruise. This group of islands having never before been even examined, I devote a few lines to them. Their central latitude is 26° 12′ N., longitude 127° 14′ E., and they are thinly populated by a lower order of Loo-chooans, while a few goats and deer range their rugged heights. The unpretending villages of these poor people are found in various seaside coves, or snugly stowed away in re-

GOING TO PAY A VISIT.

treating ravines or concealed valleys, as if they were anxious to remove as far as possible from the observation of strangers. Their year is divided into the calm and windy seasons, and it was our fortune to visit them during the former. Like most of these islands, those of this group are of volcanic origin, and offer but slight promise of agricultural yield along their steep and bare or densely-wooded sides. Some of the valleys, however, grow fine rice, and a few of the slopes were planted in sweet potato. The largest of them is not more than three miles in length by a mile in breadth, and altogether they do not number over a dozen, including islets. Some of them rise to an elevation of several hundred feet, and abound with deadly snakes: more than once we made narrow escapes from their fangs while climbing the precipitous heights to obtain angles for the survey. It was any thing but pleasant to climb those hills—often on one's hands and knees—and to grasp a bunch of grass to secure your footing, while under the very next bunch you probably saw a snake coiled snugly away. Let me relate an adventure of this kind: it will give an idea of the scenes through which we passed while thus "surveying around the world."

I turn to my journal for assistance:—

"April 14.—I came unpleasantly near breaking my neck yesterday. McCullom, Carnes, and myself left the ship at an early hour to scale three heights where we were to measure base by sound and take a round of angles. Having landed at the foot of that which had been assigned me, and seen the boat hauled up above high-water mark, I left her in charge of three of the crew, and took the remaining two along to carry the spy-glass and a signal, I myself having a sextant-box under my arm, a revolver through my belt, and a pair of six-pound expedition-boots upon my heels. The revolver I carried because it was a standing order to go armed, and the boots I dragged along because the natives had warned us of the existence of snakes whose bite always put people to sleep, which latter we interpreted as meaning death.

"Our road at first was quite navigable,—not that there *was* any road, but simply from the facts that the undergrowth was not absolutely impassable, and that the mountain-side was sufficiently sloped to let one hold on without resorting to his hands.

"At the end of a half-hour's tramp, however, things began to look different. We were about half-way up the mountain, the thick undergrowth was rapidly giving place to rock, ravines, and spare patches of grass, and what earth there was was of that crumbling nature that makes a climber *feel well* before he trusts his weight on the advancing foot. We came to a halt, set our various burdens on the ground at our feet, drew a long breath, and commenced looking around. It was our first attempt at climbing for some months, and our knees already began to shake, while the upward prospect was more *stupendous* than ever.

"'How in the world are we *ever* to get up to the top of that peak?' we asked ourselves, as the eye searched in vain for a favouring ridge or firmer foothold.

"It was a hard question,—one that could only be answered by trial; and so we resumed our burdens and undertook its toilsome solution.

LOO-CHOO COUNTRY-PEOPLE—(ANAKIRIMA GROUP.)

"Another half-hour passed, and we still gazed upward at the point of destination, and called another halt; for the friendly bushes, whose firmly-imbedded roots had heretofore offered a secure hold for our unemployed hands, had now given place to thin clumps of grass, that a good jerk would pull out, roots and all. The earth, too, had become even more crumbling and unreliable as we got higher, and the rocky ravines deeper and more frequent as well as more unsafe of approach. Again we continue the arduous ascent, and again call a halt from sheer fatigue. Now, however, we no longer halted in company; for I happened to be ahead when my knees failed, and the two men no sooner saw me down than they followed my example. It was now indeed difficult to see how we were to get along any farther; nevertheless, as the entire work of the day would be injuriously affected did we give it up, I could not well avoid making another trial. At it we went, therefore, with renewed vigour; and the way in which we progressed was after this wise:—

"I, having been joined by Rose and Burke, left my box with them and climbed some feet higher, from whence I reached down for all the burdens, and, having deposited them at my feet, climbed still higher, while Rose and Burke ascended to the place I had just left and passed them up to the new elevation. This was ticklish work, but it was also the best that we could do. I look back to it *now*, and think what a great booby I was. *Then* I regarded myself as a very energetic surveyor, generously risking my bones in the cause of science.

"At last *we could get no higher*, and, what was worse, we began to think that we might find some difficulty in *getting down* again. We couldn't well make up our minds, however, to remain all night upon the mountain's side, and so proceeded at once to make the attempt. I had often heard the expression, 'It is much easier to ascend than to descend a precipice,' and had frequently tested its truth in my own previous rambles; but I had never before glanced around me and felt that there was a strong probability of my breaking my neck within the disagreeably-short space of ten minutes.

"Each one now selected his own road down,—Burke throwing his burden ahead some hundred yards, and thus getting the use of both hands, while I was so unfortunate as to select the worst road that could have been found.

"I thought that, with only one hand to steady myself, I should do better along the rocky edge of a neighbouring ravine; but, after some little time, the projecting footholds of rock became less frequent, and their places were taken up by the crumbling earth and loosely-rooted bunches of grass. Still, as there now remained but some eight or ten feet between me and a bed of rocks, from which the ground sloped off quite safely, I determined to trust to the light soil for a partial support to my foot, hoping to sustain much of my weight from a more healthy-looking bunch of grass, whose roots felt quite solid under the grasp.

"It was a fatal mistake.

"The earth gave way entirely under my cautious foot. I tried to recover myself when too late, and was left with my whole weight suspended from the grass. Should that also fail me I should slide helplessly into the rugged and apparently-fathomless fissure, which was now just midway between me and the bed of rocks, which formed one of its broken sides. There was no time to *think*, either, for at any moment the roots might draw, and then—what?

"The rocky bed already alluded to was now some four feet lower than my feet, and about five or six feet to the right. It was full of holes, and the sharp-pointed rocks peered up here and there through a rank undergrowth in which a thousand snakes might have coiled themselves without being seen; and, as we had already killed one most villanous-looking rascal while sunning himself in a similar locality, I shuddered at the idea of springing bodily over the yawning fissure into the uninviting berth, whose only recommendation was that it was level, and whose drawbacks were so numerous. Besides, I was not certain but that I might fall short in my spring and *drop into* the fissure instead of upon its far edge; for, having no foothold to spring from, I should have to cast myself bodily from the side of the mountain by means of my elbows, chest, knees, and, subsequently, my hands and feet. It was about the tightest place that I can look back upon during that eventful cruise, and as I look back I shudder.

"That bodily leap was a most disagreeable alternative; but I had either to accomplish it or finally slip, from sheer exhaustion or the uprooting of the grass, into the fissure that was under me.

"My first thought was to tax the strength of the grass as little as possible; and, to that end, I let the box slip from under my left arm, dug my elbows and knees into the soft earth, pressed my breast close to that of the mountain, and, feeling the friction thus created relieve my arm of considerable weight, began to think.

"In the mean time, Rose and Burke were in a terrible state of excitement. The noise of the falling box caused them to look around and discover my almost-pendent position, while, from the nature of the ground, they felt totally unable to render me the slightest assistance. I do believe that their feelings were as unpleasant as my own, though probably a shade less vivid. Rose, seeing the utter hopelessness of effecting a rescue, resolved himself into a fit of spasmodic suggestiveness, commencing his advice by cautioning me to 'hold on hard,' while Burke immediately commenced reclimbing to the scene of action, singing out, 'Stand by to jump, sir, if you slip,'— both of which admonitions only served to give me a darker idea of what was before, or rather under, me.

"The fissure was at least three feet wide, and the pointed rocks upon which, if successful, I was to alight face first were any thing but inviting. I fancied, too, that every motion of the bushes that grew around them was caused by some alarmed reptile preparing to receive me, and shrank from the uncertain leap. Then at times I thought the grass was failing, and this would start the perspiration to my brow and cause a sickly shiver to pass through me, carrying with it half of my strength and courage.

"About this time, Rose asked me if I couldn't jump between two of the bayonet-like rocks; but I thought such a feat extremely improbable, and continued my occupation of getting up a certain amount of friction between myself and the mountain. I hung in this way probably as much as a minute, listening to Rose's excited suggestions and feeling far from comfortable. I felt what was to be done, but revolted from the idea. The prospect of breaking several bones, of being run through the body by one of the 'bayonets,' or of alighting among several nests of snakes, was almost as bad as that held out by a pitch down the fissure. At last I was helped to action in a most unpleasant way. My *right* hand grasped the bunch of grass, and before making the leap I must take it in my *left*, as the fissure was to my right. Cautiously I commenced the exchange, watching the straining fibres with an anxious eye, and keeping my muscles braced for the jump should they fail me before I was ready.

"Just then I caught the sullen glare of two other eyes, —sullen and leaden, and yet bright and sparkling also with alarmed rage. They belonged to the flattened head of an ugly-looking snake, whose sinuous body and uplifted front indicated an active readiness for either flight or attack.

"I gazed and shuddered. I shudder now as the mind's eye returns to those flaming specks of rage which flashed their angry light within a foot of my nerveless hand. I looked back to the commencement of time, and read the truth of Holy Writ in their expression of deadly hostility:—'And I will put enmity between thee and the woman, and between thy seed and her seed; it shall bruise thy head, and thou shalt bruise his heel.' After a lifetime of hesitation and unbelief, I ceased to hesitate, and believed that God was God and that I was but dust. The prayer of extreme peril, 'Lord, have mercy upon me, a miserable sinner,' struggled in my troubled heart and nerved me to the desperate leap.

* * * * *

"It was over. The very edge of the fissure received me on its shelving side, bruised, panting, weak as an infant, and yet with whole bones and safety. It seemed as if the strength of a dozen men had rushed through my frame and thrown me bodily from the glaring eyes of that lifted crest, leaving me with the cold drops upon my brow and a sickening feeling of overtaxed muscle throughout my limbs.

"Slowly I regained my feet, rubbed my bruised side with half-numbed hands, looked back for the now-absent snake, and at the friendly clump of grass, whose torn and drooping blades gave ample proof of the service they had rendered; and, as I picked my way through the 'bayonets' and thick undergrowth, silently vowed never again to volunteer for an exploring and surveying expedition round the world."

This and similar scenes were alarming drawbacks to our pleasure while surveying the Anakirima group; but there were also others of a repaying nature. One day, for instance, we came to an island where several of us had fine sport shooting antelope while wood was being taken in at an opposite village. Old bust-proof and his master went into ecstasies over the abundance of game, and slew them right and left. We killed something like a dozen, and then learned that they were the property of the Regent of Loo-choo, the offspring of parents that had been imported from China and put upon that and another island to breed. Having ended our work, we returned to Nappa, where we found the Vincennes and Cooper, and where we offered to pay for the slain deer; but they refused, though we subsequently had good reason to suppose that they charged for them in our wood-bill.

We now commenced to get in another supply of wood for the continuation of our voyage; and, as the Loo-chooans sent it off very slowly, we found ourselves masters of more spare time than the most sanguine had hoped for. We took advantage of these idle days to roam through Nappa and the surrounding country, and it was almost painful to see how the people shunned us. It was only those who lived near the water, or who had been thrown in contact with foreigners, that did not fly from us as if we had been evil spirits.

Upon one occasion we were following a winding street, which brought us suddenly out upon the plaza, or market-place, of Nappa; and such a stampede as ensued I never before witnessed. The plaza probably covered a space of two acres, and it was crowded with country-people, their packhorses, truck-carts, and articles which they had brought in for sale. The citizens of all ages and sexes were there also, making their purchases in their usual noiseless manner, and apparently wrapped up in their bargains. Suddenly a confused feeling of alarm pervaded the whole square: strangers had appeared among them. Those who were near the opening of the street down which we came rushed pellmell from us on either side, just as a crowd makes a passage for a mad bull. They left most of their things behind, though there was one fellow who took time to sling a pig over his shoulders, and one tall, finely-formed woman who gathered up her bundle of rice and walked off with majestic dignity. Those who were more distant from us mostly disappeared down neighbouring streets or into friendly houses, though there were some who had the courage to remain to pack their wares hurriedly before flight. The cattle, too, became alarmed at the general commotion, and added their antics to the confusion of the scene. I never before saw such a state of "undecided alarm."

Being unwilling to cause any more inconvenience than they had already subjected themselves to, we stood perfectly still and called out the names of several of their officials, hoping that the familiar sounds would quiet their fears and cause them to return to their property. In this we were eminently successful, and we soon had the pleasure of walking among them, though it was still impossible to gaze at any but an averted face.

Upon another of these occasions, when we had lost our way among the crooked, alley-like streets of Nappa, we more than once found said streets ending in private houses, to the infinite terror of their half-clad occupants; and before we had worked our way out of the labyrinth we nearly frightened to death two "unprotected females" whose fortune threw them in our path. One of these—a very old and decrepit specimen, apparently—we encountered suddenly upon turning a corner, and so startled her that she could only gaze at us in stupid wonder until we

THEY ARE ALARMED AT OUR APPROACH.

had passed her, when she gave a scream and took to flight with unlooked-for activity.

The other was "a young lady of sweet sixteen," and she came gayly around another corner just as the old woman was disappearing behind the one we had passed. Her apparel was remarkable for its extreme simplicity and uncleanliness, and she no sooner saw us than she turned her face to the wall,—which was inconveniently high to leap,—and, trembling like the restless leaf of the poetical aspen, allowed us to pass without even deigning a smile. Then, as soon as we were beyond her she followed the old woman's example, being suddenly transformed, from a shrinking figure of fear, into a flying mass composed of a thin cotton wrapper, a pair of arms and legs, and a head of dishevelled, jet-black hair.

Finally we emerged from the city into the outskirts, then into the by-paths of the fields, where we met with a Loo-choo gentleman and his servant upon their way, as we subsequently inferred, to spend the day with a friend. The boy carried his master's "chowchow-box" which contained his dinner, saki, &c., as it is the fashion in Loo-choo for the guests to carry their meals along. This gentleman directed us by the shortest cut to the high-road to the capital city of Shudi, which we were in search of, and at the end of an hour's walk we found ourselves entering under the heavy archway which is stretched across the road at the edge of the city, though there are no gates to close, and no walls extending from it to be defended. It looks more like a consular triumphal arch than any thing else. We had now walked some four miles over a road some forty feet broad, which was paved, like most of our streets, with round stones, and lined on both sides by grassy sidewalks. During this time we passed many of the country-people, similar in appearance to those on the opposite page, most of whom would drop their bundles and run from us, though there were some who had the boldness to pass us with bent forms and eyes resting on the ground. Some there were, too, of the higher classes, who encountered us as confidently as anybody; but these were mostly the officials who had mixed with Perry's squadron and become reconciled to the sight of strangers. We spent several hours walking through Shudi, but derived not the slightest benefit from it, as we could no sooner enter a crowded street than the alarm would spread like wildfire, and in the snap of one's finger it would be empty and the doors of every house strongly barred. Finally we arrived at a huge pile of gray granite, that reminded us strongly of the feudal castles of old. It was surrounded by a heavy stone wall that was thirty or forty feet high in some places and had but one gate,—that we could see. Through this gate we looked, and saw a number of officials lounging around the grounds with fans in their hands, and looking altogether quite comfortable; but, though we looked longingly through the bars, and resorted to various ingenious devices to attract their attention, we failed in our object, and returned slowly to the ship, rather disgusted than otherwise with our visit.

Our reduced squadron now began to show the effects of hard work and heavy weather. The ships looked rusty, our boats were bruised and battered, and we ourselves looked miserably seedy and overworked. We

THE OFFICIALS OF THE TEMPLE.

kept up the flagging spirits of the men by reminding them of the extra compensation which we had been assured Congress would grant us, and again put to sea.

We were now bound for Ha-ko-da-di, Japanese island of Jesso, and the Cooper was to survey the west coast of the great island of Nipon, while the Vincennes and Hancock, pursuing different routes in order to cover as much space as possible, were to attend to every thing to the eastward. The two latter vessels were also to touch at Si-mo-da, east coast of Nipon; and, before reaching that half-sheltered port, we surveyed a number of islands hitherto unexplored, and lying in the path from California to China. As we worked our way slowly through those unknown lands to the northward, we passed one active and several extinct volcanoes, and finally arrived at Ousima or Preble's Island. The Vincennes had examined the east coast of this island during her cruise of the previous year, and found it, like that of Formosa, totally wanting in harbours of any kind. It was now reserved for the two ships in company to encounter a succession of the most magnificent ports of shelter as they surveyed along its west coast.

One of these, situated upon the northwest extreme of the island, is well worthy of a passing notice. In the first place, it is undoubtedly the most sheltered anchorage in the world; secondly, it is the most convenient locality for a coal-depôt, should steamers ever run from California to China; and, thirdly, it is the dividing-line between the Loo-choo and Japanese islands. There we found both of these people, the former on the southern shore of the *double* harbour, and the latter on its northern,—the former receiving us with fear and trembling, the latter with suspicion and distrust. Upon visiting the former, we were timidly asked, through our interpreter, "Why have you arrived at our small island?" and upon landing among the latter we were obliged to intimate our readiness for fighting before they would get out of our way and let us ascend a neighbouring peak with a theodolite. Here we found fresh supplies of a magnificent raspberry, similar to some we had encountered at the Anakirima Islands, and which I neglected to speak of while writing about that group. They were of two different species, one of a brown colour and as large as a small apricot, the other yellow and about the size of a Malaga grape. The former grew on a vine that ran along the ground or twined itself around bushes; while the latter hung in clusters from small bushes that generally stood off by themselves. The leaf of the larger was often from seven to eight inches in diameter, and one which I brought home with me is always mistaken for that of the grape. We gathered quantities of these berries; and—as we had previously failed to get fresh provisions from the Loochooans, and subsequently failed to do so from the Japanese, in spite of Commodore Perry's much-talked-of treaty—I have no doubt that they warded off the scurvy from us for months. The latitude of the splendid harbour around which these berries grew is 28° 30′ N., its longitude 129° 32′ E., and it must eventually become a place of importance.

Leaving this quiet retreat, we once more put to sea and continued the survey, by separate routes, to Si-mo-da; arrived off which port, we sighted a vessel entering ahead of us, which our glasses proved to be the Vincennes. We had expected to arrive some days before her, but the "old John" had had to contend against headwinds, and had, as usual, drifted to leeward. Poor "old John"!

The Vincennes anchored in the mouth of the unprotected harbour; and, as we passed her at the astonishing rate of six knots, and answered the hail of Commander Rodgers as to the health of the ship, &c., we noticed a Whitehall row-boat towing at her stern, and several strangers in European costume mixed among the officers and assisting them to admire (?) the graceful outlines and killing pace of our poor old tub of a steamer.

As we rounded to and let go our anchor well in with the shore, we wondered what that clean-looking Whitehall boat was doing in Japan, and who those admiring strangers could be; and in regard to these two wonders our minds were soon set at rest.

Scarcely was the anchor down than they came alongside in the Vincennes' gig, and, a barge-load of Japanese officials boarding us at the same time, our hands were filled so far as entertaining was concerned. We immediately took the combined party down into the ward-room and began to find out who the former were, while the latter, with their usual prying policy, began to try to ascertain why we had visited their unfrequented shores.

Our "admiring strangers" proved to be Americans of the nomadic stamp, who had lately arrived from the Sandwich Islands with an assorted cargo destined to meet the wants of whaling-vessels, and who, upon the discharging of their vessel, were to have reloaded her with Japanese goods and sent her to San Francisco, while they themselves remained in Japan with their embryo ship-chandlery.

Their party numbered nine in all:—Mr. and Mrs. Reed and two children, Mr. and Mrs. Doty, and Messrs. Edgerton, Bridleman, and Peabody. They were at present living in a temple on shore, and invited us to make their quarters our lounging-place.

The manner in which they came into possession of this temple—in fact, the only reason why they were allowed to land at all—is worthy of note, more especially as a very wrong conclusion is jumped at on page 454 of the otherwise very truthful work resulting from the labours of the squadron under Commodore M. C. Perry. Before noticing this wrong conclusion, I will make a simple statement of the manner in which they awoke one fine morning and found themselves temporary residents of Japan. Commodore Perry's treaty had nothing whatever to do with it.

Shortly previous to their arrival, the Russian frigate Diana had been seriously injured by an earthquake while at anchor in the harbour of Si-mo-da, and had subsequently foundered while being towed to the more protected port of Hey-da for repairs; and her crew, being thus left upon the hands of the Japanese,—who feared an armed body of five hundred men,—were necessarily compelled to have quarters assigned them, and provisions furnished, until such time as a ship should arrive to take them away.

A large temple at Kaga-zaki (a small village of some hundred and fifty houses near the mouth of the harbour) was therefore placed at their disposal, which, subjected to a few alterations, made them a most comfortable residence; and they were still lounging through its roomy saloons and passages when our admiring strangers arrived, and were, to their surprise, boarded by a Russian officer instead of a host of Japanese officials. Now, these Russians had saved their small-arms, &c., as well as their lives, when their frigate went down, and, being several hundred in number, were a source of constant dread to their usually-tyrannical but now obsequious hosts, who no sooner saw the arrival of a vessel than they advocated the idea of *their taking passage in her away from Japan.*

As she was not large enough, however, to take them all at once, it was determined to let all of her passengers and cargo be landed, toward the simple end of obtaining more room in which to stow a greater number of the obnoxious Russians; and it was further determined that, as long as their schooner was employed in the transportation of said Russians, they, the Americans, should have the free use of the temple with and after the Russians, and be further granted a house in which to store their cargo. Upon the return of their schooner after her last load—*i. e.* after she had done Japan the service to rid her of her unwelcome guests—they were to restow their cargo, and take themselves off, with any Japanese goods which they might be able to sell them. And this is a correct account of the manner in which Americans first resided temporarily in Japan; although, as I have previously said, one would arrive at a far different conclusion from reading Perry's comments on the subject. In regard to this treaty I have to add another word:—it grants much more than even the most sanguine mind had reason to expect; and yet, from the utter faithlessness of the Japanese themselves, many of its articles are rendered null and void. The commodore will have to be sent back with a moderate force and full powers, and not with an overwhelming squadron and his hands tied with Government tape.

And now let us return to our mess-room, where the Japanese, the nomadics, a Russian officer, and "the mess," were opening bottles of French punch, to the especial delight of the former.

The Russian just spoken of had been left in charge of the temple with several men, when his companions had retired to the more secluded port of Hey-da, to avoid being discovered by the English and French cruisers, and he was now almost as delighted to see us as were the Americans themselves. He spoke with great feeling of the kindness of the officers of the U. S. steamer Powhatan to his shipwrecked companions, in giving them clothes and provisions, and finally became so affected by the combination of Russian gratitude and French punch that he threw his arms round Carnes, the master, declaring, in broken accents, that "he never before saw such fine sailor-men, and that we must come on shore to his house at once."

This specimen of fraternizing was not lost on the Japanese portion of the assembly, who, having drunk at least double as much as any one else, were quite prepared to take advantage of any such demonstration to relax their sober countenances and assume a "hail-fellow-well-met" style of demeanour, more in keeping with the occasion. When they had first drawn up around the table, (with the dignity of gentlemen, it must be confessed,) we had intimated, by unmistakable signs, our desires to see their swords, of the beautiful polish and temper of which we had heard so much, and they had universally refused to draw them, expressing their surprise and wonder in horrified glances and mysterious shakings of the head. Now, however, they readily gave them into our charge, making signs that they could not eat and drink with comfort while bothered with them, and pointing to the state-rooms as places of safety where they might be laid. Of course we went into those state-rooms, and with closed doors examined their beautiful workmanship and temper to our hearts' content.

"I'll tell you what it is!" said the Russian, as he watched with reluctant gaze the rapid inroads which they made in the precious punch: "these fellows talk very smoothly now, and promise you every thing you ask for; but wait until the time comes to fulfil their promises and see how they will act. The only way our admiral could get along with them was by getting the men under arms and threatening to march them upon Yeddo whenever they promised without acting; and, if you ever expect them to bring you half the provisions they have put on that list, your commodore will have to do the same thing."

And he was right; for, as long as we were in Japan, we could never succeed in getting any thing but a few eggs, now and then a tough chicken, and occasionally a quart or two of fresh beans. Rice, soya, and saki were the only three articles they ever furnished in abundance.

Tatz-nosky, the interpreter, who was seated directly opposite to our Russian friend while he thus belaboured his nation, and who understood probably about one-half of what was said, took it all in good part, but, as the party was breaking up, revenged himself by whispering, in a confidential manner, "Russe no good! Ameliken *very* good!" After which he and his companions took their departure amidst most energetic protestations of regard and friendship. The last thing Tatz-nosky did was to tell us that the governor had given us permission to go on shore for a little while, but that we must not ramble far,—a piece of information that so annoyed the captain, that he called him back and indulged in an impromptu speech to the following effect:—

"Commodore Perry had made a treaty with Japan, and we had a copy of it on board for our guidance. That treaty granted us the privilege of going on shore when it suited us; and, though we fully appreciated the attention of the governor in noticing our arrival, still, we could not look to him to regulate our movements," &c. &c.

Tatz-nosky understood enough of this very proper speech to show him that we were conscious of our rights and determined to exact them, but whether it ever reached the ears of the governor it is hard to say.

THE PRETTY GIRLS WHO WELCOMED US.

CHAPTER XII.

WE LAND IN JAPAN, AND VISIT A NUMBER OF AMERICANS AND ONE RUSSIAN—"MAHOMET AND THE MOUNTAIN" DIFFER AS TO THE MOST PLEASANT DIRECTION FOR A STROLL, AND FINALLY PART COMPANY, TO THE EVIDENT ANNOYANCE OF THE LATTER.

AND now we were in Japan, among the mysterious people who for the last three hundred years had amused themselves by tying and otherwise harshly treating all shipwrecked mariners of whatever nation, and with whom the world was now beginning to renew its acquaintance after an isolation of centuries. It was a thrilling thought—the very idea of landing among them; and, although it was raining when our guests of the last chapter left, several of us armed ourselves with umbrellas and took a boat for the beach. We landed between Ka-ga-sa-ki and the sea, and followed the beach until we reached the outskirts of the former, when we began to be struck by the great number of children and pretty girls that came forward to welcome us. They seemed quite anxious to see strangers, coming out of their houses, and lining our path with their fancifully-painted umbrellas overhead and their awkward stilt-like sandals underfoot. There was considerable pertness, too, as well as curiosity, in their glances, but as a general rule their bearing was marked by any thing but boldness. The people of this particular locality had seen so much of our countrymen, and apparently formed so favourable an idea of them during the two visits of Commodore Perry, that they now viewed us without fear: indeed, to have heard their questions and seen their pantomime, one would have imagined that the majority of them had been personally acquainted with the worthy commodore. They would pronounce his name quite plainly, (Comdo Pelly,) and ask us, by signs, if we had ever seen him, giving us to understand, in return, that they regarded him as a very powerful personage. Even the little children had now become reconciled to us, (through associations with members of his squadron, we inferred,) and approached us with perfect confidence. They would collect from all directions, as we passed, hold out their hands with the salutation, "How do *you* do?" or, "Ohio!" and, if noticed by a good-natured shake, would retire among their less adventurous companions with the steps of young heroes. They also, in many cases, evinced the utmost eagerness to pick up a few words of our language.

One little fellow I remember in particular, who learned to count as high as ten in as many minutes; and the next day I found him on the sandy beach with a sharp stick, with which he was tracing 1, 2, 3, &c. as readily and accurately as many thick-headed school-boys after a month of daily drubbings. He held in his left hand a slip of paper on which I had written him the numbers on the previous evening, and, recognising me as soon as I approached, made signs that he had no longer any use for those, and wanted me to put down some more. I looked at his childish frame and bright, sparkling eyes, and began to conceive a high idea of Japanese brains. It is needless to add that myself and friend seated ourselves on a piece of ship-timber, and wrote him down the numbers *ad infinitum*, which he had no sooner received (the lead-pencil being added, to his lively joy) than he commenced counting on his fingers as high as each number, when, as we bent our heads in assent, he put the Japanese character opposite to each, and, the whole being translated in that way, he smoothed off a place on the beach, and went to work with his sharp stick and a will that caused me to look back to my own truant-playing days and blush. But all this has nothing to do with the visit which we went on shore to pay.

A walk of some ten or fifteen minutes through the two rows of houses that lined the beach brought us quite unexpectedly in front of a large wooden structure, to which several of the crowd that followed us pointed with the explanatory exclamation of "Roos!" "Roos!" which we took to imply that it was the quarters of the Russians, and that it would be but polite in us to stop and pay them a visit. As we had gone on shore for that purpose, we took their advice and turned at right angles into the broad and shady avenue, which, after a length of some fifty or sixty yards, terminated at the foot of a massive flight of stone steps, at the top of which was an equally massive-looking portal, guarded on either hand by an unknown monster of frightful exterior, carved out of wood, and most fancifully painted.

We passed between these fierce-looking unknowns, and entered upon a square and level space of something like an acre in extent, from the back of which the thickly-wooded hill-side arose, while in the centre was built the temple. Between this latter and the hill-side—in fact, extending up into the bushes—was a Japanese graveyard,—a most singular-looking graveyard to stranger eyes, and yet incapable of being mistaken for any thing else.

It was laid out in walks and beds something after the fashion of a flower-garden, and contained thousands and thousands of small stone images that varied in size from six inches to two or three feet. These were arranged about in spots without much regard to the beauty of effect, being piled together like so many bricks, or scattered about in the most convenient corners and crevices. Some I even saw stuck up in the spreading branches of the trees, and others again that, having been put at the foot of a tree between two roots, the latter had grown around them and rendered their removal no longer possible. We were given to understand, by one Japanese, that these images contain the ashes of defunct officers; and, by another, that they were intended simply as tombstones to mark where the ashes had been laid. And this latter authority I rather incline to, though it is dangerous to believe *any thing* that a two-sworded Japanese tells you.

As we entered upon the cleanly-swept space in front of the temple and looked around us, we saw a dozen or more of these two-sworded gentry lounging about the yard, while a number of others were engaged with their pipes in the spy-house. These latter were the superiors, who, in that dreamy state of enjoyment, awaited the frequent reports that were brought to them by the former in regard to every movement of the occupants of the temple.

These informers no sooner saw us all inside of the gate, than they made a note of our number with their paint-brush-like pencils, and, as we were received on the steps of the temple by the Americans and him who "had never before seen such fine sailor-men," we saw them sink upon their knees and hand their slips of paper to the lazy smokers of the spy-house.

"You see they have counted you already," said one of our hosts, as he welcomed us to the immense mansion; "and when you go away the same thing will be done over again. From the moment you enter their ports, they station boats to watch your ships. When you leave your ships, you are counted and watched. When you land, you are followed; and when you return on board, you are again counted to see that there are none left on shore. If a less number return than landed, a search is at once got under way and the missing ones are *always found.* We sometimes amused ourselves by passing, like the Frenchman's cat, '*incessantly* ins and outs of ze cat-hole,' (a gate in our case,) thus causing these sentries to keep up a perfect stream of reports. They couldn't understand it at first, but after a while smelt a rat, and contented themselves with reporting only about every ten minutes. The children used to baffle them considerably also, for in their childish sports they would often get beyond the grounds of the temple and mix with the Japanese of their own age, much to the annoyance of the officers."

By this time we were seated in a large and spacious room, one of whose windows looked out upon several fresh-looking monuments that lifted themselves from a slight elevation on our left, while the others opened into the grand hall of the temple.

"Well, it is singular!" exclaimed one of the party, as he gazed through the former upon the civilized-looking monuments. "Look here at these granite monuments, with their emblems chiselled upon them, and the fellow's history cut in, exactly where with us would be put 'Sacred to the memory,' &c. They look *exactly* like the monuments you would see in any Christian graveyard. I thought the Japanese burned their dead and stowed the ashes away in jars?"

"So they do, as a general rule," remarked the Russian. "But these are not Japanese monuments that you see there. Four of Commodore Perry's men and one of his officers are buried under them. The monuments themselves were made by Japanese, from drawings by Americans."

"Do you remember what the name of the officer was?" asked an interested voice.

"Hamilton,—Dr. James Hamilton," was the careless reply.

I looked back to the jovial mess-room of the Kennedy, (only two short years,) and, as my eye rested on the glorious hearts that then beat around our social board, I felt it dim and moisten over the memory of more than one that was now pulseless and cold. Hardships and disease, combined with the destroying breath of the uncurbed typhoon, had even then sadly thinned our ranks. One slept his noiseless sleep among the unknown depths of the coral sea, and now the lasting monument of another, towering over the Buddhist images, proclaimed on its face a gospel truth,—strange words to be seen in that infidel land.

"Poor Hamilton!" said one pensive voice. The others passed lightly on to other subjects; and, as night approached, we took our leave and returned on board, several two-sworded officials attending us to the beach. Thus ended our first day in Japan.

We awoke the next morning with the very reasonable hope of having a fresh breakfast,—soft-boiled eggs, a broiled chicken, or something of that sort; but there was no such good fortune in store for us. We ate our usual sea-breakfast, and then began to abuse Tatz-nosky. "Well, you may abuse him as much as you choose," said Cavilosky, our Russian friend, who came on board just at the time: "did I not tell you yesterday that they would bring you nothing?" The Russian was right; for, during the several months that we were in or about Japan, we never once received fresh provisions for the crew, and only rarely a stray chicken or a duck for ourselves. Rice, soya, (a very fine fish-sauce,) and saki, (a strong and not unpleasant liquor made from rice,) were the only things they ever furnished us in abundance; and, had it not been for the former of these, we should have been in a starving condition.

Upon one occasion we saw several hundred chickens in a bamboo pen in the very centre of Si-mo-da; but, before we could find the proper person to order some sent on board, they had disappeared. Upon complaining of this to Tatz-nosky, his excuse was that they had been previously sold, but that we should certainly have some before long. This indefinite date never arrived. Upon another occasion we saw dozens of the finest bullocks ranging the neighbouring hills, and, when we wanted to buy some of them, were informed that they were used as beasts of burden, but that if we wanted *a horse* we could have one.

We had not been many hours in Si-mo-da, when Commander Rodgers was applied to by the "nomadics" to force the Japanese to respect a certain article of Commodore Perry's late treaty; but that officer very properly regarded the disputed point as a question for future discussion between the two Governments, and contented himself with making an official appeal in their behalf. The result of this was that the nomadics were informed that the treaty-phrase "temporary residence" was understood to mean a day's stroll through the city or into the country, and that they could never be allowed to settle in any part of Japan. They therefore got on board of their schooner when she returned, and sailed to Ha-ko-da-di, where, meeting a similar refusal, they returned to San Francisco in very high and just dudgeon. But I am getting ahead of my narrative.

Finding that we were unable to buy beef and vegetables, we turned our attention to articles of Japanese manufacture, such as china, lacquer-ware, &c.; and, having exacted a promise that a bazaar should be got up for us as soon as possible, we sat down patiently to await its fulfilment. In the mean time we surveyed the harbour and adjoining coasts; which accomplished, we resorted to daily walks into the interior as the most profitable way of passing the time. We were much annoyed during our first walks by the Japanese officials, who, after drinking all of our French punch on board ship, would encounter us on shore and dog our steps to prevent our communicating too freely with the country-people. Let me recall one of these walks:—

It was upon a clear and cool morning, that ushered in a warm day; and the hour was sunrise. Lawton, our chief engineer, Bridleman, one of the nomadics, and myself, stepped into the dingy and pulled for the upper landing upon the edge of Si-mo-da. The reader probably remembers the word "dingy." It is the name of a boat,—just such another small boat, pulled by two other similarly-encased small boys, as carried old bust-proof, his master, and myself on shore at Simon's Town to frighten Hottentot women and startle catbirds. In the present case we were pulling leisurely over smooth water, however, and the trousers "held their own" bravely. We were armed for a long tramp,—very large walking-sticks, heavy expedition-boots, &c. &c.; and, in addition, we carried concealed revolvers for defence, and our watches, to excite curiosity in the country-people. Finally, we had a very poor idea of where we were going or what we were going to do.

"Let's just start directly back into the country," said Lawton, "walk right straight ahead until twelve o'clock, then eat our lunch alongside of some romantic stream, throw the crumbs to the fish, and return by a new road. If we *do* lose our way and have to sleep among the Japanese, why, we'll at any rate do what no untied foreigner has done for centuries."

"I think I'd rather sleep in my bunk," I said, "unless,

indeed, we could carry a tent with us and go upon a regular voyage of discovery for a week."

"That's a good idea," said Bridleman; "but, as we are now half-way on shore, we'd better put it off to another day."

The boat here ranged up to the rocky and picturesque landing, and we stepped ashore under the heavy foliage of unknown trees, and wended our interesting path between their sturdy, live-oak-like trunks and under their sheltering arms. It was the third time we had been on shore in Si-mo-da; but we could not tire of that shady walk or of looking around every bush and corner for something new. The reflection that we were among a people who for hundreds of years had existed entirely among themselves lent an interest to every object that crossed our path, and caused the blood to flow through our veins with the nervous excitement of intense curiosity.

The first object of note that we passed was a Government spy-house,—a small bamboo building,—which had been erected near the landing, since our arrival, for the express purpose of enabling the Government spies, who occupied it, to note every American who came on shore and cause him to be followed or watched by one or more of their number. We had, upon both of our previous visits, been excessively annoyed by these spies, and had complained to the governor of being thus watched; but he excused his Government with the barefaced assertion that "they were sent along with us to keep us from getting lost, and *not* as spies upon our movements," adding that "if we did not want them we had only to *send them*

MAHOMET AND THE MOUNTAIN SETTLE A DIFFERENCE OF OPINION.

away." This was all very fair, apparently, but when we had "sent them away" they *wouldn't go*,—affecting not to understand us; and so this time we had gone on shore determined to give the first fellow who couldn't understand our signs to return, a good kicking, and, if necessary, a thumping besides. The opportunity for resorting to this practical mode of explanation soon presented itself.

We had not passed the spy-house more than a hundred yards, when a couple of two-sworded officers were observed to be following us, and before walking another hundred they were within speaking-distance. We stopped to let them come up, but they also came to a halt: it was evidently a case of "Mahomet and the mountain," and so Mahomet boldly returned to the mountain.

This action on the part of the prophet was evidently regarded in a threatening light by the two who composed the mountain: they looked just like over-curious servants detected by their master in the act of eavesdropping.

Mahomet took half of the mountain by the shoulders, caused him to "right-about face," and then made signs that *we* were going north, and that they, the mountain, were expected to move off in a southerly direction. This they "couldn't understand" through the medium of the senses of sight and hearing, and so Mahomet resorted to his heavy boot and the half-mountain's sense of feeling. I never saw such a kick in my previous life, and but one subsequently that at all approached it. It caused one-half of the mountain to tremble to his very base and then take up his uneven flight for the friendly shelter of the spy-house, where he sank exhausted upon the soft matting, and as we looked back we could see him gesticulating violently in our direction; and it caused the other half to place his hand indignantly upon his sword until Mahomet made a demonstration in his direction, when he followed his more bulky companion with alarmed activity. Our path was crossed by no more *mountains* that day,—many rough hills, and no end of watercourses and rocky roads; but no more mountains. Mahomet looked as large as *two* ordinary men after the successful accomplishment of this feat, and as we crossed the broken waters of the river Inodzu-gama by a bridge of planks nailed on the heads of numerous piles, we talked quite triumphantly of our victory, and almost wished that we had another two-sworded officer to exercise upon.

Our friend "Mahomet" was no other than Lawton; and since that kick I have entertained the most profound admiration for his understanding.

It was a beautiful valley that we were now ascending, —wildly beautiful in its strange isolation from the world, in its irregular formation, in its short and angular turnings, in the clear and limpid stream which, flowing through its highly-cultivated centre, followed its every turning and here and there approached the jutting feet of the mountains on either side; wildly beautiful in the dense and unknown foliage, in grove after grove of the wax-like japonica, in the startled flight of brilliant birds, in the sudden dash of the mountain-trout, and in the shady cottages of the unknown people.

We had much to see, more to think about, still more that was lost to us. Who ever yet saw all that was worth seeing during his first walk in the strange land of a still stranger people? Sometimes we would leave the highway that followed along the river's bank, and, following a winding footpath, come suddenly upon some rural habitation and its startled occupants. Then what a scene of noise and confusion would ensue! Dogs barking and slinking off behind corners, children screaming and clinging to their mothers for protection, while the mothers themselves, in some cases, wrung their hands and blubbered like so many children,—everybody and every thing flying from us as if destruction existed in our very appearance. By the men only were we, as a general rule, differently received; and even they often avoided us, or approached with distrustful glances, as their retreating household left them alone with the "Amelikins."

We generally commenced these interviews by exclaiming "Ohio," (good-morning,) then shaking hands with friendly energy, next addressing them as "John," and finally producing a cigar for each of the party. These they would light with great difficulty, watching our motions very closely, soon tire of smoking them, put them aside carefully, and end by lighting their own small pipes and offering us a puff, while waxing bold enough to feel the texture of our clothes, examine our boots, &c. &c. About this period of the action we would produce a watch, revolver, box of matches, or some equally, to them, unknown principle, and explain its mechanism or use; and before ending we were generally surrounded by the entire family,—women, children, and dogs,—all apparently (not even excepting the latter) equally curious to see "what the row was." What wonders the feeling of curiosity will effect! It was our most powerful lever in working ourselves into the good graces of those singular but—I mean the masses—well-meaning people.

The motion of the watch seemed to afford them more satisfaction than any thing else; and, by pointing to the sun and the hour-hand alternately, making various signs, and using a few disconnected words of their language, which we would acquire expressly for these walks, we generally gave them a very fair idea of its use and value. They were also much amazed at our revolvers, making signs that one American was more than equal to six Japanese, and that "Nipon" and "Amelika" must always be friends.

When we would get up to leave, after all this, they would press around to shake hands, and often accompanied us some distance on our walk. They seemed to pass at once from a state of distrust to one of perfect confidence, and would laugh heartily at other parties who, seeing us suddenly round a corner, would drop their baskets or bundles and run for dear life, until reassured by a well-known voice or familiar face. We could not avoid the conviction that the officials had impressed the people with the idea that we were cutthroats, &c., and that they would best consult their own safety by avoiding all communication. At any rate, they always received us distrustfully and parted from us in the utmost good-humour.

It was in this way that we continued our walk up the romantic valley until 1 P.M., when we reached a wayside tavern, where we wiped our heated brows, pulled off our heavy boots, and stretched out upon the clean-looking, cushion-like mats with which the floors of their houses are *always* spread. There are wayside taverns in Japan as well as in the rest of the world, reader, and the publican of this particular one was a fine-looking old man, with an upright frame, an expansive forehead, a mild blue eye, and a general cast of features that partook as much of the Caucasian as of the Mongolian race. He received us without the slightest hesitation of manner,—in fact, with polite self-possession, (*he* had evidently been thrown in contact with foreigners before, possibly with members of Perry's squadron at Si-mo-da,)—and drew us off several cups of saki from one of his numerous hogsheads. He also called his wife and daughters to see the "Amelikins," and they approached without the usual signs of distrust, smiling good-humouredly, and giving utterance to several connected words, which, judging from the morning compliments usually indulged in by the ladies of our own land, we concluded had some bearing upon the "general state of the weather and upon the heat of our walk in particular;" but of this we were never fully satisfied.

In the mean time, the old gentleman began spitting several fine specimens of mountain-trout and sticking them upright before the fire, intimating, by signs, that they would soon be done, and that they would agree well with the saki. We very shortly proved the truth of his signs, to our entire satisfaction.

We then, in turn, produced *our* lunch, of which they all partook sparingly, tasting each different article, such as cold ham, sardines, loaf-bread, claret, &c., and then passing it to their next neighbour. They seemed pleased with them all, save the claret, over which they made awfully wry faces—there is no denying that it *was* a little sour—and compared it to vinegar, which latter is with them an article of great consumption. We passed an hour in this way very pleasantly, and then hauled on our boots, which had previously been passing the rounds as objects of great admiration, bade our kind hosts farewell, and, leaving the river at right angles, struck over the mountain for the sea, supposing it to be distant about two or three miles.

We had a tough climb up the ravine-paths; but the work of surveying had well used us to exertion of that nature, and at the end of an hour we were looking down from a rocky pass, between two neighbouring peaks, upon the distant sea. We were surprised at its great distance,—at least three or four miles to the beach, and six or eight more along the beach to Si-mo-da. We began to think that we might have to sleep on shore after all; but, by driving steadily ahead, having the good fortune *not to get lost*, and resisting the temptation to stop at the inviting villages through which we passed, we reached our boat in good time, and took our friend Bridleman on board with us to a dinner by candlelight.

That same night the affair of "Mahomet and the mountain" spread around the mess like wildfire, and resulted in a vote of thanks being tendered the former for his gallant bearing, and a resolution that "we do likewise to the first two-sworded officer who presumes to follow us hereafter."

It was not long before an opportunity for testing our determination to "do likewise" presented itself; and this second argument was urged with even more spirit and determination than the first, simply from the fact that we now felt convinced there would be no fighting, whereas, in the first attempt, no one knew but that we might have been "catching a tartar" instead of kicking a Japanese. This second affair occurred some miles from Si-mo-da, near another roadside inn. I take the following extract, as to what followed it, from my papers:—

"Having thus, by a healthy kick and a show of further violence, relieved ourselves of our noble companions, we now passed a quiet hour with our plebeian friends and then continued our now unmolested walk. Our conversation with said 'scum of the earth' (as the officers call all of the swordless class) was necessarily carried on by the usual signs, grimaces, &c., sprinkled here and there by a few words which we knew by heart or had written on paper; and yet one would be astonished to see how well people can often get along in that way. Among other things, we had no difficulty in comprehending the following pieces of information:—

"'We are very glad that you kicked him; but, had one of *us* done so, his head would have been cut off.'

"'*We* work, and *they* walk around. *We* have to give them money to buy food with.'

"'*We* would like very much to know all about you, to buy and sell with you, but *they* won't let us.'

"'We cannot do what the officials do not want us to,' &c. &c."

Now, from the above and various other remarks,—which I do not remember,—we could not but conclude that the *people* of Japan are as ripe for revolt as the most violent flibustier could desire, while, at the same time, we were forced to acknowledge that they were *kept under* more effectually than any nation under the sun. Probably, a latent inclination to revolt among the masses first gave rise to extreme severity on the part of their rulers, as a precautionary measure. In speaking of the masses, I include merchants, (many of whom are worth more money than many of the nobles,) farmers, priests, artisans of every description, tailors, sailors, fishermen, publicans, and, in short, everybody in Japan whose birth or services to the state have not given him the right of wearing two swords stuck through his sash.

So much for strolls through the country adjoining Si-mo-da.

CHAPTER XIII.

SOMETHING ABOUT BUYING AND SELLING IN JAPAN, AND HOW THEY USED COMMODORE PERRY'S TREATY TO SWINDLE US—ALSO, HOW THEY ASK FOREIGNERS TO LET PEOPLE ENJOY THEIR MEALS IN QUIET, AND HOW A FOREIGNER FELT UNUSUALLY SMALL.

BEFORE I commence to show how it was that we went to the bazaar and how we were swindled in various ways, it will be necessary to give the reader an idea of the comparative value of Japanese and American money; and this calls for a slight digression.

It had been the "Japanese fashion," from time immemorial, to make presents of every thing that left the country; that is, a strange ship would arrive off one of their ports, and, while refusing to let her anchor, they would nevertheless furnish her, free of charge, with all such things as wood, water, provisions, &c., and then order her away. Of course I except in this the regular vessels of the Dutch, which arrived at Nan-ga-sa-ki twice every year, and with which they traded quite largely, though under certain very degrading requirements at the hands of these latter. For instance, they were confined to their ships, guarded with insulting closeness, and required to be basely deferential to their stupid customs and arrogant officials. And these sycophantic Netherlanders were, and had been since the expulsion of the Jesuits, the *most favoured of nations.*

Commodore Perry's treaty, however, having just been signed before our arrival, *we* now had the liberty, through it, of landing and walking where we would. Hence it was supposed that we had the right to enter any man's store and purchase that article which most suited our taste and pocket. But, as the merchant would in this case receive all the profit, the sleepless policy of that astute Government had taken care to introduce a defensive article in the treaty, which provided that "Americans should purchase every thing *through the officers of the Government.*" After which, vendors of all ranks and classes were given to understand that they were not to sell to any American *except through an officer*, upon pain of losing their heads. Thus they had it arranged quite smoothly for the Government, and the revenue thus resulting was at least worth the trouble attendant upon the conception and execution of the idea,—which idea amounted to the following in plain English:—

"These Americans," they said to themselves, (those of Perry's squadron,) "know a great deal about China. An American dollar is worth in China from fourteen to sixteen hundred cash, and a Japanese itzabu is worth in Japan sixteen hundred cash, also. An American dollar has a little more silver in it than three of our itzabu; so, if we can make it by treaty equal to only sixteen hundred cash, we can receive them in payment at that rate, pass them through the mint, and—presto!—they are divided into three, each of which is worth as much as what we received it for."

Now, so far as I can see, there is nothing but a very grand rascality and considerable cunning in the conception of the above idea; but it is passing singular that they should have executed it successfully against Yankee forethought, or even, indeed, against ordinary common sense.

How was so great a mistake committed by Commodore Perry? One asks in vain. We only know from sad experience *that it was* committed, and that the consequence of this depreciated value being attached to our coin results in a duty of *just two hundred per cent.* being paid to the emperor on all American silver that enters Japan from American pockets, and that we Americans are the ones who pay that duty.

When payment was made in gold we lost this same two hundred per cent., but the emperor gained little or nothing. The reason of this was that the difference between the value of gold and silver was much less than in other parts of the world. So much for the way in which Commodore Perry was weathered; and now for the fleecing consequences which it entailed on us.

We made quite a grand display as we landed from our ten or a dozen boats and formed in marching-order under the dense shade of the grand old trees that lined the landing, while two drums and a fife took the head of the column and enlivened us with "both vocal and instrumental music." We were all in uniform, swords and cocked hats being the order of the day; and, to judge from the great numbers of the fair sex that crowded the streets through which we passed, there were weak heads in Japan also, who, like two out of three similar heads in other parts of the world, were too apt to judge birds by their feathers.

And now, as we approach the bazaar, let us take a bird's-eye view of its construction and general appearance.

It was never my fortune to see either a saw-mill or pit in Japan; and yet this building was got up with *very fair pine boards* that had evidently *been sawed.* They were rough and unplaned, truly; but then that only let one see that they had been *sawed* and not *hewn.* The building itself covered about three-fourths of an acre of ground, was perfectly square, some fifteen feet in height, one-storied, and enclosed an immense square court, whose area was probably greater than that of the building itself. Its roof was thatched and sloped toward the court, and it was possessed of but one entrance. In short, it was nothing but four equally long, wide, and high sheds put together so as to form a square, and having a door left in one of said sides near one of the corners. It had, like the spy-houses, been built solely for us and since our arrival, and would, like them, be torn down after our departure.

We entered at the solitary door, and, like so many children in a toyshop with an unexpected supply of pocket-money at their disposal, looked around upon the brilliant display, and confused ourselves by wondering which we were to admire most, which we were to pass by, and which to linger over.

Two of the four shed-like sides of the building were divided off into stalls, one of which was furnished to eaeh merchant to enable him to display specimens of his wares to the best advantage; while the spaces immediately in front of the stalls were covered by boxes containing the wares, of which those on the shelves were only samples. They evidently expected us to purchase largely, thinking probably that we came as much on a speculating voyage as any thing else. Of the remaining two sides, one was vacant, while the other was divided into one large and two small apartments,—the former of which was neatly covered with cushion-like matting and given to us as a lounging-place, while the two latter were appropriated by the Government-officials who had charge of the affair as an office and spy-room. It is needless to say that the spy-room *joined the gate:* they *saw every thing.*

As we passed leisurely from one stall to another, we remarked a great sameness in their general appearance. There was but one which differed materially from the others, and there the difference consisted in its being filled with china instead of lacquer-ware. But *such* china as it was!—superior by far to the most delicate French porcelain, and infinitely more cheap, in spite of the depreciation of our money.

The other stalls were just like so many "old-curiosity shops,"—a little of every thing Japanese being to be found on their shelves, from the purchase of which the least possible amount of use was ever to flow. Like the porcelain, the lacquer-ware was of the most beautiful description, and exceeded that of China as greatly as did said porcelain the most ordinary stone crockery. One piece I remember in particular, the gorgeousness of whose colouring attracted the admiration of every one as he passed it. It was a most happy and truthful imitation of an ordinary "red-fish" (such as are caught in the Gulf of Mexico) of some eighteen inches in length; and, upon attempting to take it up by the side-fin to examine it more closely, two-thirds of its top-side was lifted off, showing it to be a dish capable of holding a large boiled or baked fish. They told us it was made to hold such a dish at the feasts of the "big bugs" of Japan, and that the lacquer was so fine that hot water exercised no power upon it. This they said of a great deal of their best lacquer-ware, and the truth of their assertion we subsequently proved at our own mess-table. From what we then and have since observed, we all came to the conclusion that they are infinitely superior to all other nations as far as regards the quality of their porcelain, lacquer-ware, and swords.

Among a number of other articles, all well worthy of a passing notice, we saw umbrellas and rain-cloaks, both of them being made entirely of the bamboo-plant and a vegetable oil the name of which I now forget. They make paper from the above useful plant which is as strong and lasting as the best calico, and which, when well oiled, becomes *perfectly water-proof.* Expose yourself to an hour's hard rain with one of those hooded cloaks on, or with one of those umbrellas over your head, and you come out of it as dry as you went in. I myself used one of the former on constant boat-service during a period of several months, and found it to answer admirably; and, at the end of that time, I drew forth warm thanks from a friend in San Francisco to whom I presented it: it was still water-proof.

There were also a great variety of a species of lithographic engraving exposed in piles for sale on some of the shelves, of which several of us purchased largely. They did not exhibit any remarkable art as far as the "getting up" was concerned; but we valued them as specimens of the art, nevertheless. We had heard much of the accuracy of the Japanese pencil and brush; but their lithographs did not argue any great beauty in the originals. They generally referred to Fu-si-ya-ma, (their sacred mountain,) to scenes from city and country life, to their various games, to distorted male and female figures, or to public buildings. These latter were apparently truthful; but all of the others partook more of the nature of caricatures than of natural appearances, and were undoubtedly calculated to impart an exaggerated and distorted idea of most of the subjects to which they referred; as, for instance:—

There was one scene of a trial of strength between two wrestlers, in which they must have weighed (comparing them with the figures of the audience) from seven to eight hundred pounds each, while their surplus fat hung about their huge necks and shoulders like the folds of the skin of the rhinoceros. These fellows were wrestling on the "sawdusted" pit of an immense amphitheatre, the seats of which were crowded with an admiring audience, while the referees stood off in two separate parties.

While we were looking at these lithographs, orders came from Yeddo to stop the sale of them; and this, of course, only made us more anxious to buy. The shopmen, however, would no longer sell, and, upon our applying to Tatz-nosky, he replied that the emperor thought they would give too good an idea of what was going on in Japan, and had ordered that they be all returned to Yeddo. Upon hearing this, we at once went through the different stalls before they had a chance to pack them away, and took under our arms every picture that we could lay our hands upon. Of course the merchants said that we could not have them; that they were not for sale, —only to be looked at; that they would not receive pay for them; that their heads would be cut off, &c. &c.: but we nevertheless carried them quietly on board, and the next day they, in as quiet, matter-of-course a manner, received payment for them, while their heads were still in their usual place.

Thus it was that pictures of every description were added to the list of articles which, by express orders of the emperor, were not to be sold, bartered, or given to persons living outside of Japan. And, while making this remark, I may as well mention as many of those reserved articles as I can recall. In the first place, then, there were their swords; secondly, every thing in the shape of an offensive or defensive weapon, all of the tools of the various trades, and the coinage of the country. Then there were these engravings descriptive of Japanese life, and a variety of other articles which I cannot now remember. And as fast as any thing was thus embargoed it was immediately packed up and sent back into the country.

It took us several hours to see enough of the varied and beautiful display of the rare specimens of their unknown workmanship that were crowded upon the shelves and floors of every stall; but the thing which surprised us most was to see the prices of the various articles marked on them in dollars and cents, just as one sees them pinned on goods exposed as samples in the windows and at the doors of our own shops. I subsequently learned the secret of this from Tatz-nosky, who—with an unabridged edition of Noah Webster's dictionary, and an immense pile of scattering pieces of information in the shape of symbols, detached words, and sentences obtained from the officers of Perry's and our squadrons, at his elbow—was rapidly, and with dogged perseverance, informing himself as to our language and customs in general. I could not but conclude that the Japanese would soon know much more about us than we ever should about them, unless another treaty should more fully open their ports. Once let Tatz-nosky and his brother-interpreters master the English language, once let books be introduced into Japan, and the day of their stupid seclusion will be past.

When I asked him how these prices had been obtained, he was candid enough to acknowledge that the different merchants had requested him to write them on slips of papers, and that they paid him quite handsomely. He had his pocket-book at the time filled with slips of bamboo-paper, on which he wrote different values in both Japanese and English as he was applied to by the merchants. Tatz-nosky was evidently wide awake as to the propriety of turning an honest itzabu.

The merchants, therefore, having to pay for these tallies, were loath to let them go with the goods. Thus, when any thing was bought, they invariably took them off and stowed them away as one would a bank-note; but many of us, wishing to pack our things *just as they stood*, objected to this practice, and were, in return, often charged from fifty to a hundred cash (three to six cents) for this luxury of letting our friends at home see their presents just as we had seen them in Japan.

They were cunning enough, too, as far as disposing of inferior goods was concerned, for they only brought out these at first, reserving the others for the last few days of our stay. We did not see any of their "number one" specimens during our first or second visit, and, when we asked in regard to them, they would insist that "we saw all; they knew of nothing else," &c. They were evidently anxious to dispose of the inferior lot first, after which they knew that we would not fail to be disgusted with our purchases as soon as the higher-priced ones should be exposed, and then we would be certain to lay out more money. And they were right; for, although the most of us returned on board the first day without making any purchases, still, we "caved in" on the second day and bought quite freely. Then, on the third day, they commenced bringing in the high-priced articles, and we began falling into the trap.

Day after day, therefore, as we returned and lounged through the crowded showrooms, new articles of unexpected beauty and rare excellence of workmanship would rise before us at every turn, cast a shade over every thing of the kind previously bought, and cause us to long for heavier pockets or more reasonable charges.

Oh! they were a cunning, a most dishonest set of fellows, those very Japanese merchants, holding up their wares before us, and tempting us to board the shrinking purser for various sums until we finally found ourselves heels over head in debt! They would watch us with "crickets' eyes," while we examined their various articles, judge with astonishing accuracy as to those with which we seemed most struck, and the next day all similar articles would be advanced in price, sometimes as much as a hundred per cent. They would take the tallies off at night, and put on others with higher marks on them, and then insist, with their usual barefaced disregard for truth, that "all the same as yesterday." This was all very provoking, truly; and yet what could *we* do? We had either to consent, in the first place, to be swindled by the treaty, and, in the second place, by the merchants themselves, or we must leave Japan without purchasing presents of their rare and beautiful workmanship for our absent friends. We chose the former of the two, and, with the unenviable feelings of men who are aware of the fleecing they are being subjected to without the most remote hope of being able to protect themselves, we continued our daily selections.

We were even denied the pleasure (?) of haggling over the price of things with any prospect of success. There was nothing like that there. There it was in bold relief, written in the plainest of both English and Japanese; so we only had to say the magic words, "Put him in a box," or, "Put him in paper," or pass on to some other article more or less expensive. Those "magic words" require a word of explanation.

As a general rule, the Japanese make neat boxes of a species of white cedar for their lacquer-ware, &c., when it is of ordinary, fair, or No. 1 quality; but for the inferior articles they use paper as wrappings. While exposed for sale, all of the former were set on the top of their empty boxes, while the latter were stowed *en masse* and treated generally with much less consideration. As soon, therefore, as a thing would be bought, we would be more than likely to say, "Put it in a box," or, "Put it in paper," or something of that sort; and their watchful ears soon caught these sounds, while their observing eyes told them that whenever they were uttered something was always bought. So, with a very imperfect idea of what "put him in a box" meant, they would watch us with their glittering eyes as we lingered over their wares, and encourage us to purchase by using that expression from time to time as they observed us to hesitate. After a while, they arrived at its exact meaning, but had got so used to it by that time, that, when any thing whose quality did not entitle it to a box was bought, they could only hold it and remark, in a manner of nonplussed inquiry, "*No* put him in a box!" which we found to mean that they could only afford to wrap it up in paper.

As we selected the different things in this way, we were followed by one, two, or three boys, as the extent of our purchase might call for. As fast as an article was bought, we entered its name (having often to coin them for ourselves) and price on our list, and passed on to something else, while our watchful attendant picked it up and followed us around as long as we lingered in his particular stall. When we had tired of one merchant, we crossed the court to the sitting-room of those who had charge of the affair, (the officials,) where we always found them sitting *à la Turque* around a metallic brasier containing live coals, at which they, from time to time, lit their diminutive pipes or warmed their sugarless tea.

They would also make a list of the articles brought by the boys who followed us, count the cost, compare their amount with ours and that of the merchant, and then receive it in silver dollars. The goods were then delivered to us, and an acknowledgment given to the merchant to the effect that the Government owed him an itzabu for each dollar that had been paid in.

As night approached and business was closed for the day, all the dollars that had been received were counted in the presence of the several officers and spies, boxed up carefully, and immediately forwarded to Yeddo, where they went into the mint as *itzabu* only, and came out multiplied by three and a fraction. An itzabu for every dollar received was then sent back to Si-mo-da, and the acknowledgments redeemed.

Thus it will be seen that if a merchant sold one hundred itzabu worth of goods, he received his money in full, and in good time; that the Government cleared a fraction over sixty-seven cents on every silver dollar that entered their ports, and that we and our poor old Uncle Samuel were really the only sufferers. For, though one hundred dollars was marked on the goods as their price, still, it was with the understanding that a dollar, though more than three times as heavy, was still only equal to an itzabu, and the same goods would have been sold to us at thirty-three dollars, could we only have converted that weight of silver into its real value equal to one hundred itzabu.

"I'll tell you what it is," I remarked to one of the officers while paying my first bill; "the first thing you know, some American will imitate your die, and come here with a shipload of itzabu to buy your goods with: then you'll *have* to receive your *own* money for what it is worth."

He smiled calmly at my evident greenness, as he replied, through Tatz-nosky, as follows:—"It is not possible for Japanese itzabu to go out of Nipon: how, then, can they ever be brought back again? If we saw you with itzabu, we would know that you had made them; hence we would not be forced to receive them. They would not be *our* coin in that case." After this "sogdollager"-like argument, he quietly lit his pipe, handed it to me, and smiled a smile of careless indifference.

I have previously remarked that silver was much more preferable to them than gold; and the reason was this: a gold-piece of theirs, valued at four itzabu, weighs about as much as one of our quarter-eagles. Hence, if an article was marked $2 50, and was paid for with a quarter-eagle, the gold received would only be equal to four itzabu; but, were it paid for in silver, this latter would be equal to seven and three-quarters itzabu, or nearly double. From this it will be seen that gold is less valuable in Japan than in other countries; and, were it not for the peculiar policy of that people, this difference might be speculated on to great advantage by outsiders; but, as there is no possibility of one's buying it up and getting it out of the country, the fact loses much of its importance.

I asked Tatz-nosky, among other questions, why gold was not more valuable; was it as plentiful as silver among them? &c. &c.: and he replied it was as hard to dig one as the other; from which I inferred that he had answered my last question in the affirmative: but, when I said something to that effect, he added an ambiguous remark that left me as much in the dark as ever:—"They are both in the ground: how, therefore, can we tell?" or words to that effect. The above gives a very fair idea of the cautious manner in which they answered our questions.

Upon one occasion, when we were making home-purchases, one of the nomadics (Mr. Edgerton) offered a gold eagle and one silver dollar in payment, and it was flatly refused. "Why do you refuse it?" he asked. "The treaty says that 'payment shall be made in gold and silver.' I fulfil its conditions by giving you ten dollars in gold and one in silver, and you break it by insisting on receiving *eleven silver dollars.* You won't be satisfied until we bring a thousand fillibusters from California to see you and teach you what's right. *Tell* them so."

Poor Tatz-nosky, at this period of the action, looked remarkably small and confused.

"Do you not see that I am only the interpreter?" he asked, in his imperfect English. "I only tell you what I am told. It is not my fault if the emperor prefers being paid in silver."

"Confound your emperor's tastes!" continued Edgerton, as he reluctantly hauled out the silver. "I came here on the strength of the treaty, bringing nothing but gold with me; and now I find it won't pass. What kind of a treaty do you call that? Commodore Perry 'll come back here some day and blow you sky-high."

"Japanese like Commodore Perry very much," replied Tatz-nosky, "but not understand him all. Japanese will do what Commodore Perry speak," &c. &c.

And yet, while thus invariably protesting their willingness to fulfil the requirements of the treaty, they scarcely ever did so. They are certainly—politically speaking, at any rate—the most dishonest and untrustworthy people in the world; and, in my opinion, a good flibustiers' drubbing is the only thing that will ever introduce them to honesty. The great bugbear of the Government is the fear of a foreign war. They are well aware of the one which the English waged so successfully against their neighbours the Chinese, and are nervously afraid of experiencing similar treatment at the hands of any nation they may be so unfortunate as to offend. There is no manner of doubt in my mind that this fear was a powerful, though unacknowledged, auxiliary in bringing them to the signing of any treaty at all. I firmly believe that they signed it as the *lesser of two evils;* that they knew at the time *exactly what it meant,* and that there was a "mental reservation" on their part to respect its provisions only so far as they should be forced to to keep out of trouble. And this is not my opinion alone, but that also of all with whom I have conversed who were there with me, and who, like me, suffered from their unfaithfulness. And now let us turn to the stalls once more.

One of the objects most worthy of admiration was an artificial bird,—an ordinary chicken-hawk; and it was decidedly the most naturally-executed thing that I ever saw. No feather-work specimen of Rio Janeiro, Madeira, or any other part of the world, ever excelled it. It was the first thing of the kind that we had seen or heard of; but we were told that they were quite plentiful in Yeddo. This fellow sat upon an ivory perch, to which he was secured by a chain of the same, and was invariably, when first seen, taken for a live bird: every thing was perfect

There was also in one of those stalls a most beautiful fabric, which, for want of a better name, we called crimped crape. It was in the form of a scarf, some four feet in length by six inches in width, was of a brilliant crimson colour, and capable of being stretched to a length of twenty feet while retaining its width unimpaired. Upon being let go, after being thus elongated, it would spring back, India-rubber-like, to its former length. We subsequently observed that the women used it largely for tying up their hair, and that after a time its elasticity became greatly impaired. "What a *sweet* spring-scarf it would make!" exclaimed a young lady of Philadelphia, upon seeing a sample of it, which I had brought home simply to show the fabric.

And now I will conclude this account of the bazaar with a general remark upon the utter uselessness of the great majority of the articles made by the Japanese for export. They themselves have no use for many of them; and, when asked why they had been made, would reply that they were copied from drawings or patterns obtained from the Dutch, and that they—the Dutch—bought them in large quantities and carried them away.

As we walked among them, such expressions as the following might be heard at every turn:—"It's a very beautiful piece of work, truly, but then what *use* can it be put to?" "I don't believe they would know what to do with it themselves," &c. &c.; and it was really singular how many things there were to which similar remarks would apply.

And now let me end this chapter by giving a rough idea of the Japanese houses. They are generally built of rough stone-masonry, or upright poles placed very close together and plastered over like laths, and they are from one to two stories in height. They are sometimes thatched, but more generally tiled, and at Ha-ko-da-di these tiles were in turn covered by tons of different-sized stones, apparently sufficient in some cases to crush in the whole roof. They are partitioned off into several mysterious apartments, and have doors hung on iron or wooden hinges and which fasten with the ordinary string-latch. The floors of all those which I entered were raised about a foot, and covered by oblong sections of stuffed matting, which fitted so snugly together that there was no danger of getting the foot into the cracks. These mats were as soft as the seat of an ordinary hair-sofa, and were always kept beautifully clean,—persons leaving their sandals in a square earthen cuddy-hole before stepping upon them.

These rooms receive light and ventilation through most ingeniously-contrived windows, and many of the partitions and doors are after the same idea. Having no glass, they are forced to use a very strong and semi-transparent bamboo-paper, which they stretch over the frames very tightly and then paste down. These frames are just like ours, only the surface of the cross-pieces is flat, to enable the paper to adhere. They work back and forth in the side of a house like folding-doors, and give more light than one would imagine. They are so strong that I have snapped my finger against the centre of the (paper) pane with considerable force and had it rebound from it as from a tightly-snared drum-head.

Of course the inmates cannot see what is going on in the streets, but then they have the satisfaction of knowing that they are equally protected. If they want air or are curious, all they have to do is to slide the frames sideways. The dwelling-houses are generally from twenty to thirty feet square; but some of the temples, with their outbuildings, cover upward of two acres. These latter are not used solely as places of worship, but are often appropriated as the quarters of the retainers of powerful princes during their journeys.

Some of the more pretending houses have piazzas, which are tiled over as usual, and slatted up along the sides so that the passion-flower and other creepers may protect them from the sun. I was once passing one of those cozy-looking two-story establishments toward the end of a solitary ramble, when, hearing music overhead, I was suddenly seized with a desire to see what was going on, and, without stopping to consider upon the breeding of the procedure, at once climbed up to the roof of the porch and looked into the open window of a room on the second floor. There I saw three musicians seated on the inner side of the matted floor, while in the centre of the room was a large lacquer-ware tray of viands, around which were seated a middle-aged Japanese and a young, highly-dressed, and very pretty girl. They were attacking the contents of the tray with unmistakable relish, and I should probably have joined them with pleasure had not the man got up with a dignity which put me to the blush and — shut the window in my face. I really felt ashamed of myself, and arrived at the end of my walk, with the determination to respect the privacy of others, even if they *were* only half civilized.

CHAPTER XIV.

SOMETHING ABOUT BATHS AND BATHING IN JAPAN, AND HOW THEY OBJECTED TO OUR SURVEYING THEIR COASTS—HOW WE OVERCAME THEIR OBJECTIONS, AND HOW TATZ-NOSKY TOOK SEVERAL LONG RIDES—HOW BUNSBY DISCOVERED LAND, AND HOW THE "OLD JOHN" CROSSED THE STRAITS OF T'SUGAR.

THERE is a wide-spread idea in regard to the profligacy and lewdness of the Japanese as a nation; and, though it must be confessed that there is little or no modesty among the middle and lower classes,—we had no opportunity of judging in regard to the higher,—still, I never during our entire intercourse with them saw any indications of a lack of practical morality. Natural depravity and impurity of taste is perceptible at almost every turn in the shape of lewd engravings and a disregard to exposure of the person; but then it must be remembered that they are half-civilized Orientals, and heathens at that. As far as their acts are concerned, the women are perfectly correct in their intercourse with strangers, which is more than can be said of the Chinese, though they do what the latter do not,—they bathe promiscuously with the opposite sex in the public baths, because, I suppose, their ancestors did so before them, and their primitive ideas recognise no harm in so doing.

These people are, like most Orientals, a nation of ducks,—their greatest luxury consisting in vapour, warm, or surf bathing,—and much of their time is devoted to their enjoyment. Even in the small town of Si-mo-da there are four bathing-establishments, where persons, for the sum of two Japanese cash, (about one-eighth of a cent,) may dip into an immense tub of warm water, or, when it is too hot, may seat themselves on beams extending over it and be subjected to the influence of the rising vapour, after which they return to the outer apartment and conclude their bath by emptying or causing to be emptied over them a dozen or more buckets of cold water.

They are, with the exception of the Malays, some of the Pacific Islanders, and the followers of Mahomet, the most cleanly people I ever saw. They are even unnecessarily cleanly; they bathe too often for health: one would think that they were anxious to make up in purity of person for the undoubted depravity and impurity of their *tastes.*

They have also hot and medicinal springs throughout the country, to which those who can afford it resort for the enjoyment of their real or supposed virtues. One of the former of these is situated about two miles up the valley that runs back from Si-mo-da, and is well worthy of a passing notice.

It is situated at the foot of a lofty hill, on the southern side of the valley, and comes boiling from a fissure in the rock with a power indicative of a bountiful source. This boiling forth, we were told, however, was by no means constant; at times there being a very limited flow, and at others a spasmodic soda-fountain-like action that projected great quantities. The Japanese made signs to us that the water was much hotter when thrown out by the soda-fountain-like action, and that persons unaccustomed

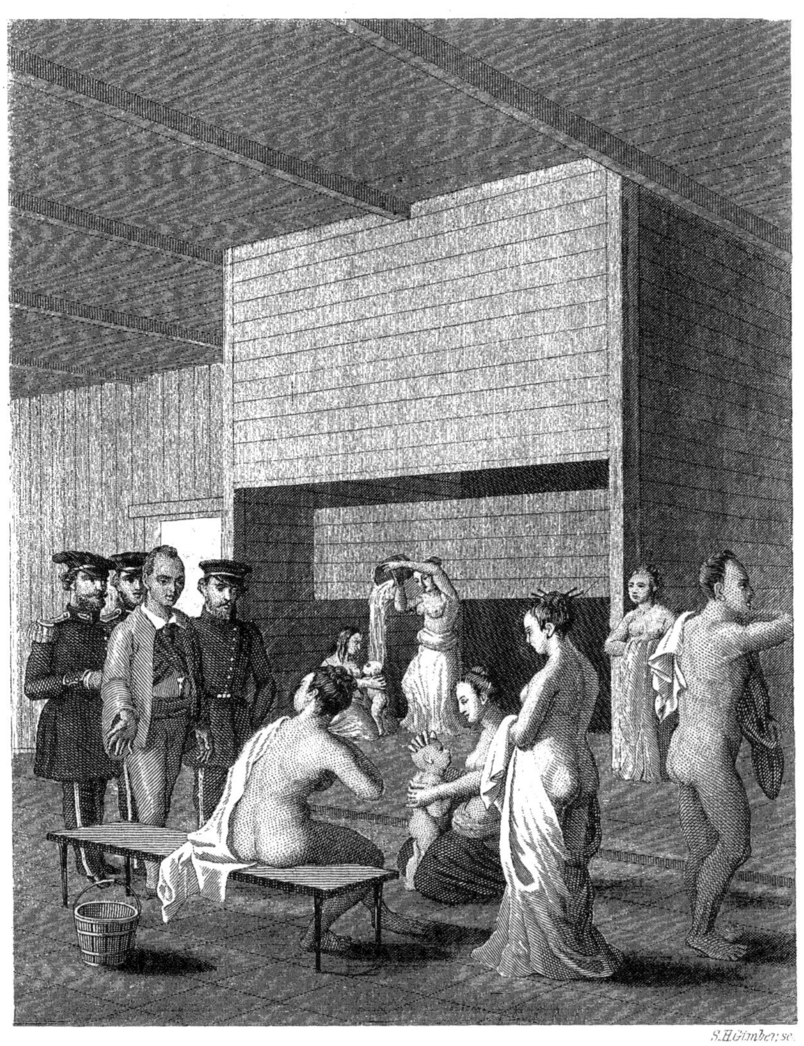

S. H. Gimber, sc.

BATHING SCENE.
IN JAPAN.

to it were wont to hold their noses on account of a bad odour that prevailed at such times. I tried to arrive at the nature of the odour, but could only learn that it was possessed of a choking sensation, and that it could be tasted in the water; and I was thinking of passing a few hours in the vicinity, hoping for an opportunity of judging in person, when one of our party drew a match across the bottom of the box to light a cigar, and the odour was immediately recognised by the owner of the bath as that in regard to which he had been making signs. It was sulphur.

I at once stooped down, and, leaning over the pool, tried to get a cupful of the water before it became tainted by admixture with that in which the bathers had been floundering all day; but, from the peculiar construction of the bathing-place, I found it impracticable. This latter was partly hewn out of the rock, and partly walled up with boards, the seams of which were tightly calked. It was some three or four feet deep, and had a bamboo joint running through the wall at that height, which acted as a constant drain to let escape the surplus water. The fountain itself was in the bottom, and consequently three or four feet under water; so it was no easy matter to get an uncontaminated cupful. At last I gave up the attempt: the risk was too great of my tasting water that had been in contact with the skin of various bathers; I was not sufficiently devoted to science to encounter it. I put my hand in it, however, more than once, and tried in vain to detect the existence of sulphur through the sense of smell.

It was quite warm enough even now, while the boiling

was so beautifully even and regular; but they made signs to us that, when it burst forth *à la* soda-fountain, the bathers took good care to give the fissure a wide berth, for fear of being scalded. They gave us also to understand that, when the water was drawn off at night and the fountain thus relieved of the pressure of the superincumbent three feet of water, it spouted forth in the form of a *jet d'eau* of several feet in height; but this we never had an opportunity of seeing.

This immense tub, or rather bathing-pool, had a bamboo house built over it, and benches of the same reed ranged round its sides; and, though we seated ourselves on those benches with the ever-existing feeling of curiosity in regard to every thing connected with those isolated people, no difference did it make to the unblushing bathers. All ages and sexes divested themselves of their garments in the most matter-of-fact style, and mixed unconcernedly in the common centre of attraction.

They not only did that much, but they also acted the part of body-servants to each other, without the slightest regard to either sex or age; and this same absence of every thing like propriety was observed, not in that place alone, but upon all other occasions where our officers had an opportunity of judging. It prevailed throughout all of the bathing-establishments of Si-mo-da and Ha-ko-da-di, and was to be observed in the every-day life of the people wherever we fell in with them. I once asked Tatz-nosky, the interpreter, if the higher classes were equally shameless; and he replied, in their usual "beat-the-bush" manner, that at Yeddo and other large cities "things were not as we found them at Si-mo-da." Golownin, the Russian captain, who was their prisoner for a long time, remarks, however, that they were woefully wanting in modesty, and makes no exception in favour of the higher classes. It was revolting to see such a total absence of that beautiful exponent of a nation's degree of civilization and purity.

While watching the bathers of the "hot spring," I heard something else denied which had always existed in my mind as a fixed fact.

"This is the way you bathe in Russia, I believe?" I said to Cavilosky, the Russian officer who had accompanied us. "I should think it productive of a most demoralizing tendency."

"My dear sir, you were never more mistaken in your life," he replied: "we are as proper in Russia as they are in any other part of Christendom. Where did you get such an idea from?"

I referred him to the "Iconographic Encyclopædia" as my authority, and added a few words in its praise as a work of standard reference.

"Pshaw! pshaw! The 'Iconographic Encyclopædia,' indeed!—the work of a musty-headed Dutchman, whose brains had long been deadened by lager-bier before the idea of getting up such a book presented itself. Give us some better authority."

I saw readily that he was prejudiced by a feeling of combined shame and annoyance at such a national characteristic being attributed to his countrymen, and so changed the subject, with the unalterable conviction that the "musty-headed Dutchman" was right and our choleric little Russian wrong.

While this conversation was going on, I searched in vain for any silicious or other matter which the water might precipitate when coming in contact with the air, and was thence forced to the conclusion that the smell of sulphur spoken of by the Japanese was owing to the escape of some noxious gas, which, finding a vent through the fissure with the water, thus produced, at times, the soda-fountain-like action before spoken of.

This was the only hot spring near Si-mo-da that we heard of; but the interpreters spoke of them as being very common in other sections of the country.

Surf-bathing seems to be peculiar to the lower classes that reside near the sea; and it is probably the attendant exposure which bronzes the skins of those who indulge in it, until the stranger wonders why the natives along the coast are so much darker than those of the interior.

I have seen as many as several hundred men, women, and children,—the entire population of villages, apparently,—rolling about in the surf in one promiscuous heap, and all the while yelling and screaming like so many savages.

The inhabitants of the cities of the interior, on the contrary, scarcely ever approach the beach, but patronize the bathing-houses twice, sometimes three times, a day. Several of us once visited one of the most respectable of these latter, to examine its arrangements, &c.; and, having been told that they were seldom frequented during the heat of the day, we chose that hour for our visit. Upon arriving at the establishment, we found it just being vacated by a most dilapidated and hideous-looking old woman, while another, who did not seem much better off so far as good looks were concerned, held open the bamboo door and motioned us to enter. Thinking, probably, that we had come to see their mode of bathing, she made signs that there were no bathers just then, but that there would be shortly, and that we had better seat ourselves around the sides and make ourselves comfortable.

We made her understand, with considerable difficulty, that our object was to see the arrangement of the hot-water apparatus, &c., whereupon she pointed to a dark-looking hole at the back-end of the room that resembled a huge, old-fashioned wood-fireplace with the back knocked out, and motioned us to pass under it and see for ourselves. So we took advantage of the permission, and, at the expense of wet feet and the inhalation of a considerable quantity of a steamy, disagreeable atmosphere, accomplished the object of our visit.

We found the inner apartment into which the chimney-like passage opened to be a room of about from eight to ten feet in size, and containing an immense caldron in the centre built around with mud and stones. It was filled to overflowing with water, from which the steam arose in clouds and circulated between a dozen or more rafters that were just high enough from the stone floor to let one walk upright under them. From what we could learn, they did not fill this caldron more than three times a day at the utmost, it being so large that the water retained its heat several hours. Then, as it cooled gradually and lost a portion of its purity with each successive bath, the price of admission decreased to a single cash.

In the corner of this apartment was also a smaller

vessel, into which a constant stream of cold water emptied through a bamboo joint that kept it in an overflowing state unless the bathers were unusually plentiful. From this they dipped bucketsful of water, which they carried into the next room to have poured over their heads after the hot part of the bathing was ended. They would hand their two buckets of water to the nearest friend, and stoop down on the concave stone flooring, while said nearest friend would get as great an elevation as possible and pour the contents over them; then the water ran through a two or three inch hole in the centre of the floor.

As we concluded our examination of the inner apartment, and again stooped under the chimneyplace-like passage-way into the outer room, we came upon several persons of all ages and sexes, who had entered since our arrival, and who were then engaged in the process of disrobing preparatory to taking a dip in the inner tub.

Our appearance did not seem to cause them either surprise or confusion; but, on the contrary, as we tried to prevail on the woman of the house to accept a dime in return for what we had seen, they crowded around in their primitive costume to see what the dispute was about. And here was another demonstration of the despotic manner in which the masses are there ruled: that old woman made signs to us that were she to accept a single cash from us her head would be in danger. And it is more than probable that half of those who crowded around us were spies, who would have reported her to the Government, had she done so.

Japan is worse than Jesuitical Rome or iron-heeled

Austria, as far as her police-department is concerned. There the friend spies upon the friend, the relative upon the relative. The word confidence is not known among them: every thing is caution and suspicion.

So much for Japanese baths and morals; and now let us pay a visit to the secluded port of Hey-da, to which the Russians had retired to avoid discovery by the French and English cruisers. When the Japanese found that the "old John" was about to go there, they objected violently, throwing themselves back upon Commodore Perry's treaty, with great apparent regard for its every feature, and giving us to understand that if we went to Hey-da it would be clearly a piece of bad faith on our part, as the treaty expressly provided that Americans were to visit no Japanese ports save those of Nan-ga-sa-ki, Ha-ko-da-di, and Si-mo-da.

To this, Commander John Rodgers replied, with equal force and wariness of regard for the provisions of the treaty, that, among other things, that instrument permitted American vessels in distress to *fly for refuge* into *any port of Japan*, and that that liberty would be worse than useless if we were not to be allowed to make charts of all such ports for the benefit of all such distressed vessels.

While running in for refuge, *without a chart*, he said, the vessels might strike upon a sunken rock, or reef, in which case they would have done much better to have remained outside in the storm. This would be a poor kind of protection to extend to American vessels in distress.

Still the Japanese refused: they always refused every

thing,—even what the treaty expressly provided for; and the only way we ever got along was to do what we wished to without asking any questions, and then refer them to the treaty for our authority.

So, if we expected to accomplish any thing by our visit, we had to act just as if we had full authority from the emperor, or make up our minds to do nothing at all; and, as we had already sailed several thousand miles to get at this work, we couldn't well go away without accomplishing it. So, *at it we went*, commencing the southern end of our survey at Hey-da, on the island of Nipon, and ending at the town of Tomari, on the northern extremity of the island of Jesso,—a coast-line of over a thousand miles, accomplished through all kinds of weather, and against all manner of obstacles that were thrown in our way by the cunning of the Japanese. But let us return to Hey-da and the shipwrecked Russians.

On the morning of the 24th of May, 1855, we left Si-mo-da before a light land-breeze, and, under all sail and low steam, worked our way slowly to the southward, keeping well in with the land and sketching in its windings from point to point. Several Russian officers, who had crossed the mountains on foot to Si-mo-da to pay the squadron a visit, took passage with us, and added to the interest of the trip by pointing out and naming various villages that we passed, and indulging us with accounts of their experience among the Japanese.

These accomplished officers and gentlemen mostly spoke French fluently, and some of them even understood our own language quite well. I had always regarded Russian officers as rather illiterate and boorish than otherwise, and was consequently now the more surprised to find them our equals in polish as well as in classical and scientific acquirements.

Our time passed pleasantly enough, as we steamed over the distance of forty miles, and we were beginning to think that some signs of the harbour ought now to be heaving in sight, when we suddenly found ourselves within a mile of its very mouth. So beautifully was it hidden from the sea, that a strange vessel might have "backed and filled" about its locality for days without imagining the existence of any such place.

"Voilà la Fu-si-ya-ma!" exclaimed one of the Russians, pointing far down the coast to a magnificent mountain, which, suddenly relieved, by a passing squall, of its dense envelop of clouds, now lifted its snowy head far into the mid-day sky.

A magnificent sight it was, truly. Imagine a vast truncated cone, whose even slope to the northward was washed by the rolling waters of the bay, while its southern base dropped gradually back for miles and tens of miles into the unknown interior. Its snow-capped crest reflecting the weakened rays of the evening sun, its uneven belt of constant clouds around its centre, and below that the distant blue of its sweeping sides, fill up the picture. I say, with the Russians, "Voilà la Fu-si-ya-ma!"

"It is their great object of reverence, I might almost say of worship," continued the Russian. "You find it stamped upon most of their porcelain and lacquer-ware, and hung in tapestry about many of their altars. Its sides, that now look so blue, are said to be remarkably fertile: its summit is always covered with snow, and is in bad weather generally hidden from view by the clouds which hang around it. It serves them also as a very reliable barometer. When several hundred of their boats were towing our crippled frigate from Si-mo-da to Hey-da, the day was beautifully clear, and we were getting along quite smoothly, when suddenly a white cloud hid it from our view and threw the whole line of boats into the wildest state of confusion. They cast off their lines and pulled for the shore in such haste that it was with difficulty that we could keep enough with us in which to save ourselves and crew. When the hurricane which the white cloud indicated broke upon us, *we* were safe in under the land; but the old Diana foundered in a few minutes. Their knowledge of the weather was all that saved us."

We were now approaching the curved and narrow entrance of the harbour; and, as is usual when entering a strange port, all hands mustered on deck with glasses and wide-awake eyes, to see what was to be seen, and to imagine a great many things which were not to be seen. And the changing panorama that presented itself on every hand was one well worthy of admiration. The day was as calm as a perfectly-motionless atmosphere could make it, and just warm enough to make it pleasant. Ahead of us there was opening a green and picturesque valley, with the *locale* of its hidden villages indicated by groves of closely-planted shade-trees, and with the glassy surface of a winding stream breaking out here and there and reflecting the slanting rays of the western sun. On our left, the southern range of mountains that formed one wall of the valley stretched their broken length down into the very sea, lifting their uneven ridge several hundred feet above its level, and telling the mariner of bold water along their rugged sides and friendly shelter under their protecting breasts.

On the right, a long, low, and curved fragment of land, some one or two hundred yards in width, and densely covered with the heaviest timber, stretched itself from the northern shore toward the mountain-range already alluded to, coming to an abrupt termination just in time to leave a passage of fair width opening into the inner harbour, and forming, with the remaining shore-line, a magnificent anchorage, in shape something like the number 6. Then, to complete the panorama, astern of us, miles away upon the clearly-defined horizon, where the dark blue of the sea and the azure hue of the heavens joined to limit the circle of vision, loomed out the undulating land that, stretching far out into the sea from the downward slope of Fu-si-ya-ma's northern side, formed a horseshoe bay of huge dimensions, whose unknown shores might, to our excited fancies, have contained a dozen such quiet anchorages as the one we were now entering.

Reader, if you have ever entered a quiet, millpond-like harbour after a week or more of hard and stormy weather, you can well imagine our feelings as we rounded up into this landlocked little cove, which was so perfectly protected that not even a ripple was to be seen upon the cool and shady-looking beach. It was so totally different a harbour from that of Si-mo-da, so infinitely superior in every respect, that we could not restrain the exclamation, —"Oh, if Commodore Perry had but selected this as one of his three ports of entry, ships arriving at Japan would at any rate be assured of safety from the elements, if nothing else." We wondered in vain why Si-mo-da had been chosen when Hey-da was so near; and we have not yet ceased to wonder.

As we steamed slowly up into this figure-of-six harbour, the Russian boats, which had been saved when the Diana foundered, were seen safely moored along the quiet beach; but the Russians themselves were nowhere to be noticed. They subsequently acknowledged that they had taken us for an English or French steamer under American colours, and repeated the oft-complained-of proceeding of the former, who had entered the harbour of Petropolowski with our flag at their peak, made a hasty survey of it, and then put up their helm and steamed out again while hoisting their true colours and firing a gun in bravado. We had not seen the act ourselves, but had heard of it so often that we finally began to regard it as having taken place beyond a doubt.

As soon as we had let go our anchor, the captain's gig was placed at the disposal of our passengers, and after they had been on shore a few minutes we began to see swarms of their countrymen crowding the beach, many of whom came off in their boats to extend the civilities of the port to us. One would have imagined it a possession of the Czar instead of a Japanese seaport town, so completely had the Russians made themselves at home. They laughed at the idea of our not visiting them at their quarters because the Japanese objected to it, and offered to take us in *their* boats if we wished to respect their foolish fancies.

That night we had them, as well as several Japanese of rank, on board, and introduced them to a bowl of hot whiskey punch; and, as this latter disappeared, we acquired considerable information of their nation at large, from the Japanese, through the Russians, some of whom had already made considerable progress in the language.

Among other things, we learned one of the great secrets in regard to the beauty and remarkable polish of their swords. It was not every Japanese sword that was good, the vice-governor told us: it was only a certain number, that had been made by a workman who lived A.D. 1750, that were so highly prized: any others could be had for a trifle,—from ten to thirty dollars.

The old fellow had drank pretty freely of the punch before expressing himself thus liberally, and another glass or two upset his reserve and dignity completely. He slapped us on the back in a most "hail-fellow-well-met" style, and drew his sword when requested, without the slightest hesitation. This latter was certainly the most beautiful specimen of steel that I ever saw: put any light fabric across it and sweep your arm through the air, and its divided parts floated upon the disturbed atmosphere. The governor seemed unusually proud of this sword: it was made, he told us, by the great maker of 1750, and had come to him from his father, who had long since retired from public life. I tried to ascertain if swords, &c. fell to the lot of the eldest son in Japan, but failed to convey the question in an intelligible form.

The party broke up at a late hour, and the next day was devoted to the survey of the harbour, which being accomplished, the restless anchor once more appeared at the cathead, and the "old John" again pointed herself for the sea.

That evening we were again at Si-mo-da, the Japanese appearing not to care a farthing about our having visited Hey-da, although they had opposed it so violently before it was accomplished.

Our stay at Si-mo-da was now drawing to a close. We had resurveyed the harbour, compared our work with the chart of Lieutenants Maury and Bent, of Perry's squadron, and found that the destructive earthquake and its attendant sea-wave which had reduced Si-mo-da to ruins since the visit of that squadron had not perceptibly altered its formation or soundings.

As an evidence of the zeal by which both officers and men were filled during this cruise, I will remark that, about this time, the idea of exploring and surveying the coast of Nipon from Si-mo-da to the northeast point of the island, and then crossing the stormy Straits of T'Sugar to Ha-ko-da-di, island of Jesso, in an open boat, was originated by some one and subsequently executed with happy success. The coast-line to be thus examined was nearly five hundred miles in length, their charts were very unreliable, and it was the season when violent gales were likely to cross their track at any moment. It was undoubtedly a most hazardous undertaking.

As soon as the expedition was proposed, volunteers sprang forward from every quarter, and, as soon as the officers and crew were selected, the boat was prepared for the unusual service and proclaimed ready for sea.

She was the largest boat carried by the Vincennes, was known as "the launch," and measured probably from four to five tons. They had built a light forecastle-deck forward, knocked up a few lockers aft, and rigged her as a sloop. She carried a twelve-pounder boat-howitzer on a pivot, one or two boxes of fixed ammunition, a change of clothes for each man, and the regular Government-ration of beef and pork, bread, rice, whiskey, &c. for twenty-one days. Her crew numbered from fifteen to twenty souls, all armed to the teeth and ready to go *anywhere* in spite of *any thing* the Japanese might say or do; for these latter, with their usual annoying policy, had strongly objected to such a thing as a boat of light draught running into all the nooks and corners where a large vessel could not go, and it was therefore necessary to do it against their wishes.

Of course we would not have persisted at the expense of life, but then we knew well enough that the Japanese were like a large, savage, but quiescent dog: walk by him in a quiet, cool, unconcerned manner, and he will probably content himself with keeping his eye upon you; whereas, if you hesitate in your advance, he will more than probably spring at your throat

And thus it was with them and us. As soon as we stopped to show them the consideration of asking their consent to the most simple measure, they would begin to clear their throats and advance more difficulties than an ordinary man could think of in double the time; and these difficulties were always so trivial, and the desire to bother and retard us so apparent, that we generally left them in anger and did what we had in view, without the slightest regard to them or their opposition.

The launch was now dubbed the "Vincennes, Jr.," and put under the command of Acting Lieutenant John M. Brooke, of the Vincennes, Sen., who had associated with him in the risky undertaking Messrs. Edward Kern, artist, and Richard Berry, sailmaker, in addition to the regular crew.

Finally, the day of sailing arrived, and we all put to sea, leaving the nomadics, their schooner,—which had now returned from Petropolowski,—and Cavilosky, the Russian, in charge of the harbour. The Hancock surveyed a group of islands on her route and then made the best of her way toward Ha-ko-da-di. Arrived near the northeast point of Nipon, we fell in with fogs and heavy weather, which made the navigation any thing but safe. Let me turn to my journal for an idea of this unpleasant navigation:—

"We were running along the northeastern coast of the island of Nipon, under both sail and steam, had had no observations for some days, were enveloped in a fog that might apparently have been 'cut with a knife,' knew that strong and unknown currents swept around us, had no chart from which to get even an *idea* of said northeastern coast, were any thing but certain as to our locality, felt that a gale of wind was coming down upon us, and were nervously anxious to reach shelter in the harbour of Ha-ko-da-di before night. This harbour was *supposed* to be some fifty miles off; that was where our dead reckoning placed it: but then dead reckoning was proverbially unreliable, and the unknown currents already alluded to only added to this uncertainty. We were steering what we also *supposed* to be the right course to make the northeast point of Nipon, before starting to cross the straits that separated it from Jesso, so that we might use it as a fresh starting-point in finding our way through the fog; but we had expected to discover it before breakfast, and it was now getting toward noon, and there was still nothing to be seen but fog, fog, and occasionally a heavy-winged sea-bird breaking through its dense folds, hovering over us for a moment, and then darting away from sight as suddenly as it had appeared.

"We were going along very fast, too, for the 'old John,'—at least eight or nine knots the hour; for the wind and sea were both astern, and, like any other collection of matter, she could not have stood still under such circumstances had she been so disposed. Besides, we had also got up steam that morning, and the boiling water under her Dutch galliot-like stern told that the propeller was also lending a hand to urge her ahead. No wonder, then, that she waddled along through the water and fog at the above unusual rate.

"This unusual rate was a very pleasant thing as long as we had reason to suppose that we were steering the right course, for the faster we went on said right course the sooner we should arrive at our port of shelter; but, after we had run for an hour or two beyond the time when we should have sighted the northeast point, we began to get anxious and to fear that we might be running blindfold toward some rock beyond the cape, or upon some shelterless lee shore, which might at any moment be discovered with unpleasant suddenness; in either of which cases it would have been a 'clew up and furl' game with the 'old John' and all connected with her. The captain and Carnes, therefore, put their heads together over the imperfect chart, and concluded to change our course so as to sight the land along which we were running, and which we *knew* to be to the westward of us, though *how far* we could only conjecture

"The helm was therefore put to starboard; some of the lighter sails were taken in; the others were braced for the wind on the port beam, and every thing kept in active readiness to change back to our old course as soon as the land should be discovered ahead. In this way we ran on for an hour or more, the first lieutenant having the trumpet on the quarter-deck, the officer of the deck, whom he had relieved, being in charge of the forecastle, to help the look-outs keep their eyes open, and to superintend things in general in case of the sudden change of course which was momentarily expected, and the crew being at their stations for 'wearing ship.'

"Suddenly, a seaman by the name of Corcoran,—with whom Dickens must have been acquainted before creating his character of 'Bunsby,'—and who stood near the officer in charge of the forecastle, looked very wise, and said he *heard* the breakers. This caused every one to listen intently and open their eyes still wider; but they heard nothing. Presently he said he *saw* them; and, as others now *heard* them just as he said he *saw* them, the officer in charge took his word for it, and bellowed out to the quarter-deck, 'Port! *har-r-r-d* a-port! Breakers ahead!' and, as the ship fell rapidly off under the influence of both propeller and sails, a long white line of boiling surf appeared along our port bow and beam, and caused us to congratulate ourselves upon the sharp senses of 'Bunsby.'

"The deep-sea lead, which had been kept going as

fast as it could be hauled in since our change of course, now gave fifteen fathoms as the depth of water! and, as the beach was not more than four hundred yards off, we did not think it prudent to close in any more, but ran along with it at about that depth and distance, keeping a good look-out on each cathead and a hand-lead going from each of the fore-chains.

"As we had closed with the land while standing in, the fog had seemed to lighten considerably, and we now ran along at our old speed, keeping the breakers *just in sight*, and straining our eyes through the fog ahead to discover our long-looked-for northeast point. This was a most trying kind of navigation. For, suppose that we should have been running before that wind and sea into a fathomless bay, where we could not have anchored; or suppose a reef had suddenly been found, making out from the land right across our path!

"'Haul by the wind and beat out of such a disagreeably-tight place,' I think I hear some seaman answer.

"'Yes; that would do very well; but, unfortunately, the 'old John' could never be persuaded to acquit herself after that style,' is my answer. She was like a crab: she always went *astern* or *sideways* in all sudden emergencies,—confound her! Suddenly, as we looked, the vague and undefined outlines of a dark detached object arose before us, and then another, farther in the fog, as the first became more distant.

"'Land ho!' sang out the look-out. 'Two islands right ahead, sir!' shouted the officer in charge of the forecastle.

"'Port!' said the ready voice of the first lieutenant to the man at the wheel. 'Brace up the head-yards! Quartermaster, let the captain know there's land reported ahead.'

"'Ay, ay, sir!' and, as the messenger disappeared down the cabin-hatch, the old ship, as if conscious of her danger, swerved slowly from her course until she brought the newly-discovered objects out upon her lee bow.

"'Steady there!' exclaimed the first lieutenant. 'How do you head now?'

"'Nor'-nor'east, sir,' replied the helmsman, as he 'met her' with the lee wheel and fired an admirable shot at a distant spittoon.

"'Very well. Keep her so.

"'Ay, ay, sir.'

"The after-yards were now braced for the wind on the starboard quarter, and we were soon running on our new course with but slightly-diminished speed.

"'That's the point we're looking for,' said Carnes: 'I know it by those islands. We're all right now.'

"'Breakers ahead! breakers on the weather bow!' shouted the startled voices of both look-outs at this moment.

"'Haul by the wind, Mr. McCullom,' said the captain, who now came on deck, 'and take in the topgallant-sails.'

"So we hauled by the wind, took in topgallant-sails, and passed the word to fire up strong. The poor 'old John' was apparently in another of her endless 'tight places,' and steam was the only thing we could ever hope to help her with.

We were now 'by the wind,' with the beach along which we had been running looming up upon our weather quarter and astern, with the three islands (another having come out of the fog as we neared them) on our lee quarter, and with what was an apparent reef of rocks, over which the surf was breaking furiously, extending from the outer of the three islands along our lee beam and well forward on the lee bow,—almost dead ahead, in fact. The wind also had increased to a young gale; that is, we felt its force much more then, that we were no longer running away from it; and, had we not got in the topgallant-sails as soon as we did, the masts would certainly have gone over the side. Our headway, too, was entirely deadened, and, in spite of the assisting propeller, it soon became apparent that we were drifting on to the reef.

"'What do you think of it, Mr. Carnes?' asked the captain. 'Is it a reef, or only the strong current breaking around the point? The sailing-directions speak of three islands, but of no reef.'

"'It looks miserably natural, sir,' replied the master, as he continued regarding it through his opera-glass;* 'but I don't see how it can well be any thing, if this is the northeast point: that's the difficulty.'

"We were at this moment in a painful state of doubt and uncertainty, and would have gladly hesitated, had it only been to gain time to think; but, as we were all the while drifting toward the reef, immediate action was what was wanted. Fortunately for our peace of mind,

* Opera-glasses are rapidly superseding the ordinary "spy-glass" on ship-board, especially at night.

the fog lifted while we were yet talking, and enabled us to discern other objects that established pretty well the fact of its being *the* point, when we at once knew that the reef must be but a tide-rip, and so determined to run through it.

"'I'd trust to the sailing-direction for there being no reef off this point, and *run through it*,' said the master.

"'So we will!' said the captain. 'Hard up the helm, Mr. McCullom, and point her for it.

"So the helm was put hard up, and in less than three minutes more we were entering the threatening streak, carrying no bottom at thirty fathoms all the while, and with the leaping waters breaking over our bulwarks in all directions, and in such quantities as to cause us to tremble for the safety of the Vincennes, Jr., whom we knew would have to round that same point in a few days, and under, possibly, similar or worse circumstances. Another minute, and the supposed danger was behind us, when we again breathed freely, set the topgallant-sails, royals, and all studding-sails, and shaped our course for Ha-ko-da-di at the rate of ten and a half miles the hour. It was a strange thing for our old craft to be moving at that rate, and I am almost afraid to tell of it; but then it must be remembered that we were under all sail and steam, and that a rising gale of wind was following us in its squally strength.

"'Well! I never seed such cruisin' as this,' remarked Bunsby, as he turned over his tobacco and looked back at the surf-like tide-rip that crossed our track. 'If the Lord, that looks out for sparrows and tailors, a'n't got this old thing under his speacil wing, I don't know.'

"A general laugh followed this characteristic ebullition. Bunsby had long since become the acknowledged 'ship's growler.' We subsequently returned to this point, and made a perfect survey of it, as well as of the entire straits.

"We were now but some forty miles from our port,—the diagonal width of the Straits of T'Sugar,—and, could we but keep up our then speed for seven or eight hours, we should get in that night. So we held on to the straining canvas and kept up full steam, for there was a five or six knot current running against us; and, though the gale continued to increase, and consequently to urge us ahead at a more headlong pace than ever, still, it also created a very high and dangerous 'chop-sea,' which broke continually over our bulwarks, flooding our decks, and in one case filling a quarter-boat so full as to create fears for her safety. We again thought of the poor little Vincennes, Jr., of her brave and adventurous officers and crew, and wished them safely across a passage which was often threatening the safety of even a ship of our size.

"That night we reached our destination in safety, but we had a hard run of it; and, if we had been forced to pass the next twelve hours in darkness and at the mercy of that gale and six-knot current, there is no telling where the thirteenth hour would have found us. As it was, we got a glimpse—and it was only a glimpse of a moment's duration—of the promontory of Ha-ko-da-di, just as the twilight was leaving us; and then we ran in after dark by *guess-work*. It is not surprising, therefore, that we should have *run on shore*, which we actually did do, though it was fortunately well inside of the capacious bay, where the water was smooth and the mud soft. That same night, however, we hauled off again, and the next morning steamed up to the regular anchorage off the town, where our store-brig, an American whaling-brig, and an English surveying-schooner, were quietly stowed away among a fleet of the clumsy-looking Japanese junks."

As day by day now rolled on, bringing in first the Vincennes, and then the Cooper, we continued to tremble for the missing launch, and to think that the risk had been almost too great.

Finally, she arrived, to our great satisfaction; and the next day brought in the nomadics also, who told us that couriers had arrived daily at Si-mo-da after our departure, reporting the launch at her various stopping-places along the coast, and causing the officials a vast deal of annoyance. Here is what we learned from the combined gossip of the two vessels. My journal says:—

"The Vincennes, Jr., left Si-mo-da on the morning of a fine day, and for some time had a continuation of pleasant weather and easy sailing. They passed the first night in a small bay some miles above Si-mo-da, with their boat anchored near the beach and their tent pitched upon a grassy knoll, before which a bright fire was soon kindled and a warm supper subsequently discussed. The natives of a small village near at hand received them quite civilly, but took care to send a courier over to Si-mo-da, reporting their arrival and asking for instructions as to what they should do. The arrival of this messenger at Si-mo-da is said to have caused no little annoyance to the pompous officials before whom he presented himself, and they immediately started Tatz-nosky in hot haste to drive our explorers to sea. They had no difficulty in recognising the launch, from the drawing which was sent of her, as the boat which had left their harbour in the morning, and to which they refused permission to survey along their coast. Tatz-nosky rode upon a Government-horse, and doubtless 'used him' as hard as Government-horses are generally used under similar circumstances; but, when he arrived at the end of his journey, the Vincennes, Jr., had stood out to sea, and he had the pleasure of riding back again. Had he been a well-read European, he would doubtless have hummed upon his return-journey the once-popular ditty of which this is a part:—

"'The King of France, with twenty thousand men,
March'd up a hill, and then march'd down again.'

"Our explorers were equally fortunate on the second evening of their cruise, so far as passing a quiet night was concerned. They found another little cove, into which they retreated before the approach of a squally night, and entailed a long ride upon a second courier; which, in turn, mounted poor Tatz-nosky again upon his Government-hack. But he had not proceeded half-way on his road this time before he was met by a third courier, who informed him that their visitors had departed with the early dawn. They were like the Irishman's flea:—'put your finger on him, and he isn't there.'

"In this way they cruised along quite smoothly, making good time during the day before favourable winds, and seeking shelter at night in quiet little coves which they generally were so fortunate as to fall in with toward evening. After a while, however, 'a change came o'er the spirit of their dream,' in the shape of a gale of wind, when they would fain have run into some of the 'quiet coves' that had befriended them so far; but unfortunately they had arrived at a long stretch of iron-bound coast by that time, that warned them that their greatest safety now consisted in keeping at a reasonable distance from the land: so they had to work through it as best they could, eating cold and uncooked provisions, being knocked about in a most dangerous manner by the heavy seas, and passing altogether any thing but a pleasant time.

"Now, as long as that state of things lasted, they were in great danger; but they were fortunately included among Bunsby's tailors and sparrows, and got to the end of the iron-bound coast in safety, after having narrowly escaped foundering one unusually stormy night. The heavy weather still continued, however, and made the rest of the passage rough and dangerous in the extreme: still, they accomplished it with safety, if not comfort, as far as the northeast point, where they encountered the tide-rip which had caused us of the 'old John' so much annoyance, but which their little craft then crossed quite easily, there being only a moderate breeze by that time, while we had had a gale following us.

"In short, she arrived safely in Ha-ko-da-di on her twenty-first night out, much to our relief and greatly to the surprise of the Japanese fishermen, who wondered greatly to see a craft of her size cruising along their stormy coasts. That same day she was unrigged and hoisted into the Vincennes again, and thus was her perilous voyage happily terminated. The foregoing is a

THE "IRON-BOUND COAST" DURING FAIR WEATHER.

very fair specimen of the manner in which we were often exposed during that surveying cruise around the world."

We were now to remain about Ha-ko-da-di from fifteen to twenty days, taking in coal and salt provisions from the Hamburg brig Greta, which we had chartered at Hong-Kong to meet us at this point, and surveying the harbour and Straits of T'Sugar, (erroneously pronounced Sangar,) after which we were to separate to meet no more until our arrival at San Francisco.

CHAPTER XV.

HOW BRASS BUTTONS ARE VALUED IN JAPAN, AND HOW PARTRIDGES ARE THERE TRANSFORMED INTO SINGING-BIRDS—HOW WE VISITED A SEA-GOD'S TEMPLE, AND HOW A GERMAN EXPLORER PREFERRED REMAINING OUTSIDE—HOW SOME AMERICANS LEANED ON COMMODORE PERRY'S TREATY, AND HOW IT GAVE WAY UNDER THEM.

WE found Ha-ko-da-di a very different place from Si-mo-da,—at least treble its size, and situated at the foot of a curved and towering promontory, which, joined to the main by a long low neck of land, forms one of the largest and finest harbours in the world.

We now turned our attention to the Greta, and several days were devoted to transferring her cargo of coal to our exhausted bunkers and replenishing our supplies of provisions for the use of the crew. As for ourselves,—the officers,—there was no such luck in store. During this time we walked over most of the surrounding country, to the infinite terror of old women and small children, and made daily hauls with our seine along the inner shore of the bay, to the great annoyance of the Japanese authorities and to *our* own especial edification about meal-hours.

During one of these walks, Hartman and myself bartered away a number of brass buttons for several articles of religious worship, and returned on board in high glee. The next day the doctor, while upon a similar excursion, met a countryman with a wicker-basket containing ten or a dozen fine plump partridges; and, as they were eating which we had not enjoyed for many months, he hauled out several silver dollars on the spur of the moment and offered to "buy the lot." The man refused, however, and was walking off, when some one exclaimed, "Try him with the buttons!" at which the doctor hauled out a handful of them and made signs that he would barter. The fellow now halted, and, after examining them, intimated that he would give a partridge for a button, and, to the delight of the party, handed over the entire basket for a dozen or so of buttons. The next day they were eaten with great gusto, and, just as we got up from the table, a high officer came on board with the interpreter, and complained that "some Americans had been many miles back in the country and bought some poor people's household gods, and that another party had forced a poor man to sell them all of his *singing-birds*:" at the end of which he hauled out *every button* that we had traded, returning them to the captain, and requested that the "household gods" and "singing-birds" be returned.

Now, here is a beautiful specimen of the cunning of those people. There was an abundance of partridges on the island of Jesso; and, had that officer come on board and demanded the return of a poor man's *birds*, we should have said, "Why do not you officers provide us birds to eat?" and he could have answered nothing: whereas, when we now asked the question, he shrugged his shoulders, and said singing-birds were never eaten.

Fortunately it was too late to return them; but, the captain having asked Hartman and myself seriously in regard to the household gods, we could not deny that we were the parties, and were consequently requested to give them up. We had great luck in seine-hauling, and this, too, seemed to trouble them considerably. They evidently envied us the boat-loads of fine salmon, trout, perch, and flounders which we daily carried on board, and determined to stop the sport. They told the captain that the people in and about Ha-ko-da-di were very poor; that they lived almost entirely upon fish, and that if we went on in that way much longer they would be in a starving condition. This was simply absurd, as there were dozens of their own seines being hauled in the harbour every day, and one of theirs was as large as half a dozen of ours would have been. Probably "absurd" is too mild a term; but, as I am "talking behind their backs" as it were, I will content myself with it.

The captain replied carelessly that if they would sell us what fish we wanted the seine should be used no more, but that if worthless or half-decayed fish were sent they would be thrown overboard and a seining-party sent on shore at once. To this the high officer replied that we should thereafter be regularly supplied with fine fresh salmon; and the next day he sent on board three of that kind of fish, which looked very well at a distance, but which we refused to accept upon a closer inspection, as their gills were already turning green and four dollars were asked for them. They were consequently thrown overboard and the seining-party once more landed on the beach.

We had not got our first haul half-way on shore when several two-sworded officials, attended by some ten or fifteen inferiors, gathered about the spot, apparently actuated only by curiosity. After a while, however, they took it upon themselves to drive off some poor people who were picking up the refuse fish, at which I beckoned to the three men nearest me, and—considerably emboldened by the action of "the prophet" at Si-mo-da—gave the officers several hearty kicks, when they ran off in great confusion, tripping over their swords and being followed by their ten or fifteen attendants. We then called the poor people back, one of whom was so delighted at the turn which things had taken that he at once commenced eating his fish raw, to our extreme disgust. He would pick a six-inch fellow up out of the sand by the tail, give him a flirt through the water to wash the sand off, and then commence by biting off the entire head, after which he went regularly down to the tail, which he only threw away to enable him to grasp another. In justice to the Japanese at large, however, I must say that this was the only thing of the kind we ever saw.

The kicking which we had administered to the officials seemed to have had the desired effect. They did not reappear to trouble us, and we shortly returned on board with a well-loaded boat, and continued our sport daily as long as we remained. In this way one boat and a dozen men supplied our entire ship's-company with fine fish; while, had we consented to be browbeaten by the arrogant officials, they would have furnished us an uncertain and stale supply at a greater cost than a butcher in the United States would charge for supplying a ship's crew with beef and vegetables.

At Ha-ko-da-di we found public bathing conducted exactly as at Si-mo-da, and in all other respects the people seemed similar. As a matter of course they were even more wild, for they had seen less of foreigners; and, if possible, the two-sworded gentlemen evinced a stronger disposition to follow our tracks, but one or two properly-applied kicks soon cured them of that weakness.

We found several objects of interest around the shores of this magnificent bay, the most prominent of which was a marine cave of vast dimensions chambered out of the rocky breast of the towering and surf-worn promontory of Ha-ko-da-di by some past convulsion of nature, and now dedicated by the Japanese fishermen to their sea-god, whose aid they there invoke to calm the raging of the sea or to bless their coast with endless shoals of salmon. The very existence of this half-submarine, half-subterranean place of worship would probably have never been known to us had our ship been any thing but a surveying-vessel; but the nature of the service required at our hands took us *everywhere*, and, if the "old John" couldn't go herself, she sent one or more of her six boats to act for her.

It was in this way that the archlike entrance to the cave was discovered,—one of our boats, while engaged in the survey of the harbour, having entered just far enough to determine that it *was* a cave, and one, too, of no inconsiderable extent. As soon, therefore, as the survey was completed, an exploring-party was organized to enter and examine it thoroughly, and to that end quite extensive preparations were necessary.

It was reported as being horribly dark, even at the mouth, could only be entered in a boat, and that the roaring of a heavy surf or waterfall had been heard from the outside. Our informant also stated that a heavy swell rolled into it, that its rocky mouth was whitened by a sulphurous vapour, and that, from the current which set into it, there was evidently another outlet: should this other outlet prove to be a whirlpool, or even an ordinary waterfall, a boat-load of human beings, without light and utterly ignorant of the locality, would find themselves most unpleasantly situated. We consequently armed ourselves with lanterns, matches, lines, knives, hammer and nails, &c. before leaving the ship, and, as the crew had been worked hard lately, took the dingy and her two boys to pull us to the scene of action.

The party consisted of nine, all told,—quite enough to crowd into a small boat that was going to *feel her way*, through a darkness like that of night, to the bottom of an unknown cave. Six of us were officers of the ship, a seventh was the German supercargo of the Greta, and the remaining two were the dingy-boys,—the same two dangerously-encased juveniles who had landed Mahomet, Bridleman, and myself so successfully at Si-mo-da upon the occasion of the former persuading the mountain to "move off" in a southerly direction.

Our German friend was quite talkative at first, indulging us with vivid descriptions of various European caves which he had explored in early life, and enlarging upon the feelings of intense interest which such enterprises were calculated to create in the inquiring mind. As we drew near to the cave, however, he became rather taciturn than otherwise, and, as we reached its mouth and the order was given to "hold water" with the oars while the plan of procedure was being determined upon, he hazarded the remark that "some vones more better make stops outside ze rocks, vile ze uzzer vones goes in;" but in this he was overruled at once, and, a deep-sea lead-line having been securely fastened to a projecting fragment of rock, we backed boldly in under the gloomy and resounding archway. Keeping a light strain on the line, to "hold on by" should the possible whirlpool prove a reality, the oars were taken in, and, with boat-hooks and hands, we urged her cautiously through the thickening gloom.

And now the German proved to be right in one thing. It was "intensely interesting to our inquiring minds," as the boat dropped slowly away from daylight, rising and falling over the heavy swell and grating harshly against unseen projections of the rocky sides. We began to think that the roof of the archway might get lower with unpleasant suddenness as we progressed, and that the next swell might inform us of the fact by mashing our heads against it; for it was so very dark that, even with our lights, we could not see the rugged walls against which we were scraping. The feeling at last became so *intensely* interesting to the supercargo himself, that he again became communicative. "Vel! vel! I don't loiks zis!" he said, nervously; "much better take some vone out of ze boat. 'Tis var small boat for so many peoples. I vaits outside for some time. I not loiks zis."

I must confess that I didn't "loik" it myself; and the feeling, passing down into my fingers, caused them to tighten their grasp around the line, until the boat came to a stand-still.

"Hillo! what's the matter?" asked Carnes.

"Slack the line, H——, and let her go in," said the doctor. (Said H——, who was seated in the bows, with his feet braced firmly against the stem, thought he'd much better *hold on* to the line until he could see where he was *going to slack her to*.)

"I feel bottom!" exclaimed Squires, who was leaning over the side with a boat-hook.

"You feel the mischief!" said Lawton. "You're feeling the *boat's* bottom."

"I suppose I know what I'm about!" retorted the indignant feeler: "darkness don't keep one from *feeling*."

"I not loiks it!" broke in the German; "much better vone, two, three, at vonce. Boat var small."

"Well, let's haul out again and leave half on the rocks," said another, who evidently began to think with him.

"Well, all right!" exclaimed several more of the party. I didn't say much, but hung back on the line with such effect as to change night into day in a most amazingly short space of time. I didn't like the gurgling noises in our rear: they sounded too much like a subterranean watercourse to make it pleasant.

"Vel, I gets out," said the German, as we ranged up alongside of the entrance.

"Oh, no! *you'd* better hold on," said he who had accused Squires of feeling the boat's bottom.

"No, but I loiks better here," replied the former explorer of European caves, as he jumped upon the rocks and advised that "vone, two, three, more better at vonce."

One by one the party followed his example, until there

were but four of us left to make the second attempt,—the doctor, the master, he who had accused him of the boat-hook of feeling the wrong bottom, and myself.

Backing in as before, we *progressed backward* quite smoothly until arrived near our former stopping-place, when the doctor wisely remarked that "we'd better hold on a minute until our eyes became accustomed to the darkness: probably we might be able to see." So my fingers again tautened around the line, and the party came to another halt. The wisdom of this proceeding soon made itself apparent, and then we began to wonder why some one hadn't thought of it before. The dark outlines of a vast and dome-like apartment became now every moment more distinct, until, with the assistance of our lights, we could see passably well. "Humph!" said one; "there's no whirlpool, after all: it's only the surf rolling in among the rocks." "I don't believe there's any current sets in, either: it's all humbug," said another. "Give her a shove astern, H——."

So I slackened the line, and, trusting to the eyes in the other end of the boat, gave her a most energetic shove.

"There it is!" "*Now* we're in for it!" "*Trim* boat!" "Haul out, H——!" "Con*found* the bats!"

These confused and excited exclamations were the result of three things. The "energetic shove" had landed the old boat's stern on a sunken rock, which we subsequently found to be located exactly in mid-channel. Secondly, the swell leaving her there, she canted over and came within an ace of spilling us all out. Lanterns were let fall, the better to enable their holders to look out for "No. 1," and the candles took advantage of the occasion

BACKING INTO THE SEA-GOD'S TEMPLE.

to go out. Thirdly, a hundred or more bats, alarmed by such unusual noises, left their various stow-holes, and, flying in our faces, added their disgusting contact to the general drawbacks of the adventure. I began to wish myself with the German, and, in order to gratify the longing, hauled heavily on the ever-friendly line, and with the next swell we righted to an even keel and surged ahead clear of the rock. We were no sooner again upright, however, than our courage returned, and we came to another halt and began feeling about for the lanterns and matches. These found and lit, we noticed that the fright had considerably sharpened our sense of vision: I suppose our eyes had by this time adapted themselves to the darkness.

We now backed in again, slackening the line with more confidence, and poling her clear of the sunken rock with boat-hooks. Once inside of that, we were all right, and the next moment the party jumped on one of the large boulders of massive granite that apparently composed the flooring of the cave, while I returned for the outsiders in a most triumphant mood.

This time we got in without any difficulty, one of those already there having remained on the boulder with his light, to warn us as to the bearing of the sunken rock, which, being between him and the entrance, was plainly visible as the swell broke over it.

Leaving one of the boys in the boat to keep her clear of the rocks, we now lit our candles and commenced climbing over the boulders toward the centre of the dome, where we could see the dim and uncertain outlines of a truncated cone, upon the top of which was perched something very much like an ordinary dog-kennel. This was by no means pleasant climbing, as one every now and then put his hand upon a king-crab, a young bat, or some object equally pleasant to the touch: still, we climbed on, and finally reached the top.

It proved to be a rugged mound, half rock and half earth, and the dog-kennel to be a grotesquely-carved josh-house, within whose closed portals we discovered a finely-executed bronze casting of their sea-god. A number of copper cash were around about his sacred feet, and a gilded serpent twined around his head and reared its wide-spread jaws over the stupid Oriental eyes of the image. Altogether it was a most singular-looking "josh," and more than one of the party (as it was subsequently acknowledged, though every one protested at the time that it would be a wanton outrage against the Japanese) came to the secret determination to get possession of it before leaving the port. No one had the face to molest it *then*, from the simple fact that we knew that the Japanese spies had kept their glasses (they get these through the Dutch at Nan-ga-sa-ki) on our every movement since leaving the ship, and that they would visit the cave immediately after night to see if we had carried off any thing. So we went away empty-handed, if I may except an unfortunate young bat which was mercilessly crowded into a large-mouthed bottle by our enterprising assistant naturalist and acting junior engineer, L. M. Squires, Esq.

While making our exit from this heathen temple, we noticed that the archway which led to it was about one hundred yards long, crooked like an elbow, from five to ten yards in width, and of an average height of about fifteen feet; while the water measured seven fathoms at the mouth, decreasing as you neared the rotunda.

Knowing all this, it was very easy for me to return for Mr. Josh a few days later: but the sleepy old fellow had disappeared; and, whether the Japanese fisherman or one of our own party had anticipated me, I have never learned to this day.

Among other shell-fish we found a very fine mussel along the shores of this bay, which took the place of inferior oysters admirably. I don't know what we should have thought of them had we had access to an ordinary market-place; but, living on salt beef as we then were, they proved any thing but unacceptable.

Having almost completed the survey of the Straits of T'Sugar, which separate the great island of Nipon from that of Jesso, the Vincennes and Cooper now sailed upon their last cruises previous to our arrival at San Francisco, while the "old John" remained quietly at her anchor. Seeing the Vincennes and Cooper thus put to sea, and knowing we were to follow their example upon the following day, the Japanese "chin-chined Josh" to an alarming extent, thanking their idols for relieving them of the foreign vessels. The sound of their huge drums and shrill wind instruments had scarcely died away, however, when a fresh arrival took place in the shape of three English war-steamers, one of which was towing a fourth. This latter we at once took to be the Russian steamer Vostock; but, as she drew nearer, she proved to be our old friend the Tartar, with whose officers we were acquainted. We therefore went on board to pay them a visit and hear the news; for the last time we had seen them (during our survey of the straits) it had been reported that the English and French cruisers had discovered the Russian squadron stowed away in the Bay of Castries, and we thought, of course, that there had been a grand battle.

Upon reaching the deck we were received by the most disgusted-looking set of warriors that I ever looked upon. We shook hands warmly, and tried to get them to tell us about "the fight;" but all we could get out of them for a long while were the following words:—"The beggars cut stick in a heavy fog, and left us sucking our fingers." After a while, however, they became more communicative, and we learned as follows:—

While Admiral Sterling, in the Winchester frigate, with the assistance of the steamer Hornet, was blockading the Russian vessels moored in Castries Bay, a fresh gale blew on shore, causing him to haul his wind for an offing; and, when this gale with its accompanying fog had passed over, the Russians had disappeared, ships and all. The Hornet immediately landed a party, who found things in great disorder, there being all the appearances of a hasty flight. Bread just done to a turn was found in the oven. Twenty barrels of good flour, a quantity of spars, and, lastly, some ladies' dresses and trinkets were also found: these latter were retained by the captain of the Hornet to be restored to their owner on a future occasion. A daguerreotype of a lady was also found which had been taken in London.

Our friends told us all this, and ended by saying that the "beggars" must be somewhere in the Gulf of Tartary, and that they would soon find them again; but we of the "old John," some three months later, learned, from one of the Russians themselves, that they passed through the head of the gulf and into the Amoor River, where they had fortified themselves in the hope that they would be followed. It had always been a received truth that there was no passage between the island of Sagalien and the mainland; hence the mistake of the Allies.

On the 29th of June, 1855, we left Ha-ko-da-di through a dense fog, in order that, when the usual clearing-away at noon took place, we should be in a position to conclude our survey of the Straits of T'Sugar, having been directed to end that work previous to proceeding up the west coast of Jesso. In order to facilitate the accomplishment of this task, I was ordered to take the armed launch, twelve men, a week's provisions, tent, &c., and follow the coast as far down as a station known as "West Point," where we were to be picked up by the ship at the end of three days.

By means of various ingenious devices — such as enlarging upon the great number of deer that we would fall in with while "camping out," &c. &c. — I was so fortunate as to secure the companionship of old bust-proof and his master for this expedition; but, before it was over, the latter lost all confidence in my predictions, and concluded to oil up his favourite and stow him away for an indefinite period when he should return on board. We also carried along with us one of the tightly-encased small boys of dingy notoriety, to take charge of the contents of our camp-kettle, &c. His name was Mr. John Jeremiah McCarty, and he was equal to all the other boys in the ship as far as juvenile rascality and activity were concerned.

The fog clearing off at noon, we left the "old John" in high glee and commenced the work. West Point proved to be about half-way between Ha-ko-da-di and the larger city of Matsmai, and was reached toward the close of the second day, when we pitched tent for the second time, and amused ourselves by breaking one of the agreements *appended* to the treaty by shooting several finely-flavoured wild ducks, with red legs and feet and pointed bills. When subsequently spoken to about thus breaking the treaty, I threw the blame on the Japanese officers themselves, who, probably from a desire to see how our guns carried, had strongly advocated the act by unmistakable signs and gestures. It is astonishing how well people can make themselves understood upon agreeable subjects, though unable to speak a word of each other's language. In this case we understood them perfectly.

Our first night at camping out was one of some excitement. We had been refused permission at Si-mo-da to do the very thing in which the launch was then engaged, and, from a most unpleasant custom of the Japanese,—*i.e.* the seizure and binding of strangers, and their removal to Yeddo,—we entertained reasonable fears of at least being disturbed in our slumbers. In order therefore to avoid as much as possible all communication with the natives, our tent was pitched at least three miles from any visible habitation. A large fire was soon kindled with drift-wood, supper cooked and dispatched, and a *ci-devant* tailor (armed to the teeth) placed upon post-with orders to call the purser and myself in case of any arrivals. I have every reason to believe that this "marinized seamster" went immediately to sleep; for, after we had vainly devoted hours to the same end, we suddenly heard voices at a distance, and, upon leaving the tent, found him seated after the fashion of his craft, and unable to answer.

Upon reaching the elevation of the bank, and looking in the direction from which the voices came, a beautiful sight presented itself to our eyes: no less than forty or fifty Japanese, each bearing one of their fancifully-painted lanterns, were moving toward us at a rapid pace. They did not seem to fear detection; but, in order to "provide against all precautions," we got under arms, six of us being at the boat and eight at the tent.

As they continued their approach, they talked in very loud tones, (to give each other courage, one of the men remarked;) but, as soon as they saw us awake and prepared, a halt took place, and one of the party advanced alone. Upon being met by me without any blood flowing, he was followed by others of his company, and, the purser now joining with bust-proof and the tent-guard, we were soon engaged deeply in the mysteries of pantomime.

It would be tedious to explain the numerous signs which the constant necessity of driving from their coasts strangers with whom they cannot exchange a word has placed at the disposal of these people: it will be enough to say that in the present case, assisted by the few words of their language picked up at Si-mo-da and Ha-ko-da-di, we made ourselves very fairly understood. And the following is the result of a half-hour's pantomime, sprinkled over with some twenty words.

Japanese, (with a look of command.)—"Put up your tent, put every thing into your boat, and sail away."

American.—"We are going to sleep here to-night and sail away in the morning."

Japanese, (look of command changing to one of affected terror.)—"You can't sleep here to-night: if you do *my* head will be cut off by the governor."

American.—"Oh, no! we have been to Si-mo-da and Ha-ko-da-di, and know that it is only one of your stratagems to get strangers away without resorting to force."

Japanese, (with a most funeral-like expression of countenance.)—"It is true: we never joke: I must lose my head."

American.—"I am very sorry: we will all cry very much. But, as the wind is against us, we will sleep here to-night, and sail away to-morrow if the fog clears away. If the fog remains, we remain."

Japanese.—"How many of you are there?"

American.—"Fourteen men, fourteen rifles, and fourteen revolvers."

Japanese, (with great vivacity of manner.)—"All right. You are going in the morning. Don't go back into the country. Go to sleep. We'll be back early. Good-night."

And, thus saying, the party retraced their steps, talking in a very lively manner, very unlike men upon the brink of decapitation. Just as they were moving off, the purser heard a noise on the bank above, and, climbing up with "bust-proof" through the rank grass, reached the summit just in time to see some forty or fifty others scampering away among the bushes. They had surrounded us without our being aware of it, although the "marinized seamster" did hold out that, if there *was* any direction in which he *had* watched, *that* was it.

True to their promise, they *did* return the next morning, and at a most fortunate moment. The day was just breaking; it had come on to blow since midnight; the launch was gradually dragging in the heavy surf, and we had either to haul her up on the beach or put out into the bay. As it was still very foggy, the former was determined upon, in spite of the danger attending it, and they arrived just in time to assist us. They found twelve of us up to the neck in the surf, while the remaining two guarded the arms; and, though the most violent pantomime failed to induce them to take to the water, while assisting us to haul, they nevertheless did good service at the end of the boat's painter. They seemed perfectly reconciled to our stay, and the head-officer laughed heartily when asked as to the method he had adopted in rejoining his head to the trunk.

They partook sparingly of our breakfast, evinced the usual curiosity in regard to every thing in our possession, understood with apparent pleasure that we were making charts of their islands, praised the accuracy of the sketches which the yeoman of the ship (who accompanied us) had made, and finally begged that we would fire one of the rifles at a mark.

Fortunately, one of the boat's crew was a really fine marksman, and there was no objection to gratifying their curiosity; so, a piece of drift-wood being put up some hundred yards down the beach, he put a ball very near the centre with "the utmost non-she-lan-cy."

This shot caused them the greatest wonder at first, but was shortly attributed to chance, and it required a repetition of the exploit to convince them of its commonplace nature.

They remained with us some time, making signs upon various subjects; and I was surprised to observe the amount of knowledge possessed by this evidently-inferior class of officers in regard to European affairs, or rather in regard to the affairs of the world outside of Japan.

They were not only aware of the existing war, but had a very fair idea of the causes which led to it. They said that Russia was very large and France and England very small, and asked "why America didn't join one side or the other and put an end to it at once."

They have an idea that the whole Western Continent belongs to the United States, and that we are more powerful than any other two nations put together: of course we did not undeceive them in this respect. They were fully aware of the railroad then in progress across the Isthmus of Panama, knew that the discovery of gold in California was a late affair, and, in short, asked so many unexpected questions, that one was forced to the conclusion of their being in more frequent communication with the outer world than is generally supposed.

In reply to their question as to America joining in the war, I told them it was peace and commerce which had made us so powerful, and that it was our policy to be friendly with all nations as long as they acted fairly by us; that, when they abused our citizens or violated treaties, then we declared war. This allusion to breaking treaties seemed to give them some uneasiness. They asked if Nipon (in speaking of Japan or the Japanese Government they always use the word Nipon) had yet broken the treaty made with Commodore Perry, and, upon being answered in the affirmative, cast their eyes upon the ground and looked hypocritically sad. They next supposed that, as Nipon had broken the treaty, America would fight Nipon as soon as the ships could come out. This was a difficult question to answer: we could find neither words nor signs to express ourselves, and therefore looked very grave and shrugged our shoulders with evident effect.

I now in turn began to question the headman. I asked him why he had caused us to be surrounded the previous night, knowing as he must that America and Nipon were friends; and his answer was characteristic of their well-known policy. They who we thought had surrounded us were poor country-people, the scum of the earth, persons to be spit upon by such as us, (he and myself,) &c. &c., and that they had come of their own accord simply to see what was going on.

His manner, however, contradicted this explanation; and, upon my accusing him and Nipon in general of insincerity in most of their dealings with us, he laughed cunningly, as if it were a fine trait we were discovering in their character, and returned to the subject of our "going away."

This pertinacity annoyed me almost to the kicking-pitch, but I contented myself with informing him that we should leave when we were ready, and not before; and that as for persons prowling around a tent at night, Americans often mistook them for wild beasts and fired their guns accordingly. This information, or rather the manner in which we were forced from lack of words to impart it, (to wit, pointing the gun at his breast, and then advancing rapidly till it came in pretty sharp contact with his fifth rib,) threw the headman into a state of indignant reserve, which proved even cherry-brandy-proof for as much as five minutes,—*i.e.* until the bottle began to look empty.

In this manner the morning passed along drowsily enough, only one thing occurring worthy of note. This was the passing by of some high mandarin and retinue, who were transporting an extensive lot of matchlocks in the direction of Ha-ko-da-di. To this "big bug" the Japanese in our vicinity went on their knees while giving what we supposed to be a history of our arrival, detention, &c.; and the "big bug" himself, after hearing said history, frowned loweringly upon our party, much to the indignation of Mr. John J., who gave vent to his feelings through various contortions of the body and countenance, accompanied by a well-known sign, supposed to be of Masonic origin, and addressed (behind my back) to the angry official. It was singular to see a dozen grown-up men on their knees before a stupid-looking official, while a stranger boy, almost a child in years, was indulging in the most ridiculous pantomime at his expense.

This party consisted of some fifty men, and probably of as many horses, many of the former carrying lacquered poles with gilded heads, to which were attached streamers

JAPANESE OFFICIAL COMMUNICATING WITH A SUPERIOR.

of different colours and shapes; while some of the horses carried the more important personages of the party, and the remainder burdens of matchlocks secured on each side in the shape of packs. And here I will remark upon the great number of horses which exist upon this island. Almost every village has several droves, some of which are used under the saddle by officers and couriers, but the greater number in the transportation of dried fish, &c. In height they average only from fourteen to fifteen hands, but are compactly built, and most mule-like in their powers of endurance. You see them travelling along the beach under their packs, in single file, and with the bridle of one fast to the saddle of another. In this manner one or two men easily drive any number. They are shod and unshod as the nature of the road demands,—not with iron shoes, but with a socket of platted grass, which, singular to say, lasts several days.

I embraced the opportunity presented by this somewhat military display, to make the best inquiries I could as to *the army* of Japan, and, from what I learned, combined with like information received from Tatz-nosky, came to the conclusion that they had no army at all. The feudal system of Middle-Age Europe prevails here with a healthy if not an increasing vitality, and in the existence of this system is found their much-talked-of army. The Government, for instance, has a fort to be taken or defended. The work is given to some particular prince or nobleman, who, with his peasantry,—or, more properly speaking, his slaves,—proceeds to obey his orders. If his force prove insufficient, a second high officer is ordered to join the undertaking; and so on. And in this lies the secret of their army of two millions, against which so many timid people in the United States were afraid to send so small a squadron as Perry's. I sincerely believe that Commodore Perry, with the force he then had at his command, could have waged a successful war against the whole empire of Japan.

At 2 P.M., the weather moderating and the fog lifting, we struck every thing in haste, and proceeded on for West Point. Just before shoving off, however, we received a present from the "headman," in the shape of two ordinary chicken-cocks, which caused us to rub our hands as the hour for supper crossed our minds. I don't know what we should have done, in lieu of rubbing our hands, had we known to what respect their extreme age and toughness entitled them: they proved impenetrable to even our scurvy-threatened teeth.

This is one of the many rewards attendant upon a cruise of that nature. We were *forced* to live upon salt beef, ditto pork, and insipid preserved meats, for (in this case) eight months, with forty gallons of lime-juice on hand to retard the arrival of the scurvy. But to return to more pleasant subjects.

Three or four hours carried us into a small cove in the vicinity of West Point, partially sheltered from the surf by sunken and other rocks, in which we dropped anchor, pitched tent, and made other preparations for passing the night. It was here that we discovered the great antiquity of our presents; and, a new set of the ever-watchful Japanese coming on us about this time, and signing us to shoot some ducks, we readily complied with their intimation, producing them a momentary gratification and ourselves a fine supper. The next day we were picked up by the elongated anchor-hoy commonly known as the "old John," and the day following saw the conclusion of the survey of the Straits of T'Sugar.

As I remarked in the last chapter, we found three foreign vessels at anchor among the Japanese junks. These were the Hamburg brig Greta, which we had chartered at Hong-Kong to bring us a supply of coal and provisions, the English surveying-schooner Saracen, who was engaged on work similar to ours, and the American whaling-brig Leveret, which had arrived some days previous, on the strength of Commodore Perry's treaty, to land her cargo and its owners and then continue on her whaling-voyage. The supercargo of the Greta, who was a very agreeable companion, in spite of his fondness for exploring caves, (?) showed us a list of liquors, cigars, &c., from which we could supply our mess for months at an advance of fifty per cent. over Hong-Kong prices. But when it came to provisions we were woefully disappointed. There was nothing in that line save the regular Government-ration; and some of the mess sighed heavily as they looked forward to eating salt pork and beef for the next several months and probably arriving at San Francisco half disabled from the scurvy.

We found the passengers by the Leveret in as much trouble with the authorities about setting up a ship-chandlery on shore as the nomadics had been in at Si-mo-da; and Commander Rodgers was now boarded by both parties, praying that he would see the governor and insist upon the treaty being respected. The result of this was a forcible appeal on our part in their behalf; but it was unsuccessful, and both vessels soon sailed in disgust, the Leveret on her whaling-voyage, and the nomadics for San Francisco.

And now I will end this chapter by showing how these unfortunates,—men who had been regularly *swindled*, by what purported to be a treaty, into investing "their all" in a venture to Japan,—I will show, I say, how our Government left them in the lurch and upheld the cunning interpretation which the Japanese placed on a phrase of said treaty.

Upon arriving at San Francisco and applying at Washington for indemnification for the losses they had sustained through the palpable treachery of the Japanese, they were informed that the phrase "temporary residence" did not mean temporary residence; that they had nothing to complain of; that the phrase meant, as the Japanese said, "a day's walk into the country," or "a few days on shore," or something equally absurd. I wonder when any more Americans will risk their capital upon this treaty, which cost us several millions?

CHAPTER XVI.

WE PASS BEFORE THE GREAT CITY OF MATSMAI, TO THE WONDER OF THE JAPANESE, CONTINUE TO THE NORTHWARD ALONG THE WEST COAST OF THE ISLAND OF JESSO, BEAT A JAPANESE OFFICER ON THE HEAD, AND FINALLY ARRIVE AT THE TOWN OF TOMARI, WHERE WE HAVE A GOOD LOOK AT THE AINU, OR "HAIRY KURILES"—THE LAST OF JAPAN AND THE COMMENCEMENT OF A HEAVY FOG.

It was on the 1st of July that we ended the survey spoken of in the last chapter, after which we continued along the west coast and anchored that night off the great city of Matsmai. There we found only an open roadstead, and we did not approach near enough to take interest in the appearance of either land or city.

The running survey upon which we were engaged was in itself a probable violation of the treaty, and the captain was naturally averse to any further infringement of it in the shape of going on shore, except for the purposes of wooding ship or obtaining astronomical observations necessary to our work. He therefore, expecting some of us to make a terrestrial demonstration, and disliking to refuse the necessary permission, anchored several miles off, evidently to discourage all shore-going parties; and this must account for my passing Matsmai with only a few words. The same inconvenient though doubtless proper restriction, being to a greater or less extent continued up the whole coast, deprived us of many opportunities of observation and relaxation, which, joined to the unavoidable drawbacks attendant upon all cruises of this nature, made us long more and more for San Francisco and a month's respite. *We* had seen enough of "Japan and the Japanese."

The next morning at an early hour we had hove up our anchor, and were again under steam, standing in for the land, intending to skirt the face of the city as close as the depth of water would permit.

Matsmai, from all that we could see of it while thus passing, is a city of considerable extent and imposing appearance. Situated in lat. 41° 25′ N. and long. 140° 02′ E. of Greenwich, its inhabitants enjoy a temperate climate and that greatest of luxuries,—an abundant supply of pure and cool water. This water, as it flows from the springs which the purser and myself found around the base of every hill, is actually *too* cold to drink in any quantity. Ice, though covering the summits of the mountains, which lift their whitened crests over the inland portion of the city, has no charms for the people of Matsmai.

Situated under the west point of the roadstead, and extending along the beach some two miles to the eastward,—having its feet washed by the surf, and retreating some half-mile back among the hills,—the elevated portions of the city rising from gentle undulations or from the summits of sloping hills studded invariably with fresh and green-looking trees,—Matsmai presents a most pleasant scene for the eye to rest upon. It is upon these hills and undulations, surrounded by regularly laid-out grounds, groves of shade-trees, and apparently-beautiful gardens, that the Government-buildings and residences of the higher class appear to be located. There was one

JAPANESE TEMPLE.

large pagoda-like structure in particular, which, with its grounds, seemed to occupy the whole of the highest hill, and which, from its imposing elevation, would make—probably *does* make—an admirable signal-station. Perched upon its very summit, the greensward, sprinkled here and there with shady groves, extended from it in every direction until a white paling-fence, (it looked strange at first to see our well-known paling *whitewashed* fence *in Japan*,) forming a circle of probably a mile in circumference around the base of the hill, seemed to bar its farther extent.

In addition to this, I counted no less than four large temples or josh-houses, each having its grounds and groves, its greater or less elevation, and its neat paling-fence. It is a beautiful spot to look at; and, in spite of my experience at Si-mo-da and Ha-ko-da-di, I could not avoid thinking that it would bear a closer inspection as far as cleanliness was concerned. We passed along before Matsmai under low steam, carrying safe water well in with the beach, and watching through our glasses the excited natives who crowded the water's edge to see "the large junk that sailed with her sails furled." Like the Chinamen on the Wan-chew River, it was "a huckleberry above their persimmon."

Leaving the master, with an armed boat and his astronomical instruments, at the point making out from the west end of the city, the ship herself devoted the rest of the day (plus four hours of the night) to the examination of two islands on the southern horizon, and, after returning for the boat, continued on to the northward with the first gleam of day. It was this kind of service which tried the powers of both men and officers,—working from daylight until dark on those long days, and then often devoting half of the night to finding a safe anchorage at which to sleep through the remaining darkness. Many persons who read these lines by a comfortable fire may possibly think that they would enjoy the excitement and novelty of an "exploring cruise around the world:" I can only say that I thought so once myself.

On the 6th inst. we found ourselves near a prominent point, and, the weather being favourable, the master landed again with his instruments. There being a hilly, well-wooded country coming down to the very beach, the assistant botanist was ordered to strap up his portfolio and land also. This point was the southwest extremity of a passably-fair bay in which we found anchorage for the night. Besides his various vegetable discoveries, the assistant botanist made several in the animal line. He chased, unsuccessfully, several hare, (such as are found in Lower California,) gave a wide berth to several savage-looking natives, and finally fell in with a gray wolf making a late breakfast from a slothful hare. This fashionable repast he interrupted through the instrumentality of a well-directed stone, and secured what was left (one hind-leg) for preservation in spirits of wine.

As I have already remarked, we anchored in that bay for the night, and there the miserable policy of the Japanese was more glaringly demonstrated than ever.

Two bateaux, paddled each by two of the lower class of Japanese, (*the people*,) came alongside after much persuasion, with great trembling and evident fear, and, mistaking our signs of welcome for applications for a few clams in the bottoms of their boats, readily passed them on board, accepted a few trifling articles in return, and were becoming quite lively and pleasant, when a third bateau, paddled also by two men, came rapidly within hail. The after-paddler of this third bateau, calling to them in a threatening and brutal tone, beckoned them off from the ship with the most violent gestures, and, not content with thus driving them away, confiscated their paddles, with which he beat them severely over the head, made their boats fast to his, and thus towed them in-shore, where a severe bambooing probably awaited them.

I had the satisfaction, ten minutes later, of using a boat-hook in conjunction with the shaven head of one of that fellow's brother-officers, who, while I was sounding around the ship in obedience to orders, had the impudence to *wave* his "ten-scull" boat to be sculled alongside of our cockle-shell of a dingy so as to render oars perfectly useless. His object was to prevent our going any nearer the shore; and, after motioning him out of the way several times without success, I resorted to the boat-hook application with most satisfactory results. These people propel their bateaux (most Japanese boats merit the appellation of bateau rather than boat) with from one to twenty sculls; and it is astonishing with what skill they will manage them. They progress either ahead, astern, sideways, or diagonally, as circumstances may call for; and, if they wish to prevent a strange boat from proceeding in a certain direction, all they have to do is *once to get alongside*, and the progress of that boat is at an end until a boat-hook or something of that sort is called into requisition. But to leave generalities. After receiving one blow they got out of the way even faster than they had got into it, and proceeded toward the ship with a caution that indicated the fear of there meeting a similar reception.

There were five mandarins in this boat, each armed with two swords, when I raised the boat-hook; and, instead of offering to draw them, they tumbled one over the other out of reach of it in a most *un*mandarin-like style, and did not resume their stupid haughtiness of manner until clear of all possible contact. I don't know that I should have been half so determined had previous experience not stamped their class as the most arrant cowards: as it was, I returned on board and blew my trumpet as a man of great readiness of action.

At this place we saw, for the third time, the Ainu, or "hairy Kurile." The first specimen was seen at Ha-ko-da-di, where he had drifted as one of the crew of a coasting-junk; the second lot received a "wide berth" from the assistant botanist; and now they were becoming quite plentiful. I will, however, defer their description until we come to a place under the northeast point of this island, where we remained a day taking in wood from their boats, and where they literally crowded our decks during that occupation.

Leaving our anchorage, after having bought some four cords of wood for as many yards of broadcloth, we continued along the coast toward Strogonoff Bay. It had been the custom of those people from time immemorial to hurry off all ships anchoring in their waters by giving them wood, water, and a few provisions, gratis, and then telling them to go to sea at once or entail upon the "headman" the unpleasant necessity of having his throat cut. And this was exactly the manner in which they now acted to us, even though the treaty says that "payment shall be made in gold and silver." After we had received the wood they positively refused to receive *any thing* in return, and the cloth was only accepted because we would not bring it on board again.

It was most amusing to see how quietly they permitted us to walk through the town on the following morning after having tried to prevent our even sounding in the bay during the previous evening: my impression is that a firm bearing, backed by even a small force, is all that is required to cause these officers (not the people) to behave with respect and consideration to any stranger.

Our *ci-devant* whaler, "Bunsby," told us that a few years back he cruised in these latitudes, and that, upon landing at Matsmai for supplies, the whole boat's crew were *forced* down upon their knees before a stupid-looking dignitary, and retained in that position until the withdrawal of the great man set them at liberty. With us, however, the case was widely different. When we landed at this last place, a dense crowd of Kuriles and the lower class of Japanese pressed from all quarters to see us, and were driven away (evidently to show us respect) with brutal blows and violent language. One fellow in particular dealt his blows around with such utter disregard to the safety of heads and limbs, that many of the shrinking crowd either jumped or were pressed off the mole; and I noticed one little girl who was thus injured so as to require being helped out of the water. But to go on with my narrative.

Running along the shore during the day, we, as usual, anchored at night near a small town, and about 9 P.M. were boarded by a bateau sculled by two Japanese, one of whom seemed, from his dress, to belong to the class of officers. He wore no sword, however; and it may here be worthy of remark that since leaving Matsmai, up to the present time, we have stopped at no village (the one of the boat-hook exploit excepted) where were persons residing entitled to wear two swords.

Well, this nocturnal arrival came over the side in an easy, lounging style that was quite new in a Japanese, and, the captain being on deck, several of us accompanied him into the cabin with the new-comer. He displayed some uneasiness when the door was closed, but regained his off-hand manner as soon as he saw a decanter and glasses join the party. The first thing he did was to take from his capacious garment a bundle of lacquered cups and saucers, which he presented to the captain, at the same time pointing to the decanter and glasses and intimating his desire to be presented with one in return. At this we all laughed heartily: the fellow had evidently boarded vessels with a like object before. Seeing us laugh, he looked a little annoyed, and gave us to understand that "it was only at night that speculating visits were permitted in Nipon." I can't imagine what he thought we laughed at. The conduct of this man gave us a good opportunity for remarking a most unfavourable peculiarity of this undoubtedly deceitful and treacherous people. While we were laughing at his expressive pantomime toward the glassware, his companion came down, and, crouching on the deck, looked anxiously in the same direction.

They were both longing to be presented with a glass; but, when one was held out to each, both shrank back in well-feigned alarm, and, holding up the right thumb, gave us to understand that to accept was as much as their heads were worth; and yet in less than ten seconds after this they both had their glasses stowed away under their garments. This they accomplished by concealing them, in apparently a hurried manner, while their heads were alternately turned away; and that this turning away of the head was "Nipon custom" there is no doubt: in fact, they told us as much. Shortly after this successful feat they took their departure, but again returned shortly after midnight, and yet again upon the following morning in company with the headman of the village. On this latter occasion one of the cruets disappeared from the captain's stand, though unfortunately the discovery was not made until too late to expose the thief. The result of this was an order to let no more Japanese boats come alongside unless upon business. That was the first and only case of theft that we experienced while among them.

We were surprised to find here immense droves of deer in the immediate vicinity of the town; and the doctor with his Kentucky rifle, and the purser with everlasting "old bust-proof," went on shore the morning after our arrival to try to bring some on board. They had seen some of the skins stretched against the sides of the houses, undergoing the process of drying; and the people had made signs to them that the dense cane-brake which backed the town was full of them, and that they were at liberty to shoot as many as they desired. They therefore entered the brake in high glee; but, though they saw a few here and there, and heard hundreds of them rushing through the canes, the growth was so dense as to render such a thing as taking aim impossible. They consequently returned empty-handed and in great disgust, to be informed by Martin, the steward, that our preserved meats were almost expended, and that, if "the gentlemen" didn't shoot something soon, we would be in a starving condition.

At this place we took in another supply of wood, saving our coal for the Okotsk Sea, and here succeeded in making payment in the shape of tea, sugar, rice, &c. Here we also caught a fair supply of small rock-cod, which rendered the breakfast-table so attractive as to open the state-room doors half an hour sooner than usual.

Continuing on to the northward with a leading wind, we passed the English frigate Winchester and brig Bittern, apparently beating down for Ha-ko-da-di. As usual, we were running quite close in with the land, and they, ever on the look-out for the absconding Russians, came well in before the unmistakable proportions of the elongated anchor-hoy convinced them that we were not the Vosgoth under American colours.

The southern corner of Strogonoff Bay gave us shelter during the following night, and the next day, taking advantage of a moderate southeasterly gale, we succeeded in sighting Cape Romanzoff, the northwest extremity of the island. We found this cape very well located on the chart; and, had the weather been clear, the eye might easily have crossed the Straits of

La Perouse and rested upon the southern shore of Sagalien. This latter island, which is larger than Cuba and smaller than Nipon, is said to be divided between the Chinese and the Japanese,—the latter holding the southern half, while the former claim the northern. Its native population are the Kuriles; but, whether they are entirely or partially subject to their double masters, I am unable to say. I conversed in Ha-ko-da-di with an English officer who had lately landed near the centre of the west coast of the island, and who spoke of them as "wild-looking fellows, very hairy, clothed in a coarse sack, and fearful of coming out of the bushes, from which they peeped at his party like so many wild cattle."

As usual, Carnes was landed at Cape Romanzoff with his instruments; and, while the astronomical observations were going on, the ship herself ran down to two islands on the western horizon, hoping to sound around them both before dark. In this, however, we were woefully disappointed, for the sun left us before the first circle had been completed, and we had the pleasure of feeling our way back through a combination of water, fog, and darkness. And here it may be well to caution all vessels passing through the Straits of La Perouse to give Romanzoff a berth of at least a mile and a half, as there is a reef making out to the north-northwest from that cape, whose length is a mile or more, and of which no indication exists on the chart. We anchored some time after midnight, and the shivering master, upon his return on board, expressed himself in emphatic language against all such nocturnal excursions.

The next day we attempted to follow the shore of Romanzoff Bay, toward Cape Soya, to the eastward, but found so many hidden dangers in the shape of reefs and sunken rocks that we gave up the idea and steered straight for the town of Tomari. Here we anchored for the night, and devoted the remainder of the day and part of the next to wooding up. Any vessel seeking shelter in this bay cannot be too careful with lookout and lead. It is the worst ground we passed over during that cruise; and yet Golownin speaks of it as "a fine large bay, having regular water and good holding-ground," &c. Possibly we may have devoted too short a time to its examination, for we found this writer generally remarkable for closeness of observation and accuracy of statement.

The town of Tomari, situated in this bay and immediately under Cape Soya, the extreme north point of the island, is one of the numerous fishing-settlements of the Japanese, which line the coast from Matsmai up. In fact, this latter city itself was settled centuries since simply to establish a firm footing on an island singularly remarkable for the quantities of salmon which fed along its shores, and which on the more northern end "were often so plentiful as to be dipped out with hand-nets and paddles." Whenever you see an indentation in the coast, there you find one or more of these villages: I don't think we could have passed less than several hundred of them. And this great population along the sea-shore certainly renders probable the assertion of Golownin, to the effect that the island of Jesso is without population in the interior, the nature of the country being unfavourable to cultivation. And, from what we ourselves have seen of the diet of these people, the sea-shore *must* be their most desirable location. I doubt if two Japanese out of three ever eat any article (rice and sweet potatoes excepted) which they do not obtain from the sea. Fish, shell-fish, gelatine, and almost every variety of sea-weed, are regarded as wholesome, and some of the latter are really very palatable. Almost every one has, when confined to a sick-room, relished a bowl of Irish or Ceylon moss; and much of the Japanese sea-weed, when cooked, resembles that preparation. May not the succession of villages along an uncultivated sea-shore, as seen by all vessels passing on their voyages, have given rise to the prevalent idea of the marvellous population of the empire? And does not this succession of mountain after mountain, of range rising above range, indicate the existence in their bosoms of great mineral wealth? I am no geologist, and therefore am not entitled to an opinion; yet, from what I saw, heard, and read while in and about Japan, I believe that gold, quicksilver, and coal exist in abundance in the mountains of Jesso. But to return to the town of Tomari.

This, as I have before remarked, was a fishing-settlement, and contained some hundred houses, with a probable population of from six to eight hundred: of these some fifty or more are Japanese, and the remainder the native Kuriles. Of these latter we had seen several hundreds at our various "wooding-up" places; and now I will proceed with my necessarily incomplete description of their general appearance, habits, &c.

Dr. Pritchard, in his excellent work entitled "The

Natural History of Man," has, upon the authority of various writers, the following page in regard to the subject:—

'The best account of the Ainos that we have yet received is to be found in the narrative of Von Krusenstern's voyage.

"Some particulars respecting them were given by La Perouse and Broughton. The former of these writers says that 'the Ainos are rather below the middle stature, being at most five feet two or four inches high. They have a thick, bushy beard, black, rough hair, hanging straight down; and, excepting in the beard, they have the appearance of the Kamtschadales, only their countenance is much more regular. The women are ugly enough: their colour, which is dark, their coal-black hair combed over their faces, blue-painted lips, and tattooed hands, allow them no pretensions to beauty.

"La Perouse says 'they are a very superior race to the Chinese, Japanese, and Mantschoos, and their countenances are more regular, and more similar to those of Europeans. . . . . The inhabitants of the Bay of Crillon were particularly beautiful and of regular features.' The same writer adds, that 'their skin is as dark as that of the Algerines.' Broughton says 'they are of a light copper-colour;' but Von Krusenstern declares that they are nearly black.

"But the most remarkable circumstance in the physical character of the Ainos is, that, though the eastern Asiatics are in general very deficient in hair and almost beardless, they are the most hairy race of people in the world. 'Their beards,' says La Perouse, 'hang upon their breasts, and their arms, neck, and back are covered with hair. I observed this circumstance,' he adds, 'as a general characteristic, for it is easy to find individuals equally hairy in Europe.

"Broughton declares that their bodies are almost universally covered with long, black hair, and that he observed the same appearance even in some young children."

The foregoing is what Dr. Pritchard says on the subject; while Golownin, writing from personal observation during his strange captivity, remarks:—

"The appearance of the inhabitants of Matsmai, (Jesso,) and of the other Kurile islands, shows clearly that they are of one race; the features, the uncommonly-brown colour of the hairy body, the black, shining hair, the beard,—every thing, in short,—indicate a common origin. The only difference between them now is, that the Ainu of Matsmai are handsomer, stronger, and more active than the Kuriles, to which, perhaps, a more active life and abundance of good food have greatly contributed; for the Japanese have traded with them for these four centuries, and bring them not only rice, but even articles of luxury, such as tobacco, sage, &c. The other Kuriles, particularly the northern ones, live in indigence, feed on roots, sea-animals, and wild fowl, of which they, indeed, are never in want; but idleness often hinders them from collecting a proper stock, so that sometimes they pass several days without food, in indolence and sleep. . . . . In trifles the Kuriles like to imitate us: thus, for example, they shave their beards and wear long tails. The Ainu, on the contrary, wear their beards, and cut their hair like the Russian wagoners, only something shorter.

Our Kuriles wear Russian dresses of all fashions, as they receive them; for the Ainu, on the other hand, the Japanese prepare a certain dress, according to the Japanese cut, and of hempen cloth, which resembles our coarse, unbleached sailcloth. The elders receive cotton and silk dresses. If one of them particularly distinguishes himself, the Japanese Government rewards him with a splendid dress embroidered with gold and silver, or with sabres in silver scabbards. . . . . The Government has ordered that the Ainu shall not work for any Japanese, not even for the crown, without payment. For every kind of work a price is fixed, with which they are, however, not content, because it is not answerable to their labour." And again:—"The Ainu live in winter in what are called jurten, or huts of earth, and in summer in straw huts, in which they have no benches or seats, but sit on the ground, either on the grass or on Japanese mats. Their food consists of rice, which the Japanese supply them with, of fish, sea-animals, sea-cabbage, wild herbs, and roots. Many have gardens in the Japanese fashion; others employ themselves in the chase: they kill, with their *spears* and arrows, bears, deer, and hare, catch birds, and also eat dogs. . . . . The Ainu are, in general, extremely uncleanly. They never wash their hands, faces, or bodies, except when they have to go into the water to do some work: they never wash their clothes. . . . . Polygamy is allowed among them: they have two or three wives, and the elders still more.

"They have no writing, and, consequently, no written laws: every thing is handed down from one generation to another. . . . . The total want of words of abuse in their language is a proof of their mildness of manners. . . . . The sun and moon are their divinities. But they have neither temples nor priests, nor any religious laws. . . . . They have here [Matsmai] oaks, firs, yew, cypress, birch, lime, various kinds of poplars, maple, aspen, mountain-ash, and many others. . . . . Of quadrupeds there are bears, wolves, hares, rabbits, deer, wild goats, sables, and field-mice; in summer, geese, ducks, and swans visit them. In general, all the same sorts of land and sea birds are found here as in Kamtschatka."

My own observations proved the gentlemen from whose works the foregoing have been so freely quoted, to have been well informed in the first case (except it be in the case of universal hairiness of body) and a true observer in the last; while, at the same time, they enable me to make a few general comments.

The hairy endowments of these people are by no means so extensive as the foregoing quotations lead one to suppose. As a general rule, they shave the front of the head *à la* Japanese, and, though the remaining hair is undoubtedly very thick and coarse, yet it is also very straight, and owes its bushy appearance to the simple fact of constant scratching and seldom combing. This remaining hair they part in the middle and allow to grow within an inch of the shoulder. The prevailing hue is black, but it often possesses a brownish cast, and these exceptions cannot be owing to the sun, as it is but reasonable to suppose that they suffer a like exposure from infancy up. Like the hair, their beard is bushy, and from the same causes. It is generally black, but often brownish, and seldom exceeds five or six inches in length. I only saw one case where it reached more than half-way to the waist; and here the owner was evidently proud of its great length, as he had it twisted into innumerable small ringlets, well greased, and kept in something like order. His *hair*, however, was as bushy as that of any other. As this individual was evidently the most "hairy Kurile" of the party, we selected him as the one most likely to substantiate the assertion of Broughton in regard to "their bodies being almost universally covered with long black hair." He readily bared his arms and shoulders for inspection, and (if I except a tuft of hair on each shoulder-blade of the size of one's hand) we found his body to be no more hairy than that of several of our own men. The existence of those two tufts of hair caused us to examine several others, which examinations established his as an isolated case.

Their beard, which grows well up under the rather retreating eye, their bushy brows, and generally wild appearance and expression of countenance, give them a most savage look, singularly at variance with their mild, almost cringing, manners. When drinking, they have a habit of lifting the hanging mustache over the nose; and it was this practice, I suppose, which caused an early writer to say, "their beards are so long as to require lifting up." Though undoubtedly below the middle height as a general rule, I still saw several who would be called quite large men in any country; and, though the average height be not more than "five feet two or four inches," they make up the difference in an abundance of muscle. They are a well-formed race, with the usual powers of endurance accorded to savages indicated in their expan-

THE AINU, OR HAIRY KURILES.

sive chests and swelling muscles. Their features partake more of the European cast than any other. They are generally regular, some even noble, while all are devoid of that expression of treacherous cunning which stands out in such bold relief from the faces of their masters,—the Japanese and northern Chinese. I cannot but agree with the author of the foregoing remark as to their superiority over those nations.

The clothing of those who came under our observation never consisted of more than three articles, and seldom of more than one. Generally, a dressing-gown-like garment, made from the inner bark of an abundant tree, reaching as low as the knee and confined round the waist by a sash of similar material, constituted their entire suit. Occasionally they wore grass sandals, sometimes even leggings of woven bark reaching as high as the knee; but these cases were rare. Krusenstern says that "they clothe themselves with the skins of dogs and other animals in winter," but we saw no signs of any such garments. Probably they clothe themselves lightly in summer in order to appreciate the warmth of skins during severe changes.

The Ainos are unpleasantly remarkable as a people in two respects,—viz.: the primitive nature of their costume and their extreme filthiness of person. I doubt if an Ainu *ever* washes; hence the existence of vermin in every thing that pertains to them, as well as a great variety of cutaneous diseases, for which they appear to have few or no remedies. There is another side to the picture, however, and it is a bright one. Their moral and social qualities, as exhibited both in their intercourse with each other and with strangers, is beautiful to behold. They are a people who, if once restored to the freedom of which they were so glaringly deprived, would be peculiarly fitted, both by superiority of intellect and natural mildness of disposition, to receive the truths of a gospel against which sensuality and innate rascality close the eyes of the nations which surround them. I am not unaware of the fact that years have elapsed since the introduction by the Russians of the tenets of the Greek Church into their more northern islands, and of the very few sincere converts which that doctrine has obtained: but what more can be expected when the priest visits his flock but annually, remains a few days, and then leaves them to the association of sailors and Russian hunters, the nature of whose lives is by no means calculated to impress them favourably in regard to their religion?

"Love to one's neighbour," true generosity of disposition, a general cheerfulness of manner, and a modest and retiring bearing, are general characteristics which strike the eye of even the passing stranger. It is greatly to be lamented that a single bold stroke of villany on the part of the Japanese should have degraded a great part of their race to an apparently-endless servitude.

I cannot account for Broughton's assertion in regard to their being of "a light copper-colour," unless he referred to a few isolated cases. As I have previously remarked, we saw several hundred men, women, and children, and these were all of a *dark brownish-black*, with one exception; which exception was a male adult, strongly suspected of being a half-breed. In regard to the several quotations which I have inserted from the truthful pages of Captain Golownin, I see nothing that clashes with my own experience. From our own observation since arriving in Japanese waters, we have all been forcibly struck with the remarkable truthfulness of the contents of that writer's pages: it is undoubtedly *the best* work extant on Japan, (Commodore Perry's not excepted,) and as such may be read with confidence by all who feel an interest in that mysterious people.

The Ainu mode of salutation at joining and parting company is worthy of remark. They bring the tips of the fingers up to the eyes, cast the latter upon the ground, and, in a low voice, indulge in quite a lengthy harangue, while stroking the beard from the eyes downward. This latter operation is repeated as long as the harangue lasts, at the end of which they glance toward the person saluted, and, if he is looking another way, the process is repeated until they catch his eye. This also seems to be their manner of returning thanks for any present received. Their sign of farewell, however, consists in a repeated elevation and depression of the extended hands, something after the manner of an *Irish* nurse dancing her charge at arm's length without regard to consequences. (I have had a latent feeling of revenge against all Irish nurses ever since one of them "danced" me out of her arms upon a brick pavement some thirty years since.) In addition to this, when one is leaving *in a boat*, they throw after her receding form curiously-carved sticks of spruce, whose fine shavings drawn curlingly to either end give them very much the appearance of a calker's paying-mop previous to saturation in the boiling pitch. What this ceremony means, or what was the nature of their mumbled words, we were never able to learn.

So much for the "hairy Kuriles:" and now for the winding-up of our survey along their coasts.

Having filled up with wood at Tomari, (for which the Japanese would receive *nothing*,) and fixed the astronomical position of Cape Soya, the northeastern extremity of Jesso, we rounded this latter under steam, and filled in the coast-line as far to the southward as Cape Shaef, when, a dense fog putting a stop to all further work, the head of the old *ci-devant* anchor-hoy was again pointed to the northward, and, after we had crossed the Straits of La Perouse, we anchored near a rock known as "dangerous" since the time of the unfortunate La Perouse. At least, our dead reckoning and the distant bellowing of seals indicated us to be in its vicinity; but whether we were or not the dense fog rendered it impossible for us to say. This was the same fog that had arrested our work on the previous evening, since which time our circle of vision had certainly not exceeded one hundred yards in diameter; and, if it was to be the exponent of the weather we were to expect throughout the Okotsk Sea, we were indeed entering upon a desperate work.

"Blindman's buff," among children, is undoubtedly a pleasant species of recreation; but, when it comes to be indulged in between vessels and rocks, its character assumes quite a different phase. We were now clear of Japan, and at anchor upon the verge of the Okotsk Sea, awaiting a fair wind to carry us across it to the southern point of Kamtschatka.

This was the 15th of July, 1855.

CHAPTER XVII.

WE REACH THE PENINSULA OF KAMTSCHATKA, FOLLOW ITS WEST COAST TO THE NORTHWARD, AND DISCOVER A COAL-MINE AND A HALF-BURIED VILLAGE—AFTER WHICH WE PROVE A NEW-FASHIONED BOOTJACK, AND TAKE A DIP INTO THE SCIENCE OF GEOLOGY—WE FIND THAT SHOWER-BATHS ARE NOT ALWAYS CLEANSING.

WE had not long to wait for our fair wind; and, though anxious to locate "dangerous rock" astronomically before leaving those unknown shores, we finally despaired of the fog clearing away, and called, "All hands up anchor!" The location of that rock would have been a most appropriate winding-up to the vast amount of work which we had accomplished since the commencement of this portion of the survey at the quiet port of Hey-da.

The end of a half-hour saw us under all sail and no steam, with the propeller disconnected, and a fine breeze on our quarter, progressing at the promising (?) rate of *four and a half knots an hour* upon our foggy path of over six hundred miles. Poor "old John!" miserable old tub! Months have passed since I and my companions in misery left your fated hull to the tender mercies of the officials of the San Francisco navy-yard, and thus deprived you of the power of drowning us some fine morning; but I saw, by the Philadelphia "Evening Bulletin" of April 30, 1856, that you have been provided with a new set of flesh-and-blood machines and sent up to Puget Sound to engage in warlike deeds with the Indians, instead of being broken up for firewood. How have those officers and men rendered themselves obnoxious to the "powers that be," dear John, that they should be thus sent to sea in such a miserable old craft as you are? Are we so plentiful and useless just at present that a few from our midst won't be missed? or is it that the Government can't *afford* to break you up and build a *safe* vessel? But my feelings are running away with me, John; and so let us return to our passage across the Okotsk Sea; which having accomplished in eight days,—sharp work for you, John!—we rub our eyes one morning about three o'clock, and, shading them with the right hand from the rays of the rising sun, gaze upon a long, low sand-beach, which our chronometers tell us is the west coast of Kamtschatka.

It was on the morning of the 24th of July that we, cautiously feeling our way with the lead toward the expected shore, discovered the low sand-beach already mentioned. Further than that there was nothing to be seen, the weather being so hazy as to shut out entirely the high land of the interior. Toward noon, however, it lighted up, and enabled us to get good observations on the beach; after which we hoisted up the boat and steered a north-by-west course along the beach, keeping it in sight at from one to two miles' distance, and carrying beautifully-regular soundings over a fine anchoring-bottom of mud and sand. These soundings we made at regular intervals of ten minutes, and for hours and hours there would not be the fourth of a fathom difference between them. It was a vast marine plain that we were sailing over, and the land itself was low and level and not elevated more than a few feet above the sea. I had expected to find a country of volcanoes and a dangerous and variable bottom. Possibly there were volcanoes in the interior and an uneven bottom farther out to sea; but, for the last few days of our passage from Japan, the lead had told us that we were sailing over a beautifully smooth and inclined plain. We were agreeably disappointed in all this; and, the heavy "chop-sea" through which we had rolled for the last week having left us, and the day still continuing beautifully clear, we began to flatter ourselves that coasting along Kamtschatka was going to be a very fine thing. But, before I follow this coasting any further, let me say a few words about the depth of water, &c. between the Straits of La Perouse and the point where we rubbed our eyes, some one hundred miles to the northward of Cape Lapatka, the southern extremity of the peninsula along which we were running.

As I have already remarked, we were engaged eight days in the passage, being under sail only, as it was necessary to reserve our coal for the actual work of surveying. During these eight days we sounded with deep-sea twine whenever the ordinary line failed to get bottom, and thus kept up the "line of soundings" with great success: only once did we fail, and then twelve hundred fathoms were run out with no sign of bottom; the breeze blew quite fresh, and caused us to drift away from the lead too fast. Both before and after this failure, however, less line brought up specimens of the ocean's bed.

These specimens generally consisted of mud and sand, dead shells, and small stones, the former often containing a singular worm, incrusted in a brittle shell resembling in form the figure 8, and which, upon being broken out of said shell, twisted about the deck in a most lively manner. They retained life in the atmosphere several minutes after being thus exposed,—longer than one would have imagined, when it is recollected that they had previously existed under several hundred fathoms of water.

Many persons have an idea that in the high latitudes of Kamtschatka and Siberia even the *summers are cold:* our thermometers during the passage gave us an average temperature of 50 degrees, while we subsequently found it uncomfortably warm. And this was in lat. 60° N. We found the weather, as a general thing, very changeable,—sometimes disagreeably cool, and then again quite warm.

On the 26th, having run some two hundred miles to the northward, we came to the first high land yet seen; and here our soundings began to lose their beautiful regularity, and the coast, taking a bend to the eastward, caused us to change our course to N. by E. Before doing this, however, we came to anchor, lowered a boat, and placed her at the disposal of the master, to enable him to land on the beach and fix the position of this point by astronomical observation. A number of the mess, curious to feel the soil of "despotic Russia" under their feet, or hoping to shoot an eatable animal of some sort, took passage with him, while we, the remainder, amused ourselves by fishing.

A number of fine flounders, and *one immense crab*, rewarded *our* exertions, while the shore-party returned shortly after noon, full of glowing accounts of black bear and gigantic salmon, but without either the one or the other: they had neither killed or caught any thing, and were in high glee at the prospect of fried flounders and lobster-salad to be made from the enormous crab, whose legs had to be broken off to get him into our largest pot.

This fellow, I think, deserves more than a passing comment; for I have subsequently searched in vain for his counterpart through various authorities, and am forced to the conclusion that they are a half-crab, half-lobster freak of nature, larger even than the latter, and existing only on those or similar unfrequented shores.

I say "they," because the shore-party reported the beach as being crowded with similar shells, the meat having been most probably scratched out by the bears, which abound along that coast in great numbers. Some of the shells seen were from seven to nine inches in diameter, almost round, and quite thick and strong. It was in the claws that the animal resembled the lobster, every thing else being more like the crab. When the fellow that we had caught alongside was spread out on the deck upon his back, his legs measured three feet two inches from tip to tip; and when we turned him over he raised himself on those tips several inches above the deck, as if to command a better view of things in general. His smallest legs were as large as one's little finger; and it was in one of these that the hook had accidentally caught, the shell being strong enough to lift him over the ship's side. Taking the taste of the bears for good authority, we immediately boiled and transferred him into a crab-lobster-salad, sufficient for the whole mess, and, unlike the lobster, remarkably juicy and tender. The doctor listened to several writhing applicants during the succeeding night.

After all, it seemed that our shore-party had narrowly escaped a most unpleasant time. Upon arriving near the beach, the surf was found to be running very high; but they went at it boldly, and, jumping out at the right time, the boat's crew ran her up "high and dry." They were very well content to get wet no higher than the knee.

The master then occupied himself with his observations, while the ramblers started with their guns and revolvers back into the country. The sight of large and numerous bear-tracks served to create a feeling of affectionate companionship which kept them pretty well together: they had no idea of attacking Bruin on his own soil, singly, and advanced with prudent caution as they neared a ridge or turned the bend of a ravine. Finally, they came to a river—a broad and noble-looking stream—whose snow-fed waters seemed alive with salmon of the largest description and capable of floating a liner for miles into the interior. They did not reach its mouth, however, and could not say if it was free or crossed by a bar: from our past observation we inferred the latter.

They found the country sandy, undulating, and miserably barren; not a sign of habitation, and, in short, a most cheerless-looking spot. They returned to the boat, after an hour's tramp, with a few semi-transparent stones as their only prizes, and were there received with the information of "a dozen or more bear" having been seen by the boat's crew farther down the beach.

"What a pity we didn't go that way!" said one.

"Maybe it's better we didn't," said another.

"*I'm* going after them now!" said a third.

"And the boat's going on board," said the master, as he closed his boxes and beckoned to the crew.

"Just like our luck!" exclaimed the last speaker, in a voice of fleeting disgust: "we might as well have stopped on board."

Ten minutes later, and the boat was at her davits, while the shrill whistle of our only boatswain's mate was ringing around the silent decks, calling the wearied crew to the oft-repeated work of heaving up the anchor, and telling of work, work, nothing but work, as long as the daylight lasted. Another ten minutes, and we were again under way, continuing through rain and wind the interminable coast-line,—a stormy end to an unexpected spell of good weather.

We had not worked along thus many hours when the wind hauled ahead and increased to a gale; so we had to heave to and let it blow by. It lasted all that night, and we were rapidly losing much of our hardly-gained ground, when the weather fortunately moderated, and we were enabled once more to close in with the beach and continue the survey. As we thus worked our toilsome way to the northward, we found the low, flat land along which we had been hitherto running, gradually changing its nature to that of bold and towering heights that lifted their snow-clad crests far into the foggy sky and shoved their rocky bases well out into the sea in the shape of rugged promontories, whose frequent ravines were filled with melting snow and dark, shapeless rocks, and whose ridges and sides were covered by a dense and luxuriant vegetation. It was singular to see the snows of the North and the rank vegetation of the South existing alongside of each other, where we had expected to find nothing but the former and a stunted growth of the arctic pine.

Every now and then we would pass a turbid stream that owed its periodical existence to the melting snows of the last winter; and we would generally see a wandering bear, or flock of geese or ducks, near its mouth, when we would amuse ourselves by sending a Sharpe's-rifle messenger to notify them of our proximity, though the distance was always too great to enable us to fire with any precision.

As we thus ran along over that unknown ground, with a good look-out, bad charts, and an active lead, as our only pilots, we would often stop off the mouths of those rivers, or under the sheltering heights of those rugged promontories, to get astronomical observations; and, upon these occasions, our assistant botanist would accompany the shore-party, and generally return with some rare or previously-unknown arctic plant, while the *gunners* of the party would often get highly excited over "fresh bear-tracks," and probably bring back with them something more substantial, in the shape of a brace of finely-flavoured ducks, or some unfortunate goose.

The observations which were thus obtained invariably proved our best charts to be dangerously incorrect. Upon one occasion I remember that we found the ship's position (on the chart) to be some distance in-shore. This we regarded in the light of a most innocent shipwreck, and enjoyed it accordingly. When this took place, we were in lat. 58° 40′ N. and long. 158° 43′ E., the beach bearing from northeast to southwest of us, and distant about five miles. We subsequently experienced many similar shipwrecks, and upon one occasion found ourselves upon the side of an extinct volcano that was actually more than sixty miles from the sea. So much for the amount of reliance that can be placed upon the best charts of that region. Those which *we* then obtained data for, and which will shortly be forthcoming from the able hands of Commander Rodgers, will consequently be of rare value to our whalers, who frequent that coast, and annually lose one or more of their fleet simply from *the want* of good charts.

As we thus made a running survey of those unknown regions, we took good care to obtain and preserve not only specimens from the hills and beach, but from the bottom of the sea also. We had two species of "patent leads" for this latter work, and they both acted admirably. One of them was intended for bringing up specimens of the bottom when the depth of water exceeded two or three hundred fathoms, and did actually once bring up a thimbleful of sand and mud from the enormous depth of three thousand five hundred fathoms. That was in the North Pacific. The other was intended to be used in from one fathom to one or two hundred, and it often brought up a pint or more at a single haul. It was curious to wash out these specimens in a bucket of water and hunt for shells and other "wonders of the deep" in mud and sand that had existed at the bottom of the ocean for centuries in their undisturbed seclusion.

It is also worthy of remark that both of these admirable inventions sprang from the brains of two of our own officers,—the shoal-water one having been made in Hong-Kong, under the immediate direction of Commander Rodgers, while the "deep-sea explorer" was got up by Passed Midshipman (now Lieutenant) John M. Brooke, the able astronomer of the expedition, and who is even now trying to bring it before the notice of Congress.

In anticipation of these leads "working well," we had provided ourselves with several hundred small vials, in which every thing worth preserving was stowed away, after which it was sealed up and labelled carefully, for future examination.

There was one remarkable fact which we noticed about the soundings along that entire coast: this was their remarkable regularity, without regard to the greater or less elevation of the land along which they were obtained. Generally speaking, (as in the case of the northern and southern shores of the Mediterranean,) soundings are found to vary with the nature of the land; that is, deep water is generally found off bold headlands, and shoal water off low ranges: but in this case we found only ten or twelve fathoms abreast of the highest points, which was no increase to what we had carried along extensive tracts of country whose greatest elevation was not probably more than fifteen or twenty feet.

These towering, precipitous, and black-looking points presented a totally different appearance, when you were abreast of them, from what they did when their sides only were exposed to view. It seemed as if they were mountains of loose black rock that had been lightly covered by a fertile soil, and then the end of them that projected into the sea broken off and transported to "parts unknown," leaving their black-looking faces in striking contrast with their green sides and snow-filled ravines. We found them occurring at intervals of several miles, invariably enclosing long strips of a shingle or sandy beach, from which the green lowland retreated into an undulating country which was itself backed by the blue mountains of the distant interior. These latter were generally either perfect or truncated cones, and combined with other unmistakable signs to establish the fact of previous volcanic action.

It was an interesting occupation to watch these changing scenes through our glasses; and as we watched them, we admired the native grandeur of those towering promontories, the shining beaches darkened here and there by mountain-torrents flowing from the ravines of melting snow, the undulating country covered by its short-lived but rank vegetation, and the distant cones of heavenly blue, and could not but regret the prevalence of those arctic winters which for eight out of the twelve months cover such a beautiful region with one vast mantle of dazzling snow. This poetical state of mind, however, received a severe shock on our first landing, through the instrumentality of thousands of swarms of the gallinipper-breed of mosquito, who, regarding us in the light of most welcome visitors, soon succeeded in stinging us into a far different mood of feeling. These attentions of theirs brought vividly before my slumbering memory the assertion of a long-unseen messmate, to the effect that "the mosquito, though a small insect, had often been known to move a man weighing over two hundred," and, further, caused us to return on board with good appetites, the result of the unlooked-for exercise which we had been forced to indulge in in sheer self-defence.

We not only saw mountains and green grass as we thus cruised along, but would often fall in with one or more wandering whale-ships, sometimes homeward bound with full cargoes, sometimes hove to under reduced sail while their boats were chasing a whale, and at other times riding to their uneasy anchor off some rocky shore while engaged in "trying out" the oil of some captured monster, whose huge carcass, after being deprived of its blubber, would be cut adrift from the ship's side and allowed to float unheeded before the wind and sea, while another of his ill-fated companions, who had all along been moored securely astern, would then be hauled up to undergo a like "stripping."

We would generally heave to or anchor near all such vessels, and communicate with them, in the hope of getting information in regard to a reported coal-stratum that we were in search of, or to give them tracings of our surveys, and were more than once amused at their peculiar mode of navigating. Upon asking one of their captains how he found the charts, he replied, in an indifferent, don't-care sort of way, "Oh, pretty fair; I don't find any thing much out:" and, upon our telling him of some of our previously-mentioned "innocent shipwrecks," he expressed great surprise, and *guessed* that he'd "better be taking another observation soon;" and, upon being pressed a little further on the same subject, he candidly acknowledged that he had not used his chronometer for a month,—having been too busy with whales to pay any attention to the position of his ship. At that we ceased to wonder over the loss of so many whalers: our only wonder was that so many ever reached home in safety.

I have already remarked that we were in search of a reported coal-mine. We had heard from a whaling-captain that it existed along the northern part of that coast, and that he had once picked up a boat-load of it on the beach, which burned beautifully in his stove, &c. &c. But unfortunately he had not taken any observations for some weeks at the time of his discovery, and was consequently unable to give us its latitude within any thing like reasonable limits. We only knew, therefore, that there was *said* to be coal along that coast at *some* point, and that, unless we found it, the "old John" would soon be left to depend upon her sails alone for motive-power and our chances of ever reaching San Francisco be alarmingly decreased. We consequently kept a good look-out as we ran along the broken shore, and in the end were amply rewarded for our pains.

It was about two hours after the noon of July 30 that we threw our maintopsail to the mast, stopped the engine, and hove to off the entrance of what promised to be a fine and extensive harbour, which we subsequently determined to be in lat. 61° 15′ N. and long. 161° 31′ E. We had followed the coast down very closely heretofore; and, as the general appearance of the land about this entrance gave greater indication of the existence of coal than any we had yet seen, the captain determined to run in for the night at any rate, and leave again the next morning should we fail in discovering any.

As we had no chart of this harbour, however, as we could see a huge pile of rocks off its mouth, and as there was a very heavy swell running in at the time, it would have been any thing but prudent to have risked the ship by entering without some previous examination; and so a boat was lowered, and I, having the watch below, was called to go in her. We had a fine time getting in after we were once started, for the light whale-boat skimmed over the heavy swells like a feather, sinking out of sight in their deep valleys, or being lifted on their rolling breasts, as the case might be. We stopped every two minutes to get a cast of the lead, until the water began to shoal to ten or twelve fathoms, when we began to cast it as fast as it could be hauled in.

As we thus pulled in toward the passage, the harbour opened beautifully, and I began to think that we were finding a magnificently-protected anchorage on those inhospitable shores, when suddenly the lead gave but four fathoms, then three, and lastly only two, as the depth of water. So we immediately turned and pulled at right angles to our former course, when the water again deepened, seeming to promise a fair anchorage under the huge pile of rocks already alluded to, and which we now found to lie right in the centre of the entrance to the bay. As we pulled in this new direction and looked back at the harbour, there could not have been presented a more promising appearance of good entry and subsequent shelter.

It was in the form of a pot-hook, the handle being represented by the mainland, and the hook-part by a towering and curved promontory, while the "huge pile of rocks," which proved to be one immense irregular mass surrounded by an infinite number of smaller ones, was situated equidistant from either of those points, and about a mile seaward of an imaginary line drawn from the point of the hook to the opposite side of the handle. At this latter extremity of the line, where it joined the mainland, were to be seen several mound-like objects, having posts and poles stuck in and around them, and looking very much like one of the half-buried villages which we had read of as being common to Kamtschatka. We could see no smoke, however, and thence concluded it to be uninhabited.

In passing the rock for which we were now pulling back, I had expected to find good water inside the hook; but, upon arriving at our imaginary line, it had shoaled, as I say, to two fathoms, and so, having given up all hope of finding an anchorage for the ship inside of the hook, we were now looking for one under the shelter of the rock. This latter, though quite small when compared with the false harbour, was nevertheless quite large enough to break the sea as it rolled in, thus creating a kind of uneasy anchorage under its lee, that was only acceptable from the fact of there *being no other;* and I therefore picked out a twelve-fathom hole, having a mud bottom and passably-smooth surface, and, having let go our little anchor near its centre, hoisted a flag as a signal to the ship, which had been following the boat slowly in, that she might come thus far, at any rate, without danger. In about ten minutes after this, she was alongside of us, when she let go her anchor, and commenced to roll with such energy that we experienced no little difficulty in approaching and climbing her rusty old sides.

The noise created by the chain in running out after the anchor, seemed to cause considerable alarm to immense numbers of a large and black duck-like bird, that had their thousand nests in the crevices of the rock under which we had anchored, and who left said nests with a sharp discordant cry, as the unusual sound startled them in their isolated haunt and caused them to fly over and about us in inconceivable numbers. They proved to be the aquatic fowl vulgarly known as the shag, and to the ornithologist as the "Phalacrocorax cristatus"—a crested, long-necked cormorant, that we subsequently shot in great numbers as an article of food, (don't start, reader,) though I must acknowledge that the captain and a few other philosophers were the only ones that ever succeeded in the treble task of swallowing, keeping down, and properly digesting their (to me) unsavory flesh. From the *immense* numbers of this bird which covered this pile of rocks, we called the principal one "Shag Rock," and, as such, included it in our survey.

We had no sooner furled sails and got the ropes laid up about the decks, than two boats were called away,—one to go in search of coal along the inner shore of the curved promontory, and the other to follow down the mainland to the bottom of the pot-hook. In the first of these boats went the captain and Lawton; while in the stern-sheets of the second reposed the master and our indefatigable doctor, with his small-bore Kentucky rifle to keep him company. Some of us also took the tomtit, (a boat smaller even than the dingy,) and pulled over to Shag Rock, with a heavy ship's musket and revolver each, where we soon commenced blazing away among the unfortunate shags and northwest parrots, with an energy of action and destructiveness of aim that promised to fill our boat before long.

Though I had pulled in from the ship through hundreds of this latter bird while feeling the way for her, I have, until now, neglected to mention them, simply because it was not until our landing on Shag Rock that we were enabled to get a close view of them. I have, since my return to the United States, searched through more than one writer on birds, hoping to find a description of this particular rarity, but without success. In the shape of its bill it approaches the puffin, and, in the arrangement of its head-feathers, the little parrakeet-auk; but in other respects it differs widely from both of these birds. The opposite sketch is a mathematical drawing of the male and female, one-sixth life-size. I must therefore conclude that it is, at any rate, a rare specimen of the feathered tribe, and hence well worthy of a passing notice. The male is about the size of a large teal-duck, is covered with dense masses of variously-coloured feathers, and has the head and bill *of a parrot*, (hence the name given it by whalers,) surmounted, in the case of the female, by a rooster-tail-like crest of several inches in length, and, in the case of the male, adorned by two side-tufts as in the engraving. It is web-footed, has red legs, and in brilliancy of plumage is not excelled by the well-known Mandarin-duck of China, or the beautiful wood-duck of our own country. It was a fine sight to see them falling around us at every shot; and, as we took them up and felt their great weight and plumpness, we looked ahead a few hours, and our mouths watered as we saw them at the head of an imaginary dinner-table, with the savory steam rising from their well-browned breasts, and the ready knife hovering over the upright fork.

But alas for all human anticipations! When we came to taste them, they were so tough, so fishy, and so musty, that it was impossible for the greatest lover of game among us to approach them: even the philosophical eaters of the less pretending "shags" shrunk aghast before this terrible disappointment, and loaded their plates with the black-looking fragments of the latter in preference.

When I say that our northwest parrot had the head and bill of the ordinary tropical bird of the same name, I must except the hole under the lower jaw, and the thick, black tongue of the latter; but in all other respects the resemblance was very close.

When we returned on board with a load of them after our impromptu shooting-excursion, we found that the exploring-parties had got back ahead of us, and that they had discovered a very accessible stratum of coal on the inner face of the promontory; also a small river, emptying into the bottom of the hook, whose mouth *was not* blocked up by salmon, as we had been led to suppose by

"NOR'WEST PARROTS"—(MALE AND FEMALE, ONE-SIXTH LIFE-SIZE.)

whalers; and they further told us that the "mound-like objects having sticks and poles stuck over and about them" had proved to be very comfortable houses, in which a number of natives were living. These latter were all males, however, and the entire apparent population of the village did not exceed fifteen souls. What they had done with their women and female children we never could ascertain, though we remained with them a week, during which time we traversed much of the surrounding country without seeing a sign of another living creature, not even so much as a bear. We finally concluded that they had some inner settlement, to which they had sent them for safe-keeping, and wisely gave up all idea of ever learning any thing on the subject. But let us return to Shag Rock.

While we were seated around our long mess-table, gazing vacantly at the overrated parrots, and slowly making up our minds to commence the attack upon a huge piece of salt pork, the quartermaster came down and reported that the tide had already fallen five fathoms, and that it was *still* falling. So, as we had heard from the whalers of these tides sometimes falling so much as to leave a ship anchored "high and dry" upon the rocks, we hurried on deck to see what it meant. Upon looking around, we were surprised to see the whole hook of the harbour some distance above the surface of the water, while pointed rocks had sprung up between us and the larger one under which we were anchored, like magic. This was the more singular, as we had noticed no upper current indicative of such a great rise and fall of tide, and we wondered without well knowing what to make of it or what to expect next. Fortunately, we still had seven fathoms under us, and, as it only fell one more, our minds were put to rest.

The morning after our timely discovery of coal, we "called all hands" bright and early, and sent Lawton, our chief-engineer, with his twelve firemen and coal-heavers, to attack it with pick and shovel, and to pronounce upon its quality.

He had orders to continue digging if he found it adapted to our furnaces, while the first lieutenant himself was ordered to have the bags and boats in readiness to bring it on board as it was dug out by the shore-party. Now, this was going to work without delay; but, as the first day would be likely to pass before they could get out enough to make it worth while to commence the transportation, several of us took advantage of the unexpected holiday to shoulder our guns and take a boat for the coal-stratum, which we proposed examining first and then starting back into the country for a bear-hunt as soon as our curiosity should be satisfied.

The wind was blowing quite fresh from seaward as we started; a heavy swell was also setting in through the channel which we had to cross, and the tide was falling so rapidly that we feared grounding inside of the hook before we should be able to reach the landing. It was quite cold, too, the air being down as low as 45° Fahr., and the water at about 48°; so that it would have been any thing but comfortable to have grounded near the middle of the extensive mud-flat and found ourselves under the necessity of wading on shore, or remaining in the boat with the retreating water breaking over us and the freshening breeze blowing it through our clothes for several hours, and, in the words of Hartman, chilling us fear*fully*. Nevertheless, this unpleasant alternative proved to be in store for us; and we only escaped it through the generosity of the boat's crew, who insisted upon jumping out as soon as we struck, thus lightening the boat greatly, and enabling them to wade her up to the nearest point of the beach. When we had thus reached the dry land, however, they paid severely for their kindness, in the shape of several severe cases of chills, which the doctor at once took in hand with professional activity and "knocked spots out of" at once. Being debarred access to his medicine-chest by a mile or more of salt water, he hauled a bottle of brandy out of his pocket, and, having divided it into six doses, told them to "drink that," after which they expressed themselves considerably "warmed up;" and, when we reached the blazing coal-fire which Lawton had already got under way, they might be said to have been in better condition than when we started.

Upon looking around us we noticed three or four coal-strata, instead of one only, and found, also, that they were quite extensive. They were from eighteen inches to three feet in width, ran at an inclination of about forty-five degrees with the surface of the sea, in a northwest and southeast direction, (which was about parallel with the trend of the valleys,) and passed entirely through the promontory. This latter was from three to four hundred feet in height, was possessed of very steep and precipitous sides, and was reared upon several most singular formations. There was feldspar, argillaceous iron-ore, and a kind of secondary sandstone,—a petrifaction evidently, for it existed in every stage of hardness. It was to be found all along the beach in the shape of perfectly-round balls of about the size of an orange, as well as in huge, shapeless fragments of rock. Some of these balls were so soft as to flatten easily under the foot, like potters' clay, while others were as hard as granite. These latter, if thrown forcibly against a large rock, would rebound with the elasticity of a billiard-ball, or shatter into a dozen fragments; and in the latter case they were invariably found to contain petrified clams, oysters, various other marine shells, and the *impressions* of a great number of ferns and other plants, many of which seemed no longer to grow on the hill-sides: at least I could not find any.

As for the shells of the clams and oysters, they were, generally speaking, perfect: they seemed to have become filled with earth, and then to have been gradually incrusted with it until they were perfectly round. In those which flattened under the foot we could seldom find shells, the half-decayed leaves and stems of plants being found to form most of their centres, around which, snow-ball-like, the outer coatings seemed to collect *as they rolled;* but how it was that they were rolled, unless by the ebbing and flowing tide, we could never imagine. It was singular to break open some of these hard, cannon-like balls and find oysters and clams inside of them, while there was not at the time to be found living specimens within miles of the spot. In fact, we never met with oysters along the whole coast. But the thing which surprised us most was the existence, in spots, of a greasy kind of clay, the like of which I had never before read of or seen. Walking along the beach, one would put his foot on what was apparently the backbone of a bed of dark-gray granite or sandstone, when, presto! instead of feeling a solid rock under his foot, he would find himself boot-top under; and, upon being assisted to haul his leg out, he would either leave his boot behind, or drag it out besmeared with a greasy paste, just for all the world as if he had stepped into a tub of soft soap. It acted the part of a bootjack for us more than once, and with admirable success.

In some places this singular substance ran from the mountain's side just like so much fat,—not in a stream, for its consistency was too great to admit of flowing; but we often found basins of it that had apparently *soaked through the earth*, and in these cases it was so thin as to admit readily of being stirred with a stick. In other places it was found in a more dense state; and in this latter stage it often proved a great drawback to us in our mining-operations, for, as it generally existed in layers over and between the strata of coal, we had to dig it away with shovels before we could get at this latter. It was so sticky that it often refused to leave the shovel, and the men complained greatly of its straining their arms. One man who attempted to heave a shovelful of it down the hill-side, while his footing was none of the firmest, had it stick to such an extent as to carry him down, shovel and all, upon the boggy pile, where he stuck horizontally upon all fours until some of his fellow-shovellers hauled him out. And there were two others who resorted to a "clinch" as the readiest mode of reconciling a difference of opinion, when the weaker party, falling upon his back with the clay under him and his antagonist on top, was left in that position by his now-satisfied foe without the most remote prospect of ever getting up through his own unaided exertions. He might just as well have been tied down, as was the great Gulliver, for even his hair stuck so fast that he could not lift up his head: all that he could do was to roll his eyes about and work his arms, which only served to "fit him" to greater advantage. Upon being assisted to his feet, he was heard to express himself against "clinchin'"—as the best mode of settling a dispute—"upon sich ground as this."

Before leaving, I rolled up a ball of the singular substance, intending to preserve it for future analyzation, but, unfortunately, lost it before an opportunity presented itself. This ball, which was at first of about the consistency of working-putty, soon became as hard as soapstone and susceptible of receiving quite a polish. It was of the colour of a yellowish-white clay, and without odour.

The general formation of the promontory was of sandstone of several different varieties. Along the beach, and projecting from the side of the cliffs, it was to be seen in the shape of huge boulders or pointed fragments, that had become blackened through the combined action of time and the elements and rendered as hard as granite; while in the beds of the ravines and gullies it was found in a secondary state, so soft that the water in running over it loosened the minute particles, and, carrying them along in suspension, rendered itself totally unfit for either bathing or drinking purposes. Catch a cupful of it as it fell clear and sparkling in the shape of a picturesque-looking cascade, and, before it was sufficiently settled to be drunk, there would have collected a teaspoonful of a greasy, paste-like sediment in the bottom; and, when we once went to take a refreshing shower-bath, as we flattered ourselves, under said picturesque cascade, it filled our eyes, ears, and hair to such an extent that we were glad to take a dip in the less-promising surf that was rolling at our feet.

The soil which existed on this sandstone as a base was of a loose sandy nature, and was sprinkled about quite liberally with patches of the "bootjack clay," which rendered running, leaping, and jumping along the mountain-side any thing but comfortable. We soon learned, however, to detect the presence of "a bog," as they shortly came to be called, and to guide our steps accordingly. These patches *on the hill-sides* almost invariably supported a hoarfrost-like growth, which, seeing nowhere else, we had but to *walk around* and keep on firm ground. Having no such warning along the beach, however, we did not fare so well. There it not only came up in the shape of a ridge of rock, as I have already observed, but it also existed in quicksand-like formations which there was no avoiding. Then, if you did not recover yourself with active readiness, you would soon be "boot-top under." I myself once "got my foot into it" so deep that, in bracing myself on the other to haul out by, the edge of the hard sand that supported me caved in and left me knee-deep, with a very small prospect of getting out without foreign help. I could lift either foot *half-way* out easily enough; but the angle made by the lower and upper parts of my leg (the knee being the vertex) would then become so small as to deprive me of the power of lifting it higher, and, when I attempted to bear my weight on it to haul up the other, I only worked down deeper.

I was glad enough when a couple of strong arms lifted me bodily out, minus one boot; and, after thanking my stalwart friend, *lay cautiously down* upon the hard part of the beach, and shoved my arm down after the missing article, which, singular to say, I drew out perfectly empty. It had collapsed as soon as my foot left it; and all that I had to do was to pull it quietly on and walk more carefully in future.

As soon as I had stamped my foot well down into the softened leather, and scraped off a pound or more of the adhering patent bootjack-mixture, I took a long stick and shoved it down the half-filled hole from which I had rescued my boot, to see how far I *might* have sunk had not a "friend in need" been at hand. It had gone down only about two feet when I felt a rock or some other hard substance; and we subsequently found that these "patches" seldom extended to a greater depth, so that, though considerably inconvenient, they were not at all dangerous.

CHAPTER XVIII.

WE LEAVE THE COAL-MINE FOR A HUNT, AND ENCOUNTER ANOTHER PARTY SIMILARLY ENGAGED—WE RETURN WITH THEM TO THE VILLAGE AND ARE HOSPITABLY ENTERTAINED—THE HEADMAN NOT AN ADVOCATE OF THE MAINE LIQUOR-LAW—HOW WE "COALED SHIP," AND HOW WE RAN A RACE WITH A FLOOD-TIDE.

THE last part of the previous chapter was chiefly devoted to the different formations about the coal-strata in general, and the "patent bootjack-mixture" in particular; and now I will leave Lawton and his dozen firemen digging away at its gum-like strength, and carry the reader along with the doctor and myself as we started to follow the swampy bank of the small river that emptied into the bottom of the hook at high-water, and which at low tide ran a mile or more over the flats of said hook, until it finally reached the sea at the imaginary line previously spoken of.

This hook, as I have already said, formed an inner harbour at high-water and an extensive mud-flat when the tide was down; and, as the river widened its channel considerably while running over it, thus decreasing its depth in proportion, there was no difficulty in crossing in a straight line from the coal-mine to the opposite village at low tides. In the present case, however, we determined to follow the river up into the mountains, in the hope of crossing the track of some bear or other game, and finally visiting the village on our return. So we left this latter on our right and the coal-mine in our rear, and trudged along through the soft and spongy turf and over the rugged tails of ridges that ran down and terminated at the river, until we had pretty well tired ourselves out, and arrived, not at the mountains, but at the conclusion that we had walked along the boggy bank quite far enough, and that if we expected to visit the village and regain the ship before night it was full time for us to be turning back and "stirring our stumps." So we took advantage of the first fordable part of the river to wade across, and soon found ourselves climbing the hills on the opposite side.

From the top of these hills we now looked toward the village over a treeless expanse of undulating land, whose broken surface was covered with a dense but dry turf, in which the foot sank over the ankle at every step, and whose occasional ravines were hidden by groves of dwarf pines, under which a long and wiry grass grew, and twisted, and turned, and retwisted itself, in such a manner as to render it any thing but an easy matter to work our way down, over, and up to the opposite heights. Still, even that was better than the muddy, spongy walking along the river's bank; and so we continued on over the yielding turf and through the tangled grass until we had crossed the last ravine and ascended to the extensive prairie-like plain upon the sea-edge of which the mound-like houses of the village were located.

We had not walked many hundred yards over this beautiful carpeting of grass before our attention was attracted by a shout upon our left, and, as we turned in that direction, we beheld a party of five persons, among whom we recognised Hartman and another of our mess-mates, while the remainder were buckskin-clad natives, who apparently had been pressed into their service as guides. These latter we found to consist of a father and two sons, the former of whom carried a smooth-bore flint-rifle, to which was attached a permanent rest in the shape of a wooden prong, pivoted at its vertex to the stock near the muzzle, while in his belt was stuck a short knife, and down his right leg, outside, in a socket worked in his leggings, a very long one. His sons were rigged out in a similar style, with the exception of having no gun; and they gave us to understand that when the old gentleman wounded a bear with his gun they drew their long knives to assist him in the conflict which followed. The short ones they used for cutting and eating.

As they joined us, we regarded them as curiously as they did us, for they were the first of their kind we had seen, though we had read much of their habits and seen many engravings of Kamtchadales in such works as Dr. Pritchard's "Natural History." I was surprised to find them entirely differing from those engravings; and my surprise lasted until we reached Ayan, when "old Frybark"—the Russian officer in command—explained it all away.

The Kamtchadales proper, he said, were mostly confined to the interior and east coast of the peninsula, while the few people found on the west coast (where we were) were a mongrel-breed, springing from Russians and the Ee-ah-couts Indians, and presenting the ethnologist with a most puzzling diversity of feature and general appearance.

These particular three whom we now joined—and, in fact, all of those whom we subsequently encountered in the village—were of ordinary stature, flat-featured, and of a sallow, olive complexion; and that is about all I can say of them. They were dressed in loose garments of reindeer-skins that had been well cured, with the hair inside, and the red and polished buckskin turned outside to bid defiance to every thing in the shape of briers, and almost to old Time himself. It was difficult to imagine how such clothes could *ever* wear out, so preserving a polish had they received from the combination of dirt and grease with which they seemed to be brought in constant contact.

Their trousers and boots—or rather, I should say, moccasins—were made in one, and a smockfrock-like garment came down half-way to the knee and was confined around the waist by a buckskin belt. This frock was provided with a hood, which usually hung down the back, but which could be hauled over both head and face at the pleasure of the wearer. When thus rigged out they were cold-proof, and in fact *water-proof* also, as long as they did not wade where it was more than waist-deep. Some of their clothes were sewed with waxed thread, obtained probably years back from wandering whalers, while others were more perceptibly, but with equal neatness and far greater strength, stitched together with threads drawn from the sinews of the reindeer or mountain-elk.

Although our examination of Hartman's companions was so very close, it was not a whit more so than theirs.

They mixed with us in perfect confidence, (though they had at first mistaken us for Frenchmen come to bombard their town, and now only had our word to the contrary,) and examined every thing about us with the greatest curiosity. And there I was surprised to see how well the *French* were known, and how totally the English were *un*known. "Franco no dobre," they would say,—French no good; but we could not get a word or even a look from them when speaking of the English. They drank a glass of brandy with undoubted gusto, and then commenced to examine our clothes, boots, weapons, &c. &c. What surprised them most, and excited their admiration to the highest pitch, was the fineness of the grains of our powder, which the father of the party could not cease comparing with his own, asking by signs if we had any to give away. We gave him to understand in return that we would give him a capful of it if he would shoot us a mountain-elk and bring it on board, upon which he danced around in frantic delight, partly from the effects of brandy and partly from those of joy, I suppose, and, when he had in a manner recovered his composure, informed us that as soon as he could get a horse in from the country he would mount him and ride away, after which we might soon expect to see him returning with a buck on said horse's shoulders. His manner of explaining to us that he was talking about a horse was simple in the extreme. He only straddled the forefinger of his left hand with the fore and middle finger of his right, neighed very horse-like, then clucked with his mouth, and, finally, belaboured an imaginary animal most unmercifully with his hide-covered heels.

After all this he went on to inform us that he should be perfectly contented when he should become possessed of so much powder; that it would certainly last him to his grave, and that when it was gone he would be willing to die. He never fired more than once at a deer, he said; and, throwing himself on the ground flat on his face, he planted his forked rest firmly, showed us how he called the deer toward him, how he took aim, motioned us to imagine him covered with bushes so that he could not be seen, and, having satisfied us fully on all these points, recovered his feet with the agility of a monkey, and followed us as we walked toward the village.

As we approached this latter, a number of shaggy dogs barked and howled at us as they retreated behind the piles of earth which we had justly taken to be the houses; and we were expecting to see crowds of women and children alarmed by said barking and coming out to see "what the row was," when our friend of the smooth-bore flint-rifle suddenly opened a door and motioned us to enter. It was a long, dark, and narrow archway, down which we peered as the door was opened; and a greasy smell of whale-blubber, half-cured fish, &c. that broke upon our noses, combined with the dim light of a murky fire in a distant apartment at its end, took away every thing that might have been pleasant in the prospect of resting our wearied limbs in a warm atmosphere. And, as we "hang back" at that door and look in one another's faces, as much as to ask, Shall we brave that odour? let me give the reader an idea of the outer appearance of those singular habitations.

They resembled the half of a long-necked gourd,—one

that has been split in half to make two drinking-cups of, and having a dozen or more pins stuck in the outside of the bottom of the cup, which, in this case, corresponds to the roof of the house. Altogether, they were most outlandish-looking houses outside; but, when you once entered them, the philosophy of their peculiar construction became beautifully apparent. The long, dark, and narrow archway down which we looked proved to be a passage of some four feet in width by forty or fifty in length, and was flanked on either side by angular spaces resembling the wings of a garret, which were admirably adapted for the storage of winter provender in the shape of dried seal and deer-meat, smoked salmon, whale-blubber, &c. &c., besides adding largely to the air-room—if I may be allowed the expression—of the house in general; and the "pins" proved to be poles connected with the cavity which answered the purpose of a chimney.

As we passed through this lengthy and gloomy passage-way, the "greasy odour" before alluded to grew stronger and stronger; and I for one had made up my mind, as we emerged from it into the spacious and bowl-like apartment, that my stay was to be of exceeding limited duration. Imagine my pleasant surprise, therefore, when I found that the air of this larger apartment was, comparatively speaking, quite pure. I drew a long breath of it as I became aware of the fact, and, advancing toward the fire, seated myself on a pile of deer-skins and began to look around me.

The first thing that I saw was a large and circular apartment, possessing a diameter of probably forty feet, a height of some fifteen in the centre, and which decreased dome-like as it neared the ground-part of the sides. In the centre of the curved ceiling there was quite a large aperture, and directly underneath this were piled a number of hearth-stones, over and about which a lately-built fire was smoking itself into a state of fitful "blaziness" in honour of our discovered approach and subsequent arrival.

Two boys, of about the ages of eight and ten, were seated upon their haunches near it, watching its growing power, and adding dry fragments of fuel as occasion called for. Like those who accompanied us, they were dressed in tanned (?) skins, with the hair inside, and, though of very small stature, were still rigged in every respect like their more elderly companions: they even had the two knives stuck in sockets worked in their trousers below the knee.

We soon found that we were in the house of the man of the smooth-bore rifle, and that these little fellows were his youngest children, while the other two whom we had first met were his elder ones,—the four constituting the male portion of his family. Where were the fair sex,—those fireside-ornaments? We looked around and asked in vain,—the only satisfaction we obtained being a wave of the headman's hand toward the mountains; and this we took to infer that they had been sent back into the country for safe-keeping.

As the fire now blazed up brightly and lit up the gloomy recesses of the extensive apartment with its uncertain light, we made the discovery that there were two rooms in one; that is, the fire was built in the centre of a circle of some twenty feet diameter, which put me very much in mind of the ring of a circus, the circumference of said circle being marked by upright posts that reached to and supported the ceiling. These posts were planted about four feet apart, and between them and the earthen sides of the house there was a raised platform of whale-ribs, rough planks, flat pieces of drift-wood, &c., over which were spread any number of bear- and deer-skins, upon which we were more than once invited to recline; but, as there were strong indications of the existence of vermin within their hairy depths, we confined ourselves to seats on the edge of the platform, which latter, being about a foot high, made a very comfortable seat as long as we kept our feet upon the earthen flooring of "the ring."

The posts to which were nailed the inner ends of the scantling upon which the platform was laid were rough logs from the dwarfed arctic pine, with the bark peeled off and the knots smoothed away with a knife; but they had been smoked for so long a time, and taken hold of by so many greasy hands, and rubbed against by so many greasy clothes, that they had become as black and polished as so many pieces of ebony.

After we had been seated a few minutes in this singular and uninviting habitation, the smoke began to get so thick as to cause us to rub our eyes and finally to weep outright; which the headman perceiving, he spoke a few words to one of his sons, who went and opened the door at the outer end of the long passage, when in less than a minute our enemy vanished through the aperture. The door was again closed, the passing current of air died a natural death, and the fire again began to warm the chilled atmosphere and to fill the room once more with smoke. They had to resort to the process of opening the door about every fifteen minutes after that; and upon one occasion they not only admitted a relieving current of air, but also the remnant of the then population of the village, consisting of two men and one small boy, who shook hands with us most affectionately, and pronounced the word "brandy" several times with remarkable aptitude, while with their hands and mouths they went through the process of drinking with equal success. There was no mistaking their meaning, and so the doctor produced a quart-bottle of French punch and gave them a pretty stiff horn all round. This they enjoyed excessively, even the three small boys crowding around to share in the unusual treat.

The doctor, however, did not relish the idea of giving strong drink to such small men, and told their father as much by signs; but the latter only laughed, and motioned him to let him have the bottle and cup a moment, when he poured out about a gill for each, and slapped them on the back as they coughed over its unexpected strength. Then he poured out all that was left, drank it down like water, and pitched the empty bottle to one of his still-choking offspring, who stowed it away in a mysterious corner for future use. It was subsequently a source of great surprise to see how much those people *could* drink and still not appear the worse for it. This headman, in particular, I once saw drink a quart-bottle of gin in less than half an hour, and the only difference it made in him was that he became more rough in his manner toward those under him and slightly unsteady in his gait. I tried to imagine how it was that they could drink so much without being made intoxicated, and could only attribute it to the greasy nature of their food and to the excessive cold of their winters, which call for a vast amount of animal heat.

Soon after the entrance of the "remnant of the population," and immediately following the destruction of the bottle of punch, the headman made signs that he was about to cook us some dinner; and, as we were both hungry and curious to see their mode of cooking, we expressed ourselves highly delighted at his hospitality. I don't suppose, however, that any of us thought for a moment of eating any thing he might get up, though we *were* quite hungry; for every thing around us looked so greasy and dirty that it was hard to imagine any thing about the premises capable of being cleaned.

There was a fine fire under way by this time; and the first thing they did was to plant a tripod-like structure over it, from the vertex of which hung a long iron pot-hook, from which, in turn, was evidently to be suspended some as yet unseen vessel. One of the small boys next rummaged this unseen vessel out of the same mysterious corner into which the empty bottle had disappeared, when, to our surprise, it proved to be a very civilized-looking iron pot, which the young explorer at once commenced to clean with great energy. This cleaning he accomplished through the instrumentality of quantities of fresh water, several handfuls of sand, and three or four bunches of clean, dry grass; and when he gave it its last rinsing out *the pot was evidently clean:* there was no fault to be found with *it.* I began to think that some of us *might* partake of their cooking, after all.

We asked them where they had got their pot from, and were told that a whale-ship had presented it to them many years back in exchange for a mountain-elk that they had carried on board, and that they would like to carry another mountain-elk on board of a ship and bring another pot on shore. So we entered into such an agreement, to our mutual joy.

Their next proceeding was to haul several halves of fine-looking salmon out of a greasy-looking sealskin bag, which they cut into pieces as long as one's hand, on a clean piece of board, washed well in a pail of water, packed into the pot, added a pint or so of water, sprinkled a little salt over all, (they collect salt from crevices in the rocks along the sea-shore at low-water and after a hot sun has shone for some hours,) put on the broken lid, and finally hung it on the pot-hook, where it soon began to simmer away in fine style and give forth an odour that was any thing but unpleasant. The fact of the fish having been taken from a greasy-looking sealskin bag was the only drawback to our appetite; and that was speedily overcome, for we had walked over many heavy miles, and it was long past our usual dinner-hour.

When the headman, therefore, took half of the lid off and picked out a piece for each one, which he put upon fragments of the "New York Herald" that one of us had carried along, we all held out our hands as he passed around, and fell to work,—cautiously at first, but, finally, with a most hearty will. The natives, too, attacking what was left in the pot with their knives, fingers, and teeth, the "several halves of fine-looking smoked salmon" were soon among "the things that were;" and, another bottle of punch being opened and pipes lit, we began to enjoy ourselves, while thus helping the expiring fire to get up the usual amount of smoke.

We all had our own pipes, fortunately, we having carried some that we had got in Japan, and our hosts having theirs, which had been obtained through the Russians. Their tobacco, however, was running alarmingly short, it seems; and I never saw men indulge in more extravagant demonstrations of joy than they did when Hartman pulled out a pound-plug and told them that he would not only give them an iron pot, but that he would fill it with similar pieces, in return for one of their long-talked-of mountain-elks.

The headman, immediately after regaining a state of comparative composure, reached for his gun, took aim at an imaginary elk, and clucked his tongue, as much as to say, "Wait until I get a chance: won't I fetch one down?" after which he replaced it carefully and intimated his readiness for another drink. In this way we rested ourselves and smoked away for an hour or more; when, after bartering a few pieces of tobacco and the second empty bottle for several of the cleanest-looking skins, we passed again through the long passage-way into the open air, and, accompanied by our hosts, crossed the mud-flat in advance of the rising tide, and reached our friends at the coal-mine just as they were about to return on board for the night. We therefore rewarmed ourselves at their blazing fire, reshouldered our guns, and skins, and accompanied them along the beach to meet a boat that was coming up with the tide to take us on board.

We soon reached her, when our native friends bade us farewell, with the promise to visit us on board and to bring with them one of their famous elk, the quality of whose meat we were anxious to compare with our usual diet of "salt junk" and sour bread. It is useless, I suppose, to repeat "the old story:"—how they got their iron pot stuck full of plugs of tobacco, how we continued to luxuriate upon salt junk and sour bread, and how the elk continued his leaps from crag to crag to the imminent terror of imaginary beholders.

The day following this ramble, Lawton reported a sufficient quantity of coal as being ready for embarkation, and "all hands" and boats were consequently devoted to that work. We soon found it to be any thing but a pleasant job, however; for, having to carry the boats to the very foot of the coal-stratum in order to fill them, and then to pull back over the mud-flat to deep water, the ebb-tide often got the start of us, and left us sprinkled about over said flat, sometimes with full boats, sometimes with empty ones, and always with the pleasant alternative of remaining in the boats to be half frozen, or of walking through the cold mud to the distant fire. Moreover, there was all this time lost, besides straining the boats if they happened to be loaded when thus left "high and dry;" and our boats were valuable in that out-of-the-way part of the world, more particularly as every day that passed only served to strengthen our minds in the conviction that the "old John" herself was destined to play us a trick before we could get her safely into San Fran-

SCENERY ABOUT THE COAL-MINE.

cisco. We were therefore naturally disposed to be tender with them, so that we should have something to depend upon when our dilapidated old craft should "turn turtle," drift upon a lee shore, founder in a sea-way, or indulge in any similar species of recreation.

It was soon determined, therefore, that some more summary process would have to be resorted to; for under the first arrangement we had to pull so far with our loaded boats before reaching the ship, that, by the time their coal could be hoisted on board and they sent back, the tide would be falling, and they consequently likely to ground on the flat before getting half-way to the mine. It was therefore thought best to get the ship herself under way every morning at daylight and run into as little as three fathoms, hovering off the edge of the mud-flat as long as there was water enough for the boats to pass back and forth, and then to return to the anchorage under Shag Rock until the rising of the next tide should allow them to move over it again.

This apparently-rational course had no sooner been determined upon than it became evident that we would have to consult the state of the tides in the selection of our working-hours; and so, as it was mostly low-water during the days, and the reverse at night, we capsized our habits of life and began to sleep during the former and to eat and work during the latter. Fortunately, darkness was not of long duration, as the twilight lingered until near eleven o'clock and the early dawn began to show itself about three hours later. It was, nevertheless, very trying to both officers and men; and, when at the end of five days the coal-bunkers were proclaimed full and the boats had been hoisted in, the captain looked around upon his exhausted ship's company, and caused the word to be passed that the next twenty-four hours would be devoted to a resting-spell, instead of to the continuation of the survey, as we had all feared.

As I looked around the decks and saw the weather-beaten frame of the old forecastleman and the half-developed form of the youthful "ship's boy" stretched side by side in the heavy sleep of protracted toil, I could not but rejoice over the order which had granted such necessary repose.

We had found little or no difficulty in getting out the coal ready for shipment; but our boats were so small, and the tides so uncertain, that we had been induced to press into service the headman of the village, its "entire population," and a huge skin boat of theirs, which, with proper management, might have been made to carry at a single load as much as all of our boats put together; but, after the first trip, the old fellow imagined that the coal would soon cut through her bottom, and consequently refused to lend her any more. We tried to bribe him by the offer of tobacco by the pound, and even did violence to our ideas of right and wrong by adding a bottle of brandy; but he made signs that their boat and harpoons were their only means of killing seal,—the meat of which is their chief article of food,—and we, of course, could not think of forcing him to hire her against his will. We had therefore to fall back upon our own boats, in consequence of which the work progressed slowly and laboriously.

This boat, which the headman was so fearful of injuring, is well worthy of a passing notice.

In the first place, she was built entirely of the skins of wild animals, and long, withe-like poles,—the former being sewed together with water-proof stitches, while the latter were joined to each other, and twisted, and bent, and retwisted, and doubled back, and finally tied into something that looked very much like the frame of an ordinary boat that is ready for planking. In sewing these skins together they used sharpened pieces of bone for needles, and fibres of the sinews of wild animals for thread; and the regularity of the stitches thus made was really astonishing. When they had thus connected together some forty or fifty skins in one immense sheet, they encased the frame in it, and allowed it to dry; and, in drying, it hardened like raw hide; after which, they gave us to understand that it never became loose or soft any more as long as they took proper care of it. Of course, that part forming the bottom of the boat became soft after she had been in the water any length of time; but that did not matter, as they stepped upon the withes when moving about in her.

This particular boat was from forty to fifty feet in length, some seven or eight in breadth, drew only about an inch of water when no one was in her, and carried her gunwales some three or four feet out of the water. Singular to say, she did not seem at all "top-heavy." A dozen or more two-inch poles that were lashed from gunwale to gunwale were the only things in the shape of seats that she offered; and on these sat the oarsmen, having under them a thick piece of bear-skin to guard against the otherwise almost certain caudal irritation. The headman himself found a similarly-dangerous seat on either quarter while guiding her course with a long and trailing oar. She floated on the water with the lightness of a distended bladder, and had a most singular way of twisting herself about, bending her long back over the short seas, seeming to be giving away under one's foot, &c. &c., and altogether imparting a feeling of unpleasant insecurity.

Upon one occasion, Hartman and myself were anxious to go on shore, while there was but one of the ship's boats alongside, and the headman, noticing our disappointment,—for we could not leave the ship without *any* boat for fear of accident, (a man falling overboard, or something of that sort,)—made signs to the effect that if we would get into his with a bottle of brandy in our pocket he would give us a passage: so we provided ourselves accordingly and stepped over the side. There was no wind blowing at the time, but there was still the same old swell setting in through the channel, and, as we rode lightly over them, she felt to us, who were accustomed to our ungiving boats, as if she would break her back at every jump. She would bend as much as fifteen or twenty degrees; and, if you happened to step anywhere save on one of the withe-like timbers, the softened skin would sink under the foot and cause you to catch for the gunwale under the suddenness of the impression that you had found a hole and were about to try the depth of the water. Then, her motion was so supple and snake-like that one could not for some time rid himself of the idea that "something was wrong," and that it behooved him to keep a sharp look-out. Altogether, she was a most singular specimen of naval architecture,—almost as singular as the "old John" herself.

At length we found ourselves safely on shore, with the headman in a fine flow of spirits, and the bottle half empty. He had attacked it at almost every stroke of the oars, refusing to give his companions even a single taste: he was evidently a very selfish old fellow, and one who knew how to keep those under him at a distance. So much for the headman and his village. And now I will say a few words about this coal, relate an adventure which several of us met with quite unexpectedly, and then leave Kamtschatka for the eastern coast of Siberia, the western boundary of the Okotsk Sea.

The importance of this combustible to the world at large has been so fully demonstrated within the last few years, that its discovery in unknown localities must ever be a source of interest to nine people out of ten. I shall stop in my narrative for a moment, therefore, to mention a few facts in regard to this which we discovered along the wilds of Kamtschatka. Most of that which came under our inspection was what is understood by "surface-coal;" but the last that we took on board came from a very fair depth, and looked as bright, and hard, and glittering, as the best anthracite. It was semi-bituminous, of several degrees of excellence, and burned with a bright blue flame, emitting little or no smell of sulphur, giving very little smoke for bituminous coal, and leaving few cinders and ashes. Much of it, upon being broken open, was found to contain a bright substance resembling amber, pieces of which, as large as a large buckshot, often fell out when it was thus fractured: as a general thing, however, it prevailed in the shape of veins of greater or less extent.

This bright substance we took to be pyrites; but whether the sulphuret of iron, copper, cobalt, or nickel, I was not sufficiently versed in mineralogy to determine. And here I must stop to ask the following question:—"Would it not have been worth the while of the Government to have offered a liberal salary—say three or four thousand dollars a year—to men of fair proficiency in the various branches, and thus obtained, as our 'right-hand men,' persons who would have been prepared at the time to take advantage of, and to explain and note for future investigation, the various freaks of nature which daily crossed our path in those unfrequented parts of the world?" We often felt the want of an able mineralogist in particular; but it seems that the Government expected its officers—men whose whole lives have been spent upon the sea—to possess a sufficient "smattering" of all sciences to answer the purpose. But to return to the coal. We were sorry to meet with this sulphuret, as that in which it is found is more or less liable to spontaneous combustion, and we had no idea of arraying another of the elements against the slim chance which the "old John" held out of ever landing us safely in San Francisco. We already had enough fire in the furnaces, without bringing any more on board in a latent state.

I have said that this coal burned with a bright blue flame, that it gave out little or no sulphur, made very little smoke, and left few ashes; and such was actually the case when it was piled on the blazing fire that kept us warm while digging it out; but, as soon as it was tried in our small-flue furnaces, its nature seemed to undergo an entire change. Instead of burning brightly, it smoked, and smothered, and ran into clinker, and gave forth sulphur in a most provoking and choking manner, the consequence of which was that it got up steam very slowly, kept it up very poorly, choked the flues with soot so as to force us to "haul fires" about every six hours to clear them, and accomplished generally a vast deal that was provoking to our tempers, injurious to the health of the firemen, and detrimental to the work of the Expedition.

As far as our experience extended, therefore, we came to the conclusion that it would never be adapted to burning in small-flue boilers, that it *might* answer well in furnaces intended for burning soft coal, and that it undoubtedly *did* burn well in the open air as an ordinary fire and in a blacksmith's forge. And now for the adventure which several of us encountered so unexpectedly.

We had been on shore, hunting all day, and the officer of the deck had sent a boat for us toward evening with orders to await our return and bring us on board. The firemen and boat's crews, having worked at the coal as long as the tide would permit, had returned on board shortly after noon for the purpose of getting a few hours' rest previous to the arrival of the next tide. Now, the coxswain of our boat, instead of keeping her at the end of the promontory, where there was always water enough to float her, had pulled in over the mud-flat and hauled her up on the beach about half-way between that point and the coal-mine, where he left her, and, with the rest of the crew, walked a mile or more along the boggy beach to the expiring fire, which had been left by the firemen when they returned on board. There they piled on a fresh supply of coal, and, seating themselves around it, began smoking their pipes, spinning yarns, and making themselves as generally comfortable as the cold air and their wet feet would allow them to. And this was the state of affairs when our party arrived and asked,—

"Well, boys, where's the boat?"

"Down along the beach, sir!" said the guilty-feeling coxswain, as he jumped to his feet and started off toward her. "We hauled her up nicely clear of the water before we came up, sir, and buried the anchor in the sand: she can't well get away."

"I suppose not," I replied. "Why didn't you stop at the point, or leave half of the crew in her to keep her afloat? There is a mile or more of mud between her and the water by this time." And such really proved to be the case; for, when we had turned a point and got her in view, we saw the whole flat before us without a sign of water near it, thus finding ourselves under the necessity of waiting for the next tide,—three or four long, inactive hours to be passed in the cold air, with our wearied limbs and empty stomachs as our only companions. The idea of dragging the boat over a half-mile of mud and rocks to the point was of course out of the question.

"A stupid piece of work altogether," remarked the doctor, in an irritated voice: "it is singular how many jackasses there are in this world!"

At this stage of the proceedings the coxswain looked

more guilty than ever, and, to hide his confusion, suddenly discovered an imaginary coal-vein in the precipitous side of the mountain on our right.

"Never mind finding any more coal," I observed: "what I want you to do now is to take two of the crew with you and go and stay by the boat until the tide rises, then bring her up along the beach as the water deepens. The rest of us will go back by the fire until then, and meet you as you come up." So we saw him fairly started for the boat, and then retraced our steps to the fire, where we piled on more coal, gathered closely around it, and tried to imagine ourselves in a very comfortable situation.

By-and-by, as we were thus seated around the blazing pile, limbs began to feel less weary under the influence of returning warmth, eyes began to grow heavy in about the same proportion, heads began to bob spasmodically from side to side, and even the breathing of some became heavy and regular. Not a word had been spoken for—— I can't say how long; for mine was one of those bobbing heads, and time had assumed a most misty appearance in its drowsy chambers.

* * * * * *

Suddenly we were aroused by shouts away down the beach; and, springing to our feet, we found that night was fast closing around us, that the fire had burned quite low, and that hurried feet were approaching us from the direction of the boat. Excited voices, too, were borne to us upon the damp night-air, telling of something wrong that had occurred, and serving to awaken us most effectually. The next moment the breathless coxswain and his two companions burst around a near point, running at full speed and exclaiming, at the top of their voices,—"Come on, gentlemen! come quick, doctor! come on, Mr. Habersham: the tide's a risin' fast, and we've come to let you know!"

I don't think I ever felt more like knocking a man down than at that moment. The doctor, too, was so furious that he could only turn pale and get off a few disjointed remarks in regard to the comparative size of the world and the number of jackasses which it contained; while Hartman actually foamed at the mouth in his desperate attempts to command enough English to convey his emotions.

"What made you leave the boat behind again?" I asked, as they joined us.

"I wonder how many more jackasses there are among us?" asked the doctor: "it's lucky we're discovering new islands: the old world will soon be too small to hold you."

"Vel! vel! vel! Vot ish it? Vot ish it? Ve don't see te boat yet! Vere *is* te boat?" foamed Hartman, with angry volubility.

To these rapid questions the coxswain and his friends had nothing to answer. They had been left by the boat with the previously-mentioned orders, and, instead of obeying them, had become frightened at the noise of the swelling tide, and wasted precious time by coming almost a mile to tell us that it was rising. And now we were left with but one alternative: we must either be content to remain where we were,—out of reach of the water,—and leave the boat to beat about in the surf and probably be drifted out to sea; or we must make a run for it and try to reach her before the tide should rise high enough to cover the beach and drown all who should not be able to swim back. We had travelled up and down that beach both by day and night, and knew well enough that there would be no use in trying to climb up those steeps—almost perpendicular walls—when the water should wash us from our feet: our only hope would then be in the untiring arm of the practised swimmer.

It was something of more than ordinary importance upon which we were now called upon to decide; and I am free to acknowledge, as I look back upon that darkening night, that we might have acted with far more prudence than we did. Still, when the doctor (?) cried out, "Let us run for it! there is yet time," I stopped to think no longer, but, dropping my gun on the beach and telling one of the men to come on with it as fast as possible, started off on a full run and was followed by the entire party.

And such a run as it was! I never engaged in any thing approaching it before; I hope never to be engaged in any thing similar again. "It vos fear-*ful*," as Hartman subsequently expressed it.

The lingering twilight of the almost endless arctic day was slowly giving place to the tardy night. The atmosphere was just cool enough to keep one from getting heated even by running for life, and the unpleasant "bootjack-mixture" that was constantly crossing our path more than once threw us down at the imminent risk of breaking some limb or even a neck. I could hear the increasing surge of the flood-tide as it rolled toward us, and the decreasing noise of my companions as they hurried after me: I was evidently distancing them slowly and nearing the tide-rip rapidly. I was either the worst-scared man of the party, or was enabled to outstrip them from the fact of having no gun to retard me; and I remember this thought flashing through my mind and causing me to smile as I looked ahead to the next breakfast-table and heard Hartman say, "Oh! but you should see H—— run: zat vos te best of it all."

I heard this speech in the future, I say, *and smiled;* but it was doubtless a most ghastly attempt. At any rate, it was of but short duration: it fled before the increasing roar of the advancing tide, and left me with a feeling of startled alarm that fortunately but added to my speed. I think now that it was even more than a "feeling of startled alarm;" I think it was much more like a very bad scare,—the feeling which possessed me as my left foot just then sunk into a streak of "the mixture" and caused me to measure my length on what fortunately proved to be good *hard sand.* A few bruises were nothing; but it would have been decidedly unpleasant to have found myself sticking up upon "all fours," as had been the case with the fireman who followed his shovel down the embankment.

The particular streak over which I now fell was fortunately a narrow one, and my momentum was sufficient to carry me over it. After picking myself up, therefore, I took time to be thankful for this as well as to rub my bruised elbows, after which I continued the race with any thing but decreased speed. There were two high points between our starting-point and the boat, that ran down across the beach to about half-tide mark, and I had now arrived at the first of these just as the advancing ripple commenced to wash it. Doubling it at full speed, and with the water already ankle-deep, I shouted to those behind, "Bear a hand! bear a hand!" and dashed along the next stretch of beach to gain the last point.

About this time I began to feel a little the worse for exercise. My skin was hot and dry, my knees decidedly weaker than at first, while my throat and chest actually burned under the constant friction of rapid and heavy breathing. My sight, too, was dimmed by the extreme exertion, and a dizzy feeling about the brain advised me to slacken my pace or risk a probable fall. Still, knowing that every thing now depended on *some one reaching the boat before she was washed away*, and knowing also that time was short and that I was the nearest one to her, I was urged to push ahead at every risk. I felt that, if I could but weather this last point, all would be well; for the boat lay just beyond it, and I could easily get into her and return for my companions. It was this conviction which, combined with my "badly-scared" condition, served to keep me up to speed, while I felt every moment more and more like fainting.

At times I thought of giving out in spite of all this; but then I cast my eyes from the inclined, wedge-like surface of the foaming waters to the dark outlines of the point, which was now only a few hundred yards ahead, and, reflecting that I had only to round the latter and grasp the boat's gunwale, straightened up nervously and threw myself bodily toward it, though my knees did tremble, my feet come down rather wildly, and my sight grow dimmer and more dim under such a combination of excitement, fear, and exertion.

Finally it was reached; and, as I waded heavily around it through the knee-deep water that broke against its rugged front, I saw the boat rolling from bilge to bilge in the rising surf a few yards ahead,—a sight which so enlivened me as to cause the expenditure of most of my remaining breath in an encouraging shout to those who followed. As it turned out, I had not arrived a minute too soon: a few moments later and she would have been afloat, probably drifting out into the bay, and leaving us to swim, climb up the steep and crumbling sides of the promontory, or——sink.

I staggered up to her unsteady side, and, grasping the gunwale with both hands, strove to keep her steady; but my strength was all gone. I felt at once that I was powerless while alone, and so contented myself with crawling over into the stern-sheets and being rolled from side to side until the lapse of about twenty or thirty seconds brought up the rest of the party, who shoved her off into deep water. The oars were now got out, and, while thus engaged, we drifted by the point around which we had so lately waded.

"Put over a boat-hook and see how deep the water is," said the doctor.

One of the crew complied, and found *four feet* where but a minute before it had been only knee-deep. We looked at the hopeless hill-side, shuddered, and felt—I hope—thankful.

"It's a great pity there are so many jackasses in

this world!" repeated the doctor, as soon as he had sufficiently recovered his breath.

"Vell, yes!—great pity!" added Hartman, spasmodically. "I don't vant to run ever so much again. Bierchaum, you run like a great fel-low; you have a great scare, I think, Bierchaum. I run also myself." And so we pulled on board, the coxswain keeping an unusual silence, and all hands feeling most miserable and used up. That night we finished coaling, and the next day was one of rest.

CHAPTER XIX.

WE ENTER THE GULF OF PENJINKS AND REACH OUR HIGHEST NORTHERN LATITUDE, AFTER WHICH WE RETURN TO THE OKOTSK, AND CROSS OVER TO THE COAST OF SIBERIA—WE NARROWLY ESCAPE SHIPWRECK, AND FINALLY ARRIVE AT A PLACE CALLED OLA, WHERE WE ARE REGALED BY THE SIGHT OF BULLOCKS AND THE TASTE OF MILK.

THE day after our successful race against time and a flood-tide, we once more hove up the anchor and continued our survey. We now, steering to the northward along the west coast of Kamtschatka, entered the Gulf of Penjinks, up which we ran as high as lat. 61° 20′ N., when, for want of time and favourable weather, we turned again to the southward, and retraced our way as far as the edge of the Okotsk Sea, when we stretched across the mouth of the double gulf for the east coast of "Siberia the frozen," and, upon sighting this latter during the following day, recommenced the survey.

We found our newly-discovered coal burning very badly. It was with the utmost difficulty that we could keep up a moderate amount of steam; and, upon rounding a jutting point of land shortly after noon, we encountered a current against which we could make no headway: in fact, we lost ground for some hours. The captain therefore determined to commence the next morning and use our good coal as long as it lasted, hoping that at any rate it would hold out until we should leave that region of rugged rocks and seven or eight knot currents. It will be seen how providential this apparently-natural decision proved before the lapse of twenty-four hours.

After struggling against the current until sunset, (9 P.M.,) it fortunately slackened up, and we were enabled to gain shelter in the bight above the point abreast of which we had been doing our best all day, after which we piped down the hammocks and felt unusually comfortable with the prospect of a quiet night's rest ahead.

* * * * * *

It was about three hours after midnight, and yet the arctic sun was already some degrees above the eastern horizon, while the "old John," as if ashamed of having overslept herself, was running under a full head of steam from the spot where, only six short hours previously, we had anchored for the night after one of our usual "day's work" of eighteen hours.

Don't smile, reader; we often worked *more* than eighteen hours out of the twenty-four, during those long arctic days.

I would not have any one understand, from the fact that the "old John" was under a full head of steam, that she was rivalling a North River steamer or even a fair sailing-scow in speed,—such, indeed, being far from the case, as six and a half knots the hour was the most that she could be prevailed upon to accomplish under steam only. The Government agents, in sending us to sea in her, doubtless thought that she was "just the vessel for the service;" but *we, the interested parties*, after some months' experience, became impressed with the unpleasant conviction that she was destined to drown us all some fine morning, either by foundering in a gale or drifting helplessly on some lee shore.

This conviction, as may be supposed, was productive of the most constant watchfulness on our part. I never saw watches kept with more praiseworthy zeal when the occasion demanded it. Even the crew, who were as conscious as ourselves of the defects of the lame old craft, worked with astonishing energy to keep her afloat until our arrival in San Francisco, and as determinedly avowed their intention of leaving her at that port, "whether or no, Tom Collins." These unreasonable beings actually looked forward to the crime of desertion, in preference to again "launching out upon the sea" in a vessel whose singular feats and annoying predilection for the shore had already sprinkled more than one head with gray.

It was a tough cruise, this very "last one" at which I am now looking back; and, though more than a year has passed since our crazy old craft returned us in safety to the "Land of the Free and the Home of the Brave," the mind still shrinks from the contemplation of past scenes, whose very dangers but served at the time to arouse its latent powers of resistance.

How many there are, who, looking back through the dim and shadowy past at the more prominent adventures of their lives, wonder in vain as to the source of those unknown because previously-untaxed powers of the mind, by which they were enabled, in times of pressing need, to bear up against and finally overcome dangers and obstacles which, in the quiet moments of after-security, seem to have been burdened with certain death and destruction. It is upon one of these "prominent adventures" that I am now looking back and wondering how myself and some seventy others passed through it without the loss of that readiness of action and self-possession so essential in moments of unexpected peril to the safety of lives or the success of an undertaking.

Our old tub, as I have already remarked, was running away from her night's anchorage under a full head of steam. The rugged and snow-patched coast of Siberia was on our right, distant some mile or more; several clustering islands dotted the smooth surface of the Okotsk Sea on our left; while ahead we could just see what might be a ship or towering rock, so distorted were all objects in that direction by the great refraction common to high latitudes. We were not long in doubt, however, as to the nature of this distorted object. It seemed to be rising bodily out of the confused horizon, and to be rushing upon *us* instead of our slowly approaching *it*. Could this be also refraction? Hardly. Suddenly we guessed the mystery: we had been anchored during the night in the eddy formed by a projecting headland, but had now steamed out into one of the fearful currents against which we had been so often warned by old (but, as we then thought, marvel-loving) whaling-captains. It was the same current with which we had measured speed during the previous day; only it was now running in an opposite direction and with evidently greater strength.

What was to be done now? To attempt to survey in such a mill-race would have been absurd. Nevertheless, we kept well in with the mainland, intending to run between it and the distorted object, which had at length resolved itself into three separate masses of towering rock.

The passage looked smooth and beautiful from the masthead at first; but, as we approached it with our mad velocity, a suspicious-looking streak of foam and broken water was gradually discovered to connect the extreme right of the black-looking rocks with the mainland. Should this prove to be a reef——but bah! why hunt up unpleasant subjects for thought?

Any one who has ever watched the flying landscape from the window of a railroad-car can form a very fair idea of the appearance which the receding objects here presented to us. Trees, rocks, patches of snow, dark and gloomy-looking caves, with here and there a huge boulder, snow-fed torrent, or wandering bear, rushed by us in their constant flight, separate and distinct at first, but finally melting into one conglomerate mass of unrecognisable objects, over which the momentarily-withdrawn eye ranged in vain for its former resting-place. This was the velocity with which we were going over ground now for the first time passed over to our knowledge,—thirteen miles to the hour probably, certainly not less than *twelve:* where would we all be in one minute of time should the "old John" suddenly find a reef or sunken rock under her already leaky bow?

Some such question as this was drifting lazily through my midwatch-worn mind, when I was startled by the voice of the captain, who, from his look-out on the topsail-yard, ordered our course changed so as to pass *outside* of the rocks, as the streak of broken water before alluded to was evidently a reef. This discovery was no sooner made than I knew that the "old John" was in another of her disagreeably-tight places; and, when I heard the rushing tide leaping up our sides in its mad fury, and reflected that we had to steam against that tide before we could round those black and towering piles of basaltic rock which blocked our path with certain death, my heart for a moment contracted with spasmodic horror; and, when it again swelled almost to bursting, it was with curses deep and bitter against *those in authority*, whose stupid ignorance or criminal carelessness had risked the safety of so many lives by detailing such a vessel for the hazardous undertaking of a surveying voyage around the world.

"If there's any speed in her, it'll have to come out now, or it's all day with us," said a voice at my elbow.

I turned with a look of gloomy inquiry to see the speaker; for the voice, though a familiar one, was so strangely modulated by emotion as to be scarcely recognisable. It was the captain, who, having nothing more to discover from aloft, had returned to the deck,—cool, calm, collected, and yet very pale; and his voice, though thus strangely modulated by emotion, was firm and bell-like, and his eye bright, partially with moisture, but more than partially with the light of that fire which burns only in the brave man's eye when dangers crowd around him, or in the eagle's glance when it meets the rays of the mid-day sun.

"Yes," he continued, in a voice whose forced cheerfulness grated harshly on the nervous ear; "the 'old John' must indeed 'scratch gravel' *now*, or we are *lost at last.* Tell Lawton to fire up: let us have all the steam he can. If the boilers won't bear it *they must burst.* Even now we are losing ground, and there is not much of it between us and those——"

He pointed to the dark and towering masses of the loosely-piled rock, up whose rugged sides the bruised and foaming sea reared its rushing surface, and through whose broken breast it urged its half-spent fury. No gravity existed there of sufficent power to drag the broken waters to a common level: they rolled, and leaped, and surged in their mad course until obstructed by those hoary upheavals of nature's past convulsions, and then pressed up their precipitous sides, or through dark and gloomy-looking archways, with a baffled power that told of ruin, and destruction, and death, to the hapless ship that should be swept with them in their mad career.

The general view which met the eye was awful to behold.

Imagine a ship drifting with the swift current of an expansive river to be suddenly arrested by an unexpected sandbank. The ship must now stand still: she is stranded. The current can sweep her no farther; it therefore rears itself against her slanting side, and, rushing around both stem and stern, forms dozens of turbid whirlpools under her lee. Now it presses up her side, now sinks below the general level, now leaps in broken masses up to her very gunwale, and all the while gurgling and foaming in the unsteady eddy under her lee. Imagine such a scene as this, I say, and then multiply it a hundredfold, and you will have a tolerable idea of the one from which our old ship was now straining every nerve to deliver us. Only in our case the "expansive river" was a moving ocean, the "stranded ship" a rough and towering mass of loosely-piled rocks, and the "gurgling and foaming of the unsteady eddy" was the surging of the tortured waters, which, as we slowly neared in spite of rising steam, was fast increasing to a deafening roar.

There are some throes of nature which God never intended man to describe. He reserves them in the wandering air, in the boiling centre of our common earth, in the fathomless depths of the slumbering ocean, or in the misty depths of the failing imagination, until such time as he sees fit to bring them before us in the shape of agents in his own vast and inappreciable schemes. What pen ever yet did justice to the raging breath of the West India hurricane, to the destroying action of the great volcano of Hawaii, or to the scenes of ruin and desolation which follow in the trail of the mysterious "bore" of the Hoogly and other Eastern rivers? My pen also fails to do justice to the scene which I have attempted to place before the reader.

As I have already remarked, there were three of these rocks,—one immensely large, the others comparatively small. They were separated by passages of probably fifty or sixty feet in width, and were gaped and undermined at the water's edge by several gloomy-looking caves, through and *down* which the rushing sea seemed finding a channel to the very bowels of the earth. It was opposite the larger of these rocks, and distant from it only some three or four hundred yards, that we found ourselves after the steamer had rounded to and commenced to measure her speed with that of this moving ocean. Immediately in our rear was the largest and most gloomy-looking of those downward-leading caves. It was large enough, had our masts been taken out, to receive the entire hull of the steamer into its capacious jaws; and toward these capacious jaws we were now being urged by a power which the advancing land—slowly-advancing, but still *advancing*—told us was greater than our means of resistance.

Send the best helmsman to the wheel. Crowd the furnaces with coal and pitch. Jam down the safety-valve. *Any thing for steam!*—for steam and close steering are now the only things that can save us.

Backward we go,—slowly backward! The old craft, as if conscious of the shattered timbers and mangled forms which but await her touching to spring into existence, trembles in every joint as the tortured boilers bear their increasing power against the whirling screw,—seventy revolutions to the minute, I think, we were then making,—and yet backward, slowly backward, toward the yawning death. It was sickening to see a patch of sea-weed, or a drifting log, pass us in their unconscious career and in less than a minute of time disappear upon the breast of the diving flood,—down, down, how far?

Even the whales that had been rubbing their huge sides against our barnacled copper for the last few days gave one plunge deeper than the rest, and left man to lean upon his whirling screw and die—alone. The numerous varieties of the arctic duck, which had heretofore spotted the calm and polished surface of the ocean in every direction, were now no longer to be seen between us and the nearing danger. There were thousands of them still drifting past; but, warned by nature's sure instinct, they, like the whale, avoided the risk of being thrown upon those pointed rocks, or sucked into those fathomless holes, by preserving a safe distance. They, too, using with ease the means of escape furnished them by an all-providing Being, left man to lean upon his broken reed and die—alone. Even the lost and wearied land-birds, which for days past had found food and shelter upon our decks, deserted us for a rocky perch just over the dark and roaring cavern toward which we were slowly drifting, as if selecting a commanding point from which to witness the approaching work of dissolution. The very dogs crouched at our feet in trembling fear as the noise of the rushing waters startled them, and howled piteously as they gazed into faces so changed by deep and terrible emotion. Millions of bats and swallows left their thousand nests at those dismal and unknown sounds, startled by the unusual proximity of man to their desolate haunts, and, circling through and around our gear and decks, added their harsh, discordant screams to the roaring of the waters, and interposed their black and crowded masses between us and the morning sun. They were like dense clouds casting their passing shadows over us,—gloomy shadows, that might be shading a more gloomy fate.

Backward,—slowly backward!

God of heaven! must we, in this quiet state of motionless inactivity, drift inch by inch into that howling cavern, or wilfully throw ourselves upon the sharp rocks of the sunken reef as the only alternative? Is man, and man only, with the vast resources of his mighty intellect to aid him, to be strangled, suffocated, mangled, *destroyed,* while the inferior animals around him swim majestically away, or hover on fearless wings over the sullen and hopeless struggle? Is time to end now, as far as we are concerned?—we who have still such strong frames, such glowing blood, such vivid recollections of the past, such yearnings of hope for the future, such nerve to struggle against this hideous fate could we but grasp it in some tangible form?

Is that bright sun now shining upon us for the last time?—*us,* whose path it was created to light? May not some wandering breeze reach us in its wayward course, to fill our idle sails and urge us forward while yet a few short yards exist between us and that rocky pile? Alas, no! The stern and lowering brow contracts in hopeless despair over a broad expanse of calm and polished ocean, while backward—slowly backward—we drop against the struggling screw.

We can no longer measure our yards by hundreds. Time is drawing to a close, and space seems shrinking into nothing as though they journeyed to a common grave. A strong arm might have cast a stone into that yawning gulf, when a single order, the first that had been given for apparently an age, told us that the desperate choice had been made.

To be thrown upon the sharp rocks of the sunken reef by the boiling ocean which swept over them, assured us of at least a sunlit grave; while the dark depths of the dismal-looking cavern, rendered doubly dark and gloomy by the contrast with the snowy foam which frothed around its mouth, resembled in their inky hue

"BACKWARD—SLOWLY BACKWARD."

the commencement of the shadow of the valley of death.

"Starboard!"

Reader, do you know what that single word meant? Would you see it drawn out into good old English?

It meant that there no longer existed a hope of being able to steam against the rushing tide with our powerless propeller and leaking boilers. It meant that we were to go to death upon the foaming reef in preference to being swept into his embrace in those gloomy depths. It meant that the throbbing brain of him whose slightest word was law even in that moment of awful suspense had decided to give up the unequal struggle and accept the hopeless alternative. It meant that by our own act we were resigning the few minutes during which the struggle might be protracted, to rush headlong upon the less revolting death. It meant that at the end of those "few minutes" certain and instantaneous death awaited us, and that at the end of those few *seconds* possible salvation for a few hours was in store for him who should grasp a broken spar or buoyant cask when the vessel's hull should be ground from under us, and the confused mass of shattered timbers, tangled gear, and mangled forms be swept over the boiling line into the fathomless water beyond. It meant that the moment was at hand when the weak man was to find a speedy end, and when the strong man was to feel his sinewy arm slowly deaden from the protracted labour of self-preservation: slowly, but surely, all flesh must sink. And it meant that brave hearts were now to die, and that fond hearts in another hemisphere were to weep their unknown fate and languish in lonely sorrow until time to them, also, should draw to a close. All this it meant; and horror, and despair, and approaching dissolution, gathered around us.

"Starboard it is, sir!" said the ready helmsman; and as he spoke the wheel turned evenly under his nervous grasp, and the old ship's head dropped slowly off. Bodily, hopelessly, broadside on, she now drifted toward the last struggle. How quickly those few seconds glide,—small seconds of time, but awful, awful taxes upon the mind's future stability! Men live through past ages in moments like those. The strained and labouring brain burns with a fire that whitens the locks of youth, or sows the seeds of future disease, through sheer intensity of thought.

It is come! Men cease to breathe, and, with half-closed eyes and muscles of iron, grasp a swinging rope or near belaying-pin with unconscious power!——

What? The reef! Where is it? A merciful Being smiled upon his helpless creatures and strengthened their broken reed in that moment of their dire extremity. Our eyes had deceived us. Eyes whose business it had been for years to discover the unknown reef, and to distinguish between that and the deceptive tide-rip, had failed for once. *No reef existed.* It was the peculiar formation of the land, combined with the fearful velocity of the rushing ocean, which created a tide-rip that might well have deceived a thousand eyes. And, as we drifted wildly over the boiling space into the "fathomless waters beyond," man's failing eye, which had been dry and hard and burning while death held out his fleshless arms, softened with cooling moisture, until those shapeless piles of towering rock grew dim and undefined in their uncertain vision.

It was with fearful speed that we had drifted around the angular corner of the in-shore rock, and it was soon left far, far astern. Men began again to look around them and breathe freely: the danger was past; we again went on our careless way.

"Blast her miserable timbers!" said our friend Bunsby, as he took the old ship in at a single indignant glance: "if she'd only them chaps in Congress as her crew, them in the Cabinet as her officers, and the old President for cap'n, I'd as soon see her sink as float,—shiver her!" And, with this emphatic expression of "an opinion as was an opinion," he wondered "how much longer we had to live *now*," and threw from his mouth a piece of exhausted tobacco which must have weighed something more than an ounce.

Indignation at being sent to sea in such a ship was evidently the paramount feeling in Bunsby's breast at that moment. What a most unreasonable being he was, truly, to indulge in such a wish as to the various heads of the Government! Who would not approve, as fair and just, the arming of a good swordsman with a bending lath and sending him to fight his battle? It was, I suppose, upon this principle that we—machines of flesh and blood whose only duty it is to *obey orders*—were armed with a miserable old craft, neither sail-vessel or steamer, and sent to battle the gales of every clime, to discover and locate the very dangers which better ships do their best to shun. Would that we were all Bunsbys, or that common sense and humanity would combine to sweep from the ocean all such man-traps as the *ci-devant* water-tank, the present "United States screw-steamer-of-war of the third class," John Hancock.

The day following this narrow escape, we found ourselves at anchor near a Siberian village, the name of which proved to be Ola. We had heard much of this settlement from whalers before reaching the coal-mine,—one of those explorers having enlivened us with the information that the natives were pleasant and friendly, and that they had quantities of beef, milk, and fish, besides a limited supply of vegetables. He further told us that they were totally unacquainted with the value of money, and that we could trade with them to great advantage by drawing largely upon the purser's store-room for flannel, silk handkerchiefs, tobacco, sugar, rice, molasses, &c. &c.,—all of which we found to be strictly the case. I had often heard of such innocent people, but never before saw human beings who had no idea of the value of money. Even the Kuriles have Japanese coin, and the Fejee Islanders buy and sell with the foreigners on their cannibal shores. But I am again wandering from my narrative.

As soon as the anchor was down, we called away three boats and started to find the mouth of the river upon the banks of which we had been told Ola was situated, and in these boats went at least half of the entire *personnel* of the "old John:" it was not every day that we had either the time or the opportunity to indulge in similar sprees, and when they thus presented themselves "hand in hand" they always found us ready.

Our three boats left the ship at the same time, and, after a longer pull than we had looked for, reached the mouth of the river. It proved to be a stream of some ten or fifteen yards in width, with a bad bar across its mouth,—so bad, in fact, that we beached our boats near its outer edge in preference to risking a ducking. We then walked a mile or more over a flat, boggy piece of land, through which ran our river, as well as several smaller streams, and, finally, arrived opposite a scattered collection of log houses, from which the people were running to welcome us. Let us see what my journal says:—

"The river being between us, they launched a couple of 'dug-outs' to ferry us over; which accomplished, we were received by a crowd of from fifteen to twenty natives in a most friendly manner; and they no sooner saw our articles of barter than they became unpleasantly so, insisting on shaking hands over and over again, and motioning us to follow them to their houses, where they had other articles which they would exchange for ours.

"We readily understood these signs, which were assisted by a few slang expressions picked up from whalers, and, with our 'peddler-packs' under our arms, followed them up from the river-bank. As we went along we gazed with longing eyes at the stunted but plump-looking bullocks and the trim little milch-cows that dotted the undulating country ahead of us, and intimated by signs that what we principally wanted to trade for was meat to eat and milk to drink. At this they laughed promisingly, and got off the expression 'bum-by' quite patly; after which they laughed heartily at their evident familiarity with our language, and became more affectionate than ever.

"What seemed to surprise and please them most was

our being dressed in uniform, they having been previously visited by none but whalers, whose universal habit it is to consult only the respective states of their wardrobe, and the temperature of the air, while putting on their variegated apparel. Most of us on this occasion wore blue flannel sack-coats with the usual abundant allowance of naval buttons; and these they were particularly struck with, making signs that they would like nothing better than to exchange their own fur 'over-alls' for them. In return, we intimated that our clothes would be too cool for them; but they only laughed and pointed to several women who now approached, some of whom were rigged out (evidently in honour of the occasion) in fancy calico dresses, while the others were, as usual, clothed in loose garments made from the skin of the reindeer.

"We found several of those women quite pretty, in spite of the ungraceful and masculine nature of their attire; and they joined the party in a very modest and retiring manner, shaking hands laughingly with each of us who noticed them, and accompanying us to the house of the headman of the village, who proved to be one of those who had received us so warmly at the landing."

And now, before I go any further, I may as well give the reader an idea of the houses of that village, and of the people who lived in them. The former were of different styles, though they were all built of logs with their crevices filled in with a mixture of mud and grass. The larger ones resembled our ordinary log cabins, with the exception of the absence of windows and chimneys,—an extensive skylight in the middle of the roof serving to admit light as well as to permit the escape of smoke.

Their flooring was the natural soil levelled off; and down the entire length of their centres ran a raised bed of earth of some four or five feet in width, that was kept from crumbling down by a framework of posts and rough planks.

Around this earthen work ran a gangway of about the same width, while around the sides of the building itself were tier upon tier of sleeping-bunks,—very much like a ship's forecastle,—the bottoms of which were filled with skins of black bear, reindeer, and other animals: these evidently answered the purpose of both bed and bedclothes, and presented any thing but an inviting appearance. In the centre of the earthen work there was kept up a constant fire, the smoke of which, curling up among the rafters, served to cure quantities of hanging salmon before effecting its escape through the "extensive skylight." From the smoke of the constant fires that were thus kept up, their interiors had assumed a smoky hue, which, assisted by the smell of fish, gave every thing a look of greasy filthiness. We soon concluded that the open air was best adapted to the business of trafficking, and "backed out" accordingly.

The second style of house was, as I have already remarked, similar to these as far as material was concerned, but no further. They were, like the Malay houses of Rangou, raised upon from four to eight posts to an elevation of several feet, but, unlike them, were floored with small saplings or rough plank. They were some ten feet square as a general rule, boasted a single door and no windows, and were without chimneys. Their floor was about three feet from the ground, so that they could be climbed into easily without the aid of steps. Of course they had no fire in them, they being used mostly as sleeping-quarters.

We did not enter any of them, but, upon looking in, saw nothing but piles upon piles of skins, which, being spread out very evenly, gave the whole apartment the appearance of one vast "field-bed." Their doors shut quite closely and worked upon wooden hinges, and they were sometimes locked with padlocks, (obtained from the whale-ships which visit them from time to time,) in which cases we generally found that they acted the part of store-houses. As sleeping-apartments they were decidedly preferable to the larger ones, as they were free from the odour of fish, and the absence of fire left their sides and contents of a reasonable colour.

When we came to buy our milk, the headman beckoned us to follow him with our bottles, and led the way to his particular "lock-up," where he opened the door with a wire key, (having lost the original,) and disclosed to our brightening eyes the long-untasted luxury ranged around its sapling flooring in tin pans and cool-looking earthen jars. We bought it *by the jar*—each one a jar—and began on the spot to make up for lost time. Who can tell how much our scurvy-threatened palates enjoyed these pro tracted draughts?

In addition to these houses, there were any number of sheds scattered about for drying fish previous to the smoking-process. These were rigged with light movable roofs, so that the fish might be exposed to the sun as well as protected from rain. They told us that, when bad weather came on, they hauled over the roofs, and built fires under them to lessen the effect of the moisture.

Dogs, children, and fish seemed to prevail to a greater extent than any thing else, though cattle and grown people were far from scarce. These latter were rather below the middle stature than otherwise, and we could not distinguish between them and the natives near the coal-mine. Their complexion was a sickly bronzed olive, features irregular, and they were dressed mostly in loose trousers, smockfrock, and hood,—all being made from the skin of the reindeer. Some of them wore the fur inside; others, out: just as the fancy seemed to strike them. The same garment could be worn either way.

Describing complexions is not my forte; and some one may ask, "What is a sickly bronze?" They looked like persons of a naturally-fair complexion who had been chronically darkened from generation to generation; for even the infants partook of the general hue. Their forms were remarkably light and sinewy, their eye bright, and the springing step of their moccasin-clad feet indicated muscles of unfailing elasticity. The more youthful of the fair (?) sex were lively, cheerful, and far from ugly, boasting hands and feet of rare mould and dimensions. Like young ladies of almost every latitude, they seemed to think that the fact of their being young and pretty entitled them to an extra amount of consideration; and I am free to acknowledge that they got as many skeins of silk, papers of needles, &c. &c. for their well-expended smiles as did their more elderly companions for their bullocks, fish, and other articles of trade.

Having now given the reader an idea of the Siberian settlement of Ola and of the people who lived in it, I will proceed to show how it was that they came there, and what they did after arriving; for Ola was not inhabited all the year round. But this subject is, I think, worthy of being introduced at the head of another chapter.

CHAPTER XX.

SOME OTHER THINGS ABOUT "OLA," SHOWING THE READER HOW AN OLD WOMAN NEARLY LOST HER FAVOURITE MILCH-COW, AND HOW THEY CATCH FISH IN THAT OUT-OF-THE-WAY PART OF THE WORLD, ETC. ETC.—WE ARRIVE AT FABIUS ISLAND, BAY OF TAOUSK, AND REGALE OURSELVES UPON WHORTLEBERRIES.

FROM all that we could learn then and subsequently, it seems that the country back of Ola is rather thinly populated, and that what people there are come down to the sea with the return of spring for the purpose of catching and curing supplies of the salmon which visit certain localities in countless shoals. They work at this business during most of their short summers, and then return before the approaching winter to their more sheltered homes with their provender, in the shape of smoked and dried fish.

When they break out from the confinement of their long winters, they emigrate, with their horses, cows, dogs, and sleighs, to some such "summer resort" as Ola, where they take possession of the houses that have been vacant all winter, and commence to catch their fish, and trade with any whaler that may visit them. They also often plant turnips from seed originally obtained from said whalers, which in the short space of six weeks will grow to double the size of one's fist; but, unfortunately for us of the "old John," they had neglected doing so the season we were there.

All that we found them able to trade with us for were, firstly, fish without end; secondly, three small bullocks; thirdly, some three or four gallons of milk; fourthly, several hundred Siberian squirrel-skins; fifthly and lastly, the coarser skins of the black bear, the reindeer, and another animal, whose name I forget. In addition to these, there were various articles of dress that they would gladly have exchanged; but, as most of them had been worn, we did not do much in that line. One very pretty girl I remember in particular, who, having fallen in love with a red silk handkerchief that I had purposely flaunted before her eyes, offered me every thing about her house, even to a pair of richly-worked buckskin moccasins, made long like a boot and having embroidered strings with which to tie them over the knee. She pointed to the large house of the headman, and made signs, as she measured one of them along her foot to show how it fitted, that she had only worn them upon one occasion, and that was when a number of whalers had landed with a fiddle and they had had a feast and a dance under its hospitable roof, and that they were not the least the worse for wear. There was only one way for me to get over this species of argument, and that was by putting my foot alongside of hers, and asking, by signs, what manner of use they could ever prove to me. And to this she replied by flinging them into a corner and snatching at the handkerchief with a determined, "have-it-whether-or-no-Tom-Collins" air that spoke her disappointment more strongly than the best English could have done. I ended by giving it to her for thirty squirrel-skins, a reindeer-robe, and the contemned moccasins; and the reader must not accuse me of having weathered the unsophisticated beauty in the trade until he or she reads further and sees what little value they attached to their articles of traffic and how great a value to ours.

We had been cautioned by various whalers as to the nature of the things they most longed for, and had taken the precaution, before leaving the ship, to load ourselves down with such. They consisted of the following articles:—fancy calicoes, cotton or silk handkerchiefs, needles and thread, brilliantly-coloured sewing-silk, (of which we had bought many pounds in China,) all kinds of old clothes, molasses, rice, tobacco, spirits, flannel, blankets; in short, almost every thing except money.

It would have been amusing to have stood off and watched the various groups as they carried on their trading. In the foreground, first and foremost in resources, stood the purser, with the Government at his back in the shape of endless supplies of flannel and tobacco, and the captain at his elbow urging upon him the necessity of securing bullocks and vegetables for the ship's company before they were bought up by the different messes. Now, as the bullocks were drifting about over the hills with natives already following them upon "fell murder intent," and as no vegetables had yet been discovered, the purser—very naturally—could not see the necessity for any further exertion on his part, and was evidently disposed to "take it easy." The elbow-jogging, therefore, only resulted in causing him to seat himself upon his wares and wait for the headman to drive up his bullocks and fix his price. The purser was a philosopher, and, at the same time, a most immovable specimen of the fraternity.

In another direction was to be seen a party of three or four exchanging a half-plug of tobacco for a jar of milk, and evincing unmistakable signs of a determination to arrive at the bottom of their purchase before engaging in any further speculation, while, at the same time, some more fastidious companion rushed toward them with the exclamation, "Don't drink it on shore! wait until we get on board and change it to a brandy-punch," or words to that effect.

Here were to be seen some of the crew, already heavily loaded with hundreds of smoked salmon, putting down their bundles and bargaining for others *simply because they were cheap;* while in another quarter was one who, having bought all that he wanted, amused himself by *giving away* the remnant of his trading-stock, thus drawing down upon his unsuspecting head the censure of those who, having as yet bought nothing, could see no prospect of bringing the natives to a trade as long as he continued said amusement.

Then, again, there was our heavily-whiskered boatswain's mate driving a bargain with the mother of the headman for her favourite milch-cow and calf, while she was all the while under the impression that he spoke of the calf only. Her surprise may be imagined when she saw him driving off the two, for which he had only given her two plugs of tobacco and a black silk neck-handkerchief. Of course she returned to the charge, and, as is usual in most disputes between the sexes, convinced him of his mistake and rescued her favourite.

And, lastly, there was the writer himself, with his red silk handkerchief and the unsophisticated arctic belle, with her embroidered boots and petulant air, to fill up the picture. It was a pleasant evening that we thus passed among those truly simple and harmless Northerners. Finally, we got through with our trading and began to walk around and indulge in a general survey of every thing worth noting. We looked upon the horses and cattle that were sprinkled around us enjoying the summer grass, and asked our hosts how they managed to feed them during their long winters. They pointed to the grass and made signs that they cut it while the sun was hot and put it up in piles; and that, when that was exhausted, they had recourse to the branches of the pine-trees, which were always plentiful, but not so good.

They also said that they fed all of their animals on the heads and backbones of fish, and, upon our laughing at this as absurd, one of them reached overhead, (we were in the headman's house at the time,) and, taking down one of them, motioned us to follow him outside, where he threw it to the old woman's favourite milch-cow, who made short work of it, and then wiped out her tongue as if asking for more.

I must say that the sight surprised me exceedingly. The idea of a cow eating fish was not only ridiculous, but almost disgusting, when one looked back upon the milk-drinking spree that we had just indulged in; but we were destined to be still further surprised by one of the natives pointing to a scrubby-looking little pony and intimating that he also was a great fish-eater.

We asked if the milk never tasted fishy, and they pointed to the grass and to the sun, which we took to mean that, during the summer and as long as their hay lasted, they were not fed on fish. I could not help going back a great many years and recalling a taste of wild onions that had saved a whole dairy of milk from the unlawful attentions of a party of wearied hunters, of whom I was one, and wondering which of the two—fish or onions—would be most calculated to afford protection to the dairymen under similar circumstances.

We had now been on shore some time, and, as it was a long walk to the boats and our purchases were far from light, we began to make up our bundles and prepare for the return. We found considerable difficulty at first in persuading a young bullock as to the propriety of accompanying us; but, finally, through the instrumentality of a strong line around his horns and three or four tough switches about his rear, he was induced to make very good time as far as the boat, where he was tied securely, stowed under the thwarts and transported on board of the "John."

On our way down we passed a small stream where some of the natives were preparing to catch their usual daily supply of salmon, and some of us lingered behind the main party to see how they succeeded and to carry a few fresh ones on board for supper.

I have seen fish caught in all parts of the world by dozens of nations and in a dozen different ways, but never did I see any thing like the scene that then came off near the mouth of this small stream.

When we arrived, the natives were stretching across this stream a heavy seine, made from the sinews of the reindeer and other animals: we found it some thirty feet wide, and only waist-deep at high water, and its current by no means as rapid as is usual in those high latitudes. We crossed to the other shore in a "dug-out," and, putting our bundles on the bank, seated ourselves upon them to see how they fished at Ola.

On either bank they had strong posts driven near the water's edge, to which the seine was to be secured; and, as the flood-tide was now pretty well done running, we were just in time to see the commencement of the sport. As we were thus seated upon the bank, we could see whole shoals of the unsuspecting salmon swimming quietly up stream with the slackening tide; and, as this latter obtained its height, the seine was drawn tightly from post to post and its foot secured to the bottom by heavy stones. Thus all of the fish that had passed up, and which would naturally return to the sea with the ebbing tide, would be stopped by this seine and fall an easy prey to their active enemies.

It was an exciting moment when the first returning shoal brought up against the unexpected barrier, the meshes of which were large enough to let the small fry pass, but at the same time sufficiently small to arrest for the time the larger ones, if not to stop them altogether. Any one who has ever seen a well-filled seine hauled upon a beach can well imagine the foaming state into which the closely-packed fish soon lashed the water; and, when a dozen or more men waded in among them with short, heavy clubs, and commenced striking right and left at the heads of the largest as they darted around, the excitement of the scene and the lashing of the waters increased tenfold. I had never before imagined that so many fish could be taken in so short a time: we were certainly not on the spot over ten minutes after they began; and yet, as we marched off with a fine salmon added to our former loads, they must have already thrown *at least a ton-weight* of noble fish upon the banks.

There they were received by the women and children, who, with a sharp knife and piece of board each, soon multiplied their original unity by the number three: that is, they would seize a salmon, averaging from eighteen to twenty-eight inches, by the gills with the left hand, lay him out on the board, and before you could snap your finger twice he would be divided into three pieces, of which the head, tail, and backbone constituted one, and the two sides the remaining. These latter were thrown in a pile by themselves, with some regard to cleanliness; but the former were pitched about in the dirt in every direction, not because they were not to be used, but simply from the fact that they were to be cured as winter provender for the dogs, horses, and cows. We had already seen vast quantities of them both hanging over the fires in their houses, and had, as I have already remarked, seen a cow crunch up a head, tail, and backbone, with evident relish. And this I do not wish to be regarded as a "fish-story," for it *is* true, though doubtless *curious*, and it is as a *curious truth* that I introduce it.

I have said that we did not remain at this scene of

wholesale slaughter more than ten minutes, and must now acknowledge that, after the first excitement of seeing so many fine fish caught had passed away, I was taken with a fit of begrudging disgust—if I may be allowed the expression—that rendered a further stay rather unpleasant than otherwise. We had been on salt provisions so long that it looked like sinful waste to destroy so many noble fish in a few short minutes, while the pools of blood about the boards and the peculiar fishy odour that pervaded the atmosphere gave rise to disgust: hence the combined feeling of "begrudging disgust."

Well, we left them, and, as we did so, pointed to the piles of fish and then to the ship, giving them to understand that if they would bring some on board we would give them tobacco in exchange. They were like the Kamtchadales of the coal-mine village,—more in favour of trading for liquor than any other article; but this we did not encourage, *simply from motives of humanity;* and it is to be greatly regretted that all ships that break in thus upon their innocent solitude should not pursue a similar course of conduct. I cannot imagine a more weighty moral responsibility than that which attaches itself to the bearing of persons visiting, for the first time, these and similarly-benighted branches of the great human family; and yet it seems to be an invariable fact that primitive savages, in their first intercourse with the more cultivated members of their genus, are offered every thing calculated to increase their degradation, while all ennobling actions and truths are further than ever removed from their reach. But to return to Ola and the manner in which the simple natives complied with our intimation in regard to sending us off a part of the fruits of their evening's labour. We had not been on board ship an hour when the quartermaster reported three boat-loads of fish as having arrived alongside, and wished to know if they were to be passed on board.

"Oh yes," replied the first lieutenant; "let them come: I suppose we can look out for them."

So we heard nothing more about it, until, happening to go on deck, we saw piles upon piles of the most superb salmon. I suppose there must have been three or four tons of them, and how we were to use them was now the question. I believe (to the best of my memory) that we paid two plugs of tobacco (two pounds) for each boat-load,—certainly not more than two or three dollars' worth of articles for the entire quantity; and, as I have already said, there were several tons' weight on our decks. I could not help thinking how fine a business some enterprising Yankee packer might drive for three or four months in the year could he only visit Ola in a small vessel filled with barrels, salt, and men who understand the business of pickling salmon. He might readily fill his ship and find a certain market along the coast of California, Mexico, and South America; or he might even run over to the coast of China, should he fail elsewhere.

Well, the question now was, what were we to do with so many fish? And, as no one could well answer it, the word was passed throughout the ship for all the messes to take what they wanted, "*without any regard to expense;*" as Hartman once remarked to a "nonplussed" waiter when calling for a glass of water:—"A glass of water, waiter, and never mind ze expense."

This word was no sooner passed around the decks than all the salt and old beef and pork barrels in the ship made their appearance about the fish-piles, and before the hammocks were piped down that night a dozen or more of them were filled with brine and cleaned salmon; and there were still so many left that, when the time came to wash the decks off next morning, the officer of the deck had to throw quantities of them overboard. It was more than a week before we could wash the ship clear of the smell of fish; and I doubt if any of the officers or crew of the "old John" will ever again relish that article of food with any thing like their former zest.

Even before thus getting our decks clear of the surplus fish, the "old John's" restless anchor was again at the cat-head, as with low steam and furled sails we continued the survey of the coast along the shores of the Bay of Taousk.

The weather was calm and clear at first, but the next day it came on to blow fresh, and we were forced to anchor again for shelter well in under the land. Finally, the bad spell blew by, and we were once more under way for Fabius Island, Bay of Taousk, where we hoped to find a plentiful supply of wood and water. Arrived at our destination, we fell in with a whaler, whose captain kindly came on board and piloted us in to a good anchorage. We found a good berth well in with the island, let go our anchor, and sent the dingy in charge of an officer to examine a spot where the whaler had told us that a stream of water ran down from the mountain into the sea. When the boat returned, her officer confirmed the statement of the whaler; and yet, as one looked at Fabius

Island, it was difficult to imagine how any amount of water could flow from its breast. It was a double peak rising bodily out of the sea and composed entirely of its rocky beach, ravined sides, and double crest. There were no signs of water as you looked upon its general appearance, and we long wondered where it could come from: our wonder was subsequently solved by the captain, who ascended to its summit and found there in the sheltered ravine, between the two peaks, an immense bed of snow, whose gradual melting supplied the valuable stream. The whole island was not more than a mile in circumference, and its elevation was probably six hundred feet; it was distant about one-half or three-quarters of a mile from the mainland, and its rocky shores were strewed with the finest drift-wood. Its sides and summits also proved to be plentifully covered with a species of whortleberry, which we gathered in large quantities and enjoyed as men only can enjoy such things who have been on the salt sea for months. I shall always remember Fabius Island as long as my appetite and taste for whortleberries last.

We were anchored there three or four days, engaged in the work of wooding, watering, &c., and during that time we got up several bear-hunts through the ravines of the island without success. There were but two indications of animal life ever having existed along its rocky sides and berry-covered heights, and these were the carcase of a dead whale that had been washed upon the rocks, and the whitening bones of some unfortunate bear, who had probably died from old age or the effects of a distant shot from some passing whale-boat. Our daily hunts, therefore, resolved themselves into whortleberry-gatherings; and I don't know but that we enjoyed these latter as much or more than we should have done a bear-steak.

This island formed quite a fine harbour with the mainland, and we made a thorough survey of it before leaving. There were no signs of habitations either on it or on the shores of the adjacent main, the nearest settlement being a place called Armen, located some seven miles to the westward; and of it I shall speak shortly.

On the second day after anchoring, and although it was well known that we were to carry the ship to Armen as soon as the wooding and watering was accomplished, the entire mess, with the exception of myself and an engineer, took our lightest-pulling boat and started to visit it without delay: we had heard from our friend the whaling-captain, who had piloted us in to our anchorage, that wild ducks were as plentiful there as fish had been at Ola; and, having our appetites thus sharpened for game, the majority of the mess became impatient and started as above in the hope of obtaining a supply.

They had a hard time of it,—much harder than any one had supposed at all probable,—and returned at midnight pretty well fagged out. They had had to pull themselves there and back, for the crew were employed fore and aft, and the first lieutenant, who himself formed one of the party, would not consent that the work should be retarded. They brought back with them, however, ample payment in the shape of sixty-three broad-billed ducks, four of which we had for breakfast, and as many more for dinner on the day following.

Our friend the whaler partook of the latter with us,

and paid for his dinner by telling us many amusing anecdotes of whaling and arctic life. Among other things he told us of a friend of his, the captain of a New Bedford whaler, who, having remained about this island too late in the season, hoping to fill his ship with oil, had got her frozen in, and been thus kept there until the spring thaw came on. During the severe winter which ensued, the whole ocean became one solid mass of ice, and the island and mainland were covered to a great depth by incessant falls of snow. While thus frozen in, his ship was often visited by bear, until they began to recognise it as an object from which they were always fired upon, after which they gave it a wide berth. He had often, he said, seen these animals miles out to seaward on the ice, as long as it was firm and solid; but as soon as it began to thaw they seemed to know that it was no longer a safe promenade, and confined themselves to the scarcely-recognisable beach.

He also confirmed previous accounts, of which we had both heard and read, as to the inordinate amount of food that is required to maintain animal heat during severe winters. Many bear had been killed from the ships, he said, whose meat proved a most seasonable auxiliary to their regular rations, which would have been exhausted long before the return of temperate weather, had it not been for that. He had heard of one man eating fifteen pounds of bear-meat in a single day; and, although Parry, Sir John Franklin, and other arctic explorers, mention a still greater quantity as a matter of every-day consumption, still, it was curious and interesting to have it confirmed in this way.

I shall never forget the feeling of intense satisfaction with which we sat down to the dinner at which we heard all of these and various other pieces of information. All that we wanted to make us *perfectly happy* was a few side-dishes of vegetables and a letter each from home. We had been without these two luxuries even longer than we had without fresh meat, and yearned for the one nearly as much as the other. We had then only a faint idea of the treat that awaited us at Armen in the shape of an abundant supply of turnips; for, though many whalers had spoken positively as to their being grown there, still, we had been told the same thing of Ola, and had been disappointed. Moreover, our party, who had succeeded in getting the ducks, had neither seen nor heard of them; hence, we were in a miserable state of doubtful anxiety. Nevertheless, as soon as we had filled with wood and water, we continued the coast-line with hopeful hearts:—with intoxicating visions of huge turnips ahead and the boiling water of the revolving screw astern.

CHAPTER XXI.

WE VISIT ARMEN AND BUY TURNIPS "BY THE PATCH," ENCOUNTER A VITUPERATIVE GENTLEMAN AND SOME VERY PRETTY YOUNG LADIES, AND RETURN ON BOARD—AFTER WHICH WE STEAM FARTHER DOWN THE COAST, PAY A NOCTURNAL VISIT TO ANOTHER SETTLEMENT, AND END BY ATTEMPTING TO WADE A SIBERIAN FORD.

WE arrived off the mouth of the river on which Armen is located, after a two-hours' run from Fabius Island, and, after having let go our anchor in four fathoms of water, called away three boats and prepared to go on shore. It was a fine day, and we had the whole of it before us; for the captain had determined to let us have one day to ourselves, if only to enable us to lay in a good supply of ducks and turnips.

Two of these boats were cutters, while the third was the tomtit, which four of us took, thinking we would be able to sail on shore sooner than the heavier boats would be able to pull. The breeze was blowing quite fresh off the land, and had got up quite a little sea; but then it was not *dead* ahead, and we expected to get along quite swimmingly by making long and short legs. We therefore, having provided ourselves with an ample supply of articles of traffic, such as tobacco, matches, gaudy handkerchiefs, old clothes, &c., stepped over the side into our little boat, and, making the boys get out, shoved off in grand style, hoisted our sail, and stood down the coast with the boldness of so many sheep.

There were four of us in this party,—the doctor, Lawton, Hartman, and myself; and the other boats contained the captain and the rest of the mess, with the exception of a watch-officer and one of the assistant engineers, who were left to look out for the "old John." Our first leg was a long one; and, when we arrived at its end and put around on the other tack, the wind provokingly hauled and knocked us off so much that it was as much as we could do to return without losing ground. We soon saw that sailing under the then circumstances was any thing but the tomtit's forte; and so, when we had sailed dead to leeward of the mouth of the river, the sail was "doused," and two of us took to the oars.

We now looked with envious eye upon the cutters, which were well in with the river, wished that we had taken passage in them instead of trusting to our little cockle-shell, and leaned back upon our oars with the determination of making the best of a bad bargain. This we soon found to be tough work, and Hartman and myself, who had undertaken to pull for the first half-hour, were glad to accept the relief of Lawton and the doctor before half the time had expired. The sea, too, was much rougher than it seemed to be while we were under sail, and, instead of spray breaking over the weather side and wetting us *partially*, we now took in whole bucketfuls, that soon soaked us to the skin. We began to wish with increased fervour that we had taken a seat in one of the cutters, and would, I doubt not, have returned to the ship had we not been afraid of being laughed at.

In this way a couple of hours rolled by, when we finally gained the mouth of the river, and were glad enough to land on the bank and track our boat up against the strong ebb-tide *à la* canal-boat; but even this was no amusement, for the bank was alternately of mud and round stones, which made the walking very bad, and we could see no signs of a village. Still, we knew that it must be on the river *somewhere*, and so continued our *pleasure-trip*. Another hour passed in this mule-like occupation, and then we rounded a point and were gratified by seeing the cutters and a strange whale-boat moored to the bank a few hundred yards ahead, and the scattering houses of a very respectable-looking village looming up in their rear. We felt tired enough as we reached the nearest boat and secured the tomtit to her by the painter, and inwardly vowed never to enter upon another pleasure-party of discovery, though, like Hartman and the rest, I expressed myself highly edified by the pull when the more fortunate passengers by the cutters asked us in regard to the "time we had had."

"Oh! it vos fine time!" said Hartman, in answer to one of their questions. "It vos fear-*ful* excellent; I hope I always go in ze Thomas Tit;" and the rest of us upheld him simply to avoid being joked.

We found the people of Armen the same exactly as those at Ola, only they lived in the houses in which we found them all the year round, instead of retreating back into the country as the winter came on. There was also living with them an aged Russian soldier, whom the officer of the strange whale-boat told us had been there ever since he had first cruised in those waters, and whom rumour (rumour exists even on those out-of-the-way shores) proclaimed to be a perpetual exile from his native land. He was evidently looked up to with great respect by the natives, had his own comfortable log-cabin, as many bear-skins as would have kept a dozen men warm, and a table that boasted cups and saucers, plates, knives and forks, a broken-topped sugar-dish, &c.

As we left our boat and climbed the muddy bank of the river, we were met by some half-dozen of the natives, who made signs to us that our friends were scattered about in the different houses, and that we could do no better than follow their example. So we trudged along with our "peddlers' packs" under our left arms, and a large bag in our right hands that was destined to hold "as many turnips as we could get." These latter, to our great delight, proved quite plentiful: we just walked into a patch of them, and, holding up a bottle of molasses, motioned the owners to mark out as large a place on the ground as they were willing to give for it, and then fell to work to transfer them, tops and all, from the ground to our bags in the shortest possible time. In this way we got a good many, for our steward had brought on shore a whole demijohn of molasses that we had never been able to use, and which had more than once been on the point of being thrown overboard, and it now sold at about the rate of a quart to a bushel of turnips, which soon filled our bags. They were very large, tender and juicy; and the whaler told us that they had been only planted about six weeks. I am nothing of a gardener myself, but it seemed to me that six weeks was a very short time for turnips to grow as large as pint-pots.

We found the houses at Armen of a single style, they being built on the ground, like the larger ones at Ola, and rigged out in the same style as far as the inner arrangements were concerned. Instead of fish, however, we here found *ducks* in profusion hung up overhead and undergoing the process of being smoked. The mate of the whaler, who had been so fortunate as to witness one of their ducking-scenes, thus described it.

"The ducks had collected in dense flocks on a low, marshy piece of ground, and were feeding very quietly, when suddenly dozens of natives rushed in among them, and, striking right and left with their clubs, soon killed a great number and put the rest to flight."

It seems that they were mostly only half fledged, and thus rendered unable to fly when hotly pursued. I did not witness one of these novel scenes myself; but I saw hundreds of smoked ducks hanging up in their houses, and the natives made signs that they knocked them down in great numbers with their sticks. We traded for a number of these smoked ducks, and found that they made a delightful hash after the fresher ones were all gone.

We found neither cattle or milk here as at Ola, although the settlement was evidently better off as far as worldly goods were concerned; but we got several baskets of very fine whortleberries that would have filled a peck-measure probably, for which we gave the almost-emptied demijohn of molasses and a half-pound of tobacco. They made signs that they would like to sell us a great many more at the same price; but, as they pointed to the hills, and as we had little time to remain, we did not encourage them to take a long walk for nothing.

These people seemed slightly more advanced than those of Ola, as far as association with the world was concerned. They had a better idea of the value of money, and had learned—in a few cases—to be impudent and presuming. They had also picked up a few words of broken English from the whalers, as well as the previously-mentioned impudence, and were evidently in the possession of more than one of our vices. One fellow I remember in particular, who, having mistaken a bottle of molasses, the neck of which protruded from my pocket, for one of brandy, beckoned me into his house, intimating, by words and signs, that he had a great many squirrel-skins that he would like to exchange for it; so I followed him, and found a house very much like that of the headman at Ola, only he had ducks instead of fish smoking overhead.

We seated ourselves on a locker-like seat that went all around the hut inside of the bunks, and he immediately began ransacking an old chest, from which he shortly produced thirty or forty very inferior-looking skins, that were worth—judging from the price of others for which we had traded—probably a pint of molasses, or something of that sort, and which he now held up and offered me for the "bot branda," as he pronounced bottle of brandy.

I took the bottle out of my pocket, and, holding it up before him, said, "Molasses,—not brandy," at which his countenance fell awfully, and he lost all relish for trading. As skins were getting scarce, however, and I still wanted some more, I took off my silk neck-handkerchief, which had cost me at the rate of six dollars the half-dozen in New York, and offered it to him; but he shook his head and put them back in the chest, muttering, "Branda! branda!"

"This cost one dollar," I said, as I opened the handkerchief and showed him that it was not worn.

Imagine my surprise—almost anger—when he turned sharply around and said, "You lie! not cost dollar,—only shillin'. You no dobre," (you are not a good man.) I immediately arrived at the conclusion that he was a worthless fellow, unworthy of further association, and so rearranged my pack and continued my stroll through the village.

We fell in here, as at Ola, with several *very pretty girls.* The men, and most of the women, as a general rule, were tanned; but these girls were of a comparatively fair complexion and possessed of as rosy cheeks as one would wish to see. *They were the most refreshing sight* that we fell in with along those dreary shores, and, what is more, they stood as high as possible in the estimation of the whalers for their modesty and general correctness of behaviour. These people all wore little crosses around their necks, and gave us to understand that they were visited once a year by their priest, who, upon these occasions, generally remain a month, to baptize the children and teach them how to be good. They, as well as all the natives whom we fell in with in that sea, hold the faith of the Greek Church.

At length the hour of departure arrived, and we took leave of them by shaking hands all around before getting into the boats. The fellow who had expressed such decided doubts as to my veracity, however, I treated with "silent contempt," and was retaliated upon, as we hoisted the sail, by his singing out, at the top of his voice, "You lie! you no dobre!" whereupon I felt very small, though it was I who had only told the truth, while he had been rude and inhospitable. I am ashamed to say that I was so weak as to experience a desire to give the rascal a good kicking with my heavy expedition-boots. The breeze, which had caused us so much hard work in the morning, was now in our favour, and soon wafted us once more alongside of the "old John," when the anchor was at once hove up, and we continued our survey toward another settlement, called Tavisk or Taousk. This was the fourth and last settlement that we fell in with from the time of striking the west coast of Kamtschatka up to our arrival at Ayan on the east coast of Siberia. There were two others that we did not reach,—a small town at the head of the Gulf of Penjinks, and the larger one of Okotsk, both of which we were forced to pass for want of time. These two latter, and the four previously-mentioned, are the only settlements that we could hear of along that entire coast-line, commencing at Cape Lapatka, the most southern point of Kamtschatka, and ending at Ayan, which is within a few score miles of the mouth of the Amoor River.

The long northern day was pretty well ended as we let go our anchor off the mouth of the river on the banks of which we had been told that Taousk was located; and night was so close at hand that we could only tell, from the reflected rays of light that beamed from the river's winding bosom, that we had struck the right place. It was so late, in fact, that we hesitated as to the propriety of attempting to land that night; but a spirit of adventure seemed to grow among us with the darkening shades, and, in less than a half-hour after the anchor was down, two boats were in the water, and every officer in the ship, save myself, the purser, and an engineer, were seated in them, and pulling through the darkness to *find the mouth of a river that they knew nothing in the world about*, and to visit a town the very existence of which we only knew from hearsay. And now, as I did not go myself, I shall have to give the account of the trip as I myself heard it the next morning after their return. I even forget now who was the narrator: but these are the facts; and it is said that facts speak for themselves. This is the sense of what we who remained on board heard the next morning after the party had returned in company with a number of natives, two of whom (priests of the Greek Church) took passage in our boats, while the others came off in their own half-bateau, half-canoe-like "dug-outs."

Shortly after leaving the ship, the night had closed around them so fast that they soon lost sight of both ship and shore; but, as they had a compass and lantern in each boat, and had obtained their course before leaving the ship, they continued pulling steadily in the direction pointed out by the needle, and, taking care not to part company, soon came within reach of the sound of breakers, along which they then pulled until a dark spot on the beach told them that they were abreast of the river. They then closed in with it cautiously, and finally found themselves entering a swiftly-running stream whose mouth was whitened by the breaking surf, and whose turbid waters came down to the sea with such violence as to drift them out more than once after they thought themselves securely entered. Upon one of these occasions they were cast upon a sand-bank just outside of the mouth and narrowly escaped being rolled over, so furiously ran the current. This was harder work than they had bargained for; and, after pulling a half-hour or more and making very little progress, they were forced to land upon the beach and resort to the process of "tracking."

This amusement my narrator described as being any thing but pleasant; for they found themselves sinking over the ankle in the mud at every step, or stumbling over loose piles of stones which the darkness hid from view: still, it was better than pulling with the oars all night against a current which they could hardly stem, and so they hung to it with the determination of necessity, and were in the end rewarded by arriving at a village on the left bank, which they rightly concluded to be Taousk. There they were received by the barking of dogs, the bellowing of cattle, and, finally, by a score of natives, who, after they had been convinced that they were not a detachment of the Allies bent upon burning their town, received them very kindly, and conducted them to the house of the priest, who, it seems, was the "headman" in temporal as well as spiritual affairs.

By this personage they were received more kindly than ever. He got them up a glorious supper of milk, butter, brown bread, cold duck, solidified reindeer-milk, &c., and, after that was over, drank a half-bottle of French punch, which the doctor or Carnes had presented him with, and, pointing to various piles of bear-skins on which they were to pass the night, retired with his half-empty bottle to seek his own repose. Our fellows found the skins any thing but uncomfortable quarters. They were, unlike those we had previously seen, very clean and sweet-smelling; and they slept soundly upon and under them until daylight, when they were aroused by the furious barking of apparently hundreds of dogs, who they subsequently learned had been alarmed by the proximity of a bear or other wild animal.

Taousk was the largest and most important settlement we had yet fallen in with. Its houses were strongly built and very comfortable: they had board floorings, tables, chairs, and windows, and a population of nearly two hundred. Beef was far from scarce; but, unfortunately, we did not take the time to get any on board: we expected soon to be at another place, called Ayan, where it was said to be plentiful.

Our party had an early breakfast, during the discussion of which the priest congratulated them upon their safe ascent of the river, giving them to understand that more than one whale-boat had been swamped in a similar attempt, and intimating that they had made a narrow escape from the sand-bank. After breakfast they walked among the scattering houses for some time, traded with the natives for some milk and a few bear-skins, and finally returned on board with the priest and his native assistant.

They were accompanied by some of the natives in a large canoe, in which the whole party returned after having been shown around the ship and regaled upon salt beef and pork, sour wheat-bread, and an abundant supply of fine strong coffee. This latter seemed more grateful to them than any thing else; and, as we still had a fair amount on hand, we gave the priest several pounds to remember us by. He was almost as delighted as the headman of the coal-mine had been when promised his cap full of powder. The people of Taousk were similar to those of Armen and Ola, with probably a little more of Ee-a-coute blood in their veins. The priest himself was a Russian, and seemed to possess great control over them.

We had no sooner seen our guests safely started for the shore than the anchor was again weighed and the survey continued. We were now gradually working our way to the southward, stopping every few days to fill up with drift-wood from the beach, and meeting with adventures without number. I will relate two of these by way of varying the narrative, but, before commencing, must indulge in a few remarks in regard to several ways of fording a river.

There is more than one mode of crossing a ford. One may accomplish the feat with great dignity on a sure-footed horse; or he may wade quietly from one bank to the other; and then again he may, like the mountain-goat, "leap from rock to rock, to the imminent terror of all beholders." But there is yet another mode,—an impromptu one, if I may so express myself,—which is characterized by any thing but dignity, and which taxes a man with unpleasant suddenness to the utmost extent of his resources, both mental and physical. I allude to the only mode which one finds at his disposal when, having waded to about the centre of a boiling rapid, he all at once feels his legs swept from under him and himself floundering in the turbid stream, carried furiously upon its uneven breast between and over jagged rocks, and possessed of a confused idea that he must get to one bank or the other before he is thrown, bruised and insensible, into the dark foaming pool which generally terminates such affairs. He has but one conviction—one point—to strive for: he must either reach the most attainable bank before he is cast against some rock and disabled, or he must be cast against that rock and subsequently drifted into the whirling pool with broken ribs or limbs, and a disagreeably-slim chance of being able to swim with those that are left sound.

I now found myself in a position such as this, and it happened after this manner.

The "old John," being still afloat, had managed to carry us into a half-sheltered bay, where she let go her anchor, and despatched her boats and crew to the beach to cut and bring on board a supply of drift-wood, to be used instead of coal, as this latter article was running quite short.

There being a certainty of the entire day being consumed in this way, several of us took our guns and struck back into the country in search of a flock of broad-billed ducks that the doctor had discovered near the beach, and which he had driven to a distant lagoon by shooting off the heads of two of their number with his small-bore Kentucky rifle. Always on the alert when there was game within reach, this indefatigable sportsman had landed in the first boat, shot off two heads, and returned on board for a double-barrelled gun, before the rest of us had made up our minds that we would hunt at all. His unexpected return, however, with a brace of brilliantly-feathered drakes, caused us to shoulder our fowling-pieces, crowd some ham and bread into our pockets, and accompany him in his search for their scattered companions. Old bust-proof and his master were again "in clover."

We landed on a quiet beach of heavy shingle, climbed up it through the piles of driftwood, and from its summit looked over a vast marsh-like plain, spotted here and there with elevations and scattering lagoons, and cut up by a perfect network of winding streams, which, springing from the melting snows of the back-mountains, worked their numerous paths toward the bay, joining each other in their progress until they finally got up quite a respectable river, that emptied its turbid volume through the rise of the beach into the clear waters of the calm and motionless bay.

No sooner had we reached our elevation of some thirty feet above the sea, than the doctor pointed out the direction which the ducks had taken, and each one started by a different path to hunt them up. The tide was ebbing at the time, and we therefore penetrated the muddy expanse without fear; moreover, many of the hillocks were high enough to afford a place of retreat should it return upon us unawares, and so we waded the various streams and lagoons, as we left the beach behind us, without a thought. Hours were passed in this way without my crossing *the sign of a duck*, and I had returned to within a few hundred yards of the wooding-party, when, from the top of a more elevated mound, I caught sight of a flock swimming lazily on the bosom of a lagoon, distant some three hundred yards and apparently of quite easy approach.

True, the *river was between us*, but then it did not look *much* larger than one I had just waded, and I did not even stop to reflect that it *might* be too deep and rapid to admit of fording. Moreover, I saw the captain's Ethiopian steward "making a straight wake" for the lagoon; and, as he was considerably in advance of me, I had to cross at once or let him have the first shot. As I say, I did not stop to think, but went down the slope at a trot and boldly entered upon the trial. I struck the stream at a point where a rocky ford, apparently knee-deep, promised a safe crossing, while both above and below the water was apparently quite deep. This ford was about a hundred yards in length by twenty or thirty in width, was an inclined plane of loose pebbles and firmly-embedded and jagged rocks, and altogether a most unpleasant-looking locality *after I had advanced too far to retreat.* The rushing water boiled and foamed among the jagged rocks with a force that made me feel quite unsteady over my five-pound expedition-boots, and caused me, for the first time, to think of retracing my steps. I came to a halt, concluded it was *deeper* ahead, if any thing, and felt that, if I could only turn without being tripped up, it would be the best course to go back.

I had a heavy ship's musket on my shoulder, and knew that, if I braced it against the bottom to support me in turning, I should lose just twelve pounds of my weight, and thus render it much easier for the knee-deep water to sweep my feet from under me; still, I could not turn without support of some kind, and began to hunt up a means of increasing my weight. A most ingenious device soon crossed my mind, but unfortunately it was purely theoretical:—could I only fill my pockets and hat with the loose pebbles that were working under my feet, I might increase my weight sufficently to enable me to dispense with that of the musket; but, upon stooping carefully down to feel for these loose stones, I was convinced of its impracticability, narrowly escaping losing my foothold, and was glad to regain an upright attitude.

I began to look anxiously around and wonder if I was destined to have my ribs broken against those jagged rocks, or if there was a possibility of my being able to steer clear of them should I cast myself with the rushing current and trust to swimming on shore after being swept into the revolving waters of the lower pool. Then again I thought it might be better to hold my ground as long as possible, until I could attract the attention of some one; and to this end I strained my lungs to their utmost, hoping that the previously-mentioned Ethiopian would hear me and be induced to attempt a rescue. In this I was fortunately successful; but the jar of the exertion nearly cost me another loss of footing, and the Ethiopian, instead of advancing to my assistance, quietly folded his hands over the muzzle of his gun and regarded my position with great apparent complacency. In the mean time the pebbly bottom was gradually working from under my feet. I began to feel uncomfortably *light*, and, finding that I should certainly be swept away in a few more seconds, determined to exert myself in *some way* while it remained optional. I therefore cautiously turned my musket muzzle down, planted it firmly against the edge of a sunken rock just below me, and, with that as a support, commenced to get myself pointed in the opposite direction.

It was only a commencement. No sooner did I expose the surface of both boot-tops to the furious current than I came down face first, was drifted barrel-like over the sunken rock, then over another, and, altogether, jerked about in a most confusing manner. It seemed as if my arms, legs, and head were being swept about in all directions at once; and I need scarcely remark that at this period of the action I let the musket look out for itself. How I ever reached the opposite shore is, and ever will be, to me a mystery. I remember, as I fell, feeling nerved by the conviction that I was in great danger, and that presence of mind and powerful exertion were all that I could depend upon; and I remember also determining, as I felt myself rolled with bruising violence over the first rock, to strike out for the opposite shore at an angle of forty-five degrees *with the current*, as the most apparent means of safety. But this, combined with a vast amount of floundering, sharp pains, and confusion of ideas, is all that I *do* remember, until I found myself crawling with painful exhaustion up the rocky beach some eighty yards below the point from which I had started. I looked in the direction of the contemplative Ethiopian, who no sooner saw me lying exhausted upon the bank than he seemed suddenly awakened to the conviction that something had happened, and that he had better make it known. So he hurriedly fired off his gun, shouted at the top of his voice that Mr. Habersham was drowning, and

CROSSING A SIBERIAN FORD.

then actually ran away from me as fast as his legs could carry him. Slowly I recovered my breath, more slowly still my strength, until finally I felt able to examine for injuries. Singular as the assertion may seem, I had escaped with a few quite severe bruises, a sprained wrist, and a good ducking; and, the captain soon arriving in a boat, I was taken on board, dosed with brandy, and covered up warmly in bed. For the next few days I was quite contented to remain quietly on board; but a week later I was induced to join in a bear-hunt, which resulted in great danger to three of the mess. I never tried the depth of another Siberian ford, however. This "bear-hunt" is the second adventure of which I spoke. As it will be a rather lengthy account, I will put it at the head of the twenty-second chapter.

CHAPTER XXII.

WE WAYLAY A SIBERIAN BEAR AND NARROWLY ESCAPE "CATCHING A TARTAR;" AFTER WHICH WE ENGAGE IN A STAMPEDE, CLIMB A VERY STEEP HILL, AND THEN DESCEND AGAIN TO OUR BOAT.

A WEEK had passed since the adventure recorded in the last chapter, and we were again at anchor in a half-sheltered bay. It was evening, and the past day had been devoted to loading our decks with a fresh supply of drift-wood and to filling our water-tanks; and, now that we had as much on board as we could stow, and it was near sunset, we concluded to remain at anchor that night and make an early start the next morning.

Immediately after dinner, and while the majority of us were at work, the doctor, Lawton, and Williams had taken advantage of our being at anchor to embark in the tomtit with their guns and the determination to employ the remnant of the day in a stroll through the woods after some wandering bear. They had often indulged in similar strolls without having the fortune to meet with the object of their search, and now vowed that they would not return *this time* without some well-riddled bruin as their travelling-companion. And now, as the day's work was over and the western sun dropped slowly behind the uneven range of the surrounding mountains, the tomtit was observed about half-way between us and the southern shore of the bay, returning at a rate whose extreme tardiness indicated any thing but a "glorious day's sport" as having been enjoyed by her Nimrod rowers.

Several of us were leaning over the quarter-deck rail, commenting upon their probable disappointment and disgust, when the quartermaster of the watch directed our attention to an immense bear, who, he said, had just appeared upon the beach from the thick undergrowth which almost hid the mouth of the river, our late watering-place. We looked in the direction indicated and saw a huge mass, of a black colour, whose well-defined outlines moved slowly toward the water's edge. There was no mistaking it for any thing *but* a bear as it picked its lumbering way through the heavy sand and scattered rocks along the rippling beach, toward the southern point of the bay. He was at least a mile, probably more, from us, and yet his huge dimensions and every motion could be seen as plainly as if he had been within gunshot. We thought how large he must be to show so plainly at such a distance, and longed to cross his path with our rifles and revolvers.

He was evidently *taking his time* to go wherever he was bound, for he walked along quite slowly, stopping every now and then with his head to the ground as if smelling or eating something, and then continuing along as before. We looked toward the bright path which had been left by the setting sun and wondered if its refracted rays would last us another half-hour, or if we would be likely to reach the beach *just as it got too dark to shoot*, and thus have a long pull for nothing. We wondered all this with excited voices, and, while wondering, cast our eyes in the direction of the tomtit, whose sharp-sighted occupants had evidently been as wide awake as the old quartermaster. We could see them lying on their oars and apparently consulting as to the rationality of returning to the beach and awaiting his arrival either from the boat or ambush behind some log or rock; and in a few moments the boat's head was pulled quickly around for the beach by Lawton and Williams, while the doctor, with a tiller-rope in each hand, leaned eagerly forward with every stroke.

"By George!—there they go back after him!" exclaimed an excited voice.

"Let's call away the Falcon" (our fastest boat) "and lend them a hand," cried a second.

"The crew have been worked hard to-day, gentlemen," remarked the first lieutenant; "and if you want the Falcon you must pull her yourselves."

"Oh, the mischief!" exclaimed excited voice No. 1.

"I've been working hard too," chimed in No. 2.

"Well, gentlemen," interrupted the captain, who was as ready for the fun as any of us, "call away the gig and get your rifles: she's handier than the Falcon. Come! let's see if we can't get a bear at last!"

In less than two minutes we were all seated in the crowded stern-sheets of the flying boat, with the eager crew bending to their supple oars and urging her headlong course toward the unsuspecting monster. There were five of us in the boat besides the crew, all armed with Sharpe's rifles and revolvers,—some even with bowie-knives,—while the crew themselves each had a carbine, ship's pistol, and cutlass,—eleven grown-up men, armed to the teeth, and in hot pursuit of a lazy old bear, who continued his lounging way along the beach without the least indication of consciousness or fear of danger. It was exciting in the extreme to every one but him.

Five minutes rolled by in this way, and then we saw the tomtit reach the beach some half-mile below the bear, when the three hunters hastily landed, hauled her up well clear of the water and concealed themselves behind a huge boulder of granite which was distant some twenty feet from the water and about the same distance from the edge of the hill-side bushes. It was, in fact, situated exactly in the centre of the beach at low-water, and the trunk of a fallen tree that had rolled down from the hill-side connected it with said hill-side bushes. Had they had both time and material at their command, it would have been impossible to have constructed a more admirable place of ambush.

This was all very favourable; but there was one consideration which acted as a powerful drawback to their hopes: they had but one round of ammunition each, (all this we learned subsequently,) and neither knife or revolver in the party. What if it should come to a hand-to-hand struggle? Nevertheless, they shut their eyes to such a disagreeable result and entered boldly upon the desperate game of waylaying a ferocious animal whose weight was certainly not less than sixteen hundred pounds, and whose kind—like the grizzly of our own Western mountains—had often been known to hug a man or horse to death after receiving a dozen wounds any one of which would have disabled an ordinary animal.

It was, indeed, a risky game to be entered into under the circumstances.

After thus stowing themselves in ambush, getting good rests for their guns, and determining exactly how far they were to let the bear come before firing, they began for the first time to calculate the chances that were against them, and to feel doubtful, even amidst their nervous excitement, as to the result. The doctor, who was renowned for shooting off the heads of geese and ducks at marvellously-long distances, may be supposed to have felt perfect confidence as to the effect of his "only ball;" but then he had not now his long Kentucky rifle, and was far from certain that he should shoot with his usual closeness with the heavy ship's musket that had been kicking his shoulder out of joint for the last few hours.

As he was, however, the most reliable shot, in spite of the absence of his favourite gun, it was determined that he should fire first, while Lawton, who was armed with a rhinoceros rifle of immense bore, was to aim at his heart and fire as soon after as possible. Lastly, Williams, who was armed with a double-barrelled shot-gun loaded with ball, was cautioned more than once to shoot right for the centre of his fore-shoulder,—a *little abaft* if any thing,—and to pay particular regard to the state of his own nerves,—*i.e.* not to *get excited* and be led into the dangerous error of shooting *over his back*.

"Now, mind what you are about," said the wary doctor: "*I* may miss with this old musket, and if you two follow my example we are certain to be hugged to death. You remember what the old priest at Taousk told us about these fellows? Confound it!" he exclaimed, as he cast his eye in our direction and saw that we were pulling hurriedly toward the bear,—"confound it! There's a boat pulling right up for the bear: they'll drive him back into the woods. Did you ever see any thing so provoking?"

"I wonder people haven't got more sense!" muttered Lawton, in an angry whisper. "They *must* know that we are here waiting for him, and yet they run that chance of driving him to the bush. I wish she'd run aground. Miserable foolishness!"

"Remember what we agreed about 'standing by' each other here," said Williams: "there's to be no running if he closes with us; *I* couldn't keep up." The doctor and Lawton laughed, in spite of their chagrin at our approach; and then ensued an interval of silence, followed by disconnected remarks as to the approaching crisis.

Bruin was now getting close enough to cause them to lower their voices to a whisper. He was about two or three hundred yards off, lumbering along about as fast as a man would ordinarily walk, and apparently unconscious of either ambush or boat. The doctor, therefore, with his usual wariness, cautioned them to silence.

"Hush! hush!" he whispered. "He is close enough now to hear. Fortunately the wind is coming from him to us and his nose will be of no use to him. If we can only keep out of his sight and hold our tongues, he will come right upon us before he suspects any thing. We will let him get as far as that bunch of grass before we fire, and then we can make a sure thing of it." He pointed with his pale but steady finger to a clump of dried sea-weed which the ebbing tide had left *just eleven feet* from the place of ambush, drew a long breath to relieve a nervous feeling of morbid hungriness that had lately attacked him, and examined the musket's cap with a doubting eye.

And now to return to our boat. There was no occasion now for the usual order of "Give way, boys!" the long sweeping oars of mountain-ash worked with the beautiful regularity of a steam-engine, under the bent backs and swelling muscles of the long-tried and excited oarsmen, and seemed to cast the boat at least her length ahead with every stroke. We were beginning to close in with the beach pretty well; and, just as we had succeeded in getting the bear between us and the shore-party, he seemed to discover us for the first time. Our gliding approach, however, did not apparently disturb him; he only turned a lazy glance toward us, snuffed the tainted air, and continued his lounging gait toward the very clump of sea-weed which the sound judgment of the Kentucky hunter had imagined he would approach in search of some fated shell-fish or other object of food. We saw that the crisis was fast approaching, and we were yet some three hundred yards from the beach: would that he might find some unfortunate crab to arrest his lazy progress until we could give a few more strokes and reach the shore!

To the ambushed hunters these were moments of thrilling excitement. They could not remain positively out of his sight without he being also out of *their* sight, and, notwithstanding his immense bulk and weight, he moved along the sandy beach with such a noiseless tread that they could not judge, from the sound of his steps, whether he continued his approach, or whether he had taken to the bushes from the noise of our oars. This state of suspense at length became so unbearable that the doctor determined to steal a cautious glance at him over the top of the boulder, and in the execution of this he was so fortunate as to get a good view and recover his hiding-place without being seen by Bruin. The feat was successfully accomplished; but he has often expressed regret at having undertaken it, simply from the fact that the unexpected size and ferocious look of the monster, combined with the startling accounts we had all heard of his desperate mode of fighting, and their own total want of defensive arms, so troubled his ordinarily-steady nerves that he felt he should have fired with a truer eye and more steady aim had he avoided looking at him until the moment arrived to do so along the barrel of his musket.

His description of his savage appearance, as observed while he was thus evidently unconscious of the presence of danger, was vivid in the extreme.

"When I lifted my eye over the boulder," he said, "I expected to see him at a distance of at least fifty yards up the beach, and to find him of a reasonable size. Imagine my surprise, therefore,—indeed, my alarm,—to find him almost under our noses and exceeding in size the largest of oxen. I must confess that I longed at that moment for one of two things,—either to feel my knife and revolver in my belt, or myself safely on shipboard. In fact, I think the latter feeling was a *little* the strongest if any thing. Of course my survey was a hurried one: still, I saw more than enough to increase my fears as to the result. See here what it was that I saw.

"His head, though quite large, was small when compared with his huge fore-shoulders, of a jet-black hue, and covered with a growth of short, sleek hair that shone as if he had just dipped it into a barrel of grease. The rest of his body was covered with long and thick *wool*, rather brownish along the backbone, but as black as his head everywhere else. His fore-legs were of an awful size, his height from four to five feet, and his length of body and limb absolutely horrifying. I calculated at the time that he could not have weighed less than fifteen hundred pounds,—possibly more; and, as I imagined myself borne down by that weight, I shuddered.

"As he still continued his approach he threw out his fore-legs with a sweeping motion, and swung his apparently-unwieldy frame something after the fashion of an over-handed swimmer; and the tracks that he thus left looked deep enough to contain a gallon-measure. A dense swarm of gigantic mosquitos hovered around his head and seemed to cause him no inconsiderable annoyance in that particular locality; and I could not help thinking what good judgment they evinced in the selection of their point of attack, as they might have worked a day through the thick wool which protected the rest of his body without reaching his skin. As he moved along with his slow and measured pace, his general appearance was prominently indicative of two things—unbounded strength, and a latent ferocity of disposition which promised an unyielding foe. I looked at him and trembled; and, as the above all flashed quickly through my brain, I drew a long breath, and felt that a moment was drawing near when courage and thought must combine with inferior muscle to equalize the pending struggle. By a violent effort I retained my self-possession, sunk quietly into my ambush, and, with firmly-set teeth and pointed musket, awaited his appearance beyond the outer edge of the rock.

"Lawton and Williams had, in the mean time, gazed anxiously in my face, there to read information which could not now be imparted by words; and, as they observed its expression of almost alarmed excitement, they became a shade paler, and grasped their guns with compressed lips and flashing eyes as they bent their steady gaze toward the clump of sea-weed.

"It seemed as if minutes had become hours as we thus awaited his appearance.

"We could hear the sounding beats of each others' hearts, and the hurried dip of your boat's oars, which, now that the end was at hand, we hailed as a promise of rescue should the probable struggle result from a misdirected ball or the bear's well-known tenacity of life.

"Slowly the moments dragged by: plainer became the sound of your oars: we could even hear the noise of the broken water under your rushing bow, when * * * *

"The deafening report of Lawton's heavy-bored rhinoceros rifle at my very ear caused me to spring to my feet and glance hurriedly around with a confused idea that concealment was no longer our *forte*, and that the time had at length come when muscle, coolness, and determination were the only reserves for us to fall back upon. The game was now evidently under way, and nothing but steady nerves and desperate fighting was to save us.

"Lawton had taken me by surprise when he fired; for

I was unfortunately so close to the rock that a small projection of its right side completely concealed the bear from my view, while his whole fore-shoulders and head were exposed to the others. In fact, *he* saw the others before I saw him; and it was a sudden demonstration of flight on his part that had caused the unexpected discharge.

"I sprang to my feet with ringing ears, and looked anxiously over the boulder, which was now between the bear and myself. The sight which met my eyes was thrilling to behold

"He was standing upright upon his hind-legs, hugging the air at random with frantic rage and fright, throwing his expanded jaws right and left with nervous jerks, writhing with strange pain, and growling with the strength of distant thunder. The heavy ball of the rhinoceros rifle had passed clean through his body in the region of the heart, and from the torn wounds thus created the red blood spouted with every agonized contortion. Its crimson hue indicated a vital source, and, as I gazed upon the spasmodic jets of the arterial stream, I felt that the day was ours. Slowly, and with deliberate movement, I pointed the musket between his very eyes while he was not more than ten feet from the muzzle. He was just about to close with us; but the ounce-ball stopped his spring. I imagined I could hear it as it crushed its resistless path through the hardened skull; but in this I was probably mistaken, as he could never have acted as he did subsequently with such a weight of lead in his brain. It doubtless glanced from the unyielding bone after cracking it and bringing him down as you saw him fall. Wasn't it done beautifully? Didn't he howl awfully?"

And now let me remember what we saw from the approaching boat. We saw the top of the medical head through the gloom of approaching night, as its owner took his cautious peep over the boulder, and expected to see the flash of his musket as the immediate consequence; but, to our joy, he as suddenly dipped out of sight again, while Bruin still continued his lazy way. We knew now that they had determined to let him get under their very noses before firing, and as the boat flew toward the scene we watched with straining eyes for the expected flashes.

The shades of evening were now being darkened by the near approach of night, but there was still a fair prospect of sufficient light to see us through the affair. It was just dark enough to let one see both the flash and smoke of a discharged piece, and to enable the huntsman to take a deadly aim without the drawback of a distracting ray. We gazed with straining eyes through this gathering gloom, as the crew swung with unfailing muscle to the bending oars.

Suddenly those straining eyes encountered two beautiful sights, while, in the same instant almost, our ears were saluted by the sharp report of a discharged rifle.

In the first place, we saw its sudden and lurid flash, and in the second, the frightened action of the stricken bear. Even before the report reached us,—in fact, simultaneously with the explosion of the lurid flame within ten feet of his lowered head,—he sprang frantically into the smoky air, came heavily down upon his powerful hind-legs, and in that upright position beat the air wildly with his sweeping paws, while, with expanded jaws, he shook his pointed head with mingled pain, rage, and fright. At that moment he offered the most perfect idea of the old expression—"looking seven ways for Sunday" —that one could imagine, and its vivid application to his painful contortions forced itself upon my mind even in that moment of wild excitement.

"*Give* way, boys! *Drive* her ahead!" exclaimed the eager voice of the captain, as with pale cheek and nervous hand he steered the trembling boat clear of the pointed rocks which began to cross our foaming path as we neared the beach. "*Give* her headway! A dozen more strokes and we are there."

"Oh, horror!" exclaimed a tremulous voice from the bow. "But this is frightful! The bear will fight! See how he settles his gaze upon the doctor and gathers himself for a spring! He will take them all with one sweep of a single paw. And *we—we are too late*!" The speaker raised himself with a gesture as full of emotion as his voice, and leaned eagerly forward over the boiling water that curled under our stern.

The large veins swelled almost to bursting on the dripping brows of the labouring crew, and the tough oars bent like whalebone under their frightened strength. The doctor had nursed kindly weak men who were strong men now, and the power of long-cherished gratitude combined with bone and sinew to drive the boat ahead and rescue his threatened life. It was not in every oar of ash to resist those hardened muscles that swelled thus with gratitude and excitement: something must fail, for the yielding oars can yield no more. Suddenly there came a crash: one of them has broken; and, as its now useless loom was swung heavily into the air by its baffled owner, he gave vent to a deep and hasty imprecation and ground his clenched teeth in bitter disappointment. Still, *on* we go: there are four more left, and only a few more yards to pass. The power of that failing oar seems to have been absorbed by the remaining four, for our speed is apparently unchanged.

Shortly we saw another lurid flame flash through the deepening gloom, as the doctor's bent head bent still lower upon the levelled barrel, and at the *same* instant the full report of a heavily-loaded musket broke upon our ear. It took no time to reach us *now;* we were within thirty yards of the thrilling scene which was apparently but just commencing, and frames that trembled with excited emotion stood upright in the boat, ready to rush into the unequal struggle as soon as her bow should touch the longed-for beach.

This last shot was a magnificent triumph of the sure eye and steady arm which guided it. The bear, having caught sight of his foe behind the boulder, had suddenly settled upon his haunches, and, with expanded mouth and open arms, commenced a spring which would, in all probability, have landed him in their very midst. But a merciful Power arrested him on its verge: the heavy ounce-ball struck him full in the head, glanced from the unyielding but cracking skull, and brought him down like a felled ox. He came down head first into the soft sand with a jar that seemed to shake the very beach, clasped his wounded forehead with both paws, and rolled his shining head to and fro with a rapid and agonized motion. We could hear his deep-toned growl and laboured breathing as he scattered the loose stones and sand in all directions, seemingly intent on burrowing a den in which to shelter himself from his relentless enemies.

A round of loud and enthusiastic cheers broke from our party as he thus came down with a shock that in itself would have been enough to break the neck of any ordinary animal, and more than one tremulous arm pointed a Sharpe's rifle toward the fallen monster.

"Don't fire!" exclaimed a voice whose owner was evidently more collected than the rest of us. "He is done for, or Williams would draw on him with his double-barrel. Another cheer for the victory."

* * * * * * *

We cheered with even more spirit than at first, and the ravined hills spread its notes far and wide upon the motionless air.

It was a most unfortunate demonstration, and they were miserable ravines to lend their aid to our more miserable rejoicing. Bruin reared his bleeding front as the strange and unknown sounds broke upon his deadened ear, and, glaring around with flaming and blood-stained eyes, seemed to regain from them a portion of his paralyzed strength as he staggered toward the boulder, behind which our three friends retreated before his threatening approach. It was then an awful sight, as it is now a thrilling recollection,—the doctor and Lawton, with their pale faces, well-braced limbs, and clubbed guns; Williams, with his flushed cheek, bent knee, and levelled double-barrel.

Now, Williams, a steady eye! Life and death hang upon those two last shots. Aim close! *Now or never!* We watched for the expected flash which was again to arrest his progress, and heard the snap of a failing cap.

A cry of anguished despair arose from our midst as the staggering monster shook his bleeding head and reeled heavily onward with returning powers to close with his foe. We leaned eagerly forward with a tumultuous feeling of excitement boiling in our breasts and clouding the vision with a species of vertigo. *Another false cap!*—another hope gone,—their last!

Suddenly our attention is called to our own safety. A sudden jar, a crash of splintering oak, a long grating sound, and the boat's bow is high and dry out of the water, her progress stopped.

* * * * * * *

We saw no more for the next few seconds. A sunken rock had crossed our path, and the boat, urged by her tremendous velocity, had run upon it high and dry. We were thrown in every possible direction,—some overboard, others along the thwarts, others piled in a promiscuous heap in the forward part of the stern-sheets. As for myself, I went overboard head first, but, by catching the gunwale of the boat with my left hand, brought up with only one leg in the water, and enough presence of mind to feel with my foot for bottom, holding my rifle well clear of the water at the same time.

I found it only knee-deep; and, as we were now not more than a boat's-length from the beach, a general rush was made for it as soon as people had recovered their legs and the depth of water became known.

I never before engaged in such a scrambling race,—through the knee-deep water, into holes that were waist-deep, tumbling over sunken rocks, and all the while the utmost noise and confusion prevailing.

As we thus regained the use of our eyes, legs, and voices, the bear seemed suddenly seized with fear. He turned short in his advance upon the desperate group that awaited his attack with uplifted guns, and urged his confused and staggering flight toward the sheltering brushwood of the precipitous hill-side.

Whether he shrank before the blazing eye of man's angry intellect at bay, or fled from the confused and unusual uproar which we created in his rear, it is hard to say. Certain it is, however, that he did fly, and, as he turned, we saw the no-longer-expected flash of Williams's faithless gun and heard the whistle of its misdirected ball. Another flash from his remaining barrel, another whistle of its uncertain messenger, and all hope of stopping the bear's flight was gone. *Their* ammunition was all expended, and *we* could not use ours from the astonishing fact that Lawton and Bruin were now *exactly in line.* This excited huntsman no sooner saw that Williams's balls had passed the retreating bear without disturbing a hair than he threw down his gun and hat and started in hot pursuit. Instead, therefore, of our party being able to stop and fire a grand volley, we were forced to join in the pursuit or let him and Bruin have it all to themselves. A general stampede, therefore, ensued, and such a stampede I never engaged in before. Bruin had evidently given up all idea of fighting, and was devoting his waning strength to secure his safety by flight; and,

WAYLAYING A SIBERIAN BEAR.

as he urged his laboured and painful retreat through the heavy sand and between fallen trees and projecting rocks, we pressed after him in the vain hope that he would outstrip his reckless pursuer sufficiently to let us fire without the risk of hitting the wrong object. But our exertions were of no avail. Lawton ran well, and was evidently gaining ground instead of losing. Nevertheless, Bruin, having considerably the start, reached the edge of the hill-side bushes, in which he disappeared for a moment, and then again broke upon the view, as, with out-hanging tongue, quick breathing, and laborious movement, he dragged his wounded body up the steep and broken hill-side.

He was now considerably *above* Lawton, and a few unsteady shots were fired over the latter's head, but with no apparent effect: the stampede had evidently unsettled our nerves. The flurried figure of the pursuer now in turn disappeared in the brushwood, and a moment later we saw him climbing with frantic strides in the very wake of the struggling and disabled monster. He was evidently gaining on him, too, and we expected every moment to see him turn and hug him in his crushing embrace.

At this stage of the proceedings I found myself and several others bursting our difficult paths through the tangled brushwood, and urging each other ahead with our voices, but in reality keeping each other back in our extreme eagerness. Suddenly we were at the foot of the hill, and, already half broken down by the run, commenced its toilsome ascent.

As we emerged from the thick brushwood and looked

up toward the chase, the sight which flashed upon our eyes was awful to behold.

Lawton was within a few feet of the bear, who still urged his painful flight; but now it was with his gory head and flaming, blood-injected eyes half turned with threatening rage upon his reckless foe, while the uplifted hand and general action of the latter indicated an intensity of mental excitement bordering upon insanity. He evidently was preparing to seize the retreating monster by his long and shaggy wool, and measure his strength with the remnant of that which we had been told could crush the bones of a horse as though they were so many dried sticks.

"Lawton, you jackass!" shouted the doctor, in a voice of frightened strength, "come back! Stop! Don't touch that bear! If he turns, he'll mash every bone in your body. *Come back!*"

But he was deaf to every thing like reason. His livid face, dishevelled hair, and furious energy of manner were terrible to behold as he threw every power of his muscular frame into a last long stride upon the retreating beast, and brought down his powerful grip into the yielding wool.

A cry of mingled alarm and warning from our scattered ranks seemed to recall him to his senses.

As the bear came to a half-halt and turned his bloodshot eyes and bared teeth more fully upon him with a threatening growl, a flash of reason seemed to illuminate his turbid brain and light him to the path of safety. He relinquished his dangerous hold upon the retreating monster, who at once resumed his flight with apparently a reviving strength that defied further pursuit. He now seemed to pass up the hill with an easy and sliding gait, while we were falling over hidden logs, or sinking knee-deep into the light, leafy soil of decaying vegetation at every step. Even at that thrilling moment, I found time to wonder how it was that he could outstrip us with his heart's blood spouting from two gaping wounds at every leap, and his wounded head also bleeding with deadly freedom.

Lawton gazed after him with clenched and uplifted hand, and a look of wild disappointment gleaming from his unsettled eye. He was evidently now conscious of the madness of his former pursuit, and contented himself with devoting the remainder of his strength to calling vehemently for a loaded gun.

"A gun! a gun! Give me a loaded gun! Why don't some of you shoot? The bear will get away! Follow him, some of you! I can go no farther." And he sank upon the shelving hill-side in the weakness of overtaxed muscles and lungs.

"There's no use following him any farther," exclaimed the broken-winded master. "He's got away from us, and it's too dark in these bushes to hunt for him. You can't see now ten feet around you; and he might *turn the tables* by waylaying *us* behind some rock or clump of bushes. My ribs are not over and above strong. I'm going back." He spoke word after word with a rapid and broken utterance, as he leaned his rifle against a decayed log, wiped his dripping brow, and puffed and blew like a grampus in shoal water.

"Yes; but he can't go far," gasped the exhausted

pursuer. "He's got two ounce-balls through him,—one through his heart, the other through his brain. How can he hold out long? Look here at the great clots of blood that burst from him as he jumped this log! How long can he live *now?*" He pointed to the large, water-lily-like leaf of an arctic plant, whose polished and concave surface contained probably a gill of hardening blood. "Look at *that*," he continued, "and tell me that it's no use to follow him. I'm only waiting to get my breath again."

"Oh, you jackass!" replied the breathless doctor, as he gained our stopping-place. "Suppose that bear had hugged you: where would you have been now?"

"There's more truth than either poetry or delicacy of expression in your salutation, doctor," said the now rational and reviving Nimrod. "I believe I was a jackass up to the last moment: it wouldn't have done to have held on to him any longer, *I don't think.*"

"Oh, by George!—*what* a climb!" gasped exhausted Williams, as he staggered against a tree and threw down his gun in the rank undergrowth at his feet. "Why *couldn't* I hit him? What *miserable* luck!"

"Yes, you may well ask that," said the disappointed voice of the irritated pursuer. "Why didn't you give your gun to the doctor if you couldn't shoot yourself? *You* talk about hunting bear!"

"Everybody can miss *some*times, I suppose," retorted the chagrined hunter. "*You* fired from a rest, and while he was standing still: anybody could have done *that.*"

Here the discussion was interrupted by the arrival of

the less agile members of the chase, and a hurried consultation resulted in a determination to follow the bear as far as the crown of the hill at any rate. We therefore separated into seven parties of two each, spread ourselves out to the right and left, and renewed the ascent with a distance of ten or fifteen feet between each couple. In this way we finally reached the top of the hill; but, though we had beat every bush with our guns and peered behind every rock and log, we could see no further sign of him,—not even the print of his heavy foot upon the yielding soil, or a drop of his wasting blood upon the hanging leaves. He had evidently given us the slip; and, as we once more joined company upon the bare and breezy height, we looked down the gloomy path we had just ascended, and wondered if he might not still be among some of those dense bushes or behind one of those large boulders, ready, at a moment's warning, to hug any one passing within his reach. It was now quite dark enough to make our position unpleasant as we looked and wondered in this way.

"What a pity we hav'n't an extra hour of daylight to follow him up!" exclaimed one.

"Let's come ashore the first thing in the morning and bring Jack and Brag (our two dogs) to track him to his den," said another.

"Yes; they'd track him with a vengeance," remarked a third. "They've got too much sense for that."

"Let's look around *a little* longer," said Lawton, who had now possessed himself of one of the men's carbines and felt more eager than ever; "he *can't* be far off."

"It's no use going any farther!" remarked the captain, as he peered anxiously through the increasing gloom. "We'd better be getting down to the boat before it's too dark to see our way. If it's a foggy day to-morrow and we can't continue the survey, we'll come back and hunt him up by daylight. *Allons!*"

And so we returned on board with our wearied limbs and disabled boat, and left old Bruin to drag his battered hull to some quiet corner, there to stuff his wounds with leaves and growl through the long and feverish night.

The next day was unfortunately beautifully clear,—"just the weather for surveying;" and so we continued our work and left our wounded foe to whiten upon the mountain's side, or drag through heavy weeks and months of slow recovery.

CHAPTER XXIII.

WE ARRIVE AT AYAN AND FALL IN WITH SOME OLD ACQUAINTANCES—AFTER WHICH WE NARROWLY ESCAPE BEING FEASTED TO DEATH BY THE RUSSIANS, ARE TOLD SOME "STUNNING" YARNS, SEE A WHALE STRUCK, AND FINALLY GET SAFELY TO SEA.

AT last we were "making the best of our way" for Ayan, and it would be almost impossible to imagine what a cheerful feeling pervaded the ship at the prospect of spending a week in such a port as we supposed that to be. When it was first determinately known that we were to pass the summer of 1855 along the inhospitable and dreary shores of the Okotsk Sea, we were hanging to a quiet anchor in the harbor of Hong-Kong, engaged in the pleasures of recreation after a stormy cruise of six months, as well as in the labour of refitting again for sea.

We immediately began to hunt up authorities on the subject of that sea in general, and were surprised that we could neither find individual or book possessed of the desired information. There was a woeful falling-off, too, in the charts of that frozen part of the world; and the consequence of all this was that when we left Hong-Kong our only idea of the ground we were going to was that it was the Okotsk Sea; that we would be there likely to fall in with hundreds of whale-ships; that millions of wild geese and ducks, flying from the heat of tropical summers, took refuge in its extensive lagoons and marshes; that they were so tame while thus away from the "haunts of man" that a good stick would do more service among them than a double-barrelled shot-gun; and that upon the eastern coast of Siberia (its western boundary) there existed a large and flourishing city, whose streets were lit by gas, whose stately mansions were filled by hospitable Russians, and whose name was Ayan. A report was also spread that a Russian count there awaited the arrival of the "Ringgold Expedition," loaded with charts and instructions from the emperor at St. Petersburg, the former being an imperial present of all previous surveys of Russian officers in those waters, (designed to assist us in our work,) while the latter made it the especial duty of the said Russian nobleman to leave no stone unturned to render the stay of the Americans *as pleasant as possible.* I need scarcely say that much of all this subsequently proved to be disagreeably tinctured with romance; but there was also in it a very fair amount of truth. We certainly *got the charts*, and, if not treated well by a nobleman, were at least nobly treated by two men, in the persons of the accomplished governor and his Falstaff-like second in command,—"old Frybark," as Hartman soon came to pronounce his name. But more of him anon.

It was toward the close of the evening of the 31st of August, 1855, that we stood boldly in for the port of Ayan, under all sail and steam; for, though coal was scarce, we could well afford to burn it now, as we were running for a city "whose streets were lit with gas" and where coal at any rate must be abundant. Besides, we had a four or five knot ebb-tide setting out against us, and the "old John" would scarcely have stemmed that had we not had steam to help our sails.

It struck two bells (5 P.M.) in the first dog-watch as we called "all hands bring ship to anchor;" and half an hour later all our sails were furled snugly to the yards and the "old John" herself (the tide having slackened as we got in-shore) was steaming slowly, through quite a fleet of American whalers, to a more inner anchorage. Five minutes more, and she rounded to with her usual grace (?), let go her anchor in a quiet part of the harbour, entirely removed from the strong tide and surrounded in part by the "snow-clad mountains of Siberia," and, as usual, commenced rolling heavily to the swell which set into the mouth of the harbour.

We found these "snow-clad mountains" without a vestige of snow or ice near them, covered by a luxuriant undergrowth and supporting as healthy-looking forests of spruce and birch as I ever saw. From a distance the entire scene had much more of a tropical than of an arctic aspect; and the unlooked-for attentions of several wandering mosquitos served to help us to the conclusion that the "snow-clad mountains" of Siberia were not always the bleak and frozen heights of which we had read in our school-boy days, and that, after all, "Siberia the frozen" might be a very pleasant place. To test the truth of this conclusion, several of us took a boat when the work was over, and started for a point of the harbour around which one of the whalers told us we should find Ayan; and as we rounded the point and shot into the pond-like cove from the rippling beach of which a scattering and streetless town ran back a half-mile or more, we could not avoid giving vent to our disappointment. Instead of thanks to a merciful Providence who had conducted us thus far in our coffin-like craft with safety to our bones and lives, we indulged in such ejaculations as the following:—

"Why, hillo!" said one: "this can't be the place we've been looking forward to with such pleasure for such a long time."

"I don't see any streets *to be lit* with gas!" put in a second.

"I wonder if that's the population waiting for us on the wharf?" asked a third.

"That big fellow looks very much like a Russian count," remarked a fourth.

"More like a whale!" put in a fifth.

"Hush! he'll hear us!" said another. "I'll tell you what, he looks as if he lived well. I hope his larder is solid."

Here the boat's keel grated sharply on the shelving beach of slaty shingle, and as we got out we were warmly received by four persons in European costume, while some half-dozen others, in strange dress and with the strongly-marked features of the Cossack, lingered in the rear.

The gentleman who looked like a Russian count, according to one of our party, and like a whale, according to another, addressed us in perfectly good English, introducing himself as the agent for the Russian Fur Company, Mr. Freighburg, and one of his companions as Dr. ——, of the same service. The remaining two, much to our surprise, proved to be old acquaintances,—members of that numerous tribe of restless Americans who live in all parts of the world, turning over their nimble sixpences or attempting to establish new forms of government over dilapidated states,—the same, in short, who, when last seen by us, were leaving the Japanese port of Ha-ko-da-di in high dudgeon at the authorities for refusing to let them land their cargo of "Yankee notions" and establish a store at that port. They now pointed to an immense block-house, telling us that the Russians had received them very kindly and given them the use of that building as a storehouse, and that, having landed all of their stores, &c., they had sent the Leveret on a whaling-voyage, and were now prepared to meet any reasonable calls upon their invoice. The Russians, they said, had bought *every thing* from them at a certain price, but left them at liberty to sell to others provided said others would *pay higher*. This we thought very liberal in the Russians, but indicative of higher prices than naval officers on a thousand dollars a year would be likely to relish. But to return to Ayan and "old Frybark."

"Any coal in Ayan, Mr. Freighburg?" asked Lawton, as the jovial old fellow took two of us by the arm and urged us toward his house.

"Any beef in Ayan, Mr. Freighburg?" asked the purser: "we've been living on fish until we're getting scaly."

"Beef, yes! coal, no! But we have plenty of liquor. We will go to my house first and take 'twenty drops,' after which we will talk about beef and coals. I suppose the whale-ships may have plenty of coals."

He was a large and powerful man,—the most perfect ideal of a strong man, I think, that I ever saw, weighing about three hundred, perhaps more,—looking as if he was all flesh, but feeling as if he was all iron, and carrying his weight with a light, firm step, while the drops of exertion rolled from his heated brow. As we walked along the broken edge of a dry watercourse, he uncovered his head and fanned himself with his broad-brimmed Panama hat, until I buttoned my pea-jacket closer around me and shivered before the disturbed air.

"Why, my good sir, you button your coat: you are cold? We find it very warm to-day." And, sure enough, when we reached his house we found the windows and doors all open, though we had left the thermometer at forty degrees on shipboard, and that, too, before the setting sun had left the air without his warming rays.

"Yes, Mr. Freighburg, it is quite cool for us," remarked one of the party: "we find our coats quite comfortable."

"Ah, yes! quite cool. Well, we want 'twenty drops:' they will warm us."

And, "suiting the action to the word," he brought out one of the largest gin-bottles I ever saw, filled a dozen or more large wine-glasses, and, drinking off one,—"to test its quality," as he observed,—took up another, and, motioning us to do likewise, continued:—

"Well, now then! we drink to Russia and America, —always friends!"

We drank the toast with as little of wry in our faces as possible, and, with a choking sensation about the throat, lit cigars and walked out to see "Ayan."

We found it composed of some fifty or sixty log-houses, most compactly put together, to guard against the excessive cold of their long winters, and of various plans and dimensions. The roofs were all painted red, without a single exception; and, though they were log-houses, they were *such* log-houses! Their walls were of huge pine logs, smoothly planed, and made to fit one over the other like the bowls of so many spoons; and the cracks thus left were tightly calked and then puttied. They were mostly of one story; but then such "one stories" as they were! Some of them covered a vast extent of ground,—the governor's mansion in particular, in which, if I remember rightly, I counted twenty-three apartments. "Old Frybark's" domicil was the only one that boasted a second floor, and he acknowledged that to be more for summer use than any thing else.

We noticed that every room was provided with a huge fireplace, and that the windows were all double, the glasses being separated about six inches apart, and containing between them an ordinary brick, upon which was raised a small pile of table-salt. The object of this salt, they told us, was to absorb the moisture which penetrated through the outer window before it could enter through the second into the apartment.

"Oh!" exclaimed our jovial host, as we lounged through the twenty-three rooms of the governor's vast mansion,—"oh! it is such a pity that the fear of the Allies drove the governor and his family into the country! See here this fine rosewood piano: you should hear his beautiful daughters sing to its deep-toned sound, or see them dance with the doctor and the aide-de-camp around this large room."

We could not avoid acknowledging our deep participation in his regrets, as he thus showed us what we had missed. We had not heard the rustle of a lady's dress for more than six months, and wanted something to make us feel civilized again.

And thus we lounged from room to room, every thing deserted and cheerless; for the governor had retreated, with the entire population, hundreds of miles into the interior before the expected demonstration of the combined fleet, burying every thing that they could not carry, and leaving Mr. Freighburg (who was a non-combatant) to look out for things in general and the buried articles in particular. We subsequently saw long trenches which the Allies had dug in the (not always vain) search for cannon, *nominally*, but, in reality, for any and all public property worth taking away. (It must be remembered that Ayan was a depôt of the Russian Fur Company, and not the property of the Czar, hence *private property*, at any rate, should have been respected.) With rare politeness, the retreating governor had left orders with Mr. Freighburg to put his house and billiard-table at the disposal of the allied officers.

"I am sorry that I cannot extend to you the same civility," remarked our host: "the English officers took away all the balls and cues when they left. *Voilà* the table!"

"Unheard-of vandalism!" exclaimed the master. "And how acted the Frenchmen?"

"Oh!—the Frenchmen? Always gentlemen. You see, the governor valued this table very much; for after it commences snowing we are confined to the house so much that one must have something to make amusement. After a shell freezes over the snow, then we dig our way out, hitch up our dogs to the sleighs, and are our own masters. Then we cut streets through the snow from house to house, and begin to be sociable. But come; let us walk a little more: then we shall want 'twenty drops.'"

So we walked on, turning now up the valley toward the small but neat-looking Greek church, whose red steeple and pendent bell looked more like home and civilization than any thing we had seen for a long, long time. We walked on and on, until the pale Northern moon shone upon our evening path, and then turned and (for want of another road) retraced our steps to the two-story house, where "twenty drops" were poured out, as a matter of course, cherry-stemmed pipes loaded with good Turkish tobacco, and family-looking old rocking-chairs filled by wearied limbs. One, two, three hours in these sleepy old rockers, the yawning "good-night," a chilly pull in an open boat, the hoarse hail of "boat ahoy!" from the watchful old quartermaster, the flash of a side-lantern in our eyes, a steep climb up the rolling side, and we were again upon the deck of our wandering home. I went to bed, and dreamed that the entire English nation were condemned to an eternal game of billiards; and I hope sincerely that this book may reach England, if it be only to let them see how some of the officers of H. B. M. frigate Sibyl requited the high-bred and considerate courtesy of the Russian Governor of Ayan during the summer of 1855.

We were so much pleased with "old Frybark's" Turkish pipes and tobacco, as well as with his "twenty drops" and off-hand hospitality of the previous evening, that, when he came on board the next morning and told us that "he expected all hands to dine with him that day," there was not a face that did not sparkle, or a tongue that tried to excuse its owner. Probably the fact of said tongues having tasted nothing but salt provisions or insipid preserved meats (the fish and turnips of Taousk Bay excepted) for several months, combined with our host's promise that his table should groan under the delicacies of the Ayan season,—probably, I say, this combination may have had something to do with our sparkling faces and consenting voices. But let facts speak for themselves.

As the appointed hour for dinner approached, we called away two boats, and, leaving the "old John" in charge of the best bower, a good scope of chain, the officer of the deck, and engineer of the day, the remainder of us packed ourselves into them and started for the quiet landing on the slaty beach that bounds the smooth waters of the inner harbour. We were received this time by the yelping of hundreds of sleigh-dogs, who, being absolutely necessary during the winters for travelling-purposes, are well taken care of when the summers arrive, in anticipation of future need of their services. We looked in the direction whence these howls and yelps proceeded, and saw a large log-house, around which hundreds of these dogs were lazily basking in the sun, and thought it would be a good idea to pay them a visit on our way up. We therefore crossed the dry and rocky bed of a periodical watercourse, and approached their commodious kennel. These watercourses are worth a passing notice.

The immense quantity of snow and ice which covers

that whole country at the end of their long and severe winters, melting sometimes with destructive rapidity during the first spell of warm weather, rushes down to the sea in swollen streams that uproot trees, dislodge huge rocks, and most effectually put a stop to all travelling until the green patches once more appear upon the hill-sides, and the turbid streams, gradually decreasing in dimensions, finally disappear entirely, leaving their uneven beds spotted here and there with silent pools as the only indication of their short-lived existence. It was over one of those uneven and spotted beds that we now picked our way, and, as we climbed the opposite bank and came suddenly upon the various groups of dogs, they raised their shaggy heads and howled most piteously. And that was the extent of the notice that they deigned us. There was no wagging of tails, no bristling of the backs, not even any skulking behind corners,—nothing but the protracted howl, and a sleepy indifference to our proximity; and, as they turned their vacant eyes upon us, we were convinced of the truth of the character ascribed to their peculiar breed,—*i.e.* that they are utterly worthless in every point of view, except as regards their docility and power of endurance before a sleigh. Their kennel, as I have already observed, was a large log-house, and in it they were locked up at night, while around it they were fed and watched during the day. They had their regular keepers, whose only duty consisted in attending to their wants and keeping them from wandering away. They gave us a parting howl as we left their unsavory locality, and again crossed the dry bed of the vernal torrent on our way to "old Frybark's" two-story domicil.

Arriving in good time at the door of that hospitable mansion, we were actually received with *open arms.* The old fellow looked as if he longed to embrace us all, but contented himself with shaking hands *crushingly*, calling loudly for the doctor, and hurrying us up to his outer chamber, where several bottles of various sizes, shapes, and colours, gleamed before our affrighted eyes.

"Well, now, come on! A little too late for a Russian dinner, but 'better late than never.' We will now take 'twenty drops,' then go over to the governor's house and eat our caviare, ('Tis caviare to the general.' See Hamlet,) after which we will drink some champagne and have dinner. My house is so small that I have set the governor's table, and after dinner we will have the horses at the door and take a ride into the country. It will shake down our dinner and get up a good appetite for supper."

"Supper!" exclaimed one of the party: "you don't expect to keep us to supper, too?" he continued, with a look of dismay, for he had lunched heartily upon a tempting beefsteak before leaving the ship, and shrank aghast before the rapid enumeration of what was yet before him.

"Keep you to supper? Yes! and to a champagne-dance after supper, too. We shall be in want of music and ladies, but then we can whistle for ourselves and imagine that some of us are the governor's beautiful daughters. *Allons!* let us go and take our caviare."

We went, and *such* a lunch as it was!—equal to an ordinary meal. And then the dinner! Nothing to be seen on the long, narrow table, save wines and vases of flowers, plates, knives and forks, and piles of glasses. But then just cast your eye into the kitchen, and see there the dozens of huge dishes loaded with—as "old Frybark" had promised—the delicacies of the Ayan season, and awaiting their turn to be introduced to the already half-sated guests. Salt and fresh water fish done up in every imaginable style; beef looking more unlike beef, in its numberless modes of preparation, than I had ever before seen it; vegetables here and there, and pastries without end. I never again wish to attend a dinner at Ayan, with "old Frybark" as the host;—at any rate, not until some cure for apoplexy is discovered, or the Russians lose some of their relish for fraternizing with Americans. I was so unfortunate as to find myself alongside of a miserably-hospitable priest of the Greek Church, who, finding himself unable to entertain me in a conversational point of view, divided his attention between keeping my plate and glasses full and his own *empty*. In spite of his large appetite, he was a fine-looking, middle-aged man, rather below the ordinary stature, dressed in a flowing robe of black silk, and wearing his dark and curling hair divided down the middle and hanging over his shoulders in flowing ringlets. His dark and silky beard reached almost to his waist, and his hands were as delicate as those of a lady. He had a smile of great sweetness, and was treated by the Russians with good-natured respect and consideration. He was a married man, and had returned from the interior with his family only the night before. On the whole, we had a very pleasant time alongside of each other, seeing that neither of us spoke a word of each other's or any common language.

At last this *abundant dinner* was ended, and, singular as

the assertion may seem, we did *ride into the country* immediately after it. "Old Frybark" was in the best imaginable spirits; we were all lively from the effects of good champagne, and one of the restless Americans, before alluded to, even beyond that point. It was amusing to see our host mount his tough-looking little horse. I think he must have weighed nearly three hundred *before dinner*, and how much more as he got on horseback I should be afraid to say. Taking wines at eight pounds to the gallon, and viands at something less, I should say that the horse must have capered under at least *three hundred and twenty or thirty* as he touched him with his spur and pointed him at the steep breast of one of the towering hills by which the city is enclosed.

Our ride was both an exciting and pleasant one,—exciting to the confused ideas of the restless American, who "couldn't for the life of him tell what was the matter with his horse" until he had been thrown twice, when he arrived at the very tardy conclusion that "that champagne must have been very strong,"—and pleasant to us, who had been aware of, and guarded against, said strength. Our road took us over mountains, along patches of hard sea-beach, up valleys, across streams, and, finally, brought us *vis-à-vis* with his excellency the Governor of Ayan and *suite*, who were coming in on a hand-gallop from their country-retreat to do us the honour of visiting the "old John" and assisting Mr. Freighburg in the duties of hospitality. His excellency received us with great warmth of manner, and told us, through our now excited host, that he had been expecting us for some time, and that if we had only arrived before the Allies he might have received us in a manner more in keeping with his feelings; but, as things now stood, we must excuse any apparent neglect, and take the expressed will for the impossible deed.

We replied, with equal suavity of manner, that we had already been almost feasted to death by his accomplished (here "old Frybark" blushed scarlet, and looked in other respects quite overpowered) representative, and that if he did not mercifully interpose his authority there was no telling what grave consequences might ensue. At this point we all laughed, as a matter of course, and, giving the reins to our fretful little horses, galloped back to Ayan; the governor and captain leading off, "old Frybark" and our doctor next, then the Russian doctor and Carnes, and, finally, "the crowd in general" bringing up the confused rear, while the restless American darted about in all directions upon his irritated horse, with the evident desire of attracting the admiration of his excellency to his superior (?) horsemanship

And thus we re-entered Ayan, where a fresh edition of Turkish pipes and tobacco, of "twenty drops," and of pressing invitations to partake bountifully, occupied the time that must yet elapse before the promised supper.

Fortunately, we were spared that promised supper for the present, but with the express understanding that it was to come off on the following night. "Distance lent enchantment to the view," as we settled back into the old arm-chairs, and talked about the war, the late vandalisms of the English officers, the manners and customs of the several tribes of Eastern Siberia, the price of furs, and of statistics in general. The governor spoke quietly, but feelingly, of the great losses and hardships which he had been forced to entail on the population by taking them away from their homes into a comparative wilderness, and gave us several interesting anecdotes of Siberian country-life. There was nothing in this prolonged conversation that surprised us more than a remark of Mr. Freighburg's in regard to the high prices which the company realized for many of their furs. He told us, among other things, that their hunters were sometimes so fortunate as to take a species of beaver—never more than two or three during the whole season, however—whose skins sold in St. Petersburg for the enormous sum of one thousand rubles, (nearly *eight hundred* dollars,) and that the silver fox often sold as high as *three* hundred.

We expressed our surprise that a *beaver's* skin should sell for so large a sum, remarking that in the northwestern sections of the United States they were quite plentiful, and the fur comparatively cheap.

"Ah! but, my dear sir," he replied, "you have not this beaver of which I speak in your country. We have the inferior kind of beaver here, too, but it is a very different animal from the one I speak of. The skin of this one is just large enough to make a fine high collar for a winter cloak, and the Russian noblemen who want such collars must pay their one thousand rubles or *go without.*"

We had every reason to believe "old Frybark" to be a man of strict veracity, and his assertion was, moreover, sustained by the others present, who spoke of it as a matter of course; still, I hesitate to publish such an unheard-of price for a beaver's skin, and must refer all skeptics on the subject to "old Frybark" himself. I myself believe that the price was as he stated.

And now, if the reader will imagine twenty-four hours passed, (during which time the governor had returned to the inner settlement, leaving his aide to assist "old Frybark" in entertaining us,) and pretty much the same party reassembled in our host's "second-floor sitting-room," in company with Turkish pipes and tobacco, numerous bottles of "twenty drops," and the prospective supper which was at length at hand,—if he will imagine us in that room, I say, and himself as a listener, he will hear what we listened to upon that occasion, and doubtless be as much surprised as we were.

"You talk about beef!" said "old Frybark," as he refilled his huge pipe and drew a match across the bottom of the box. "You say you had too much yesterday, and yet you want whole bullocks now to take on board ship! Well, the natives will drive three in for you this evening. When the English came we had to drive them all back into the country."

He lit his large pipe and puffed away complacently, with his gaze riveted upon the bottle of "twenty drops" as Dickens says old John Willett was wont to admire the kitchen boiler.

"You talk about eating and drinking as if we ate and drank a great deal," he at length continued: "you should see one of these Tongouse [Tongouse Indians] drink butter if you want to see how much a man used to cold weather can drink."

"*Drink* butter!" exclaimed one of the party. "Why don't they *eat* it?"

"Because they like to drink it better," was the reply. "I have seen one of them drink forty pounds and then go to sleep."

"Did he ever wake up again?" asked a surprised voice.

"None of your marines' yarns here, old gentleman," remarked another.

"Oh, Mr. Freighburg!" exclaimed a fourth, in a deprecatory tone,—"*forty* pounds?"

"Forty? Yes; any one of these Tongouse that you see will drink *twenty* as an everyday affair; but there is one fellow in particular, who, as I say, *once drank forty* and then went to sleep. I pledge you my honour."

"*You* didn't *see* him, Mr. Freighburg?" I asked, in a hesitating voice; for, after commencing the question, I suddenly remembered that he had *already* pledged his honour to its truth.

"Yes I did, though," he replied; "and I'll tell you how it was. A friend of mine was as skeptical as you are, and so I just said to him, 'Mr. Henry, I see that you don't believe what I tell you.'

"'Not a bit of it,' he said.

"'Well,' said I, 'you pay for forty pounds of butter that is in the Company's warehouse, and give it to him, and if he doesn't drink it all before noon (this was about nine o'clock in the morning) I'll pay you back the money.'

"'Agreed!' he exclaimed, and commenced to feel at once for his pocket-book; but I told him, 'Never mind the money yet a while,' and sent my servant to hunt up the Tongouse.

"After a while he came; and when he heard what it was all about, and saw the butter, his eyes sparkled, and he rubbed himself, as if he already had it in him. He just warmed it a little to make it run, and then set to work. At noon he had drank it all and was asleep in the sun, with the butter running from his pores in the shape of greasy perspiration."

"Ugh! horrible!" exclaimed a disgusted voice: "what beasts they must be! Are they fit for any thing but to drink butter and sleep?"

"Yes; they drink whale-oil almost as well, and fight bears much better than you or I could. You were speaking of your encounter with a bear up the coast the other day: had one of these Tongouse been there instead of your three fellows with their clubbed guns, he would not have got away as he did. Those three fellows had a narrow escape:—you don't know *how* narrow. Had not the bear been frightened by the outlandish noises you made in rushing to the rescue, he would have made short work of them. You might as well expect to stun a whale by hitting him over the head with a boat-hook, as to stop a bear with a clubbed musket. You should have had a Tongouse there: they do not know what fear is. They attack the bear single-handed, with a long knife as their only weapon, and always win the battle unless he runs. They are generous as well as brave. Their mode of warfare you will doubtless look upon as foolishly liberal. They always hunt with this knife,—which, with the handle, is from three to four feet long,—and if they come upon a bear asleep, instead of killing him at once, they catch him by his wool, give him a shake to wake him up, and then step back out of his way and tell him to come on. If he moves off instead of fighting, they throw stones at him to make him angry, and then when he rushes up to hug they receive him on one knee, with the butt of the knife braced against the ground, and the point ready for his heart. I suppose *that* sounds strange too, but *it's true*."

"You are quizzing us, Mr. Freighburg," remarked one of the party, dryly.

He glanced quickly at the speaker, and said, earnestly, "I assure you, upon my honour, that I am only telling you *facts*. *Voilà* M. the Governor's aide: ask him."

"Well, I beg pardon," replied the doubter, with a smile that started the old fellow's tongue as loose as ever. "Give us some more: it's quite edifying."

"Yes, but I take 'twenty drops' first. Smoking is dry work, and, when you come to talk too, it's parching." He knocked the ashes from his pipe, laid it on the table, and, as usual, filled *all* of the glasses. I, having already burned my throat with his modest "twenty drops," got the start of the party by complaining of a sick headache—which I really had—and begged to be excused from joining. Some offered one excuse, some another, and others manfully reached for their glasses, but with the air of martyrs. He cast a most reproachful glance at us who had declined, emptied his glass, refilled his pipe, and continued.

But before I proceed any further I must add a word in regard to the "butter-drinking feat" of the Tongouse. I published it some time since in a Philadelphia weekly paper, and shortly after met an old acquaintance,—a purser in the navy, and who is at this very time stationed at the Philadelphia Navy-yard.

"Look here!" he said to me, after we had indulged in the usual remarks *as to the state of the weather:* "that was quite interesting about the butter. But you don't expect people to believe it, do you?"

"I can't say I do," was my reply. "Still, it is my own belief that it is true."

"Oh, yes, I know," he returned. "And now I'll tell you something singular. I had a nephew who once went in a whale-ship for his health, and when he returned *he told me that same yarn as having happened to himself. He* must have been the 'Mr. Henry:' that wasn't the true name, was it?"

I candidly acknowledged that, having forgotten the name, I had taken that of Henry for want of a better; and now, like "old Frybark" referring to the governor's aide, I can only say to any skeptic of Philadelphia who may read this book, "*Voilà* M. the purser of your navy-yard: 'ask him.'" And now let us return to the enlightening conversation of our Falstaff-like host.

"That affair of the butter was a good thing for all concerned," he continued. "I sold forty pounds for the Company, the Tongouse got a fine dinner, and Mr. Henry saw something that he would never have believed *without* seeing. Now, don't some of you want to pay for *twenty* pounds? I'll show you two men at once who'll fight for the liberty to drink it."

Before any one could accept or decline his offer, the door opened, and in walked a most singular specimen of the *genus homo.* He was below the ordinary height, and possessed of immoderately-thin long arms and legs. He had a huge head resting upon a cornstalk-like neck, a large and flabby-looking mouth, a most disagreeable countenance, and a manner at once obsequious and presuming. His complexion was horribly sallow, and his huge feet moved over the creaking floor without seeming to leave it at all. His general appearance indicated a long ride accomplished, as he advanced to Mr. Freighburg and spoke a few words in Russian. When he had ended he was presented to the party as Mr. ——, just arrived from St. Petersburg.

"Just arrived from St. Petersburg!" exclaimed several voices in a breath. "Why, Mr. ——, how long have you been on the road?"

"Rather longer than usual," was the smiling—such a *smiling!*—reply. "To-morrow will be nine months since I left, but my health has been bad, and I travelled by short stages. I have only ridden forty miles to-day, but that is much for me." He, too, spoke English quite well, and, as he took a seat, crossed his pipestem-like legs, and folded his long hands over his knee, I expected to hear him add, "But I'm very 'umble," so much did he remind me of an old acquaintance,—one Uriah Heep, of David Copperfield memory.

"Don't imagine that it's such a *very* terrible journey, after all!" exclaimed "old Frybark." "The Government Post does it in sixty days, and when the news of the war came it was only fifty-eight on the road. You can easily make the trip in eighty days at a cost of five hundred dollars: in fact, it is only a pleasant travel. You go from here to —— river on horseback,—a distance of some six hundred miles; then take a boat for several hundred more; then leave the river and travel several hundred farther in light wagons or on horseback: you cross many rivers and mountains, follow the windings of numerous valleys, and see a splendid country and many singular people, during this part of the trip. Then you begin to arrive at a more cultivated region and to see signs of civilization, and in a week or so more you are at St. Petersburg. You see this tobacco, that champagne, that loaf-sugar, that tea, that caviare?—they all came over that long road, sewed up in raw hide, and always arrive in the good condition you see these in."

"What a fine trip it would be if we could only run the 'old John' on a safe rock, step quietly on shore, and go home by St. Petersburg!" exclaimed one of our party: "she couldn't drown us *then*,—confound her!"

Here our host was called out to see another arrival, and the next moment we heard his large voice calling for all who wanted to see how the Tongouse travelled on reindeer to come down. A general rush was now made for the door, where the new arrivals—in the shape of two Tongouse Indians—were leaning against their clean-limbed reindeer-bucks, whose branching antlers seemed in themselves heavy enough to bear down the elevated heads and arched necks of their fleet-looking owners. They had travelled seventy miles that day and yet looked fresh and lively. The saddles were girthed well upon the fore-shoulders,—almost on the neck,—and a single thong of hide served as a bridle. One of our party tried to mount, as any one would mount a horse; but the animal bent to the ground and became restive under the unusual proceeding. The Tongouse now mounted into the saddle by climbing up over his neck, and he stood as firm as if a feather only had been blown against him. They seemed to be very strong in the fore-shoulders and just the contrary in the back and quarters. For our edification the second Tongouse now mounted, and a short race ensued, in which they seemed to get along quite well, but by no means as swiftly or gracefully as many of our ordinary horses: probably they would have shown to better advantage had they not already travelled seventy miles.

"It's a mystery to me, Mr. Freighburg," I remarked, "how you manage to feed your stock during such long winters,—these hundreds of horses and dogs which we see, and the numberless reindeer which you say are owned farther in the interior. I don't even see sheds to shelter them under."

"Why, bless your heart!" answered the old fellow, "we let our horses and reindeer go free as soon as the cold weather commences, and they wander about in droves of hundreds and thousands, finding plenty to keep them from starving during the winter. They dig down through the snow for dried grass, &c., and it is only toward the spring, when the snow thaws and then freezes again, thus covering the ground with a solid mass of ice,—it is only at that time that we have to feed them until the weather gets warm and melts the ice away. Now, *one* horse alone could not clear away the snow for food, and thus you find them in large droves, as I say. Their great number also adds to their security from the attacks of wild beasts. Now, as to sheds for sheltering them from the cold, we have none at all; and, though the centigrade thermometer often sinks as low as twenty-five degrees below zero, we seldom hear of any of them freezing to death. You see, when it is so *very* cold we really do not feel it as much as if it were warmer; for the air is always perfectly still and dry, and it is with the sharp, damp winds that we suffer most."

And thus passed another evening; and the next day they were to dine with us, and upon the following we were to lunch with them, and then——to sea once more in our miserable old rattletrap.

The next day came and the dinner passed off finely; and then the short night and supper on shore followed, and the early sun ushered in "the last day." This last day in port was remarkable for two things,—the first of which was fear*fully* important, as Hartman expressed it, while the second was exciting in the extreme to all who witnessed it. The first was the purchase of an air-tight hogshead of fine flour from a charitable whaler, that was sufficient to insure us good bread until our arrival at San Francisco; and the second was the striking of a large whale within gunshot of our ship. But let my journal give us a few pages in regard to this latter:—

"We had been at anchor three days. Our field-books were full of data for the harbour-chart, and the next morning's early sun was to see us under way for the river Amoor. During these three days we had worked hard in our boats with sextant and lead-line, and during the three nights still harder at the Russian governor's table with knife and fork. In fact, we had been almost feasted to death by these fraternizing Northmen, and had determined to remain on board this day at least, to repair damages and recover from the effects of their overdone hospitality and roast beef, in spite of the promise they had extracted from us to attend another lunch.

"They were a glorious set of fellows, those very Russians,—strong-framed, large-hearted, and with astonishingly-capable heads and stomachs, if one might judge from the quantity of wine and viands which they destroyed at most frequent and outlandish periods. They would drink three or four wine-glasses of raw gin or whiskey before each meal,—calling it by the modest combination of "twenty drops,"—and raise their brows in surprise at our remarkable abstinence, we only indulging in one glassful. They would eat an ordinary meal just before each regular repast, calling it by the simple expression of "getting ready," and accuse us of not liking some particular dish, simply from the fact of our slackening up after having already eaten as much as two ordinary *men* before it was brought on the table. In short, they were men who could eat, drink, and keep late hours without experiencing any of those annoying results which too often present themselves in the shape of nightmare, unpleasant pains about half-way between one's head and heels, &c. &c.; and, such being their powers of endurance, they had no idea of letting us recover quietly in our rooms from the effects of the previous night's supper, when, as they said, they were to lose our company the next day. They therefore came off to the ship in a body, and had pretty well persuaded some of the more seasoned of the mess to return with them according to promise, when the cry was raised on deck that a school of whales was entering the harbour, and that the whale-ships were all lowering their boats preparatory to commencing work. There were some seven of these ships, all Americans, each one being manned with not less than four boats; hence the sport promised to be amusing, and the cry of 'whales in harbour!' no sooner reached us than all idea of leaving for the shore at once took wing.

"The entire party now rushed up from below,—up, up,—some into the rigging, some on the yards, others into the tops,—every one seeking an elevation from which to look down upon the coming contest between man and the giant of the deep,—between mind and instinct.

"It was curious in the extreme to watch the wary old bulls and cows as they drove the young calves into shoal water and there left them to feed, while they themselves, from the fact of drawing too much water, were forced to remain farther out, cruising back and forth, across and about the entrance, diving under ships, lying on the surface as if sunning themselves, motionless, apparently asleep, and yet sinking suddenly, like a lump of lead, dropping *perpendicularly away* from the sneaking boats, just as one of them would get close enough to make the harpooner brace himself for the deadly heave. Of calves I suppose there were a dozen or more, accompanied by an infinite number of grampus, amusing themselves in the shoal water; and there were probably as many as fifteen or twenty of the bulls and cows 'backing and filling' in different parts of the harbour, each of the former having one—sometimes two—boats dogging his wake or cutting across his course with silent, cat-like movement.

"The harbour being small, the water smooth and polished, the day beautifully bright, and our positions quite elevated, we could follow most of their motions while under water nearly as well as when they swam on the surface; and the manner in which they would turn from danger was really astonishing. In their doublings they put me in mind of the fox. One old gray-backed fellow I remember in particular, who, while swimming leisurely along from a pursuing boat, suddenly turned a deep somerset without disturbing the surface of the water at all, and a minute later breached some three or four hundred yards directly astern. Two boats—one of which had been sneaking upon him from either bow—had evidently caused this retrograde movement.

"No sooner had this old fellow's huge body breached again to view, than the three boats, who seemed to be devoting their particular attention to him alone, crept swiftly back toward him with their noiseless paddles; but, while yet some distance off, his body, which had since his reappearance floated lightly and motionless on the surface, seeming suddenly deprived of every thing that was buoyant, dropped perpendicularly out of sight, leaving nothing to tell of his previous sunning process save a few curling eddies. As a round-shot would have sunk, so sank he from the eyes of his pursuers, and when next seen was pretty well in with the calves and grampus, more than half a mile from his former position. The boats, however, judging with singular accuracy as to his submarine course, had followed him with such effect as to be within less than half that distance of him, as he blew his steam-like spout and again resumed his motionless position on the surface.

"In the mean time, the other fifteen or twenty boats were similarly engaged, and, an hour or more having now passed without any change in the programme, we began to think that our sport might not come off, after all, when suddenly old Grayback, who had been cruising under water for some time, lost his reckoning and rose under the very bows of one of the motionless boats, and, before aware of his dangerous locality, received the ready harpoon into his unsuspecting blubber.

"I think he must have sprung at least ten feet clear of the water, and for more than a second his huge frame, bent and doubled up by surprise or agony, was encircled by air only. Then he came down, and "oh, what a splash was there, my countrymen!" It reverberated over the whole harbour, and raised a swell over which the boat rose and fell as in a sea-way.

"'Starn all!' It was the clear, *nasal* voice of the Down-east boat-steerer, which came to us across the water almost as soon as the weapon had left his powerful grasp.

"And it was time to 'starn all;' for, though the light boat sprang like a thing of life more than her length from the effects of the looked-for leap, yet she had nothing to spare: the writhing monster struck the water within a few feet of the bow, and then turned for deep water with fearful velocity. At first they 'give him line,' then slowly 'check him,' and, finally, boil along in his foaming wake, as the powerful sweep of the trailing steering-oar turns the boat as upon a pivot and guides her after the tautened line.

"I do not think that her speed at the first jump could have been less than thirty miles the hour; and only think of a boat being dragged at that rate through the water! At times, I really believed that she was below the level of the sea; but so great was her speed, that the water, instead of pouring into her, was thrown from her gunwales in curling masses, that left a wake very much like that of a young steamboat.

"No sooner was boat No. 1 thus fastened to old Grayback, than Nos. 2, 3, and 4, all belonging to the same ship, dropped the silent paddles and, with their long, sweeping oars, took part in the exciting race; while the remaining whales, as if conscious of the mishap which had overtaken their imprudent leader, rushed about in wild disorder, and, before recovering from their fright, another of their number had leaped bodily into the air, descended with a splash, and rushed wildly out to sea, with the barbed weapon in his side and the buoyant boat thundering along in his rear.

"There were now two boats fastened to their flying prizes, while some half-dozen others were pulling vigorously in various directions, intent upon cutting off one or the other of the monsters—should the opportunity present itself in one of their many turnings—and fastening a second harpoon in case the first should draw out. Old Grayback, however, seemed fully aware of the game that was being played, and evinced a decided indisposition to being 'caught foul' a second time. He was now apparently cooled down by his 'two-forty' pace, and

THE "TWO-FORTY" PACE OF "OLD GRAYBACK."

seemed determined to limit his exertions to keeping out of harm's way,—now and then indulging in unpleasantly-sudden dives or dashes along the surface, as if merely to let them know that he was still 'about.' After running some miles to seaward, the old fellow had turned and retraced his track to within half a mile of the spot where he had been struck, and we thus had a fair view of his motions most of the time; but the other whale had dragged his boat with lightning speed around the north point of the harbour and disappeared entirely.

"Upon old Grayback, therefore, we fixed our admiring eyes, and some adventurous spirits even advocated the idea of our joining in the fun with our own boats; but, as the majority of us still had in distant contemplation a mundane meeting with absent friends, the proposition to 'take a boat and pull ourselves' (the crew having been worked hard the last few days) met with little encouragement. 'Every man to his own trade,' I thought to myself, as old Grayback made one of his playful dashes, turned suddenly at right angles to his former course, and came toward us with frightful velocity. 'Every man to his own trade. What would become of that boat now if I had the management of her? I think I'd much rather be seated on this topsail-yard with my spy-glass to amuse myself with.'

"It was a fearful jerk—a bold outlay of his husbanded strength—which the leviathan made in that sudden dash and short turn; but the quick eye of the boat-steerer had caught the movement, and with one mighty sweep of his trailing oar turned the boat as on a pivot, just as she felt the tautening of the line. Onward she surged in his boiling wake. Onward, onward. A breaking reef crossed their mad career; but old Grayback had evidently again lost his reckoning, for he rushed steadily upon it. Another second or two, and he must either turn at right angles or butt out his brains. He chose the former, as any sensible whale must have done, and seemed to fly with renewed velocity. Skirting the reef with a considerable portion of his huge head exposed, he passed so close to one of the ambushed boats as to furnish the long-looked-for chance of fastening a second iron. But the harpoon, though well directed, and urged by the power of a strong arm nerved by the moment's excitement, glanced harmlessly from his polished side, and was slowly hauled in by the disappointed whaler. The unexpected attack, however, seemed to lash him to perfect madness. Bounding off violently from the reef, he tore the first harpoon from its deep-seated hold, renewing his furious flight, which bade defiance to further pursuit, and leaving behind him a turbid wake of bloody foam. Old Grayback had saved his blubber, and the Sally Ann, of New Bedford, was minus her two hundred barrels.

"'Come on! come on!' said the governor's aide, who was by me on the topsail-yard. 'The whale has got away; he has doubtless gone for his lunch after so much exercise: let us follow his example.'

"So we went down to the deck, and another half-hour saw us entering the spacious mansion of the governor, and four hours after that we were again seated in the 'second floor-parlour,' and two or three hours later we were shaking hands for the last time."

How singularly mournful such partings often are!—such abrupt terminations of unexpected but pleasant associations of a few days! Our jovial host lost his laughing roughness as he emptied the ashes from his last pipe, and his voice softened, and I thought his eye was more brilliant than usual, as he bade us farewell,—we who had broken in upon their silent solitude and helped them to pass so many pleasant hours.

"I'll tell you what it is," he said, slowly, as he passed from one to the other with outstretched hands, "you fellows don't know what a serious thing you are about to do. You are going to leave us here to our solitude just as the long winter is coming over us. You are going to return to your friends and homes in the civilized world, while we are to be frozen in here with our useless billiard-table and the stores we bought from the Leveret. Don't you think that furs *ought to* sell high when Christian men have to live such a life to get them? I wish they were twice as dear: then my pay would be double, and I should only have to stay here half as long."

And thus we parted, and the next morning's sun shone upon the "old John" as she steamed slowly away from those isolated but truly hospitable mansions toward the scene of future work.

After all that has been said, it would be needless to add that we did not find any coal at Ayan. And now for a parting word in regard to that slightly-known place. I forgot its exact position, but its latitude is about 56° N. and longitude 138° E., and it is about half-way between the larger town of Okotsk and the mouth of the Amoor River. It contains some thirty or forty scattering houses, a Greek church, and a rough specimen of a ship-yard, where a small steamer, destined for the navigation of the Amoor River, was being built previous to the visit of the Allies. It is inhabited by three or four hundred persons, consisting of Russians, German-Russians, Cossacks, and the Tongouse Indians, and is the principal depôt of the Russian Fur Company in those regions. It is frequently visited by whalers, annually by a ship of the Company to carry the more ordinary furs to Europe, and seldom or never by any other vessels. It may be well here to add that the more costly furs are packed in water-proof bales and sent across the country to St. Petersburg in the same way in which "old Frybark's" white sugar and caviare were obtained. And now I have done with Ayan and—glorious "old Frybark."

CHAPTER XXIV.

WE VISIT THE TSCHANTAR ISLANDS, PARTAKE LARGELY OF WILD RHUBARB, AND CAPTURE ONE OF THE INHABITANTS—AFTER WHICH WE SAIL FOR THE AMOOR RIVER, WHERE WE FALL IN WITH THE BOATS OF THE RUSSIAN SQUADRON, FAIL TO PASS THROUGH INTO THE GULF OF TARTARY, AND FINALLY RETURN INTO THE OKOTSK SEA.

THE day after leaving Ayan we sighted the Tschantar Islands, and toward night let go our anchor in the principal harbour of that of Fekilzoff. This was the only one of the group upon which we landed; but, upon steaming around the others, we found them exhibiting the same general appearances, from which we concluded that "in seeing one we had seen all." Their central latitude is 55° N., their longitude 138° 30′ E.: they are covered with dense forests of spruce and birch, are rather hilly than mountainous, are watered by clear and numerous streams, and yet are not possessed of a single human inhabitant, as far as we could learn from our own observation and from conversing with whalers.

In fact, animal life of every description seemed scarce, though the soil is remarkably rich and vegetation consequently luxuriant. In conversing with whaling-captains in regard to these islands, they had held out most startling and sport-promising pictures to us. One of them said, for instance, that he had been anchored in one of their bays in company with two hundred other whale-ships, and that black bears were as abundant in the forests as one could desire. A boat's crew of his, he said, had once attacked and wounded one of them, when he gave chase, and not only ran them into their boat but swam out into the bay after them. They then turned on him with their lances and harpoons, and made short work of him.

Another captain told us the most marvellous yarns about the rise and fall of the tides along these shores, and of the shoals of whale which had frequented these bays "last season." He said—and others confirmed the story—that he had struck whales in six fathoms water, and dug clams out of the sand directly under his boat two hours later. And yet we passed three or four days in those waters, and did not see a clam, a whale, a bear, or any thing remarkable in the rise and fall of the tides. The currents that ran through the passages that separate the islands, however, were of astonishing rapidity, rendering the navigation full of peril even for a steamer.

When we let go our anchor in the Bay of Fekilzoff, we found several whalers already there, busily engaged in the work of wooding and watering ship. They complained greatly of the scarcity of whales, and talked of going to the northward in search of them. One by one they left us until we were alone in the silent bay.

Upon the morning after our arrival, two boats had been detailed to sound out the harbour, while the others were employed in wooding and watering ship. This left our indefatigable Nimrod, the doctor, at liberty, and he was soon upon the hill-sides with his rifle; but, after walking all day and finding nothing but two squirrels, he returned on board in great disgust and with a very poor idea of the veracity of the whaler who told us that "black bears were as abundant in the forests as one could desire." I must not forget to add that both bust-proof and his master accompanied him upon this excursion, and shared in his bitter disappointment. These squirrels were of totally-different species, though they were both amply provided with fur against the excessive cold of their winters. One of them was about as large as an ordinary gray squirrel, of a dark grayish colour, and with a jet-black and flowing tail, while the other was much smaller, of claret hue, with narrow brown stripes running down his back, and possessed of very little tail at all. The former fell a victim to bust-proof, and the latter was run down by the doctor and caught alive. These animals seemed to live on a little nut which we found in great quantities in the burr of the shaft-like spruce pine, whose growth was the densest I had ever witnessed in forest-trees. We subsequently bought whole baskets of these nuts from the natives at the mouth of the Amoor, partly as food for the doctor's pet, and partly because they were very fine for us to nibble at ourselves. They were about the size of a buckshot, of irregular formation, and tasted very much like the meat of the hickory-nut. Their covering was more of a skin than a shell, and might be swallowed without inconvenience. The trees on which this nut grows were, as I have already remarked, very abundant and straight; and, as we expected soon to give out of coal and have to carry sail quite heavy in consequence, we cut and rafted a number of them to be worked into spars in case of necessity. A hundred thousand ships might have loaded with similar timber from that single island. The second evening after our arrival, the wooding-party returned on board, bringing with them several bundles of a most refreshingly-green-looking vegetable, which they said a whaler had recommended to them as a grand substitute for spinach. It proved to be wild rhubarb, and when cooked in the form of greens was any thing but unacceptable. It had a sharp, acrid taste, truly; but then the doctor spoke very strongly in favour of that particular property as an anti-scorbutic, and one or two trials sufficed to reconcile us to the taste. We soon became very fond of it, and, before leaving for the Amoor River, took care to cut a good supply. It grew in great abundance along the sides of the hills, and has for many years been known to scurvy-threatened whalers.

The general formation of these islands is worthy of a passing notice.

Unlike most elevated and solitary formations, they present no indications of owing their origin to the action of subterraneous convulsions. You find no bold water around their shores, neither do you notice the cone-like peaks which generally lift themselves over a volcanic region. On the contrary, they are connected to the main-land by quite moderate and regular soundings, while banks, and reefs, and isolated rocks, render the navigation any thing but pleasant. The tide also washes their shores with the rare velocity of from five to seven knots the hour, and adds its perilous uncertainty to the lesser dangers. Periodical gales of destructive violence also devastate their lordly forests and drive the sea in foaming surf along their rocky shores. Then comes a long and cheerless winter, which sinks the thermometer more than one score of degrees below zero, and drives animal life into its burrowed home for shelter against its boundless intensity.

Wherever we landed, or while sailing along their silent shores, the whole country presented the appearance of a dense canebrake-like growth of spruce pine, extending from the sea to the summit of the highest ranges, and showing us at a single glance forest upon forest of the most beautiful spars for shipping. Seldom was it that we saw a crooked tree there: they were all as straight and branchless as the most fastidious spar-maker could desire, and will doubtless be duly appreciated when their owner, the Czar, sees fit to call into requisition their vast resources.

When we were on the coast of China, at Hong-Kong and Shanghae, we had seen such spars as these selling at the unheard-of price of from fifty to two and three hundred dollars; and, as we now walked between their lofty and shaft-like trunks, we could not help thinking how easy a fortune might be made by some enterprising Yankee, with an old timber-drover and a dozen or more good wood-cutters at his command. All he would have to do would be to cut and square some thousand or more of them, fill up his ship at the cost of time and labour only, and then run quietly to a ready market at either Hong-Kong, Shanghae, Manilla, or one of a dozen other ports. In the language of modern advertisements, "here is a rare chance for an enterprising man to make a fortune."

It took us four days to end our combined work of wooding, watering, and surveying; when we again got up steam and anchor and continued on our way for the mouth of the Amoor, through a storm of rain, wind, and drifting fog-banks that soon rendered our navigation so uncertain and dangerous that we were glad to gain an anchorage under the sheltering heights of another of the group until the return of clear weather. The next day it had improved considerably, and we again got under steam and ran along down the coast, hoping to be able to pass through between the island of Sagalien and the mainland into the Gulf of Tartary, and, following the west coast of Sagalien, finally get out into the Pacific through the Straits of La Perouse and then shape our course for San Francisco. In this, however, we were destined to fail, as the reader will see.

While at Ayan we had been presented by "old Frybark" with a large number of Russian charts, several of which related to the mouth of this river. These several charts embodied the latest surveys of that region, but were given to us by Mr. Freighburg with the warning remark, "Don't trust too much to their accuracy, for the channels there sounded out have long since been filled in by shifting sand-banks, and even we have to trust entirely to pilots." We therefore proceeded with our usual caution, and, while thus feeling our way with lead and lookout over the unknown ground, we were forced to anchor at night and continue with returning light the previous day's work. It was a running survey that we were making of this coast, and we had consequently to steam well in along the land in order that Hartman might sketch in the coast-line as we proceeded. We found the water shoaling perceptibly as we neared the latitude of the river, and were finally forced to run along in as little as three fathoms, or keep so far out to sea that the indentations of the land, the existence of rivers, &c. would no longer be discoverable. Of course we chose the former course, which, though entailing considerable risk, still guaranteed the accuracy of our future charts, which was, after all, the grand object of the Expedition.

Running along in this way upon the morning after leaving the Tschantar group, we sighted a sloop-rigged vessel ahead, and, the wind being quite light, soon steamed up to her, in spite of her evident exertions to get into shoal water beyond our reach. A boat was lowered, despatched to board her, and shortly returned with her commanding officer, who came on board in high glee upon the discovery that we were an American and not an English steamer. She proved to be a Russian gunboat that had run the gauntlet of the Allied fleet at Petropolowski, and reached in safety the port of Petropskie, (off which we had anchored the previous night,) where said commanding officer lived, and who as a Government pilot had taken charge of her, and was now working her around into the Amoor to turn her over to the Russian admiral, there fortified with a squadron of five sail. This old gentleman wore a tarnished and threadbare uniform, looked as if he had seen much hard service, and spoke English quite fairly. We had no difficulty in comprehending each other, as, with the table strewed with charts, cigars, and the captain's last bottle of wine, he pointed out the numerous errors of the former, and gave us a vast amount of general information that it would have taken us months of hard work to collect. For the benefit of persons interested in the present movement of the Czar as regards colonizing the banks of that river, I may as well introduce here a short synopsis of what we learned from the Government pilot, as well as a few remarks in regard to our own experience, which, while proving some of his information to be correct, encourages us at the same time to put confidence in other of his assertions the truth of which we never found ourselves in a position to test.

He told us, then, as he smacked his lips over the long-untasted wine and puffed away at the equally-rare Manilla cheroot, that charts would never be of much value as far as the mouth of the Amoor was concerned. Even he himself, he said, who had acted the part of a pilot in those waters for several years, had to trust to his lead and a good look-out, the sandbanks were so extensive and so liable to constant changes. There were two passages, he continued, but it was hard to choose between them,—the northern one (where we now were) being a bad lee shore in case of a northeast gale, besides having very little water, while the southern, though carrying twelve fathoms over what had long been regarded as an isthmus connecting the island of Sagalien with the mainland, soon led to patches of banks and shoals over and through which only ten feet could be carried, and that with the greatest difficulty. He gave us a full description of the manner in which the Russian squadron had escaped the Allies at Castrie's Bay and passed through this passage; and it seems that upon arriving at these banks and shoals they had to throw overboard their guns, &c., put casks under their larger vessels, and were even then several weeks in working themselves into the river, so often was their progress checked by shoal water. They subsequently recovered their guns by means of their boats, and were then well fortified in anticipation of a visit from the enemy.

On the whole, he rather seemed to think that the southern passage was the best; "for," said he, "even if ships cannot enter the river they may anchor off its mouth, and discharge and receive cargo by means of flat-bottomed boats without such great exposure to northeast gales. Then they pass down the Gulf of Tartary to the Straits of La Perouse, and are soon in the Pacific." The old fellow was evidently trying to set things in the best light, doubtless thinking that the war would last for years, and that, if we spoke lightly of the difficulties of landing cargo when we arrived at San Francisco, ships would be more likely to bring them stores. And this reception of supplies from California was their only hope, he told us, as long as the war lasted, as the resources of the country around them consisted almost entirely of berries, fish, the flesh of several wild animals, and a few roots. Though the soil was fine, they had not had time to plant any vegetables, he said, though they hoped to have some California potatoes in the ground next spring, until which time they must be content with roots instead.

After getting through with the charts and wine, we went on deck, and the captain, pointing to a vessel apparently at anchor under the dimly-seen shore of Sagalien, asked him if he knew what she was, &c.; but he had been at Petropskie so long, he said, that he could not tell any thing about her. She had arrived since he left the settlement on the Amoor, and was probably an American bark that had been long looked for with supplies from San Francisco.

"How many fathoms can we carry in a straight line from here to where she is anchored?" continued the captain.

"You may steer straight for her and have three fathoms until within a mile of her, when you will find the water shoaling; and you must then keep to the southward until she bears ——, when you may steer again for her. You will find her anchored in about three fathoms water, though you will have to pass over as little as 'a half two.' She has got the best berth for riding out a northeast gale; and you had better anchor near her, as there is a bank to seaward that will break the sea and give you a comparatively quiet time."

We thanked the old fellow for his information, and offered to tow him that far on his route; but he had the modesty to decline, and we subsequently had cause to admire his foresight, for the tide ran so strong as we struck out into the stream that the "old John" had as much as she could do to drag herself through it. We were determined to make him some return for his kindness, however, and so stuffed his hat and pockets full of cheroots and sardines as he went over the side.

It took us several hours' hard steaming to reach the stranger, and there is no telling how much longer we might have been had not the flood-tide set in and given us a lift. The sun was just dropping behind the lowland to the westward as we let go our anchor and lowered a boat to board her. She proved to be the American bark Palmetto, of San Francisco, with provisions and stores sent by the Russian consul to his countrymen in the Amoor; and she was surrounded by a perfect swarm of boats from the Russian men-of-war in that river, who, imagining us to be one of the Allied cruisers, took up a hasty flight, with both sails and oars. As soon, however, as they made out our flag, they seemed to gain courage, and, calling a halt, despatched one of their lighter boats to take a closer look at us.

This fellow pulled around us several times, gradually lessening the diameter of his circle until he was within hail, when the captain bellowed at him through a trumpet to the effect that we were friends,—Americans,—and that he had better come alongside.

"Yes! That'll do very well!" sang out the officer, in a doubting voice, at which there was a burst of laughter fore and aft our decks, which, reaching his ears, seemed to satisfy him of our friendly nature much better than the captain's hail. At any rate, he now pulled up alongside of us and came on board, and, after carefully looking round the decks for a moment, signalled his companions, who at once followed his example. The party was commanded by the captain of the frigate Aurora, and had been sent out by the admiral with orders to get the Palmetto into the river if possible; but, as they had now been at it some six weeks without making any headway, it was difficult to see how they were to succeed. In the mean time the northeast-gale season was rapidly approaching, and the captain of the Palmetto was, naturally enough, getting anxious either to get in or away. We remained in company with him three or four days, during which time we sounded around for miles in search of a channel; but, finding that the Russians were evidently opposed to our proceedings on account of the existing war, the captain finally ceased work, and the next day we left them and were well clear of the dangerous ground. Before leaving, however, the Russians, apparently ashamed of the indisposition they had evinced to our continuing the survey, offered to pilot us through into the Gulf of Tartary and fill our bunkers with coal, if we would take the Palmetto in tow; but, as they were evidently unable to find water enough even for her, we did not see much prospect of their taking our ship, which drew a foot more, through in safety. Moreover, we could not well have consented had there been oceans of water, for the Allies would have had just cause to complain of a violation of our neutrality. So we left them to their fate and steamed back into the Okotsk.

CONCLUSION.

WE COMMENCE OUR HOMEWARD-BOUND VOYAGE AND ARE STOPPED BY A NORTHEAST GALE, AFTER WHICH A WESTERLY HURRICANE COMES TO OUR ASSISTANCE AND FRIGHTENS THE "OLD JOHN" INTO UNUSUAL ACTIVITY —WE ARE ATTACKED BY THE SCURVY, ARRIVE AT SAN FRANCISCO, AND HEAR VARIOUS KINDS OF NEWS—THE LAST OF THE "OLD JOHN," AND AN IDEA OF THE RESULTS OF THE CRUISE.

It was now the 15th of September, 1855; and, as we steamed back into the Okotsk Sea, we rubbed our hands and felt as only men can feel who have a hard cruise in their rear and the sight of their native land and the joys of home in their front. Our work was over, and we were at length bound for the longed-for haven of San Francisco. We had been a year without even letters from our relatives,—wanderers along the shores of strange and unfrequented lands.

We had accomplished a vast deal of work during this time,—particularly toward the latter part of it. Bad charts had been corrected without number, the data for new ones obtained, and our continuous line of deep-sea and other soundings followed us from ocean to ocean like the endless trail of the luminous circle whose broad and starry breast meets the upward gaze from every longitude. We did what I suppose no vessel ever did before:—we sounded around the world.

And now, as we were commencing our homeward-bound voyage, with something over a month's provision in the ship, with only enough wood and coal in the bunkers to last us some ten days, and with our worn-out sails and crippled spars to take us the rest of that long and weary way, we looked doubtingly ahead at the prospect of adverse gales, and trembled over the miserable ship in which we felt no confidence. We had at least four thousand miles to accomplish: we had to work our way through the Okotsk Sea, and between the Kurile Islands by the "fifty-passage," and finally to cross the expansive breast of the North Pacific to San Francisco during the stormiest of seasons. We allowed forty days to do all of this in, and determined to steam until we had entered the Pacific, and then to save our fuel until within a few hundred miles of San Francisco. Thus we had to depend upon our sails alone to accomplish the intervening distance of over three thousand miles. Now, as the reader already knows how the "old John" was wont to acquit herself under sail alone, he will readily see that we should have starved before reaching our port, had she been opposed by headwinds. Fortunately, such was not the case: our "broken reed" was again strengthened by Him who counts the hairs of our heads and notes the fall of the smallest sparrow.

* * * * * *

We had rounded the north cape of the island of Sagalien, and were stretching across that portion of the Okotsk for the "fifty-passage," when we were met by a northeast gale which caused us to fear for the safety of the Palmetto and to congratulate ourselves upon our own absence from her dangerous anchorage. This gale soon blew by, and then we again commenced working for the passage. This we reached in a few days, but were unfortunately encompassed by fogs after the breaking up of the gale, so that one stormy evening found us in pretty much the same dilemma as we had been in a year back while running out of the Yellow Sea: we apparently had another case of blindman's-buff ahead of us. We could not well avoid running, however, for a westerly gale was evidently brewing astern, and, were we to heave to, we would certainly drift upon the Kuriles as a lee shore. Our best chance, therefore, was to continue on our course while we still had a fair idea of our position; so we crowded on all sail and steam, hoping to enter the passage before night. In this we failed; but, fortunately for our peace of mind during the hours of darkness, the fog lifted just after sunset and showed us high land on our starboard bow; then it shut in again, night came on, and we were more blindfolded than ever. Still, we had seen enough. The passing glimpse of a well-marked peak had told us that the open channel was ahead of us, and beyond that the open ocean: so we kept steadily on before the freshening gale, and the next morning at daylight were well out on the Pacific: the fog was all gone, the Kuriles had sunk below the western horizon, and we were now to see no more land until that of California should rise over the opposite board.

During this first day in the Pacific, we were passed by several deeply-loaded whalers steering for the Sandwich Islands; and, toward night, the fresh westerly breeze before which we had been running for the last two days had worked itself into quite a gale,—so stormy, in fact, that we were down to double-reefed topsails before midnight, and the next morning we found it necessary to reduce sail still further. The following night it had increased to a storm, and the day after that found us scudding before a fearful hurricane under a close-reefed maintopsail and fore storm-staysail. This lasted a week or more, and, as we got farther and farther from under the lee of the Kurile Islands, it raised a heavy rolling sea which threw us ahead at a most glorious rate. It was the "old John's" *forte*,—this thing of running away from a gale,—for she was so long that there was not the most remote danger of her "broaching to;" and, upon the old principle of accomplishing a thing through main strength and stupidity, she was often known to travel at the rate of twelve knots the hour while thus urged bodily before a sea and gale.

This was all very fine for the first day or two; but, as the hurricane approached its climax, the seas, which had hitherto only roared under our flying stern or occasionally boarded us over either waist, began to tumble in over the taffrail and warn us of the necessity of battening down the hatches. The old ship herself, too, began to complain badly about that time. The furious rate at which she was being driven ahead, combined with the violent spells of rolling which she indulged in about every five minutes, and the jarring power exerted by the propeller on account of the unusual rate at which the ship's speed caused it to revolve, made her decks open so much that we might as well have had an oblong sieve overhead. The water came through them into our apartments in such quantities as to saturate our beds, ruin our books, and keep the lower deck constantly afloat.

"Old bust-proof" was particularly unfortunate. His master had given him a good oiling, stowed him away securely overhead, and then left him to sleep quietly through the passage. Alas for human forethought! his double muzzle was elevated higher than the breech: water will run down hill, and the consequence may well be imagined: upon our arrival at San Francisco he was found half full,—irreparably ruined. We looked at him and sighed: we feared he would lose all right and title to his redoubtable name at the very next discharge. His ultimate fate is shrouded in impenetrable mystery.

I don't think any of the mess will ever forget that long, wet, dreary week. I feel it now in the shape of a passing rheumatic pain. It was "fear*ful*," as Hartman expressed it, when we one morning ate our breakfast (luke-warm tea, cold bread, and fried pork) with high india-rubber boots on to keep our feet dry. At the end of the third day, just as the hurricane was about at its height, the captain started the idea of lying to and allowing it to "blow by." He entertained the very natural fear that we should run into the centre of the storm if we continued before it any longer, in which case we should certainly have foundered with the sea that was then running. He and the first lieutenant differed, however, as to the nature of the tempest, and it was fortunately determined to continue scudding. I say "fortunately," for, in the end, it proved to be the safest as well as most comfortable course, and we moreover continued logging our two hundred and fifty miles daily toward San Francisco, which was in itself a most important feature, as the scurvy was by that time making great inroads into our numbers and adding daily to the crowded sick-list.

Finally, we ran into moderate weather, then through an ordinary gale, and, in the end, awoke one "fear*fully* fine mor-r-ning," according to Hartman, to find ourselves within a few hundred miles of the land. We then got up steam to help our sails, and were so fortunate as to enter San Francisco during the night of the 19th of October. We found the Vincennes and Cooper both in ahead of us by a week or more, and some of their officers boarded us that same night to offer their congratulations upon our safety and tell us the news of the last ten months. It seemed that very grave fears were beginning to be entertained for the welfare of our miserable old tub.

Who can tell how much we enjoyed those first few days in a civilized port? There were our letters of the past year to be read, the news of the world to be talked over, and some of the finest beef, mutton, and vegetables of the world to be attacked: the very recollection of it all is glorious. Upon comparing notes as to the accomplishments of the different vessels since our separation, it appeared that we had each done more than the other two had deemed probable. The Vincennes had touched at Petropolowski, skirted the shore of Asia up to Behring's Straits, and there left Lieutenant Brooke, Mr. Kern, and a boat's crew, to make astronomical observations, while she herself pushed on into the Arctic and obtained a higher latitude in a northwesterly direction *than any previous* navigator. Finally, she was arrested by vast masses of ice, which, combined with the wide-spread existence of scurvy among her crew, forced her to return to the southward, after having found blue water where a previous English explorer had located high land. She had also made many other valuable discoveries, and collected material for the construction of charts the want of which had been severely felt by whalers for the last few years. Returning through Behring's Straits, she picked up the astronomical party, and continued her line of deep-sea soundings to San Francisco, where she arrived shortly before us, with half of her crew disabled from scurvy. I quote the following extract in regard to her cruise from our late summary to Congress showing what work we had accomplished, and asking that we be compensated for the unusual service, as was the similar expedition which sailed under Wilkes some eighteen years since:—

"The Vincennes passed up along the coast of Asia, (after leaving us at Ha-ko-da-di,) determining prominent points and headlands. She then entered Behring's Straits, where, on the peninsula of Yerguine on the Asiatic coast, among the warlike and barbarous *Tschuktchis*, she left a party of ten persons for the purpose of making astronomical, magnetic, and other observations, and to complete the survey of the Straits of Seniavine, and to investigate the flora and fauna of that country. On leaving that place for the North, the Vincennes had on board but three month's wood and provisions.

"To accomplish the survey in the limited period during which the Arctic is open, it was necessary to carry all the sail the ship would bear, through fog and mist, thus incurring the danger of wreck on shoals, bergs, or rocks, (for the Arctic is not deep.) She visited *Herald Island*, and sailed over the position assigned land claimed to have been discovered by H. M. ship Herald. She reached a higher point of latitude (72° 05′) than was ever before attained north of Eastern Asia, and disproved also the existence of *Wrangell's* land in the position assigned it.

"All that portion of the Arctic available for whaling-purposes was carefully explored and sounded. At this time, in consequence of the want of provisions and of exposure, the scurvy appeared, and the major portion of crew and officers was attacked by it. Returning toward the straits, an obstinate east wind was encountered, and for many days it was doubtful whether the ship would make good her escape from the Arctic before the rapidly-gathering ice would imprison her,—an event certain to result in the destruction of all concerned.

"Embarking the shore-party, with the valuable results of their labours, she sailed for San Francisco, where she arrived after a tempestuous passage, and was joined by the Hancock and Cooper, bringing the results of their extensive surveys. Having communicated with the Department, the Hancock and Cooper were transferred to the navy-yard, and the Vincennes sailed alone, continuing the work of survey on the route home, where she arrived in July, 1856, from Otaheite, having made the quickest passage on record.

"In the execution of these various works, the officers and men have been separated from the civilized world for periods of ten months at a time; they have been exposed to great hardships and dangers not inferior to those of war. Many of them have been permanently injured by exposure, and all have been impoverished, for the ports at which they were obliged to procure supplies for their long voyages were of the most expensive character,—the Cape of Good Hope, Sydney, in Australia, Hong-Kong, and San Francisco.

"With a *reduced* complement of officers, the labour of surveying has been performed, in *addition* to all the duties of actual service at sea, in regions of the most tempestuous character."

Thus it will be seen that they had been less fortunate even than we of the "old John," as far as fresh provisions and recreation were concerned; for, while we had met with beef, milk, berries, fish, and turnips in the Bay of Taousk, with beef, recreation, and flour at Ayan, and with spinach in the shape of wild rhubarb at the Tschantar Islands, they had been forced to depend solely upon the Government-ration of salt beef and pork, and bend their constant energies to severe and dangerous labour, &c. They were still rubbing their hands and talking of the end of work and of the fine California potatoes when we arrived.

And now, reader, if you are so unfortunate as to be a member of Congress, I take the liberty of asking you to think a moment over these last few pages, and see if you cannot reconcile it with your ideas of equity to vote for a bill which is now before "your honourable bodies" for the relief of the officers and men of the North Pacific Surveying and Exploring Expedition; and, if you decide against us, I can only hope that, if you ever find yourself on the sea, it may be in just such an old coffin as the everlasting "old John." And now for the little Cooper.

With this vessel, things seemed to have gone some what better: they found an abundance of sweet potatoes at the Aleutian Islands, while surveying their rugged coasts, and began to think they were going to have quite a fine time, when one day they were encountered by a severe gale which came very near casting them on shore. They .had anchored before its commencement, and now let go a second anchor; but she dragged them both with their chains veered out to the bitter ends,—the sea was so very heavy that passed them and broke upon the black-looking rocks not more than twenty yards astern: *they were dragging upon a lee shore.* The crew became very much alarmed, but were calmed by the admirable firmness of their officers, (Lieutenant-Commanding Gibson and Lieutenant Kennon,) and, just as all hope was about leaving them, they were rejoiced to find that the schooner had "brought up." One of the anchors, while dragging along the bottom, had caught under a rock and arrested them upon the very verge of destruction. *Their* reed also had been strengthened.

There were three pieces of news which reached us that first night, any one of which would have been sufficient to put any disease but scurvy to an ignominous flight. In the first place, our friends, as a general thing, were well. Secondly, a naval retiring board had been ordered by Congress, had already acted, and we were now "commissioned" instead of "warrant" officers. And, lastly, the "old John," whose reputation had at length worked its way through the walls of the Navy Department,—"*the old John*" was ordered to be turned over to the navy-yard, and such of her officers as were not wanted to fill vacancies on board the Vincennes and Cooper were to be ordered home over the Isthmus. I say all of this was great news; but then it was all darkened by some unpleasant drawback. Our friends were mostly well, but many had been confined to the bed of sickness. We had all been promoted, but it was to bogus elevations and to bogus pay. Our professional prospects, as far as pay and subsistence were concerned, had actually been changed for the worse. And this assertion I am prepared to prove in the cases of at least two bogus promotions out of three, though it is the prevailing opinion that the entire "active list" of the navy has been *immeasurably benefited.* And, lastly, the pleasure of our cruise, being at an end, was chilled (to one at least) by the very unpleasant reflection that he had to pay his own expenses home.

A few days after our arrival, we all went up to the navy-yard at Mare Island, when our crew were discharged or transferred to the Vincennes and Cooper, the captain and first lieutenant ordered to the Vincennes, the rest of us ordered home, and the old tub herself turned over to the yard, with the charitable warning that "she would be more likely to sink than swim if she ever went to sea again." Two of us came home by way of Nicaragua, the others *viâ* Panama, and both parties arrived at New York within a few days of each other. We now scattered to our widely-spread homes,—north, south, east, and west,—and after the first few days began to look in the papers for any stray notices in regard to the movements of the Vincennes and Cooper. One day I picked up a paper that was both amusing and informing:—the Cooper had also been turned over to the yard, the Vincennes was ordered to New York *viâ* Cape

Horn, and the poor "old John" was again being fitted for sea. She was to be sent up to Puget Sound to engage in warlike deeds against the Indians, and men were found to go in her: our warning had evidently been forgotten. Two weeks later I took up another paper: there was something more about the everlasting old coffin: she had become restive under strange hands and amused herself by blowing out the bottom of one of her boilers. Whether they succeeded in patching her up and reaching their destination in safety I am unable to say; but it is to be hoped that the undertaking was abandoned, and that she will be allowed to pass the remnant of her days in peace and quiet. And now, as I am about to leave her to that doubtful repose, I cannot but acknowledge a feeling of gratitude toward the shaky old bridge which "carried us safely over," in spite of the many anxious moments which she caused us during that rough and stormy cruise. Farewell to thy miserable but faithful old timbers!

Several months later a rusty and weather-beaten sloop-of-war anchored off the New York Navy-yard. It was the summer of 1856, and the vessel was the Vincennes. She brought home with her the remnant of our Expedition, and a vast amount of matter for the construction of charts, the advancement of science, and the enlightenment of the inquiring mind: she was the grand storehouse in which had been stowed, from time to time, the dearly-bought work of the several vessels that had composed the squadron. The cruise was at an end, and men returned to strange-looking homes, with bent frames that had been straight, and with whitened locks that had been dark. Who among those men will again volunteer for a surveying and exploring voyage around the world? I have but one more remark to add in regard to the achievements of the Expedition, and that will give the reader a fair idea of the extent of our collections. I was informed by Mr. Stimpson, our Naturalist, some three months since, that he had brought back with him *nearly five* thousand varieties of animal life—mostly marine—which were previously unknown to the scientific world. What a vast field is there opened for the naturalist and his microscope!

And now I have but to dip once more into the inkstand to return my thanks to Messrs. Edward Kern and Geo. G. White, of Philadelphia, and to "fear*ful*" A. E. Hartman, of Dresden, Saxony, for the aid of their able pencils in the way of illustrating my very imperfect MSS., and to express the hope that Congress may call upon Commander John Rodgers, our *ci-devant* leader, to prepare an *official* account of the cruise which shall spread the result of our work before the world, and do that which it has not been in my power to accomplish in a simple narrative of this nature:—*i.e.* to do justice to an undertaking which was originated by the necessities of commerce, which has progressed in silence, accomplished vast results of which little or no notice has been taken, (from the fact that we returned during the violent excitement preceding the late presidential election,) and which has not been blown into notoriety by the brazen trumpet of an Antony Van Corlear.

THE END.

LIPPINCOTT'S PRONOUNCING GAZETTEER OF THE WORLD, OR, GEOGRAPHICAL DICTIONARY,

Comprising nearly **2200 Pages,** *including a greater amount of matter than any other single volume in the English Language; giving a description of nearly* **One Hundred Thousand Places,** *with the correct* **Pronunciation of their Names,** *being above 20,000 more Geographical Notices than are found in any other Gazetteer of the World.*

EDITED BY J. THOMAS, M.D., and T. BALDWIN,

Assisted by several other Gentlemen.

TESTIMONIALS.

From the Hon. Edward Everett.

"This work has been evidently prepared with great labor, and as far as I can judge, from the best materials and sources of information. . . . The principles adopted in ascertaining the pronunciation of proper names (as stated in the Introduction) appear to me correct. This is a matter attended with some difficulty and uncertainty, but it is treated with great ability, and in a very satisfactory manner, in your Introduction. I have no doubt your Gazetteer will be found an extremely useful work, well calculated to supply a want which must have been severely felt by almost every class of readers."

From J. E. Worcester, L.L.D., Author of Worcester's Critical Dictionary.

"Having made some examination of 'Lippincott's Pronouncing Gazetteer,' more particularly in relation to Pronunciation, I take pleasure in expressing a concurrence, generally, in what is said by the Hon. Edward Everett, of the value and excellence of the work. The difficult subject of the pronunciation of geographical names appears to me to have been attended to with great care, good taste, and sound judgment; and this feature of the Gazetteer must add greatly to its value."

From the Hon. Robert C. Winthrop.

"I know of no Gazetteer so complete and comprehensive. . . . I entirely concur with Mr Everett in the opinion he has pronounced of the work, and sincerely hope that it may receive an amount of public patronage in some degree commensurate with the magnitude and costliness of the undertaking."

From Washington Irving.

"I fully concur with the opinions given by Mr. Everett and Mr. Winthrop of its merits, and with their wishes for its wide circulation."

From J. Addison Alexander, D.D., Prof. Oriental Languages and Literature, Princeton Col.

"On the subject of Geographical Orthography and Orthoepy, this is not only the best, but the only systematic work with which I am acquainted. In examining this work, I have received an indirect and incidental, but very strong impression of its great superiority, in fulness and accuracy, to any Dictionary of Geography with which I am acquainted."

From Dr. B. Sears, President of Brown University.

"Your work must prove an invaluable guide to the student of geography, and if generally adopted, could not fail to remove that discrepancy and confusion which now so generally prevail, in regard to the pronunciation of geographical names."

From M. B. Anderson, L.L.D., President of the University of Rochester.

"I hesitate not to say that it is altogether superior to any book of its class accessible to the American public."

From Prof. C. A. Goodrich, of Yale College, Editor 'Revised Edition' of Webster's Dictionary.

"Your Pronouncing Gazetteer of the World appears, from the examination I have given it, to be a work of immense labor, very wisely directed. I consider it as of great importance to Teachers."

From the Hon. George Bancroft.

"I have formed a very high opinion of the merits of your Complete Pronouncing Gazetteer; especially for its comprehensiveness, compactness, and general accuracy. I wish you the success which you so richly deserve."

A DICTIONARY OF SELECT AND POPULAR QUOTATIONS,

WHICH ARE IN DAILY USE.

TAKEN FROM THE LATIN, FRENCH, GREEK, SPANISH AND ITALIAN LANGUAGES.

Together with a copious Collection of Law Maxims and Law Terms, translated into English, with Illustrations, Historical and Idiomatic.

NEW AMERICAN EDITION, CORRECTED, WITH ADDITIONS.

One volume, 12mo.

This volume comprises a copious collection of legal and other terms which are in common use, with English translations and historical illustrations; and we should judge its author had surely been to a great "Feast of Languages," and stole all the scraps. A work of this character should have an extensive sale, as it entirely obviates a serious difficulty in which most readers are involved by the frequent occurrence of Latin, Greek, and French passages, which we suppose are introduced by authors for a mere show of learning—a difficulty very perplexing to readers in general. This "Dictionary of Quotations," concerning which too much cannot be said in its favour, effectually removes the difficulty, and gives the reader an advantage over the author; for we believe a majority are themselves ignorant of the meaning of the terms they employ. Very few truly learned authors will insult their readers by introducing Latin or French quotations in their writings, when "plain English" will do as well; but we will not enlarge on this point.

If the book is useful to those unacquainted with other languages, it is no less valuable to the classically educated as a book of reference, and answers all the purposes of a Lexicon—indeed, on many accounts, it is better. It saves the trouble of tumbling over the larger volumes, to which every one, and especially those engaged in the legal profession, are verv often subjected. It should have a place in every library in the country.

RUSCHENBERGER'S NATURAL HISTORY,

COMPLETE, WITH NEW GLOSSARY.

The Elements of Natural History,

EMBRACING ZOOLOGY, BOTANY AND GEOLOGY:

FOR SCHOOLS, COLLEGES AND FAMILIES.

BY W. S. W. RUSCHENBERGER, M. D.

IN TWO VOLUMES.

WITH NEARLY ONE THOUSAND ILLUSTRATIONS, AND A COPIOUS GLOSSARY.

Vol. I. contains *Vertebrate Animals.* Vol. II. contains *Intervertebrate Animals, Botany, and Geology.*

GREAT TRUTHS BY GREAT AUTHORS.

GREAT TRUTHS BY GREAT AUTHORS;

A DICTIONARY

OF AIDS TO REFLECTION, QUOTATIONS OF MAXIMS, METAPHORS, COUNSELS, CAUTIONS, APHORISMS. ETC.,

FROM WRITERS OF ALL AGES AND BOTH HEMISPHERES,

ONE VOLUME, DEMI-OCTAVO.

"I have somewhere seen it observed, that we should make the same use of a book, that a bee does of a flower; she steals sweets from it, but does not injure it."—Cotton.

STYLES OF BINDING.

Ultramarine cloth, bevelled board, price $1 50; Ultramarine cloth, bevelled and panelled, gilt sides and edges, $2 00; Half calf, or Turkey antique, fancy edges, $2 50; Full calf, or Turkey antique, brown or gilt edges, $3 50.

THE LIFE AND OPINIONS OF TRISTRAM SHANDY, GENTLEMAN.

COMPRISING THE HUMOROUS ADVENTURES OF

UNCLE TOBY AND CORPORAL TRIM.

BY L. STERNE.

Beautifully Illustrated by Darley. Stitched.

A SENTIMENTAL JOURNEY.

BY L. STERNE.

Illustrated as above by Darley. Stitched.

The beauties of this author are so well known, and his errors in style and expression so few and far between, that one reads with renewed delight his delicate turns, &c.

THE LIFE OF GENERAL JACKSON,

WITH A LIKENESS OF THE OLD HERO.

One volume, 18mo.

LIFE OF PAUL JONES.

In one volume, 12mo.

WITH ONE HUNDRED ILLUSTRATIONS

BY JAMES HAMILTON.

The work is compiled from his original journals and correspondence, and includes an account of his services in the American Revolution, and in the war between the Russians and Turks in the Black Sea. There is scarcely any Naval Hero, of any age, who combined in his character so much of the adventurous, skilful and daring, as Paul Jones. The incidents of his life are almost as startling and absorbing as those of romance. His achievements during the American Revolution—the fight between the Bon Homme Richard and Serapis, the most desperate naval action on record—and the alarm into which, with so small a force, he threw the coasts of England and Scotland—are matters comparatively well known to Americans; but the incidents of his subsequent career have been veiled in obscurity, which is dissipated by this biography. A book like this, narrating the actions of such a man, ought to meet with an extensive sale, and become as popular as Robinson Crusoe in fiction, or Weems's Life of Marion and Washington, and similar books, in fact. It contains 400 pages, has a handsome portrait and medallion likeness of Jones, and is illustrated with numerous original wood engravings of naval scenes and distinguished men with whom he was familiar.

WASHINGTON,

AND THE

GENERALS OF THE AMERICAN REVOLUTION.

Two volumes complete in one. With finely Engraved Portraits.

NAPOLEON,

AND THE

MARSHALS OF THE EMPIRE.

Two volumes in one. With finely Engraved Portraits.

THE YOUNG CHORISTER;

A Collection of New and Beautiful Tunes, adapted to the use of Sabbath-Schools, from some of the most distinguished composers; together with many of the author's compositions.

EDITED BY MINARD W. WILSON.

Types of Mankind,

OR

ETHNOLOGICAL RESEARCHES,

BASED UPON THE

ANCIENT MONUMENTS, PAINTINGS, SCULPTURES, AND CRANIA OF RACES

AND UPON THEIR

NATURAL, GEOGRAPHICAL, PHILOLOGICAL AND BIBLICAL HISTORY

ILLUSTRATED BY SELECTIONS FROM THE INEDITED PAPERS OF

SAMUEL GEORGE MORTON, M. D.,

(LATE PRESIDENT OF THE ACADEMY OF NATURAL SCIENCES AT PHILADELPHIA)

AND BY ADDITIONAL CONTRIBUTIONS FROM

PROF. L. AGASSIZ LL.D.; W. USHER M. D.; AND PROF. H. S. PATTERSON, M. D.

BY

J. C. NOTT, M. D., and GEO. R. GLIDDON,

MOBILE, ALABAMA. FORMERLY U. S. CONSUL AT CAIRO.

WITH FOUR HUNDRED ILLUSTRATIONS.

One volume, quarto. Price, Five Dollars.

Iron Tables, Price 25 Cents---A Useful New Work.

WEIGHT TABLES

OF DIFFERENT LENGTHS OF

ROUND, SQUARE, AND FLAT BAR IRON, STEEL, ETC.

BY A PRACTICAL MECHANIC.

This is one of the most useful works published for Dealers and Workers in Iron. So correct are he calculations, that any person can safely sell and buy with the book, without even weighing the on and Steel.

THE RACE FOR RICHES,

And some of the Pits into which the Runners fall.

SIX LECTURES,

APPLYING THE WORD OF GOD TO THE TRAFFIC OF MEN

BY WILLIAM ARNOT,

MINISTER OF FREE ST. PETER'S, GLASGOW.

With a Preface and Notes,

BY STEPHEN COLWELL, AUTHOR OF "NEW THEMES," ETC.

One volume, 12mo. Price, 62 cents.

www.ingramcontent.com/pod-product-compliance
Lightning Source LLC
LaVergne TN
LVHW021232110826
845150LV00002B/311

9781425562847